THE FUTURE
OF MEDIA

THE FUTURE
RESISTANCE AND REFORM IN THE 21ST CENTURY
OF MEDIA

EDITED BY
ROBERT W. McCHESNEY
RUSSELL NEWMAN
BEN SCOTT

WITH A FOREWORD BY
BILL MOYERS

SEVEN STORIES PRESS
NEW YORK · LONDON · TORONTO · MELBOURNE

Seven Stories Press
140 Watts Street
New York, NY 10013
http://www.sevenstories.com/

In Canada: Publishers Group Canada, 250A Carlton Street, Toronto, ON M5A 2L1

In the UK: Turnaround Publisher Services Ltd., Unit 3, Olympia Trading Estate, Coburg Road, Wood Green, London N22 6TZ

In Australia: Palgrave Macmillan, 627 Chapel Street, South Yarra, VIC 3141

College professors may order examination copies of Seven Stories Press titles for a free six-month trial period. To order, visit http://www.sevenstories.com/textbook/ or send a fax on school letterhead to 212.226.1411.

Designed by Phoebe Hwang
Cover designed by POLLEN, New York

LIBRARY OF CONGRESS CATALOGING-IN-PUBLICATION DATA
The future of media : resistance and reform in the 21st century /
Robert W. McChesney, Russell Newman, and Ben Scott, eds.—1st ed. p. cm.
Includes bibliographical references.
ISBN-10: 1-58322-679-6 (pbk. : alk. paper)
ISBN-13: 978-1-58322-679-7 (pbk. : alk. paper)
1. Mass media—United States—Forecasting. I. McChesney, Robert Waterman, 1952–
II. Newman, Russell. III. Scott, Ben, 1977–

P96.F672U624 2005

302.23'0973'01—dc22   2005003794

Printed in Canada

9 8 7 6 5 4 3 2 1

CONTENTS

PART 4: TOWARD A NEW MEDIA AGE: THE POLITICS OF CONVERGENCE, NEW MEDIA, AND INNOVATION

PART 5: THE FUTURE OF MEDIA IN A GLOBAL AGE

FOREWORD

BILL MOYERS

I must confess to a certain discomfort, shared with other journalists, with the term "media." Ted Gup, who teaches journalism at Case Western Reserve, articulated my concerns better than I could when he wrote in *The Chronicle of Higher Education* (November 23, 2001)

> that the very concept of media is insulting to some of us within the press who find ourselves lumped in with so many disparate elements, as if everyone with a pen, a microphone, a camera, or just a loud voice were all one and the same. . . . David Broder is not Matt Drudge. "Meet the Press" is not "Temptation Island." And I am not Jerry Springer. I do not speak for him. He does not speak for me. Yet "the media" speaks for us all.

That's how I felt when I saw Oliver North on Fox reporting from Iraq, pressing our embattled troops to respond to his repetitive and belittling question, "Does Fox rock? Does Fox rock?" Oliver North and I may be part of the same "media" but we are not part of the same message. Nonetheless, I accept that I work, and all of us live in, "medialand," and God knows we need some "media reform." I'm sure you know those two words are really an incomplete description of the job ahead. Taken alone, they suggest that you've assembled a convention of efficiency experts who are tightening the bolts and boosting the output of the machinery of public enlightenment, or else a conclave of high-minded do-gooders applauding each other's sermons. But we need to be—and we will be—much more than that because what we're talking about is nothing less than rescuing a democracy that is so polarized it is in danger of being paralyzed and pulverized.

Alarming words, but the realities we face should trigger alarms. Free and responsible government by popular consent just can't exist without an informed public. That's a cliché, I know, but I agree with the presidential candidate who once said that truisms are true and clichés mean what they say (an observation that no doubt helped to lose him the election). It's a reality: democracy can't exist without an informed public. Here's an example: Only 13 percent of eligible young people cast ballots in the 2000 presidential election. A recent National Youth Survey revealed that only half of the fifteen hundred young people polled believe that voting is important, and only 46 percent think they can make a difference in solving community problems. We're talking about one quarter of the electorate. The Carnegie Corporation conducted a youth challenge quiz of 15–24-year-olds and asked them, "Why don't more young people vote or get involved?" Of the nearly two thousand respondents, the predominant answer was that they did not have enough information about issues and candidates. Let me rewind and say it again: democracy can't exist without an informed public. So I say without qualification that it's not simply the cause of journalism that's at stake today but the cause of American liberty itself. As Tom Paine put it, "The sun never shined on a cause of greater worth." He was talking about the cause of a revolutionary America in 1776. But that revolution ran in good part on the energies of a rambunctious, though tiny, press. Freedom and freedom of communication were birth twins in the future United States. They grew up together, and neither has fared very well in the other's absence. Boom times for the one have been boom times for the other.

Yet today, despite plenty of lip service on every ritual occasion to freedom of the press, radio, and TV, three powerful forces are undermining that very freedom, damming the streams of significant public interest news that irrigate and nourish the flowering of self-determination. The first of these is the centuries-old reluctance of governments—even elected governments—to operate in the sunshine of disclosure and criticism. The second is more subtle and more recent; it's the tendency of media giants, operating on big-business principles, to exalt commercial values at the expense of democratic value—that is, to run what Edward R. Murrow forty-five years ago called broadcasting's "money-making machine" at full throttle. In so doing they are squeezing out the journalism that tries to get as close as possible to the verifiable truth; they are isolating serious coverage of public affairs into ever-dwindling "news holes" far from prime time; and they are gobbling up small and independent publications competing for the attention of the American people.

It's hardly a new or surprising story. But there are fresh and disturbing chapters.

In earlier times our governing bodies tried to squelch journalistic freedom with the blunt instruments of the law—padlocks for the presses and jail cells for outspoken editors and writers. Over time, with spectacular wartime exceptions, the courts and the Constitution struck those weapons out of their hands. But they've found new ones now, in the name of "national security." The classifier's Top Secret stamp, used indiscriminately, is as potent a silencer as a writ of arrest. And beyond what is officially labeled "secret," there hovers a culture of sealed official lips, opened only to favored media insiders, a culture of government by leak and innuendo and spin, of misnamed "public information" offices that churn out blizzards of releases filled with self-justifying exaggerations and, occasionally, just plain damned lies—censorship without officially appointed censors.

Add to that the censorship by omission of consolidated media empires digesting the bones of swallowed independents, and you've got a major shrinkage of the crucial information that thinking citizens can act upon. People saw that situation coming as long as a century ago, when the rise of chain newspaper ownerships, and then the concentration in the young radio industry, became apparent. And so in the zesty progressivism of early New Deal days, the Federal Communications Act of 1934 was passed. The aim of that cornerstone of broadcast policy, mentioned over a hundred times in its pages, was to promote the "public interest, convenience and necessity." The clear intent was to prevent a monopoly of commercial values from overwhelming democratic values—to assure that the official view of reality, corporate or government, was not the only view of reality that reached the people. Regulators and regulated, media and government were to keep a wary eye on each other, preserving that system of checks and balances that is the bulwark of our constitutional order.

What would happen, however, if the contending giants of big government and big publishing and broadcasting ever joined hands? If they ever saw eye to eye in putting the public's need for news second to free-market economics? That's exactly what's happening now, under the ideological banner of "deregulation." Giant, megamedia conglomerates that our Founders could not possibly have envisioned are finding common cause with an imperial state in a betrothal certain to produce, not the sons and daughters of liberty, but the very kind of bastards that issued from the old arranged marriage of church and state.

Consider where we are today.

Never has there been an administration so disciplined in secrecy, so precisely in lockstep in keeping information from the people at large and—in defiance of the Constitution—from their representatives in Congress. Never has so powerful a media oligopoly—the word is Barry Diller's, not mine—been so unabashed in reaching, like Caesar, for still more wealth and power. Never have hand and glove fitted together so comfortably to manipulate free political debate, sow contempt for the idea of government itself, and trivialize the people's need to know. When the journalist-historian Richard Reeves was once asked by a college student to define "real news," he answered, "The news you and I need to keep our freedoms." When journalism throws in with power, that's the first news marched by censors to the guillotine. The greatest moments in the history of the press came, not when journalists made common cause with the state, but when they stood fearlessly independent of it.

This brings me to the third powerful force—beyond governmental secrecy and megamedia conglomerates—that is shaping what Americans see, read, and hear. I am talking now about that quasi-official partisan press ideologically linked to an authoritarian administration that, in turn, is the ally and agent of the most powerful interests in the world. This convergence dominates the marketplace of political ideas today in a phenomenon unique in our history. You need not harbor the notion of a vast right-wing conspiracy to think this collusion more than pure coincidence. Conspiracy is unnecessary when ideology hungers for power and its many adherents swarm of their own accord to the same pot of honey. Stretching from the editorial pages of *The Wall Street Journal* to the faux news of Rupert Murdoch's empire to the nattering nabobs of know-nothing radio to a legion of think tanks paid for and bought by conglomerates—the religious, partisan, and corporate right have raised a mighty megaphone for sectarian, economic, and political forces that aim to transform the egalitarian and democratic ideals embodied in our founding documents.

Authoritarianism. With no strong opposition party to challenge such triumphalist hegemony, it is left to journalism to be democracy's best friend. That is why so many journalists joined together in questioning Michael Powell's bid—blessed by the White House—to permit further concentration of media ownership. If free and independent journalism, committed to telling the truth without fear or favor, is suffocated, the oxygen goes out of democracy. And there is no surer way to intimidate and then silence mainstream journalism than to be the boss.

If you doubt me, read Jane Kramer's chilling account of Silvio Berlusconi in *New Yorker* magazine. The Prime Minister of Italy is its richest citizen. He is also its first media mogul. The list of media that he or his relatives or his proxies own, or directly or indirectly control, includes the state television networks and radio stations, three of Italy's four commercial television networks, two big publishing houses, two national newspapers, fifty magazines, the country's largest movie production and distribution company, and a chunk of Italy's Internet services. Even now Berlusconi is pressing upon parliament a law that would enable him to purchase more media properties, including the most influential paper in the country. Kramer quotes one critic who notes that half the reporters in Italy work for Berlusconi and the other half think they might have to. Small wonder that he has managed to put the Italian state to work to guarantee his fortune—or that his name is commonly attached to such unpleasant things as contempt for the law, conflict of interest, bribery, and money laundering. Nonetheless, "his power over what other Italians see, read, buy, and, above all, think, is overwhelming." The editor of *The Economist*, Bill Emmott, was asked recently why a British magazine was devoting so much space to an Italian prime minister. He replied that Berlusconi had betrayed the two things the magazine stood for: capitalism and democracy. Can it happen here? It can. By the way, Berlusconi's close friend is Rupert Murdoch, and on July 31, 2003, programming on nearly all the satellite hookups in Italy was switched automatically to Murdoch's Sky Italia.

The issues we're addressing here are bigger and far more critical than simply "media reform." That's why, before I go on, I want to ask you to look around you. I'm serious: look to your left and to your right. Look for your allies in one of the great ongoing struggles of the American experience—the struggle for the soul of democracy, for government "of, by, and for the people."

It's a battle we can win only if we work together. In early 2003, the FCC, heavily influenced by lobbyists for the newspaper, broadcasting, and cable interests, prepared a relaxation of the rules governing ownership of media outlets that would allow still more diversity-killing mergers among media giants. The proceedings were conducted in virtual secrecy and were generally ignored by all the major media, who were, of course, interested parties. In June, then-Chairman Powell and his two Republican colleagues on the FCC announced the revised regulations as a done deal.

They didn't count, however, on the voice of independent journalists and concerned citizens. Because of coverage in independent outlets—including PBS, which was the only broadcasting system that encouraged its journalists to report what was really happening—and because citizens took quick action, this largely invisible issue burst out as a major political cause and ignited a crackling public debate. Independent journalists and activists exposed Powell's failure to conduct an open discussion of the rule changes save for a single hearing in Richmond, Virginia. Their efforts led to a real participatory discussion, with open meetings in Chicago, Seattle, San Francisco, New York, and Atlanta. Then the organizing that followed generated millions of letters and "filings" at the FCC, opposing the change. Finally, the outcry mobilized unexpected support for bipartisan legislation to reverse the new rules that cleared the Senate—although House Majority Leader Tom DeLay still holds it prisoner in the House. Who would have thought this cause would win support from such allies as Senator Trent Lott or Kay Bailey Hutchinson, from my own state of Texas? We have moved "media reform" to center stage, where it may now become a catalyst for a new era of democratic renewal.

Working journalists have something special to bring to this movement, and, therefore, have important questions to ask. What laws are needed? What advocacy programs and strategies? How can we protect and extend the reach of those tools (such as the Internet, cable TV, community-based radio and public broadcasting systems, alternative journals of news and opinion) that give us some countervailing power against media monopoly?

Without passion, however, without a message that has a beating heart, these tools won't be enough. That's where journalism comes in. It isn't the only agent of freedom, obviously; in fact, journalism is a deeply human, and therefore deeply flawed, craft—yours truly being a conspicuous example. But at times, it has risen to great occasions, and at times, it has made other freedoms possible. That's what the draftsmen of the First Amendment knew, and it's what we can't afford to forget. So to remind us of what our free press has been at its best and can be again, I will call on the help of unseen presences, men and women of journalism's often checkered but sometimes courageous past.

Think with me for a moment on the reasons behind the establishment of press freedom. It wasn't ordained to protect hucksters, and it didn't drop like the gentle rain from heaven. It was fought and sacrificed for by unpretentious but feisty craftsmen who got their hands inky at their own hand presses and called themselves simply "printers." The very first American newspaper was a little three-page affair put out in Boston in September of 1690. Its name was *Publick Occurrences Both Foreign and Domestick* and its editor was Benjamin Harris, who said he simply wanted "to give an account of such considerable things as have come to my attention." The government shut it down after one issue—just one issue!—for the official reason that printer Ben Harris hadn't applied for the required government license to publish. But I wonder if some Massachusetts pooh-bah didn't take personally one of Harris's proclaimed motives for starting the paper—"to cure the spirit of Lying much among us"?

No one seems to have objected when Harris and his paper disappeared—that was the way things were. But some forty-odd years later, when printer John Peter Zenger was jailed in New York for criticizing its royal governor, things were different. The colony brought Zenger to trial on a charge of "seditious libel," and since it didn't matter whether the libel was true or not, the case seemed open and shut. But the jury ignored the judge's charge and freed Zenger, not only because the governor was widely disliked, but also because of the closing appeal of Zenger's lawyer, Andrew Hamilton. Take a look at this! His client's case was:

Not the cause of the poor Printer, nor of New York alone, [but] the cause of Liberty, and . . . every Man who prefers Freedom to a Life of Slavery will bless and honour You, as Men who . . . by an impartial and uncorrupt Verdict, [will] have laid a Noble Foundation for securing to ourselves, our Posterity and our Neighbors, That, to which Nature and the Laws of our Country have given us a Right,—the Liberty—both of exposing and opposing arbitrary Power . . . by speaking and writing—Truth.

Still a pretty good mission statement!

During the War for Independence itself, most of the three dozen little weekly newspapers in the colonies took the Patriot side and mobilized resistance by giving space to anti-British letters, news of Parliament's latest outrages, and calls to action. But the clarion journalistic voice of the Revolution was the onetime editor of the *Pennsylvania Magazine*, Tom Paine, a penniless recent immigrant from England, where he left a trail of failure as a businessman and husband. In 1776—just before enlisting in Washington's army—he published *Common Sense*, a hard-hitting pamphlet that slashed through legalisms and doubts to make an uncompromising case for an independent and republican America. It's been called the first best seller, with as many as a hundred thousand copies bought by a small literate population. Paine followed it up with another convincing collection of essays written in the field and given another punchy title, *The Crisis*. Passed from hand to hand and reprinted in other papers, they spread the gospel of freedom to thousands of doubters. Why I bring Paine up here is because he had something we need to restore—an unwavering concentration to reach ordinary people with the message that they mattered and could stand up for themselves. He couched his gospel of human rights and equality in a popular style that any working writer can envy. "As it is my design," he said, "to make those that can scarcely read understand, I shall therefore avoid every literary ornament and put it in language as plain as the alphabet."

That plain language spun off memorable one-liners that we're still quoting. "These are the times that try men's souls." "Tyranny, like hell, is not easily conquered." "What we obtain too cheap, we esteem too lightly." "Virtue is not hereditary." And this: "Of more worth is one honest man to society and in the sight of God than all the crowned ruffians that ever lived." I don't know what Paine would have thought of political debate by bumper sticker and sound bite, but he could have held his own in any modern campaign.

There were also editors who felt responsible to audiences that would dive deep. In 1787 and 1788 the little *New-York Independent Advertiser* ran all eighty-five numbers of *The Federalist*, those serious essays in favor of ratifying the Constitution. They still shine as clear arguments, but they are, and they were, unforgiving in their demand for concentrated attention. Nonetheless, the *Advertiser* felt that it owed the best to its readers, and the readers knew that the issues of self-government deserved their best attention. I pray that a goal of the media reform movement includes a press as conscientious as the *New-York Advertiser*, as pungent as *Common Sense*, and as public-spirited as both. Because it takes those qualities to fight against the relentless pressure of authority and avarice. Remember, back in 1791, when the First Amendment was ratified, the idea of a free press seemed safely sheltered in law. It wasn't. Only seven years later, in the midst of a war scare with France, Congress passed and John Adams signed the infamous Sedition Act. The act made it a crime—just listen to how broad a brush the government could swing—to circulate opinions "tending to induce a belief" that lawmakers might have unconstitutional or repressive motives, or "directly or indirectly tending" to justify France or to "criminate," whatever that meant, the President or other Federal officials. No wonder that opponents called it a scheme to "excite a fervor against foreign aggression only to establish tyranny at home." John Ashcroft would have loved it.

But here's what happened. At least a dozen editors refused to be frightened and went defiantly to prison, some under state prosecutions. One of them, Matthew Lyon, who also held a seat in the House of Representatives, languished for four months in an unheated cell during a Vermont winter. But such was the spirit of liberty abroad in the land that admirers chipped in to pay his thousand-dollar fine, and when he emerged his district reelected him by a landslide. Luckily, the Sedition Act had a built-in expiration date of 1801, at which time President Jefferson—who hated it from the first—pardoned those remaining under indictment. So the story has an upbeat ending, and so can ours, but it will take the kind of courage that those early printers and their readers showed.

Courage is a timeless quality and surfaces when the government is tempted to hit the bottle of censorship again during national emergencies, real or manufactured. As many of you can recall, in 1971, during the Vietnam War, the Nixon administration resurrected the doctrine of "prior restraint" from the crypt and tried to ban the publication of the Pentagon Papers by the *New York Times* and *The Washington Post*—even though the documents were a classified history of events during four earlier Presidencies. Arthur Sulzberger, the publisher of the *Times*, and Katherine Graham of the *Post* were both warned by their lawyers that they and their top managers could face criminal prosecution under espionage laws if they printed the material that Daniel Ellsberg had leaked—and, by the way, offered without success to the three major television networks. Or at the least, punitive lawsuits or whatever political reprisals a furious Nixon team could devise. But after internal debates—and the threats of some of their best-known editors to resign rather than fold under pressure—both owners gave the green light, and were vindicated by the Supreme Court. Score a round for democracy.

Bipartisan fairness requires me to note that the Carter administration, in 1979, tried to prevent Erwin Knoll, editor of the *Progressive* magazine, from running an article called "How to Make an H-Bomb." The grounds were a supposed threat to "national security." But Howard Morland, the reporter, had compiled the piece entirely from sources open to the public, mainly to show that much of the classification system was Wizard of Oz smoke and mirrors. The courts again rejected the government's claim, but it's noteworthy that the journalism of defiance by that time had retreated to a small left-wing publication like the *Progressive*.

In all of those cases, confronted with a clear and present danger of punishment, none of the owners flinched. Can we think of a single executive of today's big media conglomerates showing the kind of resistance that Sulzberger, Graham, and Erwin Knoll did? Certainly not Michael Eisner; he said he didn't even want ABC News reporting on its parent company, Disney. Certainly not General Electric/NBC's Robert Wright; he took Phil Donahue off MSNBC because the network didn't want to offend conservatives with a liberal sensibility during the invasion of Iraq. Instead, NBC brought to its cable channel Michael Savage whose diatribes on radio had described nonwhite countries as "turd-world nations" and who characterized gay men and women as part of "the grand plan to cut down on the white race." I am not sure why it was the GE/NBC executives calculated that Donahue was offensive to conservatives, yet Savage was not.

And then there's Leslie Moonves, the chairman of CBS. In the very week that the once-Tiffany network was celebrating its seventy-fifth anniversary—and taking kudos for its glory days, when it was unafraid to broadcast "The Harvest of Shame" and "The Selling of the Pentagon"—the network's famous eye blinked. Pressured by a vociferous and relentless right-wing campaign and bullied by the Republican National Committee, and at a time when its parent company had billions resting on whether the White House, Congress, and the FCC would allow it to own even more stations than currently permissible, CBS caved in and pulled a miniseries about Ronald Reagan that conservatives thought insufficiently worshipful. The chief honcho at CBS, Les Moonves, says that taste, not politics, dictated his decision. But earlier this year, explaining why CBS intended to air a series about Adolf Hitler, Moonves sang a different tune: "If you want to play it safe and put on milquetoast then you get criticized . . . . There are times as a broadcaster when you take chances." This obviously wasn't one of those times. Granted, made-for-television movies about living figures are about as vital as the wax figures at Madame Tussaud's—and even less authentic—granted that the canonizers of Ronald Reagan hadn't even seen the film before they set to howling; granted, on the surface it's a silly tempest in a teapot; still, when a once-great network falls obsequiously to the ground at the feet of a partisan mob over a cheesy miniseries that practically no one would have taken seriously as history, you have to wonder if the slight tremor that just ran through the First Amendment could be the harbinger of greater earthquakes to come, when the stakes are really high. And you have to wonder what concessions the media tycoons-cum-supplicants are making when no one is looking.

So what must we devise to make the media safe for individuals stubborn about protecting freedom and serving the truth? And what do we all—educators, administrators, legislators, and agitators—need to do to restore the disappearing diversity of media opinions? America had plenty of that in the early days, when the republic and the press were growing up together. It took no great amount of capital and credit—just a few hundred dollars—to start a paper, especially with a little political sponsorship and help. There were well over a thousand of them by 1840, mostly small-town weeklies. And they weren't objective by any stretch. Here's William Cobbett, another hell-raiser like Paine, shouting his creed in the opening number of his 1790s paper, *Porcupine's Gazette*. "Peter Porcupine," Cobbett's self-bestowed nickname, declared:

> Professions of impartiality I shall make none. They are always useless, and are besides perfect nonsense, when used by a newsmonger; for, he that does not relate news as he finds it, is something worse than partial; and . . . he that does not exercise his own judgment, either in admitting or rejecting what is sent him, is a poor passive tool, and not an editor.

In Cobbett's day, you could flaunt your partisan banners as you cut and thrust, and not inflict serious damage on open public discussion, because there were plenty of competitors. It didn't matter if the local gazette presented the day's events entirely through a Democratic lens. There was always an alternate Whig or Republican choice handy; there were, in other words, choices. As Alexis de Tocqueville noted, these many blooming journals kept even rural Americans amazingly well informed. They also made it possible for Americans to exercise one of their most democratic habits—that of forming associations to carry out civic enterprises. And they operated against the dreaded tyranny of the majority by letting lonely thinkers know that they had allies elsewhere. Here's how de Tocqueville put it in his book *Democracy in America*:

> In democratic countries . . . it frequently happens that a great number of men who wish or who want to combine cannot accomplish it because they are very insignificant and lost amid the crowd, they cannot see and do not know where to find one another. A newspaper then takes up the notion or the feeling that had occurred simultaneously, but singly, to each of them. All are immediately guided toward this beacon; and these wandering minds, which had long sought each other in darkness, at length meet and unite. The newspaper brought them together, and the newspaper is still necessary to keep them united.

No wandering spirit could fail to find a voice in print. And so in that pre-Civil War explosion of humanitarian reform movements, it was a diverse press that put the yeast in freedom's ferment. Of course there were plenty of papers that spoke for Indian-haters, immigrant-bashers, bigots, jingoes and land-grabbers proclaiming America's Manifest Destiny to dominate North America. But one way or another, journalism mattered, and had purpose and direction.

Past and present are never as separate as we think. Horace Greeley, the reform-loving editor of the *New York Tribune*, not only kept his pages "ever open to the plaints of the wronged and suffering," but said that whoever sat in an editor's chair and didn't work to promote human progress hadn't tasted "the luxury" of journalism. I liken that to the words of a kindred spirit closer to our own time, I. F. Stone. In his four-page *I. F. Stone's Weekly*, Izzy loved to catch the lies and contradictions in the government's own official documents, and amid the thunder of battle with the reactionaries, he said, "I have so much fun I ought to be arrested." Think about that. Two newsmen, a century apart, believing that being in a position to fight the good fight isn't a burden but a lucky break. How can our work here bring that attitude back into the newsrooms?

The era of a wide-open and crowded newspaper playing field began to fade as the old hand presses gave way to giant machines with press runs and readerships in the hundreds of thousands and costs in the millions. But that didn't necessarily or immediately kill public-spirited journalism. Not so long as the new owners were still strong-minded individuals with big professional egos to match their thick pocketbooks. When Joseph Pulitzer, a one-time immigrant reporter for a German-language paper in St. Louis, took over the *New York World* in 1883, he was already a millionaire in the making. But here's his recommended short platform for politicians:

1. Tax Luxuries

2. Tax Inheritances

3. Tax Large Incomes

4. Tax Monopolies

5. Tax the Privileged Corporation

6. A Tariff for Revenue

7. Reform the Civil Service

8. Punish Corrupt Officers

9. Punish Vote Buying

10. Punish Employers Who Coerce Their Employees in Elections

Also not a bad mission statement. Can you imagine one of today's huge newspaper chains taking that on as an agenda?

Don't get me wrong. The *World* certainly offered people plenty of the spice that they wanted—entertainment, sensation, earthy advice on living—but not at the expense of news that let them know who was on their side against the boodlers and bosses.

Nor did big-time, big-town, big-bucks journalism extinguish the possibility of a reform-minded investigative journalism that took the name of muckraking during the Progressive Era. Those days of early last century saw a second great awakening of the democratic impulse. What brought it into being was a reaction against the social Darwinism and unrestrained capitalistic exploitation that is back in full force today. Certain popular magazines made space for—and profited by—the work of such journalists as, to name only a few, Lincoln Steffens, Ida Tarbell, Upton Sinclair, Samuel Hopkins Adams, and David Graham Phillips. They ripped the veils from, among other things, the shame of the cities, the crimes of the trusts, the treason of the Senate, and the villainies of those who sold tainted meat and poisonous medicines. And why were they given those opportunities? Because, in the words of Samuel S. McClure, owner of *McClure's Magazine*, when special interests defied the law and flouted the general welfare, there was a social debt incurred. And, as he put it, "We have to pay in the end, every one of us. And in the end, the sum total of the debt will be our liberty."

Muckraking lingers on today, but alas, a good deal of it consists of raking personal and sexual scandal in high and celebrated places. Surely, if democracy is to be served, we have to get back to putting the rake where the important dirt lies, in the fleecing of the public and the abuse of its faith in good government.

When that landmark Communications Act of 1934 was under consideration, a vigorous public movement of educators, labor officials, and religious and institutional leaders emerged to argue for a broadcast system that would serve the interests of citizens and communities. A movement like that is coming to life again, and we now have to build on this momentum.

It won't be easy, because the tide's been flowing the other way for a long time. The deregulation pressure began during the Reagan era, when then-FCC chairman Mark Fowler, who said that TV didn't need much regulation because it was just a "toaster with pictures," eliminated many public-interest rules. That opened the door for networks to cut their news staffs, scuttle their documentary units (goodbye to "The Harvest of Shame" and "The Selling of the Pentagon"), and exile investigative producers and reporters to the underfunded hinterlands of independent production. It was like turning out streetlights on dark and dangerous corners. A crowning achievement of that drive was the Telecommunications Act of 1996, the largest corporate welfare program ever for the most powerful media and entertainment conglomerates in the world—passed, I must add, with support from both parties.

And the beat of "convergence" between once-distinct forms of media goes on at increased tempo, with the communications conglomerates and the advertisers calling the tune. As safeguards to competition fall, an octopus like GE-NBC-Vivendi-Universal will be able to secure cable channels that can deliver interactive multimedia content—text, sound, and images—to digital TVs, home computers, personal video recorders, and portable wireless devices like cell phones. The goal? To corner the market on new ways of selling more things to more people for more hours in the day, and in the long run, to fill the airwaves with customized pitches to you and your children. This will melt down the surviving boundaries between editorial and marketing divisions and create a hybrid known to the new-media hucksters as "branded entertainment."

Let's consider what's happening to newspapers. A study by Mark Cooper of the Consumer Federation of America reports that two-thirds of today's newspaper markets are monopolies. And now most of the country's powerful newspaper chains are lobbying for coownership of newspaper and broadcast outlets in the same market, increasing their grip on community after community. And are they up-front about it? Hear this: in December 2003 such media giants as the *New York Times*, *Gannett*, *Cox*, and *Tribune*, along with the trade group representing almost all the country's broadcasting stations, filed a petition to the FCC making the case for the cross-ownership that the owners so desperately seek. They actually told the FCC that lifting the regulation on cross-ownership would strengthen local journalism. But did those same news organizations tell their readers what they

were doing? Not at all. Not one of them on that day believed they had an obligation to report in their own news pages what their parent companies were asking
of the FCC. As these huge media conglomerates increase their control over what
we see, read, and hear, they rarely report on how they themselves are using their
power to further their own interests and power as big business, including their
influence over the political process.

Take a look at a book called *Leaving Readers Behind: The Age of Corporate
Newspapering*, published as part of the Project on the State of the American
Newspaper under the auspices of the Pew Charitable Trusts. The people who
produced the book all love newspapers—Gene Roberts, former managing editor of the *New York Times*; Thomas Kunkel, dean of the Philip Merrill College
of Journalism; Charles Layton, a veteran wire service reporter and news and
feature editor at the *Philadelphia Inquirer*, as well as contributors such as Ken
Auletta, Geneva Overholser, and Roy Reed. Their conclusion: the newspaper
industry is in the middle of the most momentous change in its three-hundred-
year history—a change that is diminishing the amount of real news available
to the consumer. A generation of relentless corporatization is now culminating
in a furious, unprecedented blitz of buying, selling, and consolidating of newspapers, from the mightiest dailies to the humblest weeklies. It is a world where
"small hometown dailies in particular are being bought and sold like hog futures.
Where chains, once content to grow one property at a time, now devour other
chains whole. Where they are effectively ceding whole regions of the country to
one another, further minimizing competition. Where money is pouring into the
business from interests with little knowledge and even less concern about the
special obligations newspapers have to democracy." They go on to describe the
toll that the never-ending drive for profits is taking on the news. In Cumberland,
Maryland, for example, the police reporter had so many duties piled upon him he
no longer had time to go to the police station for the daily reports. But newspaper
management had a cost-saving solution: put a fax machine in the police station,
and let the cops send over the news they thought the paper should have. In New
Jersey, the Gannett chain bought the *Asbury Park Press*, then sent in a publisher
who slashed fifty-five people from the staff and cut the space for news, and was
rewarded by being named Gannett's Manager of the Year. In New Jersey, by the
way, the Newhouse and Gannett chains together own a total of thirteen of the
state's nineteen dailies, or 73 percent of all the circulation of New Jersey-based
papers. Then there is *The Northwestern* in Oshkosh, Wisconsin, with a circulation of 23,500. Here, the authors report, is a paper that prided itself on being in
hometown hands since the Andrew Johnson administration. But in 1998 it was
sold, not once but twice, within the space of two months. Two years later it was
sold again: four owners in less than three years.

You'd better get used to it, concluded *Leaving Readers Behind*, because the real momentum of consolidation is just beginning; it won't be long now before America is reduced to half a dozen major print conglomerates.

You can see the results even now in the waning of robust journalism, in the dearth of in-depth reporting as news organizations try to do more with fewer resources, in the failure of the major news organizations to cover their own corporate deals and lobbying as well as other forms of "crime in the suites," such as the Enron story, and in the failure to help people understand what their government is up to. The report by the Roberts team includes a survey in 1999 that showed a wholesale retreat in coverage of nineteen key departments and agencies in Washington. Regular reporting of the Supreme Court and State Department dropped off considerably through the decade. At the Social Security Administration, whose activities literally affect every American, only the *New York Times* was maintaining a full-time reporter and, incredibly, at the Interior Department, which controls five to six hundred million acres of public land and looks after everything from the National Park Service to the Bureau of Indian Affairs, there were no full-time reporters around.

That's in Washington, our nation's capital. Out across the country, there is simultaneously a near blackout of local politics by broadcasters. The public-interest group Alliance for Better Campaigns studied 45 stations in six cities in one week in October. Out of 7,560 hours of programming analyzed, only 13 were devoted to local public affairs—less than one-half of 1 percent of local programming nationwide. Mayors, town councils, school boards, civic leaders get no time from broadcasters who have filled their coffers by looting the public airwaves over which they were placed as stewards. Last year, when a movement sprang up in the House of Representatives to require these broadcasters to obey the law that says they must sell campaign advertising to candidates for office at the lowest commercial rate, the powerful broadcast lobby brought the Congress to heel. So much for the "public interest, convenience, and necessity."

So what do we do? What is our strategy for taking on what seems a hopeless fight for a media system that serves as effectively as it sells, one that holds all the institutions of society, itself included, accountable?

There's plenty we can do. Here's one journalist's list of some of the overlapping and connected goals that a vital media reform movement might pursue.

First, we have to take Tom Paine's example—and Danny Schechter's advice—and reach out to regular citizens. Many of us reading this book speak a common language about the "media." We must reach the audience that's not here—carry the fight to radio talk shows, local television, and the letters columns of our newspapers. As Danny says, we must engage the mainstream, not retreat from it. We have to get our fellow citizens to understand that what they see, hear, and read is not only the taste of programmers and producers but also a set of policy decisions made by the people we vote for.

We have to fight to keep the gates to the Internet open to all. The Web has enabled many new voices in our democracy—and globally—to be heard: advocacy groups, artists, individuals, nonprofit organizations. Just about anyone can speak online, and often with an impact greater than in the days when orators had to climb on soap boxes in a park. The media-industry lobbyists point to the Internet and say it's why concerns about media concentration are ill-founded in an environment where anyone can speak and where there are literally hundreds of competing channels. What those lobbyists for big media don't tell you is that the traffic patterns of the online world are beginning to resemble those of television and radio. In one study, for example, AOL Time Warner (as it was then known) accounted for nearly a third of all user time spent online. And two others companies—Yahoo and Microsoft—bring that figure to fully 50 percent. As for the growing number of channels available on today's cable systems, most are owned by a small handful of companies. Of the ninety-one major networks that appear on most cable systems, seventy-nine are part of such multiple network groups such as Time Warner, Viacom, Liberty Media, NBC, and Disney. In order to program a channel on cable today, you must either be owned by or affiliated with one of the giants. If we're not vigilant, the wide-open spaces of the Internet could be transformed into a system in which a handful of companies use their control over high-speed access to ensure they remain at the top of the digital heap in the broadband era at the expense of the democratic potential of this amazing technology. So we must fight to make sure the Internet remains open to all as the present-day analogue of that many-tongued world of small newspapers so admired by de Tocqueville.

We must fight for a regulatory, market, and public-opinion environment that lets local and community-based content be heard rather than drowned out by nationwide commercial programming.

We must fight to limit conglomerate swallowing of media outlets by sensible limits on multiple and cross-ownership of TV and radio stations, newspapers, magazines, publishing companies, and other information sources. Let the message go forth: No Berlusconis in America!

We must fight to expand a noncommercial media system—something made possible in part by new digital spectrum awarded to PBS stations—and fight off attempts to privatize what's left of public broadcasting. Commercial speech must not be the only free speech in America!

We must fight to create new opportunities, through public policies and private agreements, to let historically marginalized media players into more ownership of channels and control of content.

Let us encourage traditional mainstream journalism to get tougher about keeping a critical eye on those in public and private power and keeping us all informed of what's important—not necessarily simple or entertaining or good for the bottom line. Not all news is *Entertainment Tonight*. And news departments are trustees of the public, not of the corporate media's stockholders

In that last goal, schools of journalism and professional news associations have their work cut out. We need journalism graduates who not only are better informed in a whole spectrum of special fields—and the schools do a competent job there—but who also take from their training a strong sense of public service. We also need graduates who are perhaps a little more hard-boiled and street-smart than the present crop, though that's hard to teach. Thanks to the high cost of education, we get very few recruits from the ranks of those who do the world's unglamorous and low-paid work. But as a onetime "cub" in a very different kind of setting, I cherish H. L. Mencken's description of what being a young Baltimore reporter a hundred years ago meant to him. He wrote:

> I was at large in a wicked seaport of half a million people with a front seat at every public show. . . . [B]y all orthodox cultural standards I probably reached my all-time low, for the heavy reading of my teens had been abandoned in favor of life itself. . . . But it would be an exaggeration to say I was ignorant, for if I neglected the humanities I was meanwhile laying in all the worldly wisdom of a police lieutenant, a bartender, a shyster lawyer or a midwife.

We need some of that worldly wisdom in our newsrooms. Let's figure out how to attract youngsters who have acquired it.

And as for those professional associations of editors, they might remember that in union there is strength. One journalist alone can't extract from an employer a commitment to let editors and not accountants choose the appropriate subject matter for coverage. But what if news councils blew the whistle on shoddy or cowardly managements? What if foundations gave magazines such as the *Columbia Journalism Review* sufficient resources to spread their stories of journalistic bias, failure, or incompetence? What if entire editorial departments simply refused any longer to quote anonymous sources, or refused to give Kobe Bryant's trial more than the minimal space it rates by any reasonable standard, or refused to run stories planted by the Defense Department and impossible, for alleged security reasons, to verify? What if a professional association backed them to the hilt? Or required the same stance from all its members? It would take courage to confront powerful ownerships that way. But not as much courage as is asked of those brave journalists in some countries who face the dungeon, the executioner, or the secret assassin for speaking out.

All this may be in the domain of fantasy. And then again, maybe not. What I know to be real is that we are in for the fight of our lives. I am not a romantic about democracy or journalism; the writer André Gide may have been right when he said that all things human, given time, go badly. But I know journalism and democracy are deeply linked in whatever chance we human beings have to redress our grievances, renew our politics, and reclaim our revolutionary ideals. Those are difficult tasks at any time, and they are even more difficult in a cynical age such as this, when a deep and pervasive corruption has settled upon the republic. But too much is at stake for our spirits to flag. In 2003 the Library of Congress gave the first Kluge Lifetime Award in the Humanities to the Polish philosopher Leszek Kolakowski. In an interview Kolakowski said, "There is one freedom on which all other liberties depend—and that is freedom of expression, freedom of speech, of print. If this is taken away, no other freedom can exist, or at least it would be soon suppressed."

That's the flame of truth this movement must carry forward. I am older than many of you and am not likely to be around for the duration. But I take heart from the presence in this movement, unseen, of John Peter Zenger, Thomas Paine, the muckrakers, I. F. Stone, and all those heroes and heroines, celebrated or forgotten, who faced odds no less than ours and did not flinch. I take heart in efforts like this book and the networks of people it represents. It's your fight now. Look around. You are not alone.

INTRODUCTION

Russell Newman and Ben Scott

When Michael Powell announced his imminent departure as chairman of the Federal Communications Commission on January 21, 2005, it marked the end of the first phase of a sea change in media policymaking in the United States. Stepping down was an industry champion, one who expressed great confidence in "free markets" even as he railroaded media-ownership rules that undermined them; one who spoke of "competition" as he sought to dismantle it; one who made his probusiness proclivities known early on in his tenure, and made good on them. But he was also one who expected to be able to accomplish these goals in a business-as-usual fashion—that is, behind closed doors, without a mention in the mainstream media or a single citizen's voice in the mix—as had been done for decades at the Federal Communications Commission. To his surprise, and to the surprise of the telecommunications political complex that lobbies in Washington, Powell's tenure witnessed the greatest surge in public participation at the Commission in generations. Following his departure, media policymaking in the United States would never be the same again.

Powell's brazen attempt in June 2003 to loosen media ownership rules so that one entity could own a market's monopoly cable provider, the monopoly newspaper, three major television broadcast outlets, and eight radio stations—a story that will be told in the course of this book—set off a wave of discontent that took no one by surprise more than Powell himself. However, it is important to note that the firestorm provoked by Powell's audacity did not stem from a newfound resistance to a change in the status quo. Instead, it reflected an already dissatisfied mindset, a pent-up powder keg of anger that required just the right spark to explode. And explode it did. Perhaps more importantly, it kept on exploding in response to high-profile scandals in the corporate news media.

It will come as news to few Americans that we are now in the midst of a full-blown journalistic crisis in the United States. The cheerleading news coverage of the war in Iraq, both before and during the conflict, has led to widespread public disaffection. The exposure of economic and political influence on the reporting of

1

major newsrooms has badly injured the credibility of the "free press." Americans have been driven to the BBC and the international press to obtain trustworthy news on American foreign policy. The *New York Times* felt it necessary to publish a long apology for its mistaken coverage of the Iraq war, but only necessary enough for a page-10 appearance.[1] Postelection discoveries about columnists who received lucrative undisclosed contracts from the Bush administration to promote unpopular policies further undermined American confidence in the fourth estate.[2] Another black eye on the national press corps appeared when online bloggers discovered and broadcast the fact that a partisan hack, with no journalism experience, appeared to have received help from administration sources to be granted exclusive access to White House press gatherings, serving up softball questions to the President and his spokesman, aimed at bolstering their policy objectives.[3] When it took a collaborative effort of independent online activists to finally call attention to this scandal, what trust should the public have in a "free press" that is supposed to shield them from such activities?

Critically, in the public debate, this crisis in journalism is explicitly tied to the dangers of consolidating media ownership and the corruption of lawmakers by big media. With each successive display of political censorship, the media draw greater public scrutiny and rehash more discussion about public-interest protections. CBS has been at the center of these exposures. In the fall of 2003, the network canceled the broadcast of a television movie about the life of Ronald Reagan after GOP leaders judged it insufficiently laudatory. Then, in the run-up to the Super Bowl, CBS refused to sell advertising time to the progressive group MoveOn.org, claiming that the network does not accept political ads—a ridiculous claim from a company that rakes in millions in advertising revenues during every election season. Finally, the "Tiffany Network" became embroiled in allegations that falsified records lay behind a news exposé of President Bush's military service. Journalistic credibility was badly damaged, despite a raft of apologies and an internal investigation.

The Sinclair Broadcast Group went one better, demonstrating its complete indifference to the taboo against political censorship on a broadcast station. In May 2004, Ted Koppel dedicated one episode of *Nightline* to reciting the names of American soldiers who had lost their lives in Iraq. Sinclair, which owns several ABC affiliates, refused to air the program, claiming that "the action appears to be motivated by a political agenda designed to undermine the efforts of the United States in Iraq."[4] Sinclair did not mention in its explanation that it stood to gain millions from Bush administration policies that would loosen ownership rules. Nor did it mention that many of Sinclair's top executives are major GOP campaign donors or that it had compelled its entire on-camera news staff—including the weather forecasters—to pledge their support to the President over the public airwaves. Robert McChesney reacted strongly: "What we see in Sinclair . . . with its cozy and corrupt relationship to the Bush administration is TV journalism that is anything but independent of the government. It is a commercial version of *Pravda*, and it is an outrageous and entirely unacceptable use of the public's airwaves."[5]

The dismay caused by the changing face of the American media system is not the exclusive province of angry citizens. A May 2004 Pew Research Study that surveyed 547 national and local journalists from print, online, and broadcast media revealed that 66 percent of national news workers and 57 percent of local journalists believed that their profession was "going in the wrong direction." The principal reason for this dissatisfaction has nothing to do with declining standards of professionalism or loosened reportorial ethics: these reporters "believe that increased bottom line pressure is 'seriously hurting' the quality of news coverage."[6] The sickness is deep and widespread, as evidenced by such establishment-media voices as *Washington Post* editors Leonard Downie and Robert Kaiser in their recent book, *The News about the News*, a scathing critique of commercial pressures on contemporary news media.[7] But such is to be expected, perhaps, when newsgathering becomes just another way to generate profits within ever larger conglomerates that are equally eager to sell consumers dishwashing detergent as they are to hawk an airplane engine or a battle tank. (General Electric, owner of NBC, offers all of these items.)[8]

In effect, the media reform movement, born from many years of organizing and catalyzed by the impudence of Powell's FCC in June 2003, has developed a momentum of its own. Citizens who learned of the corruption in media policymaking have now connected that political debate with the crisis in journalism. Each periodic scandal in news columns or on TV news shows reiterates this problem and calls to mind the larger meaning of the dilemma facing the media system. Over time, this is the kind of knowledge that seeps from activist groups into local communities as conventional wisdom. It is the kind of development in the political culture that produces serious, progressive change.

The digital convergence of traditional print media, broadcasting, telecommunications, and the Internet now promises to drive a series of major policy changes that will substantially reshape the media of the future and with it, the future of our society. These changes will go well beyond deciding who owns what networks and newspapers; they will determine—if not overtly select—who will control access to public information and who will gain access to the very means of communications. Most importantly, these policies will establish whether or not the public will be involved in the governance of our own media. Most Americans are as yet unaware of these larger processes at work.

The reality is that we stand at the precipice of perhaps the most critical time in decades for active citizen involvement in shaping future media policies. Though the biggest fights still lay ahead of us, the public has now shown that it is a political force to be reckoned with in media policymaking. This by itself is an enormous step forward, but special interests within the media industry have been anticipating these debates for years. They are ready, and they are working quietly to make sure that the public's efforts will be trumped in the next policy fight the same way they have been in past fights. Big business is working to make sure the issues remain opaque and policy discussion limited to a handful of lawmakers and regulators.

This is no conspiracy theory but is simply the way the American system works today. Democracy has lost track of its citizens. People are increasingly frustrated by policies of war and peace, the economy, healthcare, environment, civil rights, and media but find no venue to challenge the status quo and no voice for public advocacy. Through media policy fights, we find not only a worthy arena for democratic participation, with many groups organized for action, but realize a challenge where the fruits of our labor create not only better media policy, but also a better democracy.

When the broadcast ownership fight made headlines in 2003, it was often the policy advocates in Washington who gave interviews and received the national spotlight. But this attention obscures the true source of the political energy that fuels media reform—grassroots groups. It is high time we explicitly recognized that this movement is fundamentally "bottom-up" and started talking about it that way, strategizing around this great strength. Perhaps no force is stronger than people coming together in local organizations to stir involvement around issues that matter most to the principles of democracy: public information, open debate, social justice, and the right of all citizens to free expression and a diversity of viewpoints. This book, largely comprised of chapters written by policy experts, owes its significance to the citizens who advocate these ideas in towns and cities across the country. Grassroots champions of the public interest, such as San Francisco's Media Alliance and Youth Media Council, Philadelphia's Media Tank and Prometheus Radio Project, Seattle's Reclaim the Media, Chicago Media Action, Independent Media Centers across the nation, Fairness & Accuracy In Reporting, community radio and TV stations, media-justice activists and other networks of media reform have all been driving this fight for years. These groups provided the local flashpoints of political activism that packed the halls when Commissioners Michael Copps and Jonathan Adelstein toured the country. They energized communities with media-literacy training, independent media, stories ignored by the mainstream outlets, biting media criticism, and alternative viewpoints on important social issues.

The purpose of this book is to prepare readers for tomorrow's media reform fights. It attempts to chart the frontline struggles over journalism, democracy, social justice, intellectual property, free speech, and their relationship to the big business battles over cable, Internet, copyright, and radio spectrum. The goal is to help shed light on the most important problems in the media system, emphasizing the ways in which public participation can help to change things for the better. Too often these debates are shrouded in the language of technocracy, hidden by bureaucracy, and left uncovered by mainstream media riddled with deep conflicts of interest. When our policy advocates in Washington and our grassroots organizers across the country invoke the will of the public on whose shoulders they stand, an informed and outspoken populace—one ready to take action to protect democratic media—must rise to the occasion. It is our hope that you, the reader, will be excited by the range of issues and ideas presented in the pages ahead and that you will be inspired to join the fight to insure that the future of the media is a just and democratic one.

The enthusiasm and energy to drive this movement is readily apparent. This book's origins can be found at the first National Conference for Media Reform, held in Madison, Wisconsin, in November 2003. When Free Press began organizing this affair, it was expected that only several hundred people would attend. Instead, close to two thousand came, featuring FCC Commissioners, members of Congress, and a broad swath of those who sought media that served the public. It was an incredibly energizing experience for a number of reasons. One, conferencegoers realized that they weren't alone in their concern, seeing others as enraged, as troubled, and as ready for action as they were. Secondly, the full breadth of what an effective media reform movement—a global one—actually looks like was finally made known. Activists for the reform of intellectual property, broadband, spectrum, media ownership, social justice, and beyond were all under the same roof for several days. The call to arms issued during Bill Moyers' powerful keynote address, delivered to an absolutely packed house in downtown Madison, is an appropriate opening to our discussion. The energy and power that resonated after the applause died can still be felt today, as the gauntlet he threw down that evening is increasingly being taken up by citizens across the country.

We intend this book to be the first stab at harnessing the power that emerged from that conference—a users' guide to winning back our media, written by those who are fighting the battles firsthand. It's also an attempt to begin dialogues among the disparate activist movements at work. Many of the most crucial questions have yet to be asked, and many answers to questions already posed are yet unformed. What is also becoming clear is that as we seek to reshape our media, we must also examine who are the entities making reforms and in whose favor reforms are being made. If it is social justice we seek, it will not be obtained if the "reformed" media still feed and propagate existing structures of power in our society.

The challenges are large, but the rewards are much larger. For a brief, defining moment, the future of our media is about to be determined. Even better, citizens now realize that they have a role in shaping it; whether they will choose to do so, it's up to us. Here's our chance.

Notes

1. The Editors, "The Times and Iraq," *New York Times*, May 26, 2004, p. A10.
2. Frank Rich, "All the President's Newsmen," *New York Times*, January 16, 2005; Anne Kornblut, "Bush Prohibits Paying of Commentators," *New York Times*, January 27, 2005.
3. Katharine Seelye, "Democrats Want Investigation of Reporter Using Fake Name," *New York Times*, February 11, 2005.
4. Margot Habiby. "Sinclair to pre-empt 'Nightline' on ABC stations, cites politics." Bloomberg.com, http://quote.bloomberg.com/apps/news?pid=10000103&sid=aqg09j99xhd4&refer=us.
5. Free Press, Press Release, "Free Press Announces Plans to Challenge Sinclair License Renewals in 2004 and Links Decision to Political Motives," April 30, 2004, http://www.freepress.net/news/article.php?id=3351.
6. "Bottom Line Pressures Now Hurting Coverage, Say Journalists," Pew Research Center Study, available at http://people-press.org/reports/display.php3?ReportID=214.
7. Leonard Downie Jr. and Robert G. Kaiser, *The News About the News* (New York: Alfred A. Knopf, 2002).
8. A full breakdown of conglomerated media properties is available at http://www.freepress.net/ownership/.

PART 1

THE THREAT TO A FREE PRESS

THE EMERGING STRUGGLE
FOR A FREE PRESS

Robert W. McChesney

Our press system is failing in the United States. To reverse course, we must make media policymaking a core political issue in this society, much as environmental issues were driven by an organized movement into the accepted realm of public debate of politicians and citizens in the last decades. It is an issue that can be a winner for the public. In fact, if it isn't a winner, our chances for positive social change on all our other fronts are greatly undermined.

There is now a severe crisis of viable self-government in this country. Depoliticization and demoralization are rampant; voter turnout ranks among the lowest in the world. In the United States, voting is determined significantly by class. The richer you are, the more likely you are to vote. Over time, this political debility reinforces a growing inequality that undermines the foundations of democratic self-governance, breeding corruption and cynicism. In the absence of anything like a real public debate in the media on critical social issues, there is little chance that the nation will remedy its deplorable status quo. Even before turning to the question of the media, even before we consider how the media system is structured, how it operates, and why it is failing democracy, the bankruptcy of our political culture is enough to suggest that the media system and the journalism it generates are far from satisfactory. When we look even cursorily at media performance on core issues facing the nation, the abject failure of mainstream journalism confirms the validity of the critique.

Consider the matter of going to war, perhaps the most significant undertaking in which a government can engage. The United States has had several major wars involving ground forces over the past century, and three points have been true of nearly all of them. First, the White House was determined to go to war while the general population was far more reluctant. Second, the White House and its allies lied to generate popular support, knowing that the truth would be insufficient to generate the backing necessary to carry out the war. And third, the news media, by and large, went along uncritically with the propaganda campaign. Indeed, United States press coverage of the buildup to World War I and Vietnam rank among the darkest moments in the history of American journalism. The media were complicit in wars that are now generally regarded as tragic mistakes.

With this legacy, one might have imagined that when President George W. Bush began beating the drums for invading Iraq, with his claims about weapons of mass destruction, imminent threats to the United States, and the central role of Iraq to the terrorist threat, the news media would approach these claims with heightened skepticism and demand hard evidence. Instead, much of the news media, including the *New York Times*, gave official claims only mild review and even participated in exaggerating them. Some of the media, such as the Fox News Channel and much of talk radio, ridiculed and attacked anyone who dared question our maximum leader. History repeats itself. The American people approved a war under false pretenses, and by the end of 2004 the war was already proven to be an unmitigated disaster.

Or consider the coverage of elections. It is beyond debate that much of what government does is beyond the purview of the bulk of the citizenry. But through elections, citizens can control who gets to be in power and how long these people stay there. It is arguably the prime evidence that we have a democratic system of governance. So, even if our media fail to provide analysis of the preponderance of what government does, they can, at the least, make it possible for citizens to effectively monitor the electoral campaigns of public officials.

Yet, our electoral system appears to be corrupt beyond repair. The cost of elections has skyrocketed. Running for office is prohibitively expensive for all but the richest Americans. Billions were spent on federal campaigns in 2004 alone. The money comes overwhelmingly from the rich and powerful in return for political favors. In this context, depoliticization appears not as an irrational choice, especially in the downward drift to the working class and the poor.

Our media are not solely or even primarily responsible for the corruption of the electoral process—though the windfall of TV political ads has made the corporate media's relationship to campaign finance similar to the NRA's relationship to gun control. It is clear that our news media reinforce the rule of big money over our elections. Much TV news coverage of elections has been gutted over the past few decades; after all, why give away time to candidates through news coverage when you can sell it to them through ad spots at such great profit? Radio news barely exists anymore outside of NPR. And our print journalism tends to acknowledge as legitimate only those candidates with big war chests. It also allows big money candidates to dictate the themes of their campaigns through TV ads. In short, the news media pour gasoline on the fire.

The problem with the media for a democratic society extends well beyond journalism. Consider the commercial tidal wave in our media that marinates every available second or pixel with some form of sales pitch or branding effort. The crisis is most blatant and disturbing with the commercial carpet-bombing of our children, beginning at the earliest ages. Study after study shows that this commercial indoctrination of children is clearly leading to a wave of serious problems, from obesity to attention deficit disorder. The practice is so indefensible that many nations have banned TV advertising to children. But because it is extraordinarily profitable, it proceeds unabated in the United States.

And that point gets to the heart of the problem. In the United States, the media system is set up to maximize profit for a handful of large companies. The system works well for them, but it is a disaster for the communication needs of a healthy and self-governing society. The core problem is not with poorly trained or unethical journalists. In fact, I suspect that this generation of journalists may well be as talented and ethical as any generation in memory; it is the context in which journalists work that is the problem. Nor does the problem reside with nefarious or corrupt owners; even if Rupert Murdoch and Sumner Redstone were to quit their jobs, change their names, and move off to Utah to do yoga and share a bong all day in a mountain cabin, the operations of News Corporation and Viacom would not change appreciably. Whoever replaced them would follow the same cues, with more or less success, as the logic of the system would remain intact. No corporate executive would place the public-interest priorities of a democracy ahead of the profit-making needs of the company. To do so in the absence of similar altruism by every other corporation would be to invite bankruptcy. Only policy changes governing the structure of the system can alter the nature of the beast.

If we want to correct the failures of media content, we have to change the system that breeds them. And following my logic, the stakes are very high. We must change media content radically if we are going to have a viable self-governing society. The media system is not the only variable in the struggle for progressive social change, but it is an unavoidable variable if we wish to transform this society for the better. As former FCC member Nicholas Johnson likes to put it when speaking to activists and progressives: whatever your first issue of concern, media had better be your second, because without change in the media, the chances of progress in your primary area are far less likely.

Where does our media system come from? In "free market" mythology, our media system is the result of competition between businesses fighting to best meet public needs. In reality, civic needs aren't even on the radar. Our media system is the result of competition between businesses and a wide range of government policies, regulations, and subsidies. Each of the twenty or so giant media firms that dominate the entirety of our media system is the recipient of massive government largesse, or what could be regarded as corporate welfare. They receive (for free) one or more of the following: (1) monopoly licenses to scarce radio and television channels; (2) monopoly franchises for cable and satellite TV systems;

(3) copyright protection for their content. When the government sets up a firm with one of these monopoly licenses, it is virtually impossible to lose money. As media mogul Barry Diller put it, the only way commercial broadcasters can lose money is if one of their employees steals from them. Ironically, even if we were to have a deregulated, "free market" media system, it would require media policies to put such a system in place.

If policies establish the nature of the media system, and the nature of the media system determines the nature and logic of media content, then the nucleus of the media atom is the policymaking process. And it is here we get to the source of the crisis of media in the United States. In the United States, media and communication policies have been made in the most corrupt manner imaginable for generations. Most Americans have had no idea that media policies were made in their name but without their informed consent. Instead, these policies were created by extraordinarily powerful corporate lobbies fighting it out behind closed doors in Congress and at federal regulatory agencies. And the resulting policies reflect this process: they are set up to serve the needs of a small group of commercial interests. And the public has no way of knowing about them because to the extent that these policies are covered in the press, they are treated as business stories of importance to owners and managers, not as political stories of interest to citizens in a democracy. Corporate media giants are content to promulgate the notion that this is a "natural" media system, beyond the purview of policymakers.

Perhaps the best way to capture the media policymaking process in the United States is to consider the 1974 Oscar-winning film, *The Godfather II*. Roughly halfway through the film, a bunch of American gangsters, including Michael Corleone, assemble on a Havana patio to celebrate Hyman Roth's birthday. This event occurs in 1958, pre-Castro, when Batista and the mob ruled Cuba. Roth is giving a slice of his birthday cake, which has the outline of Cuba on it, to each of the gangsters. As he does so, Roth outlines how the gangsters are divvying up the island among themselves. Roth triumphantly states how great it is to be in a country with a government that works with private enterprise.

That is pretty much how media policies are generated in the United States. But do not think it is a conspiracy where the corporate interests peacefully carve up the cake. In fact, as in *The Godfather II*, where the movie revolves around the Corleone-Roth turf war, the big media trade associations and corporations are all slugging it out with each other for the largest slice of the cake. That is why they have such enormous lobbying arsenals and flood politicians with campaign donations. But what they all agree on, like those gangsters in Havana, is that it is their cake and nobody else gets a slice.

The solution to the media crisis requires widespread, informed public participation in media policymaking. Corrupt power grabs are much more difficult to perpetrate under the bright light of public scrutiny. By simple virtue of awareness, public activism in policy debates will lead to better policies and a better system. There are no magic cure-all systems, and even the best policies have their weaknesses. But informed public participation is the key to seeing that the best policies to emerge are ones serving broadly determined values and objectives.

Imagine, for example, that there had been a modicum of public involvement when Congress lifted the national cap on how many radio stations a single company could own in 1996. That provision—written, as far as anyone can tell, by radio industry lobbyists and slipped into the bill by a compliant legislator—sailed through Congress without a shred of discussion or press coverage. It is safe to say that 99.99 percent of Americans were unaware of the legislation. As a result, radio broadcasting has become the province of a small number of firms that can own as many as eight stations each in a single market. Clear Channel owns over 1,200 stations nationally. Because of this single change in policy, competition has decreased, local radio news and programming have been decimated (too expensive and much less competitive pressure to produce local content), musical play lists have less nutrition and variety than the menu at McDonald's, while the amount of advertising has bloated. This is all due to a change in policy, not to the inexorable workings of the free market. "There is too much concentration in radio," Senator John McCain stated on the Senate floor in 2003. "I know of no credible person who disagrees with that." Radio in the public interest has been destroyed. A medium that is arguably the least expensive and most accessible of our major media, that is ideally suited for localism, has been converted into a Wal-Mart-like profit machine for a handful of massive chains. Such a development can only happen when policies are made under the cover of darkness by a tiny band of self-proclaimed power brokers. *Welcome to Havana, Mr. Corleone.*

Radio is also instructive because it highlights the propagandistic use of the word deregulation. This term is often used to describe the relaxation of media ownership rules, even by its opponents. The term "deregulation" has come to imply something good—that people will be less regulated and enjoy greater liberty. Who could oppose that? Radio broadcasting is the classic case of a "deregulated" industry. But just how deregulated is it? Try broadcasting on one of the 1,200 channels for which Clear Channel has a government-enforced monopoly license. If you persist, you will find yourself in a federal penitentiary. That is very serious regulation. In fact, all "deregulation" means in radio is that firms can possess many more government-granted and government-enforced monopoly licenses than before. When you see the term "deregulation" used in media policy debates, the wise course is to substitute what is really taking place: "re-regulation purely to serve large commercial concerns without any pretense of serving public interests."

As the radio example indicates, we have a very long way to go to bring widespread and informed public participation to media policy debates. The immediate barrier is the standard problem facing democratic forces in the United States: the corporate media political lobby is extraordinarily powerful and is used to having its way on both sides of the aisle in Congress. In addition, press coverage, which tends to be of marginal quality on any issue in which big money faces off against public interest, is utterly appalling in the case of media policy debates. The track record is clear: while the process may be complex, in the final analysis corporate media use their control over the news to limit, distort, or trivialize public awareness of media policy debates.

Moreover, corporate media power is protected from public review by a series of very powerful myths. Four of these myths in particular need to be debunked if there is going to be any hope of successfully infusing the public into media policy debates.

The first myth is that the existing profit-driven United States media system, for better or for worse, is the American Way, and there is nothing we can do about it. The received wisdom is that the Founders crafted the First Amendment to prevent any government interference with the free market. In fact, this belief could hardly be more inaccurate. Freedom of the press was seen more as a social right belonging to the entire population than as a commercial right belonging to wealthy investors. While the state was prevented from prior restraint, it had a commitment to make a free press possible through enlightened policies. The measure of a free press was in the caliber of the political culture, not in the commercial success of its publishers. Indeed, the first generations of the republic saw the use of printing contracts to subsidize major newspapers that would have had difficulty prospering, perhaps even surviving, left to the whims of the free market.

The most striking public policy came with establishment of the United States post office. In the first generations of the republic, newspapers accounted for between 70 and 95 percent of post-office traffic, and newspapers depended on the post office for distributing much of their circulation. A key question facing Congress was the charge of mailing newspapers. No one at the time was arguing that newspapers should pay the cost of shipping. The range of debate was between those who argued for a large public subsidy and those who argued that all postage for newspapers should be free, to encourage the production and distribution of a wide range of ideas. The former position won, and it contributed to a massive flowering of print media in the United States throughout the early nineteenth century. What is most striking about this period is that there was no rhetoric about free markets in media or the sacrosanct rights of commercial interests. That came later, when powerful commercial media interests emerged and used such jargon to protect their privileges and subsidies.

The second myth is that professional practices in journalism will protect the public from the economic influence and political biases of concentrated commercial control over the news media. Therefore, we need not worry about the media system or the policies that put it into place, because the iron conscience of professional journalists will protect us. In reality, the notion of professional journalism is only around a century old in the United States, and its viability has been hotly contested throughout that period. The constant crisis of professionalism stems from the fact that it was invented to paper over the conflict between the needs of democratic public debate and the demands of the commercial media marketplace.

Through the late nineteenth century, American journalism was explicitly organized along partisan lines. The owners of newspapers made their politics explicit in their pages. This situation was satisfactory in competitive markets, where there was a wide range of viewpoints. It became a problem by the end of the nineteenth century, as newspaper markets became increasingly concentrated and economic barriers to entry prevented new newspapers from being launched successfully. In this environment, partisan journalism turned the democratic public debate of many voices into the propaganda campaigns of a few. Adding to the problem was the tremendous commercial pressure on publishers to lower prices in order to draw a larger readership and increase advertising rates. The results were predictable—cost-cutting measures that favored style over substance. Sensational fare with a propensity for lying and the bribery of reporters became the norm. Readers began to lose confidence in the press, threatening to destabilize the market and undermine the value of newspapers as instruments of political debate, however skewed. In short, consolidating markets of partisan news produced a crisis for the media system that threatened to make the entire enterprise illegitimate in the public's eyes.

The solution to this problem—then as now—was professional autonomy for journalists. Trained, professional reporters and editors who were politically neutral would cover the news in an objective manner. The political views of the owners and advertisers would be irrelevant except on the editorial page. This was the revolutionary idea of separating editorial from business, like the separation of church and state. There were no schools of journalism in 1900; by 1920, all the major schools had been established, often at the behest of major publishers. Professionalism emerged haltingly as a compromise, providing the public with the appearance of a trustworthy free press, and leaving publishers with the credibility to continue raking in profits and shape political opinion.

Professional journalism as it evolved in the United States was far from perfect. In reality, journalists had little autonomy on the most important issues of political economy. Editors often practiced self-censorship to avoid violation of unspoken news policies set by the owners. Reporters followed standard practices, which rarely permitted severe criticism of the status quo or took up the central struggles of class politics. To a significant degree, professionalism failed to make the newsroom a sacrosanct venue for objective reportage. Rather, it simply internalized and institutionalized the commercial needs and political interests of media owners, making journalists oblivious or resigned to the compromises with authority built into their code.

One striking problem, for example, was the dependence upon official sources for a legitimate news story. This practice has made much of professional journalism stenography of debates among those in power. On issues where those in power tend to agree on the basics, like most United States wars, the press coverage is dreadful. Journalists who question the proceedings are dismissed as partisan, ideological, and unprofessional. Yet even with its flaws, professional journalism made some positive strides, and it looked awfully good compared to what it replaced. At its high-water mark, in the 1960s and 1970s, it was a barrier of sorts to commercial media ownership.

But the autonomy of journalists was never written into law, and as media companies grew larger and larger, there has been increased pressure to generate profit from the news. That policy meant slashing editorial budgets, sloughing off on expensive investigative and international coverage, and allowing for commercial values to play a larger role in determining inexpensive and trivial news topics. In short, the autonomy and integrity of United States journalism has been under sustained attack. Linda Foley, president of the Newspaper Guild, the union of newspaper journalists, states that the main concern of her members, far beyond salary, is the way commercial pressures have undermined the ability of journalists to practice their craft. It is why journalists rank among the leading proponents of media reform. They know firsthand how the media system is overwhelming their best intentions and their professional autonomy, and unless the system changes, there is little hope for viable journalism.

The third myth is probably the most prevalent, and it applies primarily to the entertainment media, though with the commercialization of journalism it is being applied increasingly there as well. This is the notion that as bad as the media system may seem to be, it gives the people what they want. If we are dissatisfied with media content, do not blame the media firms; blame the morons who demand it. This is such a powerful myth because it contains an element of truth. After all, what movie studio or TV network produces programming that people do not want to watch? The problem with it, as I detail in my book *The Problem of the Media*,[1] is that it reduces a complex relationship of audience and producers to a simplistic one-way flow. In oligopolistic media markets, there is producer sovereignty, not consumer sovereignty, so media firms give you what you want, but only within the range that generates maximum profits for them. Supply creates demand as much as demand creates supply.

And some things are strictly off-limits to consumer pressure. Media content comes marinated in commercialism, although survey after survey shows that a significant percentage of Americans do not want so much advertising. Most recently, an April 2004 survey by Yankelovich Partners revealed that 65 percent of

Americans believe that they are "constantly bombarded with too much" advertising. But don't expect a mad dash by media corporations to respond to that public desire. It is difficult, if not impossible, to use the market to register opposition to hypercommercialism in the market. Since this is where the policymaking process is imperative, citizens can potentially apply the full range of their values to determine media practices.

Most important, the media system clearly generates many things that we do not want. Economists call these externalities to identify the consequences of market transactions that do not affect the buyer or seller (and therefore the market pays no attention to them). But they have a significant effect and can level massive costs upon society. Pollution is the classic externality in industry. It requires policy intervention to reduce pollution, as otherwise competitive pressures force firms to keep on polluting. Externalities can be positive, but firms have a greater incentive to capitalize upon those; it is the negative ones they wish to avoid paying for.

Media generate huge negative externalities. What we are doing to children with hypercommercialization is a huge consequence that will almost certainly bring massive social costs, affecting everyone in society. Likewise, dreadful journalism will lead to corrupt and incompetent governance, a situation that will exact a high cost on all our lives, not just those who are in the market for journalism. The long and short of it is that the market cannot effectively address externalities; that task will require enlightened public policy.

The fourth myth is that the Internet will set us free. We have no reason to worry about corrupt policymaking, corporate control, lousy journalism, or hypercommercialism because the advent of the Internet ends the problem of broadcast scarcity (that is, more people want to broadcast than there is space on the airwaves) and means that everyone communicates on a relatively equal playing field. Who cares if Rupert Murdoch owns film studios and satellite TV systems and TV stations and newspapers? Anyone can launch a blog or website to finally compete with the big guys. It is just a matter of time until the corporate media dinosaurs disappear beneath the tidal wave of new media competition.

The Internet and the digital communication revolution are in fact radically transforming the media landscape, but how they do so will be determined by policies, not by magic. The Internet itself is the result of years of heavy public subsidy, and its rapid spread owes to the open-access "common carrier" policy forced upon telecommunication companies. How the Internet develops in the future will have everything to do with policies, ranging from the application of copyright law through the allocation of spectrum for open wireless systems to policies that assist in the production of independent media content on the Internet. The one point that is already clear is that merely having the ability to launch a website does not magically transform the media system.

Once again, the moral of the story is clear: If we wish to change the nature of media content, we have to change the system. If we wish to change the media system, we need to change media policies. And if we wish to change media policies, we have to blast open the media policymaking process and remove it from the proverbial Havana patio. My sense is that the more widespread public participation there is in media policymaking, the more likely we are to have policies encouraging a more competitive and locally oriented commercial media system, as well as a much more prominent and heterogeneous nonprofit and noncommercial media sector. But if there is a legitimate public debate, I will certainly live with the results, whatever they might be.

Nonetheless, there have been a handful of key moments when media policymaking became part of the public dialogue. In the Progressive Era, the corruption, sensationalism, and probusiness partisanship of much of commercial journalism produced a crisis that led to widespread criticism of capitalist control of the press and even to movements to establish municipal or worker ownership of newspapers. In the 1930s, a fairly significant movement arose that opposed the government's secretly turning over all the choice monopoly radio channels to owners affiliated with the two huge national chains, NBC and CBS, and called for the establishment of a dominant noncommercial broadcasting system. I will not keep you in suspense; these movements failed.

But following World War II, media policymaking has increasingly gravitated to the Havana patio. When the choice monopoly licenses for television were doled out in the 1940s, public debate played no role whatsoever. The FCC chair who orchestrated the process would leave the FCC to triple his salary as an executive at NBC three months after the TV allocation plan was announced. Since then, regulation of commercial broadcasting has degenerated to farcical proportions, as no leverage forced commercial broadcasters to do anything that would interfere with their ability to exploit the government-granted and -enforced monopoly licenses for maximum commercial gain. The crisis I described earlier is the result.

The prospects for challenging the corrupt policymaking process seemed especially bleak by the 1990s, with the ascension of neoliberalism—the philosophy that dogmatically equates profit maximization with the maximization of human happiness. Even many Democrats abandoned much of their longstanding rhetoric about media regulation in the public interest, and accepted the "market über alles" logic.

So when the FCC announced that it would review several of its major media ownership rules in 2002, nearly everyone thought that it was certain that they would be relaxed or eliminated. After all, a majority of the FCC was on record favoring new rules permitting media firms to expand—even before any study of the matter was conducted. The media giants hated the old rules and were calling in all their markers with the politicians to undertake mergers and acquisitions, reduce competition and risk, and become more profitable. The existing ownership limits under attack were essentially the last form of media regulation that had any teeth. They were backed by widespread public antipathy toward media concentration and strong support for the idea of local media. Further, the smaller commercial media sector knew that it could not survive in a market without ownership limits on broadcast and cable companies.

In June of 2003, the Republican FCC dramatically relaxed the limits on ownership.

Through the remainder of the year, the FCC's decision on media ownership rules caused a spectacular and wholly unanticipated backlash from the general public. Literally millions of Americans contacted members of Congress and the FCC to oppose media concentration. By the end of 2003, members of Congress noted that media ownership was the second-most discussed issue by their constituents, trailing only the invasion and occupation of Iraq. It is safe to say that media issues had not cracked the Congressional "top twenty" list in decades. What was also striking was how much of the opposition came from the political right, as well as a nearly unified left. In September 2003, the Senate overturned the FCC's media rules changes by a 55:40 vote. The probusiness House leadership blocked a similar vote while the courts reviewed the matter after a group of public-interest organizations filed suit. On June 24, 2003, the Third Circuit Court of Appeals struck down the FCC's rule changes, sending them back to the agency on the grounds that they defied logic and reason and lacked justification for better serving the public interest. The ruling was a major victory for a politically activated American public.

It is critical to point out that what drove millions of Americans to become active on media ownership in 2003 was not a belief in the status quo. To the contrary, the movement was driven by explicit dissatisfaction with the status quo and a desire to improve the system. Years of frustration burst like an enormous boil when Americans came to the realization that the media system was not "natural" or inviolable, but the result of explicit policies. Surveys showed that the more people understood media as a policy issue, the more they supported reform. Once that truth is fully out in the open, all bets are off. Organized people can defeat organized money.

There is extraordinary momentum coming from the struggle for media ownership. Scores of groups organizing media reform campaigns have emerged over the past few years—local, national and even global in scope, organized around a wide range of issues. In the coming few years, expect to see major progressive legislation launched: to restore more competitive markets in radio and television; to have antitrust law applied effectively to media; to have copyright returned to some semblance of concern for protecting the public domain; to have viable subsidies that spawn a wide range of nonprofit and noncommercial media; to have a wireless high-speed Internet system that will be superior to and vastly less expensive than the system envisaged by the giant cable and telephone companies; to have real limitations on advertising and commercialism, especially that aimed at children; to have protection for media workers, so that they can do their work without onerous demands on their labor by rapacious owners. The list goes on and on. Once we realize, like the nation's Founders, that building a free press is the job of a free people, the sky is the limit for what we can accomplish.

All these measures would have been unthinkable just a year or two ago but are now in play. One of the exciting developments of the last year has been the recognition that media activism is flexible politically. Unlike campaign finance reform, where anything short of fully publicly financed elections leaves open a crack that big money exploits to destroy the reforms, media activism allows for tangible piecemeal gains. We may well get several hundred additional noncommercial FM stations on the dial soon, largely as a result of sustained activism. Those stations will be a tangible demonstration to people of what they can achieve and will spur continued activism. And media reform allows for a broad array of alliances, depending on the issue, as the 2003 fight for media ownership demonstrated. Indeed, media activism might just be the glue to sustain a progressive democratic vision for the nation's politics.

But it will not be an easy fight, since the forces guiding the status quo have considerable weaponry in their arsenal and will stop at nothing to protect their privileges. This is a long-term struggle, a never-ending one in many ways. What we know is that it is impossible to have a viable democracy with the current media system and that we are capable of changing this system. The future depends upon our continued success.

Note

1. New York: Monthly Review Press, 2004.

THE FIGHT FOR THE FUTURE OF MEDIA

RUSSELL NEWMAN AND BEN SCOTT

Looking back on the last few years of public activism in the politics of media reform, the story that emerges is nothing short of astonishing.

It began ominously. When President George W. Bush elevated Michael Powell—son of Secretary of State Colin Powell—to the chairmanship of the Federal Communications Commission (FCC), the writing was on the wall. Staunchly aligned with big-business concerns, the Powell Commission seemed uninterested in the constitutional principles of citizen control over public communication. Industry lobbyists, long accustomed to significant influence at the FCC, salivated at the prospect of realizing a regulatory system that openly proclaimed total private control of broadcasting, telecommunications, and the public airwaves as commensurate with the public interest.

On June 2, 2003, then-FCC Chairman Powell made good on their desires. He moved forward with plans to further increase commercial control over the media system in a historic evisceration of regulations protecting citizen and consumer rights. He led the charge at the FCC to downsize public-interest limits on media ownership. Under his vision, new rules would allow one entity to own a city's monopoly cable provider, its monopoly newspaper, eight radio stations, and three television stations. In many ways, his zeal caused his undoing. These proposed changes—some of the most sweeping in American history—were rammed through a sharply divided Commission. The strident objections of Democratic Commissioners Michael Copps and Jonathan Adelstein were summarily dismissed, prompting the two Commissioners to tour the country against Powell's wishes to talk directly with the public about what was really going on in Washington.

Powell himself attended only the *official* public hearing, a one-off event he called before bringing the new rules in for a quick vote at the Commission. This hearing, held in Richmond, Virginia, was notable for the large number of broadcasting executives in attendance, juxtaposed with the conspicuous absence of their news cameras. Despite Republican efforts to keep the proceeding quiet, over 750,000 public protests came pouring in to the FCC, with appeals from over 100 members

21

of Congress shortly thereafter. None was heeded; even the pretense of a democratic process was discarded.

Consequently, the FCC's decision to muscle through giveaways for broadcasters resulted in an unprecedented backlash. It is safe to say that June 2, 2003, will not be remembered, as it was intended, as a golden moment for commercial media interests. It will, instead, be remembered as the day the public was awakened to the fox in the henhouse. This outcome surprised Chairman Powell perhaps more than anyone. As Brian Lowry wrote in *Variety*, "I keep picturing a boxer who was assured the bout was fixed, only to have his opponent get off the canvas and nail him with a sharp right cross."[1] If the public delivered the sharp right cross, the courts delivered the knockout blow.

On June 24, 2004, the U.S. Third Circuit Court of Appeals ruled in favor of public-interest attorneys led by the Media Access Project, reversing the FCC's best efforts to hand over the people's media system to private commercial interests. The public's right to a diverse, competitive, and representative media system was upheld in what most observers consider nothing short of a David-versus-Goliath victory for the public. Not only did the court judge the FCC's attempts to jettison media-ownership limits unjustified and unreasonable, the decision also noted that, contrary to GOP political dogma, the law held no presumption in favor of loosening ownership limits. Powell, believing that he was following the intent of Congress, had approached the public-interest rules with the presumption that they should be eliminated unless proven absolutely necessary. No longer. Thanks to the court ruling, the burden of proof for removing public protections now lies on the opposite side. This ruling all but assures that future Commissions will have far more difficulty changing rules to favor commercial interests over democratic principles.[2] The second Bush administration gave a nod to this fact by declining to appeal the Third Circuit's ruling to the Supreme Court, choosing instead to leave to the Commission the job of starting anew in its analysis of media ownership.

This series of remarkable events is truly historic in a political and legal context that seldom yields success stories. However, this momentous event must be put in perspective. After such a terrific win, it is certainly difficult to recognize that this moment is but step one on a longer journey toward a truly democratic media system. We have averted disaster, and we should celebrate. But more importantly, it is now time to start thinking ahead. In the grand scheme of things, there are bigger fish to fry than control over broadcasting, a technology whose golden age has long since passed. This is not to say that broadcast ownership rules are not important. However, they are no longer the frontlines of the battle for democratic media. The struggle has only entered a new phase, and the stakes have become exponentially higher.

Awareness For Change Gains Momentum

Right wing ideologues and market fundamentalists often accuse media activists of possessing "utopian visions," by which they typically mean that we have the audacity to demand "democracy." It is inspiring to witness people gathered together to fight for their rights. Pent-up frustration, anger, hope, and perhaps even a few "utopian visions" made themselves known in San Antonio on January 28, 2004, in the midst of the debate over media ownership. The court had not yet handed down its ruling, and the fate of public-interest protections was largely in doubt. On this date the second of six FCC Localism Task Force hearings scheduled across the country throughout the year took place.

Chairman Michael Powell created the Localism Task Force and called for six public hearings in August 2003. At these hearings, citizens would have the opportunity to tell the Commission directly how well their community broadcasters were serving localism and diversity. The creation of the Task Force, a move widely perceived as backpedaling after his new ownership rules sparked a firestorm of opposition, afforded Powell a measure of political cover. It was largely an empty gesture; even as Powell set out to study localism and diversity across the country, he made no effort to suspend the ownership ruling these hearings would retroactively inform. Powell took time to listen to the public only after the Commission's decision was already made. Commissioner Michael Copps spoke in no uncertain terms about Powell's new diversionary tactic.

> This proposal is a day late and a dollar short. It highlights the failures of the recent decision to dismantle ownership protections. To say that protecting localism was not germane to that decision boggles the mind. The ownership protections, as well as the other public interest protections that the Commission has dismantled over the past years, are all designed to promote localism, diversity and competition. We should have heeded the calls from over 2 million Americans and so many Members of Congress expressing concern about the impact of media concentration on localism and diversity before we rushed to a vote. We should have vetted these issues before we voted. Instead, we voted; now we are going to vet. This is a policy of "ready, fire, aim!"[3]

San Antonio was probably chosen as a hearing site because it was the hometown of radio giant Clear Channel Communications, a company that had benefitted tremendously from the elimination of radio-station ownership limits as part of the Telecommunications Act of 1996. At the time of the hearing, the company owned 1,200 stations and proved to be an outspoken supporter of the Bush administration, both in media coverage and in campaign contributions. A hearing in Clear

Channel's backyard was effectively a hearing in the belly of the beast, a safe haven for Powell outside the Beltway. Perhaps this is why all three of the Republican Commissioners deigned to join the two Democrats. Commissioners Kevin Martin and Kathleen Abernathy had rarely attended public events, though they were regulars at industry conventions. All of the Commissioners were in for a surprise.[4]

On the appointed day, citizens began arriving at the Municipal Plaza Building at 3:45 AM, well over twelve hours before the hearing was scheduled to begin. By noon, there were upwards of forty people in line, with more arriving as the hours went by. As they waited, local citizens helped each other to prepare testimony. Caught off guard by the early arrivals, representatives of the National Association of Broadcasters (NAB) met inside with hearing officials, attempting to eliminate the need for their members to wait in line with the people.

The reason the lineup began so early was to prevent local activists from being shut out of the proceedings. At the first Localism Hearing in Charlotte, North Carolina, broadcasters had arrived early enough to pack the main hearing room, relegating most citizens to overflow rooms. These people, whether they had comments or not, were not heard or seen during the evening, so the hearing took on the appearance of a balanced debate. The NAB's efforts to skip the line were rebuffed in San Antonio, and throughout the day, paid "waiters" appeared in line to hold places for industry representatives. (This little-known practice is commonplace on Capitol Hill, where lobbyists hire legions of low-wage placeholders, sometimes overnight, to avoid the long lines outside congressional hearing rooms. In Washington, as in Charlotte, the effect is to preclude public attendance.)

By early afternoon, numerous news trucks were parked in front of the Municipal Plaza Building. Reporters interviewed those in line while helicopters circled overhead periodically. Around 3 PM, the AFL-CIO held its own press conference elsewhere in the city to announce its report detailing the unsavory business practices of Clear Channel.[5] From this press conference, they marched to the hearing site, followed by a loud throng. Once there, multiple speakers gave speeches to the huge crowd now gathered outside.

Meanwhile, the NAB hosted a dinner for those who were to testify on their behalf. Unfortunately for them, the restaurant was nearby, and activists found out about it. Demonstrators sent a flying column to picket the industry representatives outside the restaurant. There was no denying that the people of San Antonio meant business.

The hearing itself was raucous. Reading the press reports, one might come away with the impression that a "stimulating debate was had by all." Hogwash; it was a war zone. After hearing his opening remarks, a well-informed crowd greeted Commissioner Michael Copps with a standing ovation. Perhaps never before had a federal regulator been greeted as a hero so deep in the heart of Texas. By contrast, representatives of big media cracked under audience pressure. Powell was hissed, and Clear Channel's representative was booed outright.

The tone was set at the open microphone when Michael Marinez of the Esperanza Peace and Justice Center of San Antonio looked to each of the Republican Commissioners and told them individually, "*You* are not doing things in my best interest." Other local activists echoed this sentiment and provided concrete evidence of the consequences of broadcasters' abandoning public-interest responsibilities and shouldering citizens off their own airwaves. T.C. Calvert, president of the Neighborhood First Alliance, delivered a fiery speech to the Commission:

> I live along an area called the Salado Creek, and we had a 100-year flood that came to my neighborhood, Brother Powell. You should have seen the water coming. It was scary. People were scrambling for their lives. The fire department had put their lives on the line. The police department had put their lives on the line.
>
> Our television stations in our area, the fiber optics, and the cable was shut out. Our TVs went black. The people in the community listened to a Clear Channel Communication [station] called KSJL radio. You know what they were doing while the flood waters were coming? They were bopping the music, hits and oldies, instead of warning our people that the flood waters were coming. Will you let your light shine? [Applause]
>
> Now that problem not only holds true in San Antonio, Texas, but it holds true in Oklahoma, Louisiana, New Mexico and all the communities where Clear Channel Communications has urban contemporary stations. So, I'm here to challenge this Commission to change your rules. We want to see low-powered radio stations in our community controlled by the people in this community. [Applause]
>
> We could talk about all the boards we want to. We're sick and tired of blue ribbon committees. We're sick and tired of these boards. We want ownership and we want the FCC to let its light shine. Thank you.[6]

It was an inspiring event. Citizens who had come to express outrage outnumbered the industry representatives ten to one. All were local citizens who devoted nearly an entire day of their own time to attending and speaking their minds at a hearing convened by a federal agency most had never heard of a few months earlier. Such a display of democracy in action is rare these days in the United States, and the Republican Commissioners hardly knew how to respond. Abernathy and Martin had no closing remarks when the lashing was through. By contrast, Copps and Adelstein, both instrumental in organizing and inspiring this grassroots movement, left San Antonio in a blaze of glory.

The media reform movement is gaining force. Copps' prediction in his dissenting statement to the June 2 ruling has come true: "This Commission's drive to loosen the rules and its reluctance to share its proposals with the people before we voted awoke a sleeping giant," he wrote. "American citizens are standing up in never-before-seen numbers to reclaim their airwaves and to call on those who are entrusted to use them to serve the public interest. . . . The media concentration debate will never be the same. This Commission faces a far more informed and involved citizenry. The obscurity of this issue that many have relied upon in the past, where only a few dozen inside-the-Beltway lobbyists understood this issue, is gone forever."[7]

Expanding Our View to the Bigger Picture

Looking to the future, the energy of the media reform movement's gathering momentum, fully on display in San Antonio, is very encouraging. *Broadcasting and Cable*, an industry trade magazine, headlined its story on the hearing, "The Public *Is* Interested."[8] It was almost as if another article had been penned weeks in advance, predicting that the Commissioners would be greeted by a room half-filled with a uniform mass of dark suits and headlined, "The Public Couldn't Care Less." The old days of ignorance and apathy are gone. Instead, we now find outpourings of anger, frustration, and a heightened level of *awareness*. The meeting changed the nature of the political contest in Washington. Throughout, people are realizing that no matter what they are fighting for, be it environmental protection or economic and social justice, they will gain little ground without media that report their view and message fairly. Perhaps even more importantly, they realize that changing media content to include and constitute the views of all Americans requires changing the media policies that sustain the status quo. To win just media, we must deliver just media *policy*.

The fight over media ownership has energized a media reform movement. Yet the biggest question facing the movement today is where it will go next. Will the public-interest campaign in broadcasting extend to other media-policy issues? The daunting truth is that the broadcast ownership rules we fought to protect for almost two years are small potatoes compared to what looms ahead. Big media and their government allies are mobilizing for a dramatic rewrite of the communications laws that govern all public speech. Should they act without public involvement, it is certain that we will have much more to worry about than monopoly control over television and radio. We will have lost control over the ways citizens access and use their media, period. It will be nearly impossible to go back once this multiyear legislative process is complete.

We stand at a truly remarkable moment, one which large media interests and citizens alike are faced with the task of reconfiguring and reassessing media that do not fit old paradigms and constraints. The pressing task is to sustain the energy of the broadcast-ownership debate and expand it outward onto other media issues with similar principles at stake. Public media values—such as diversity of viewpoints, empowerment of underserved communities, localism, children's programming, citizen participation in media production, reasonable access, and control of public assets (such as spectrum) through democratic processes—must extend into tomorrow's policies of media governance. The regulatory regime that will preside over this not so distant future has yet to be decided. If we are not careful, the public-media values we have fought to protect will fade with the broadcast system and play only a little role in the future of American media.

Technologies are changing to such an extent that the time has come for immediate action. We must not stop at curbing the excesses of monopoly capital's control over our media system. Let us demand a new system by blowing apart the old models and starting again. That goal may sound utopian, but over the long term it can be accomplished in earnest. The power of public participation in the media system must now prompt us to begin to ask larger questions, develop more aggressive tactics, and aim higher in our ambitions. Ultimately, we are not out to change the way the system works, we are out to change the system itself. The public has been excluded from determining the course of its own media, and the people must be returned to the seat of chief decision-maker. Democracy demands this simple but seemingly idealistic proposition. There has never been a better time than right now to think big and act boldly. Further, now may very well be the *only* time for the foreseeable future when we will be able to venture such proactive aspirations, since our window of opportunity is already closing.

Media Policy Fights in the Twenty-first century

Tomorrow's debate on media policy will still be about ownership, but they will not be about station ownership or even about the ownership of a network of stations. These battles are going to involve the ownership and control of the conduits themselves—the wires (cable, copper, and fiber optic) and the airwaves (radio frequency spectrum)—over which *all* media—audio, video, voice, data, and access to the Internet—are delivered to citizens. The gatekeepers of yesterday decided what shows would air and what articles would get published; the new gatekeepers will determine how information flows and what information citizens can access. Three trends are already becoming apparent.

The first consists of efforts by content, cable, and telecommunications giants to consolidate and concentrate control over these conduits with outright takeovers and mergers. Barring congressional action, these maneuvers will dwarf even the biggest corporate marriages we've experienced over the last two decades, creating completely, vertically integrated production-to-distribution powerhouses. Comcast's attempted hostile takeover of Disney in early 2004 marks only the end of the first salvo, begun when Rupert Murdoch successfully purchased a

$6.8 billion controlling stake in the satellite provider DirecTV. "No other media company controls such a potent mix of programming and the means to deliver it to households from Melbourne to Maine," *BusinessWeek* announced shortly after Murdoch had added the crown jewel to his collection. "Murdoch is girding for a battle that will pit satellite against cable for supremacy as the carrier of choice—and in the process could shift the balance of power in the industry his way. . . . Not since William Randolph Hearst in the first half of the Twentieth century has one man had such means to shape mass media."[9]

Though the Comcast-Disney deal was not closed, it is likely that mergers of huge distribution networks and content providers will define the future of American media. The power of such media titans over public information would be unprecedented. It is worth noting that of the 70 percent of Americans who receive television via cable, nearly a quarter buys it from Comcast.[10] The implications are not lost on the primary players. Murdoch predicted a future of media megamergers the day after Comcast proclaimed its intentions regarding Disney: "In three years the media scene will have at least three very big competitive companies in Comcast, News [Corporation] and Time Warner, and several very good and well-run smaller companies such as DBS and Cox."[11]

The second trend rapidly emerging involves the efforts of telecommunications and cable companies to eviscerate such democratic controls as presently exist over communications infrastructure—the system of wires and fiber optic cables that bring media from network hubs and the Internet out to individual households. Of increasing importance in this context are "franchise agreements" between local communities and providers of video programming (cable companies mostly, but soon to be phone companies as well). In return for granting companies access to dig up city streets and occupy public rights-of-way, these agreements give communities the opportunity to require that certain services be provided to residents in return. These agreements have historically consisted of a franchise fee to the local government, a small number of public-access channels, and sometimes "I-Nets," which wire schools, libraries, and public buildings with high-speed Internet access.

However, given the impending switch to digital broadcasting and the increasing importance of broadband access to social mobility and economic growth, communities are realizing how important it is to ask for much more—not merely access channels, but a package including a percentage of available bandwidth and a revenue stream to service a community's media needs. This bandwidth could be used to multiply the number of available access channels, providing not only opportunities for residents to create their own media but also the means to broadcast noncommercial and independent content not available elsewhere on the cable system. Some public bandwidth could be set aside for broadband delivery, to help set up community Internet access centers for low-income residents. The possibilities are as endless as the technological needs (and desires) of the community.

These interests are set against a background of telecommunications and cable giants eagerly seeking to provide all-in-one "bundled" services across their respective conduits. Cable companies seek to extend their product line past video television services and broadband Internet access into voice telephony via "Voice Over Internet Protocol." Similarly, telecommunications giants seek to expand their own capabilities past voice telephony and broadband into video television services. To that end, such telecom giants as Verizon and SBC are going head-to-head with the cable giants state by state, deploying new fiber-optic networks that promise to offer the "triple play" bundle—voice, video, and Internet access. In the ensuing battle between these behemoths, the ultimate losers are citizens: both sectors are working to take control out of citizens' hands under the guise of "promoting competition."

Cable companies across the country have already established a lengthy history of fighting local skirmishes to clamp down on democratic community control under this justification. At the time of writing, Comcast has launched a prominent televised public-relations campaign painting the company as consumer-friendly, but its actions betray its true motivations. For example, throughout late 2003 and 2004, Comcast flexed its muscles and fought a number of battles against communities looking to keep pace with technological change by bringing their franchise agreements up to date. Some communities tried to back out of existing franchises altogether after promises from the company were not fulfilled. San Jose, California, was one that chose to do so. After years of such broken promises by a number of cable franchises, the city decided to terminate its agreement with Comcast to broker new terms. Comcast responded with a lawsuit claiming that San Jose's actions were illegal, violating Comcast's "free speech rights." The "onerous" requests that San Jose made included community access to the Internet, a 10 percent set-aside of system bandwidth for public use, an institutional network for city buildings and schools, sufficient fiber-optic lines to serve the entire community, compliance with the city's living wage, nondiscrimination rules, and minority outreach requirements.[12]

Comcast's suit failed in late 2003, but the company continued its hardball tactics. In a legal brief filed in January 2004, Comcast went beyond trying to prevent the break with San Jose by threatening to *take away* public-access channel allotments provided in earlier agreements. "…[I]t is clear that new technology has eliminated much of the need for cable operators to subsidize video soapboxes," the brief stated; presumably the newly freed-up channels would favor more profitable uses.[13] Following up on the brief, Comcast hired an astounding team of two lobbyists for each council member of San Jose's City Council.[14]

In the meantime, even as telecommunication providers advance apace in expanding their new fiber-optic networks, it is still legally unclear whether these new networks require franchise agreements. Some, like Verizon, have so far played it safe by applying for cable franchises as they go. Others, such as SBC, take their chances with complex legal defenses for why they should be franchise-free.[15] Competitive proclivities between Big Telecom and Big Cable aside, their common disdain for negotiating deals with local communities is unmistakable. Big telecom certainly has no desire to be held to seeking local franchises, and big cable envies it its present ambiguous status. Both have discovered that state and local legislatures are often pliable when it comes to their demands, and they apply pressure accordingly.

Verizon, expanding its new fiber network into Virginia, fired a dramatic shot across the bow in January 2005. Its lobbyists successfully introduced legislation in the statehouse that would have torn up all local franchise agreements across the state—franchises resulting from years of negotiation—for any incumbent provider of communications services, cable providers included. These agreements with local communities would be replaced with a blanket, state-negotiated agreement that would last either twenty or forty years, depending on which version of the bill passed. The disadvantage to local governments, most of whose franchises lapse every ten years or less, would be enormous.[16]

Verizon's attempt to lock out competition for decades was ultimately unsuccessful—this time. Opposition to the bills was mounted by incumbent cable monopolies, threatened by Verizon's entrance into the market, and local governments, many of which stood to lose franchise-operator fees.[17] However, Big Telecom and Big Cable's tactics will certainly adapt; they will continue to learn from each other's successes and failures. Where Verizon's overreach ultimately stalled in Virginia, the cable lobby wasted no time in introducing legislation in Arizona that would attack the common "problem" of local franchising by whittling away at it piecemeal. This particular bill would "lower bills for customers" by slashing the franchise fees cable providers pay to cities and limiting the number of public access channels these providers could be made to offer.[18] We can expect more of such bills to appear across the country, with similar promises of consumer satisfaction in exchange for severing all public accountability, access, and control. The bottom line is that as new technologies emerge, communities are finding themselves in tougher battles with cable and phone companies to maintain public-interest media policy.

The third trend in this new phase of the debate about media consolidation centers on who will have access to tomorrow's communication networks. We are moving into a two-wire world, where cable and phone companies control the media marketplace. All video, voice, and data traffic will move over their networks, largely through Internet protocol. The question is whether these networks will be open to all users on a nondiscriminatory basis. Will they be "common carriers" of all media traffic, regardless of its origin or character, or will the owners of the networks have the exclusive power to set the terms of their use? It should come as no surprise that both cable and telephone companies are currently lobbying hard to scrap all common-carrier requirements. The regulatory scheme that would permit such an anticompetitive, anticonsumer reality is the next evolution of the "what is good for shareholders is good for democracy" assumption pushed by big business. Predictably, the results will be disastrous.

We are currently in the midst of a heated debate over how tomorrow's communications infrastructure will be regulated. Under the old regulatory regime, wires were stupid: they passed information, unadulterated, from one end of a network to the other, with all content uniformly accessible at equal speeds. The owners of the network could not interfere, nor could they deny access to any bona fide party. Under such an "open" system, innovation and competition flourished. A giant phone company might have monopoly ownership of a network in a given city, but it is required by law to sell access on a nondiscriminatory basis. That is why we all have numerous choices regarding who provides our Internet service along a common set of wires.

At least we do for the moment. When cable companies began offering broadband Internet access, they argued that, since there were two networks (phone and cable) in most communities, there was no need for them to live by open-access rules. Public-interest-advocates protested that two players in the marketplace do not make for healthy competition, much less a reason to scrap a century of successful common-carrier regulation. Eliminate the protections of common-carrier regulation, and suddenly the wires begin to discriminate. The owner of the wires no longer needs to treat a competitor's content the same as its own and no longer needs to remain compatible with other technologies. The implications are staggering. A heated debate began to rage in Congress, in the courts, and at the FCC. Once again, it was Commissioner Michael Copps who sounded the alarm in a speech given at the New America Foundation in October 2003:

> Think about what would happen if your broadband Internet provider could limit or retard your access to, say, certain news sources or political sites. Or what if your provider decided that you couldn't make use of new and improved filtering technology to prevent your children from cruising unprotected through the more obscene alleys of the Internet because it wasn't their filter? Or what if it prevented you from using some superior spam-jamming technology that could eliminate all that clutter from your in-box because it could block their spam? Or what if your broadband Internet provider decided that it wanted to impose usage restrictions to prevent the use of Virtual Private Networks by small businesses and telecommuters? Or streaming video? Guess what? Some of this is already happening. And I am told there is already a healthy market out there for so-called "policy-based routers" that allow providers to do all this.[19]

Despite Copps' warning, the FCC ruled that cable companies would not be subject to open-access rules. The phone companies immediately petitioned that their open access regulation should be stripped as well. As of early 2005, the question has been taken to the Courts.[20] Regardless of the outcome in the legal system, we should fully expect both the cable and phone lobbies to lean on Congress to legislate the changes once and for all. The Internet's open nature is under direct threat. Worse still, most Americans haven't the faintest idea what this is all about. By the time they do, it may be far too late.

What will this mean for the average person? Higher prices, fewer choices, and a total loss of control over how content is transmitted over twenty-first century networks. "Open Access" regulation is what made competition among independent service providers over dialup modem possible: one could be a local telephone customer of Verizon while purchasing dialup Internet access from Earthlink. No longer. Broadband options will consist of deciding between Big Cable or Big Telecom, if the option exists at all, with all the potential implications for control of online content that this entails. The Indymedia battle cry of "Hate the media? *Be* the media!" will ring hollow if "being the media" requires signing a contract with Comcast or Verizon to have a mass-media mouthpiece in tomorrow's media system.

Yet, even if we manage to protect "open access" on the Internet, it is still not at all clear that citizens will be able to afford the price of connection. Increasingly, a class divide is appearing in telecommunication services. The idea of ensuring "universal access" to means of communication is fading into history, as public discourse is now a commodity on the open market. As technologies converge, the divisions between the "haves" and "have-nots" will increase. High-speed full-content access will become a luxury item, available only to those with financial resources, or those with lower incomes willing to bear a disproportionate economic burden. Case in point: since passage of the Telecommunications Act of 1996, cable rates have skyrocketed by 40 percent and more.[21] The act "deregulated" much of the cable industry, explicitly with the goal of lowering prices. Clearly this was a wolf in sheep's clothing. In 2005, when Congress plans to begin rewriting the Telecommunications Act, we can expect a similar performance unless a strong campaign is mounted by public-interest advocates. Only, this time, it will not be simply cable television prices, but broadband Internet and other basic telecommunication services that are at stake. In years to come, that could mean that basic access to information—and even the ability to communicate, period—would be threatened for many.

The reopening of the Telecommunications Act may well be the single most important event in media policymaking in several generations. It is likely to be a long, hard political fight lasting several years before final legislation is signed into law. This policy contest will determine not only which industry is best positioned to own and control the wired networks of the future; it will also determine which industry is best positioned to control the public airwaves (also called "spectrum") and on what terms. The public airwaves may well become a central delivery system for all forms of media in the future, particularly for so-called "last mile" services—from the end of the wired network at the curbside to the back of the TV. "Last-generation" spectrum license holders will try to choke off new technologies that promise to utilize spectrum far more efficiently. They fear that opening up new value in the public spectrum will destabilize old business models by permitting broader access. In contrast, that is precisely our hope.

Present regulation of the spectrum sections off the airwaves for specific uses as if it were carving up a piece of land: radio, television, cellular phone service, garage-door openers, and remote controls, all are allocated to specific frequencies within the public airwaves. But this regimen demands a tacit assumption that spectrum is scarce, that to avoid "interference," the airwaves need to be divided up among those who intend to use them. However, new technologies are emerging, highlighted by Michael Calabrese and Matt Barranca in this volume, that effectively negate the problem of scarcity and the need for exclusive licensing of public spectrum. An entirely new paradigm is on the horizon for how we manage the airwaves that tosses aside the old dictum of spectrum scarcity. In the digital age, by using "smart radios," it's possible to share. This is perhaps the biggest conceptual shift to occur in media policy in decades, with broad implications for citizens who have classically been underserved or misrepresented altogether by the mainstream media. The means exist for all to have their voices heard, if only those making the rules allow it to happen. Spectrum could become more akin to a public park, sidewalk, or thoroughfare, rather than a gated community.

Forces are at work to make sure citizens never come to this realization, taking these airwaves out of public hands altogether. As the media *content* giants become even more enormously powerful *conduit* giants, the issue of citizen access to spectrum quietly disappears from the radar screen. Already, proposals have been floated that would replace the current setup whereby corporations lease access to the public airwaves with *permanent property rights*; the market would then be relied upon to "work its magic." The airwaves need never find their way into citizen hands that way—unless, of course, you're wealthy enough to buy some.[22]

Frustratingly, it seems that in Congress there is simply no time (or, more likely, perspective) for reflection about the public good when spectrum sales and propertization of the airwaves stand to send billions of dollars to federal coffers. "In the past, we robbed banks; now we rob spectrum," Senator John McCain has said, and correctly so.[23] The rush is on, as a plan by the FCC to accelerate the digital television transition—and, with it, the return to the federal government of spectrum broadcasters use to deliver "analog" signals—is receiving enthusiastic support from members of Congress. ". . . [R]eclaiming the channels—and selling them off to new technology business—is the government's priority," said Representative Joe Barton, the powerful chairman of the House Energy and Commerce Committee.[24]

What the public may expect to gain from this corporate spectrum grab remains an open question. Numerous excellent ideas are being offered by public-interest organizations, such as the New America Foundation and the Media Access Project. No one on Capitol Hill has yet suggested at what point the public will be invited by Congress to comment on the future of the media system and the usage of its airwaves. However, it is certain that a place at the decision-making table will be hard won and much needed for public interest advocates. The networks of the future will be built according to the policies of today.

Alternatives Worth Fighting For

A large number of public-service-oriented projects are already underway for providing alternative choices for future media policymaking. Among the most promising are municipal broadband systems and community wireless networks (all of which may be thought of under the banner of Community Internet). Desirous to provide affordable, ubiquitous access and up-to-date technology, municipalities have attempted to establish broadband systems more akin to public utilities than the expensive commodities.

Perhaps the largest public broadband project is Utah's $470 million UTOPIA (Utah Telecommunication Open Infrastructure Agency) project, described by the *New York Times* as "a twist on Roosevelt-era public works projects." If Utah's cities can raise the money to complete the package, Utah would deploy to homes and businesses fiber-optic cable capable of delivering data at speeds "100 times faster than current commercial residential offerings," providing digital television and telephone services to boot. "The cities involved argue that reliable access to high-speed data is so important to their goals that the project should be seen as no more controversial than the traditional public role in building roads, bridges, sewers and schools—as well as electric power systems, which are often municipally owned in the Western United States."[25]

This project, and others like it, are under attack from all sides. At a local level, telecommunications corporations, gun-shy of a nonprofit competitor that offers quality service for low cost, are pressuring city-council members to reject funding for such projects. At a state level, these companies besiege pliable legislators to pass laws restricting the ability of municipalities to provide their own broadband and telecommunications service.[26] The Supreme Court recently weighed in on this issue as well. In determining the will of Congress on the matter of publicly operated broadband, the Court gave states an open invitation to disallow such endeavors if they saw fit (or, more accurately, if convinced by powerful moneyed interests).[27]

Jim Baller, legal counsel for the Missouri Municipal League, took heart nonetheless. "Only a handful of states currently have barriers to municipal entry. . . . Some states have already reversed or relaxed barriers enacted in the past, and we hope that this trend will continue as well." He added, "We also hope that state legislators everywhere will realize that without the involvement of local governments, our nation cannot achieve our national goal of rapid deployment of truly advanced and affordable telecommunications services and capabilities to all Americans, including those in rural and high-cost areas." While remaining hopeful, he also expects that before states are able to demonstrate the benefits of a more public-utility approach to telecom and broadband, the federal government will witness a major legislative battle on the question.[28]

Public-interest providers of *wireless* broadband may offer a way to get around the power of the cable and telecom lobbies. The possibilities of utilizing the public airwaves to provide high-speed access via shared, "unlicensed" spectrum (as opposed to sectioning it off for different uses, as is presently the case) are immense. Low-cost wireless connections offer broadband access where there has been no investment in a wired network, such as in rural areas. Wireless also serves as a cost-effective alternative to wired networks in all locations. It offers the possibility for universal broadband access to television, voice, and Internet at a fraction of current rates. Sascha Meinrath, in his chapter on community wireless networks, outlines the enormous possibility of these technologies for public-service media and the challenges they face.

Naturally, commercial wireless providers oppose public-service networks and are working hard to offer their own for-profit systems at prices similar to their wired competitors. Importantly, however, such community wireless networks in all their forms reveal a thrilling weakness of the media giants. Citizens, for now, have a chance to appropriate new technologies to suit public-interest purposes. The race is on: we can let commercial interests define the use of these new technologies to serve their own purposes, or citizens can do so to suit theirs.

We may take great heart from the campaign for low-power FM radio (LPFM) that has been waged now for over a decade. In 2000, the FCC authorized the licensing of several hundred noncommercial community radio stations across America. The National Association of Broadcasters went to Congress to shut down the service, wielding false allegations of interference and legitimate fears that real local radio would siphon listeners from the cookie-cutter formats of chain radio networks. In a last-minute deal, the lobbyists succeeded in curtailing LPFM, leaving only a few hundred station licenses available. Congress justified the betrayal by ordering a study of the claims of interference.

In the last five years, these stations have grown to become some of the greatest success stories of alternative media. Thanks in no small part to a tireless group of activists at the Prometheus Radio Project in Philadelphia, LPFM stations are constructed at a rapid clip, providing a unique community medium that is a tribute to the people who operate the stations and their loyal listeners. Schools, churches, community groups, and talented artists are among the many local broadcasters that have made LPFM such a success. In 2005, the LPFM community launched a major campaign to bring grassroots lobbyists to Washington, to tell the FCC and the Congress about America's community radio and to demand that the service be expanded to license more stations. Their demands are backed by the congressional study ordered in 2000, which completely discredits the NAB's interference charges. Boasting bipartisan support and a passionate grassroots force that takes the halls of Congress by storm each time it comes to the Capital, LPFM may finally find the justice in the law that it has earned in the field.

Looming over all these major questions of domestic media policy is the arena of global trade and the prospect of taking the democracy out of democratic policymaking altogether. Policy victories that favor citizens over the bank accounts of the largest global giants are rendered powerless when brought into the realm of the World Trade Organization and made subject to other multilateral or bilateral trade agreements.[29] As Lori Wallach and Chris Slevin explore in their chapter, despite assurances from trade representatives that bringing media and cultural industries into global trade deals will do nothing to eliminate public checks on corporate power, the results of actions already taken demonstrates otherwise. Protections for public broadcast systems, subsidies for independent media and arts, ownership rules that protect diversity and localism—all of these become barriers to trade in the eyes of new global distribution and megamedia giants. Unsurprisingly, these are the parties that have influence in the writing of trade deals. They structure them accordingly.

Essentially, governments face a choice: defend national media interests at a steep price of millions of dollars in fines, or give up these protections. It doesn't take long to realize which side wins in this tug-of-war. We must pay attention to domestic media policies, for certain, but media activists in the United States must join hands with those around the world as a new global regulatory regime is put in place by "slow motion coup d'état."[30] Sasha Costanza-Chock discusses the means of citizen activism on global issues in his chapter.

Intertwined with many of the media-policy issues of digital broadcasting, wireless broadband, and global trade are questions of digital rights management or, more broadly, copyright and intellectual property. Copyright law was originally intended by the United States Constitution to accomplish two aims. First, it meant to provide incentive for creators to create again. Second, it aimed to balance the rights of creators with the interests of the general public, giving society access to common cultural forms so as to build on past achievements. Today, copyright has been utterly corrupted. Originally, copyright gave authors a fourteen-year monopoly on their writings, after which the public would share the work and use it to create cultural products for the next generation. Now, at the behest of corporate copyright holders, the term of copyright has been extended to ninety-five years. (It is barely a jest to say that copyright terms are extended virtually every time

Mickey Mouse is set to enter the public domain.) Further, these special interests argue that the constitutional premise of balancing the needs of authors with the needs of the public in respect to copyrighted ideas should be abolished in favor of permanent property rights. Spurred by high-profile clashes over Internet file sharing, the copyright debate has come off its moorings and threatens to encourage terrible policymaking that will harm innovation and public culture for generations. As Lawrence Lessig describes in his book, *Free Culture*, it is time that we recall the democratic principles that brought us libraries, used-book and used-record stores, collaborative invention, and the ability to share ideas in society.[31]

Undoubtedly, there is much to be done. Commercial interests have invested heavily in the business of controlling government policymaking, yet public-interest advocates and grassroots organizations have a newfound power and a seat at the bargaining table. When the Telecommunications Act is reopened—in its entirety, or, more likely, piecemeal—several years of fierce political battles over the most central media-policy issues of the nation (and indeed of the world) will be decided for many years to come. It is essential that the American public come to terms with the issues at stake—with the future of network technologies, and their ownership and control. It is essential that we put our energies into building alternatives, demonstrating that viable paths exist outside of the corporate-controlled status quo. Finally, it is essential that we continue to agitate, build coalitions, and participate in the democratic process, such as it is.

Conclusion: Putting the Public Back into Media Policy

On May 26, 2004, the Federal Communications Commission held its third Broadcast Localism Hearing in Rapid City, South Dakota. After several days of activities that Chairman Powell attended—a Tribal Consumer Forum, radio appearances, a demonstration of satellite service at the Upper Midwest Aerospace Consortium, and other events—when the scheduled time came to hear from the public, he mysteriously ducked out, leaving Commissioners Adelstein and Copps holding court at the hearing. That's right: not one of the Republican Commissioners came to hear what citizens had to say.

The questions the FCC invited the public to respond to were also highly instructive. Released ahead of time, the "Five Questions You Can Help the FCC Answer" were:

1. How do your broadcasters use radio and television to respond to the community's needs and interests? What are they doing well?

2. Are there certain kinds of local programming that you believe should be available but that are not being provided by local broadcasters? If so, what are they?

3. Are broadcasters well informed about important issues and events in the community?

4. Are there any segments of the local community that you believe are not being adequately served? How could broadcasters meet the needs of such groups?

5. What, if anything, should the FCC do to promote more localism in broadcasting?[32]

Underlying each and every one of these questions is the assumption that those who presently control the airwaves are the ones who *should* control the airwaves. Entirely and conspicuously absent is any mention of an inquiry as to whether citizens thought this should be the case in the first place.

San Antonians were very vocal in decrying the very illegitimacy of the present system. They didn't want to be merely placated by their media; instead, they demanded a voice in deciding who owns and operates the media. They wanted to see and hear themselves on their own airwaves. It was truly as if someone had thrown a match into a dry haystack: whole new constituencies suddenly realized that if they weren't being served by their media, they could do something about the situation. Their rage resonated with similar groups of people across the country.

In light of the battles ahead, the questions posed to Rapid City's citizens truly stand as a greater insult than even the absence of the Chairman who had called the meeting in the first place. Powell's escape to D.C. was, perhaps, a means of avoiding another public humiliation. However, it also indicates the disdain and dismissive attitude of the Washington establishment for citizens who meddle in the policies of media governance.

It is the same attitude that has alienated the public from its government for generations. It is also not surprising that almost two years of public outcry over broadcast ownership would be insufficient to cleanse the politics of broadcast regulation of its antidemocratic penchants. But Powell made the mistake of waking up the American public. Our challenge now is to focus the energy of this movement on creating policies that will serve the information and communication needs of the next generation. As far as the emerging conduit giants are concerned, the faster the airwaves are propertized, the faster the Internet becomes a series of gated communities, the sooner upstart competition is wiped out, the faster media protections are eliminated at a global level and locked-in for good, the better. Congress will follow along as long as the money backing special interests is not countered by the political sentiment of the electorate. Great potential lies in the gathering media reform movement to counter these corporate efforts to usurp ultimate control over our media. The maxim that only organized people can defeat organized money lies at the heart of our campaigns to buck existing trends, reverse tradition, and establish a truly democratic system of media governance in this country.

These are issues that media activists will need to quickly answer. As Congress begins negotiating the future of the media landscape, we must demand media regulation that ensures not only a diversity of voices, but also broad and unrestricted access to all forms of information, the means to communicate and create media, and the ability to use this information in exactly the way the public chooses. As we progress from the era of media giants rapidly into the era of the conduit giants, time is growing short for citizens to map out what this new terrain will look like, lest it be mapped out for them. There's not a moment to lose.

Notes

1. Brian Lowry, "Powell's Doomed Power Play," *Variety*, September 28, 2003. Available at http://www.variety.com/article/VR1117893062?categoryid=1682&cs=1&s=h&p=0.
2. For the full text of the Circuit Court Ruling, see: http://www.ca3.uscourts.gov/staymotion/033388p.pdf.
3. Statement of Commission Michael J. Copps, August 20, 2003, available online at http://hraunfoss.fcc.gov/edocs_public/attachmatch/DOC-238079A1.pdf.
4. What follows is an eyewitness account from Russell Newman, except where noted.
5. Maria Figueroa, Damone Richardson, and Pam Whitefield, "The Clear Picture on Clear Channel," Cornell study for the AFL-CIO, January 28, 2004. Available online at http://www.aflcio.org/issuespolitics/ns01302004.cfm.
6. A full transcript of the event can be found at http://www.fcc.gov/localism/hearing-sanantonio012804.html.
7. Statement of Commissioner Michael J. Copps Dissenting, *2002 Biennial Regulatory Review—Review of the Commission's Broadcast Ownership Rules*, June 2, 2003, p. 22, http://hraunfoss.fcc.gov/edocs_public/attachmatch/DOC-235047A9.doc.
8. Bill McConnell, "The Public *Is* Interested," *Broadcasting and Cable*, February 2, 2004, http://www.broadcastingcable.com/article/CA378531?display=Top+of+the+Week.
9. Ronald Glover, "Rupert's World," *BusinessWeek Online*, January 9, 2004. Available at http://www.businessweek.com/magazine/content/04_03/b3866001_mz001.htm.
10. Jeff Chester, "700 Channels and Nothing On," April 29, 2004, Center for Digital Democracy, available at http://www.democraticmedia.org/news/700Channels.html.
11. Jane Schulze, and Geoff Elliott, "Big Three Will Run World's Media, Says Murdoch," *The Australian*, February 12, 2004, available at http://www.freepress.net/news/article.php?id=2538.
12. Jeff Chester, "Comcast Claims Its Corporate Interests More Important Than Those of Citizens and Communities," January 6, 2004, Center for Digital Democracy, available online at http://www.democraticmedia.org/news/marketwatch/comcast2.html.
13. Ibid.
14. "Comcast's Lobbying Dream Team," *San Jose Mercury News*, February 29, 2004, p. 4P.
15. Anne Veigle, "Verizon Applies for Cable Franchises in 3 States," *Communications Daily*, January 5, 2005, pp. 3–4.
16. NATOA Press Release, "NATOA Announces Opposition to Virginia HB 2534," January 21, 2005.
17. Greg Edwards, "Verizon Fails to Gain Entry to Cable Business," *Richmond Times-Dispatch*, February 8, 2005.

18. Howard Fischer, "Cable Customers May Soon See Smaller Bills," *Arizona Daily Star*, February 8, 2005.

19. Michael J. Copps, "The Beginning of the End of the Internet." Talk given to the New America Foundation, October 9, 2003, http://www.newamerica.net/Download_Docs/pdfs/Doc_File_194_1.pdf.

20. Mark Wigfield, "Appeals Court Hits FCC Broadband 'Unregulation' Policy," *Dow Jones Newswire*, April 1, 2004, http://www.freepress.net/news/article.php?id=2970.

21. For an excellent critique of cable policy, see: U.S. PIRG, *The Failure of Cable Deregulation: A Blueprint For Creating a Competitive, Pro-Consumer Cable Television Marketplace*, August 2003, http://uspirg.org/reports/failureofcabledereg.pdf.

22. See for example, Thomas Hazlett, "Property Rights and Wireless License Values," AEI-Brookings, March 2004, available at http://www.aei-brookings.org/admin/authorpdfs/page.php?id=771.

23. Quoted in Jim Snider, "The Citizen's Guide to the Airwaves," New America Foundation, July 2003, p. 2, available at http://www.newamerica.net/templets/ssl_forms/download/airwaves.pdf.

24. Bill McConnell, "Spectrum Return Trumps DTV," *Broadcasting and Cable*, June 3, 2004, http://www.freepress.net/news/article.php?id=3725.

25. Matt Richtel, "In Utah, Public Works Project in Digital," *New York Times*, November 17, 2003.

26. Jeff Chester, "Tale of Two Broadband Cases Illustrates Battle Over Net's Future," Center for Digital Democracy, April 6, 2004, http://www.democraticmedia.org/news/marketwatch/TwoCourtCases.html.

27. Marguerite Reardon, "Broadband for the Masses?" CNET Online, April 14, 2004, http://news.com.com/2008-1037-5190220.html.

28. Ibid.

29. Lori Wallach and Patrick Woodall, *Whose Trade Organization?* 2nd Edition (New York: The New Press, 2004).

30. Ibid.

31. Lawrence Lessig, *Free Culture* (New York: Penguin, 2004).

32. This document is available at the time of writing at http://hraunfoss.fcc.gov/edocs_public/attachmatch/DOC-247489A2.pdf.

MEDIA REFORM FROM THE INSIDE OUT:
THE NEWSPAPER GUILD-CWA

LINDA FOLEY

Nestled in the middle of the First Amendment to the United States Constitution is the golden rule of media and democracy: "Congress shall make no law . . . abridging the freedom of speech, or of the press." In today's complex world of terrorist threats, extremist politics, and global economics, freedom of the press is one of our most important national values. And yet, it has never been more imperiled.

By 2004, the traditions of a free and independent press were threatened, not only by the dangerous willingness of a post-9/11 American populace to allow government to curtail freedoms, but also by an enormously powerful corporate sector that has hijacked and coopted nearly every facet of modern society, including our most revered democratic institutions. In this age in which corporations and government are becoming one symbiotic force, we must fight corporate power, as well as government abuse, in order to preserve our First Amendment freedoms.

That's what The Newspaper Guild-CWA and its members do every day. The Newspaper Guild, a union representing journalists and other print media workers since 1933, has been one of the most enduring and effective media-reform organizations in the United States.

Heywood Broun, a crusading journalist who was the most popular and most highly paid newsman of his day, launched the Guild during the Depression when, according to biographer Richard O'Connor, he called upon "newspapermen to take a more practical view of their working conditions and organize against the rapacity of publishers."[1]

At the time, the "rapacious" publishers were fighting federal regulation of minimum wages and maximum hours for newsroom workers set by the National Recovery Act, a sweeping reform program introduced in the first administration of President Franklin D. Roosevelt. The publishers resented any intrusion upon their ability to administer draconian employment practices. In what would become an all too familiar refrain throughout Guild history, the publishers demanded exemption from the NRA on the specious constitutional grounds that their First Amendment rights would be violated if they were required to adhere to such restrictive employment rules as the forty-hour work week. They reasoned that any government policy that cost them money impeded their ability to speak freely.

In an August 7, 1933, *New York World Telegram* column, Broun tacitly acknowledged the elitism of a press corps that even then often identified more closely with its bosses than with other workers of similar economic standing. Nevertheless, he wrote, "the fact that newspaper editors and owners are genial folk should hardly stand in the way of the organization of a newspaper writers' union. There should be one. Beginning at nine o'clock on the morning of October 1 I am going to do the best I can to help in getting one up. I think I could die happy on the opening day of the general strike if I had the privilege of watching Walter Lippmann heave half a brick through a *Tribune* window at a non-union operative who had been called in to write the current Today and Tomorrow column on the gold standard."[2]

Broun's column inspired journalists all over the country to rise up in opposition to the power amassed by robber-baron publishers. They rallied around Broun's call for a labor union that would speak with one voice for all newsmen and newswomen—"A union of individuals," as author Daniel J. Leab would later characterize it.[3]

Thus, the American Newspaper Guild was born.

Since 1933, the Guild has grown to represent more than 35,000 reporters, photographers, editors, advertising sales representatives, customer service professionals, and other media workers, not just in the United States, but also throughout Canada and in Puerto Rico. In the 1970s, we dropped "American" from our name to more accurately reflect our geographic reach and became simply The Newspaper Guild, or TNG. In 1997, we merged with the Communications Workers of America, a union that already represented hundreds of thousands of workers in telecommunications and media, to become The Newspaper Guild-CWA.

From our early days and throughout our history, Guild members have been on the front lines in the struggle to keep the media and their owners credible and honest. As such, our members constantly face new challenges. As consolidation of the media landscape accelerates, they are the first citizens to experience the antidemocratic effects of concentrated power in the media industry.

Consider the impact on print media workers of the industry consolidation of the past few decades. In 1950, there were 1,774 daily newspapers in the United States. By 2002, that number had shrunk to 1,457, an 18 percent decrease. Over the same period, the number of newspapers with circulations over 250,000 increased by 8.5 percent, while total newspaper circulation was falling.[4] The number of daily newspapers, and hence the number of print voices, declined while the number of large newspapers increased. Bottom line: Our members have lost jobs.

The Newspaper Guild-CWA, along with three broadcast unions that also represent journalists, conducted a poll of our members in late February 2004. Among those surveyed, 76 percent responded that they knew of at least one coworker who had lost a job in the last five years. One in five reported being laid off themselves.[5]

Another study by the Pew Center for Excellence in Journalism, titled *The State of News Media 2004*, reported that twenty-two companies now control 70 percent of daily newspaper circulation; just one company, Clear Channel, owns more than 1,200 radio stations; ten companies own 30 percent of all television stations, reaching 85 percent of all TV households; and network TV owners are all "giant corporations for whom television, let alone television journalism, represents only a small part of their revenues," less than 30 percent.

Although profits for media companies are up, investment in newsgathering is down. The networks, for example, have cut their number of correspondents by one-third since the 1980s. Newspapers today have 2,200 fewer full-time newsroom employees than they did in 1990—while ad revenues rose by 60 percent and profits jumped by 207 percent during the same period, according to the Pew study.

Thus, the study concludes, "many traditional media are maintaining their profitability by focusing on costs, including cutting back in their newsrooms." Journalists' workloads have increased, and space for news has decreased.[6]

According to our survey, job loss merely begins the litany of stresses media consolidation puts on people who bring you the news. Media workers, particularly journalists, are keenly aware that the quality of their work has been denigrated by consolidation and corporatization of their industry.

In our survey of media workers, 53 percent of those polled reported that employee morale had declined over the past two years, while only 20 percent thought that it had improved. More than 70 percent believed that understaffing was undermining the quality of news coverage, and 68 percent were highly concerned about the lack of time they had to do a professional job.

The most serious problem, according to 83 percent of those surveyed, was too much emphasis on the bottom line, along with the influence of ratings and circulation on news coverage, a loss of credibility with the public, and a decrease in the overall quality of journalism.

The vast majority of reporters will tell you that they entered journalism because they wanted to make a difference in the lives of ordinary people. Yet our poll indicates that 65 percent of media workers believe news organizations do not give enough coverage to stories that are meaningful to average Americans.[7]

The Pew report also pointed out that in June 1985, nearly 80 percent of the public trusted what it read in daily newspapers. By 2002, less than 60 percent did so. The trend was mirrored by public perceptions of each of the major television networks' news operations.[8]

Press critics and others who denounce balanced reporting as "liberal bias" might be tempted to blame this loss of credibility on the likes of the former *New*

York Times reporter Jayson Blair, Stephen Glass of the *New Republic*, USA *Today's*
Jack Kelley, and other individual reporters who have misrepresented facts or lied
to readers and viewers. But that's way too simplistic. Too often, those who advocate
media reform forget that media workers themselves are on the frontlines of the
battle they are waging. Too often, plans to agitate for media reform can degenerate
into disparagement of individual reporters.

No matter how many Jayson Blairs out there are exposed and eradicated, the
credibility of journalism won't be restored until the tolerated culture of deceptive
and manipulative news coverage is reversed. Professor Bartholomew Sparrow
observes that reporters are "employees of complex organizations," who feel "the
invisible hand" of the newsroom's social control.[9]

It's true that Blair, a Guild member while at the *Times*, apparently went to
some lengths to make his bosses and readers believe that he was at the scene of
various stories when, in fact, he wrote them without ever leaving New York City.
It's also true that the media giants Clear Channel and Sinclair Broadcast Group
try to mislead audiences about the origin of their broadcasts. Both companies
would have listeners and viewers believe that their news operations are actually
located in the cities and towns they service. In reality, Sinclair's News Central
produces "local" TV news for sixty-two stations in such places as Flint, Michigan,
and Rochester, New York, from a megastudio outside Baltimore. Clear Channel,
meanwhile, uses deejays in centralized regional studios to feed what is portrayed
as local programming, including news and weather, to stations hundreds or even
thousands of miles away. It shouldn't be surprising that the culture of the boardroom filters down and influences the culture of the newsroom. No wonder many
good journalists are leaving the profession.

The Newspaper Guild-CWA and the right of journalists to have a union voice is
so important in the struggle to maintain democratic and independent mainstream
media in this country. Reporters must have some ability to fight for stories that they
know need to be written. They must be able to challenge corporate owners and to
demand adequate resources to cover the news. They need the ability to stand up
for both journalistic principles and for themselves. As their union—their voice
and advocate at work—the Guild allows them to do just that.

Our collective-bargaining agreements contain provisions that protect an
employee's right to speak out about abuses while they guard against arbitrary dis-
cipline or dismissal. A media employer can't retaliate against a Guild-represented
journalist just because the reporter wants to pursue a story. Our contracts require
that employers have "just and sufficient cause" before someone is dismissed or
disciplined. Simply put, media employers who have Guild-represented employees
cannot use reporters as scapegoats for bottom-line policies that shortchange the
public's right to full and fair news coverage.

A sad tale out of the *Cincinnati Enquirer* illustrates the importance of the "just and sufficient cause" stipulation. Until the late 1990s, the Guild represented newsroom workers at Gannett Co.'s *Cincinnati Enquirer*. A company that has a history of union-busting and antiunion policies, Gannett spent more than a decade fighting the Guild's existence at its Cincinnati paper. (This despite the fact that the *Enquirer's* partner in Cincinnati's joint operating agreement, Scripps-Howard's *Cincinnati Post*, still enjoys a relatively calm and productive relationship with the Guild.) Eventually, Gannett succeeded in getting the Guild to relinquish representation of *Enquirer* employees. Within two years, the consequences of being without union protection became all too clear.

In May 1998, the *Enquirer* ran a special section that featured a comprehensive investigative story about Chiquita Brands International, a company controlled by Cincinnati's most powerful corporate figure, Carl Lindner. The story, written by Mike Gallagher, an ace reporter, detailed alleged questionable and possibly illegal business practices of the banana giant, citing charges of bribery, environmental abuses, and conspiracy to evade various laws. The story was accompanied by an editor's note that praised Gallagher's "thorough reporting" job. The *Enquirer* seemingly was on its way to a Pulitzer Prize.

Not so fast. Chiquita Brands, with its powerhouse of high-priced lawyers, immediately launched an assault on Gallagher. The company accused him of having surreptitiously and illegally obtained proprietary e-mails and voice mails and threatened to sue Gannett.

In what ranks as one of the most gutless acts by a modern newspaper company, Gannett caved in and totally abandoned the reporter and his story. On June 28, the *Enquirer* ran a front-page apology to Chiquita, which included language accusing Gallagher of "theft" of information "in violation of law." (Mind you, this was an apology, not a retraction.) Gannett also allegedly paid Chiquita $10 million to stay out of court.

Gallagher wasn't so lucky. He was fired, of course, and faced trial in a criminal court. He eventually cut a deal with prosecutors and fingered the source who had fed him the so-called illegal e-mails and voice mails. The source, a former low-level corporate officer at Chiquita, was also eventually tried and convicted. It's been several years, but back when I was in journalism school, we called what Gallagher did to get the Chiquita Brands story investigative reporting. But then again, when I was in journalism school, reporters went to jail to protect the identity of their sources, not the other way around.

What was lost in all this—besides the career of a promising journalist and the sanctity of his source—was the substance of the original story. The story's main allegations were never disproved or disavowed. Chiquita Brands, as far as I know, was never held accountable for its questionable business practices. And Gannett continues to publish and reap profits from the citizens of Cincinnati via the *Enquirer*. Ironically, Gannett recently announced its intention to end the joint operating agreement with Scripps' *Post* in 2007, probably leaving the *Enquirer* as Cincinnati's only daily newspaper.

Had the Guild still represented Gallagher and his colleagues at the *Enquirer*, the process, if not the outcome, would have been much different. A collective bargaining agreement with the *Enquirer* would have required Gannett to prove that it had "just and sufficient cause" before hanging Gallagher out to dry. The contract would most likely have contained a clause obligating the *Enquirer* to protect the identity of Gallagher's news sources, and union representation would have ensured that someone could stand up to defend the story and the journalist who produced it. Perhaps an arbitrator hearing the case under a collective bargaining provision would have upheld Gallagher's dismissal, but at least Gallagher would have had a fair chance to give his side of what happened.

Less dramatic, but no less important, versions of what happened to Mike Gallagher can potentially occur in newsrooms throughout America every week. Ensuring that reporters have the freedom to aggressively cover the news, even if it means taking on their own employer, is the Guild's most important contribution to media accountability.

A Guild contract provides other protections for reporters who want to do a credible job of covering the news. For example, most of our collective bargaining agreements codify the right of reporters to disassociate themselves from a story by removing their byline. Contracts also protect a reporter's right to maintain the confidentiality of news sources. Many allow reporters to engage in activities outside of work that do not conflict with their jobs. Nondiscrimination clauses and equal-opportunity provisions ensure that newsrooms are diversity-friendly workplaces. And of course, there are provisions that guarantee adequate rates of pay, benefits, and time off.

Speaking with one voice and creating power through solidarity of workers across the media sector is another necessary component of media reform. It is one reason the Guild, the CWA, and the AFL-CIO have actively campaigned against the Federal Communication Commission's repealing meaningful media ownership rules.

Jay Harris, the former publisher of the *San Jose Mercury News* who became a journalism folk hero when he resigned rather than implement budget cuts demanded by his paper's corporate parent, Knight Ridder, once observed that journalists find themselves in a profession that is dedicated to public service but is situated in an industry committed to increasing profits for its owners. Similarly, in a 2001 critique of foreign news coverage, the syndicated columnist Molly Ivins wrote, "A news organization has only one way to cut costs, and that is to cut news gathering. As the ownership of American news media becomes more and more concentrated, with all outlets subject to judgment by some 25-year-old hotshot on Wall Street as to whether they 'meet earnings expectations,' the pressure to cut news gathering gets worse. As far as the media conglomerates are concerned, newspaper and television networks are just 'profit centers.'"[10]

Journalists cannot sit on the sidelines of the current debate over the policy on media ownership as they tend to do on so many issues. Journalists and others who work in the news and media industries can't leave the fight for media reform to surrogates—not when their livelihoods and profession are at stake.

The Newspaper Guild-CWA, collectively representing thousands of media workers, can help define what separates our members' interests from those of the media corporations and moguls. Still, more individual journalists and media workers need to speak out about media reform and against public policy that facilitates ownership concentration.

So what can media activists, individual journalists, and The Newspaper Guild-CWA do to help curve consolidation and bring about media reform? The short answer is that they can agitate on the inside and congregate on the outside. Or, as AFL-CIO President John Sweeney puts it, they can engage in the "streets and suites approach to collective action."

It's an approach that has worked to preserve media diversity in at least one community. Honolulu today has two independently owned newspapers because local media workers and concerned citizens joined forces five years ago to thwart the announced shuttering of the *Honolulu Star-Bulletin*.

The effort began again with Gannett. In the fall of 1999, Gannett, owner of the *Honolulu Advertiser*, and Liberty Newspapers, a small company owned by Rupert Phillips, announced that Liberty was closing the *Star-Bulletin*—the weaker, afternoon partner in the Honolulu newspapers' joint operating agreement. The move would end the JOA and turn Honolulu into a one-newspaper town. Gannett agreed to pay Liberty an undisclosed, but reportedly lucrative, sum of money to end their arrangement.

The Guild and other unions representing workers at the *Star-Bulletin* and the *Advertiser* implored the Hawaii attorney general to step in. Eventually, he did, and with the help of a citizens' group called Save Our Star-Bulletin (SOS), he filed suit in federal court claiming Gannett and Liberty were conspiring to violate antitrust laws. A federal judge agreed and issued an injunction prohibiting the closure of the *Star-Bulletin* until the antitrust suit was decided. The injunction eventually was appealed and upheld by the Ninth Circuit Court of Appeals on the mainland.

Meanwhile, citizens and *Star-Bulletin* workers joined forces on the streets of Honolulu, staging daily protests and sign-waving demonstrations in support of their afternoon paper. Local officials, political leaders from both parties, and congressional representatives all joined in a collective call to keep the *Star-Bulletin* alive.

David Black, a Canadian publisher, eventually stepped forward to buy the *Star-Bulletin*. Under court supervision, he and Gannett finally came to an agreement about how to divide the assets of the joint operation so as to keep the *Star-Bulletin* viable. Black continues to publish the daily *Star-Bulletin*. And the owners of both the *Star-Bulletin* and the *Advertiser* have newfound respect for the community they serve. SOS, meanwhile, continues to meet and discuss local media issues.

Honolulu is an example of a kind of "convergence" in media reform. Citizens and media workers can work collectively to foster diverse media voices in their community. Debates over policy in Washington often crowd out other news generated by developments around media reform. But real changes can and do occur in local communities where people care about the quality and diversity of the information they are receiving.

Establishing collective bargaining rights at media companies is essential to our ability to reform those companies. An organized workforce is the first step toward providing a voice for media reform. Therefore, supporting and demanding collective bargaining rights for media workers should be incorporated into any media reform plan. As we have seen from the history of The Newspaper Guild-CWA, an organized media workforce can become a powerful tool for media accountability, but the workers need community support in order to pull their effort off effectively.

As Guild founder Heywood Broun told a 1933 NRA hearing (somewhat tongue in cheek), "Quite inadvertently, I am sure, some of the publishers have allowed the feeling to grow and spread that newspapermen and women who join organizations of their own creation will be subject to penalties. . . . You can't call it a free press that rests upon the fears and apprehensions of reporters who are frightened and who feel that they have good reason to be frightened."[11]

Media workers need to separate themselves from corporate bosses who don't represent their interests, either as workers or as citizens. Alliances with community activists will enhance their journalistic endeavors, not conflict with them.

The founders of our country recognized the importance of collective action and its direct connection to a free and independent press. That's why immediately after protecting freedom of the press, the First Amendment goes on to enshrine "the right of the people peaceably to assemble and to petition the government for a redress of grievances."

We all need to challenge elected officials to develop and enforce media policies that will force media companies, large and small, to live up to their responsibilities and obligations to inform the public, educate the citizenry, and give wide exposure to diverse points of view. They can start by living up to their responsibilities toward their own employees.

The First Amendment, and our commitment to its values, requires no less.

Notes

1. Richard O'Connor, *Heywood Broun, A Biography* (New York: G.P. Putnam's Sons, 1975), p. 181.

2. Ibid, pp. 181–182.

3. Daniel J. Leab, *A Union of Individuals, The Formation of the American Newspaper Guild 1933–1936* (New York: Columbia University Press, 1970).

4. "Facts About Newspapers," Newspaper Association of America, 2003.

5. "A Survey of Media Workers," February 2004, conducted by Lauer & Associates for The Newspaper Guild-CWA, NABET-CWA, Writer's Guild of America East and the American Federation of Television and Radio Artists.

6. "The State of News Media 2004," 24 May 2004, Pew Research Center for the People and the Press in collaboration with the Project for Excellence in Journalism and the Committee of Concerned Journalists, http://www.stateofthenewsmedia.org/index.asp.

7. "A Survey of Media Workers," February 2004.

8. "The State of News Media 2004."

9. Bartholomew Sparrow, *Uncertain Guardians: The News Media as a Political Institution* (Baltimore: Johns Hopkins University Press, 1999), pp. 107–108.

10. Molly Ivins, "All the News That Turns a Profit," *Austin American Statesman*, Oct. 26, 2001, available at http://www.commondreams.org/views01/1026-06.htm.

11. O'Connor, p. 184.

MEDIA BIAS:
HOW TO SPOT IT—AND HOW TO FIGHT IT

Peter Hart

Over the past several years, the movement for media democracy has grown by leaps and bounds. Compare the level of activism that opposed the Telecommunications Act of 1996 to the 2003 public-comment period at the Federal Communications Commission (FCC). In the space of a few short years, the movement for media reform became much more popular and more unified. A combination of factors made this development possible, including (but not limited to) an independent media network that popularized the concerns of media activists, and the expansion of the Internet as an advocacy tool.

But underlying these developments is public frustration—even anger—with the state of major commercial media. Meager public-affairs and local programming, cookie-cutter radio formats, the near invisibility of quality children's programs, and the often inane chatter of twenty-four-hour cable channels, all contribute to the sense among everyday citizens that it is worthwhile to imagine real alternatives.

Going to the Source

There are different ways to measure or highlight the worst problems in mainstream journalism. One way is through qualitative criticism: identifying examples of poor reporting, neglected context, and the reluctance to challenge status-quo notions and conventional wisdom. Often this kind of case-by-case monitoring serves to identify larger patterns of media bias.

Another way to study media is to do quantitative research into media patterns. For example, over the years numerous "source studies" have been conducted that look at the audience the media are talking to when they cover important stories; the findings consistently point to a media environment dominated by official sources and establishment elites. This fact explains why corporate-friendly economic policies are rarely challenged and substantive criticism of United States foreign policy is often overlooked, since guests who might challenge the two-party consensus are few and far between.

Fairness & Accuracy in Reporting (FAIR), the organization where I currently work as activism director, conducted a study in 1989 that still stands today as a model of media criticism. FAIR analyzed forty months of *Nightline's* programming, and found that the guest list was dominated by elite, conservative guests. The top four guests typified this trend: Nixon aide Henry Kissinger, Reagan officials Alexander Haig and Elliott Abrams, and far-right evangelist Jerry Falwell. Of the top nineteen guests, all were men, all but two were white, and thirteen of the nineteen were conservatives. In total, 80 percent of the United States guests were government officials, professionals, or corporate representatives, while only 5 percent represented public-interest groups (peace groups, civil-liberties advocates, environmental organizations, and the like). When the show turned its focus to the economy, more than one out of three guests (37 percent) were corporate representatives; only one in twenty represented labor.

FAIR's study was widely covered by the mainstream media and elicited a response from ABC anchor Ted Koppel. This is a key part of FAIR's mission: to take the critique to the mainstream and hopefully to engage journalists—particularly those whose work is under scrutiny—in a discussion about what we consider to be their professional obligation of offering a more diverse discussion of major issues.

Unfortunately, the patterns revealed in the *Nightline* study can be found throughout the media. More recently, FAIR commissioned a study of one year of programming on the network newscasts (ABC *World News Tonight*, NBC *Nightly News*, CBS *Evening News*). The study analyzed over 14,000 sources appearing on network news shows in 2001 and found that:

- 92 percent of all United States sources interviewed were white, 85 percent were male;

- Where party affiliation was identifiable, 75 percent were Republican, and 25 percent were Democrat;

- Corporate representatives appeared about 35 times more frequently than did union representatives (a sad irony, given the state of the economy at the time of the study);

- Women made up 15 percent of all sources, and were rarely featured as experts.

- Racial imbalances in sourcing were dramatic: 7 percent of sources were black, 0.6 percent of all sources were Latino, 0.6 percent were Arab-American, and 0.2 percent were Asian-American. Out of a total of 14,632 sources, only one on-camera source was identified as Native American.

In other words, the network newscasts were largely populated by guests and experts drawn from the elite and powerful classes, while voices who might challenge their views were given severely limited access to the airwaves. Consequently, their perspectives remained largely unknown to the tens of millions of Americans who rely on evening newscasts for their information. This situation presents a dangerous problem for a democratic society: When important issues are under discussion, can a democracy properly function when critical ideas are excluded from popular debate?

Restricting Debate on Trade and Health

The question of restrictions on discussions of trade and health is especially relevant when the establishment-supported "consensus" position on a controversial topic has been more or less agreed upon by leaders of both major political parties. In such cases, the media debate is essentially shut off, even when public-opinion polls suggest that elected officials and elite opinion-shapers are out of touch with everyday citizens. Economic and trade issues are prime examples. Take the debate over the North American Free Trade Agreement (NAFTA) in the early 1990s. FAIR studied the sources available in news reports in the *New York Times* and *The Washington Post* from April through July 1993. The study found that out of 201 sources, only six (3 percent) represented the environmental movement. Not a single representative of a labor union was quoted during the four-month period. Spokespersons for all public-interest or civic-action groups—including ones who endorsed NAFTA—made up only 7 percent of named sources.

On the other hand, United States government representatives made up 51 percent of sources in the two papers, 62 percent of sources in the *Times*. They were overwhelmingly pro-NAFTA (81 percent), as were other government sources (mainly Mexican and Canadian) that made up another 11 percent of sources. In all, 68 percent of quoted sources had pro-NAFTA positions, with 66 percent in the *Times* and 71 percent in the *Post* in favor. Only 20 percent of the two papers' sources were opposed to NAFTA—24 percent in the *Times*, 17 percent in the *Post*. In other words, almost three times as many sources were defenders of NAFTA than were critics of the trade agreement in the reports of the *New York Times*; in the *Post*, the ratio was more than 4 to 1.

But try telling that to the media. In August 1993, the *New York Times* reported that business groups were stepping up their efforts on behalf of NAFTA "after months of letting unions and environmental groups dominate the debate." It makes you wonder which debate they were tuning in to—certainly it wasn't the one presented in their own newspaper. But the public was, in fact, much more divided over NAFTA; they just weren't able to see a reflection of that position in the mainstream media.

An issue like NAFTA is covered this way because the political and business establishments were nearly unanimous in their support of the "free trade" agreement. Therefore, journalists were less likely to include the perspectives of those who were erroneously seen as far outside the mainstream.

National health-care policy is another area where the majority position fails to elicit much media interest. In 1993, there was a serious debate about changing the health-care system in this country. The mainstream media, though, largely embraced corporate-friendly "managed care," a system in which private insurance companies provide medical care through giant HMOs. Some outlets announced early on that the media had won the debate: the *New York Times* editorialized that "the debate over health care reform is over" in October 1992. But that "victory" in such outlets as the *Times* had more to do with shutting out alternative proposals, such as a Canadian-style "single payer" system, which FAIR found to have received significantly less attention in the *Times* than its favored "managed care" option.

The media seemed to argue that they were merely paying more attention to options they determined to be more "politically viable." But this decision means that news judgments are based on elite preferences, not on popular opinion: the *New York Times*' own polling at the time had consistently found majorities—ranging from 54 percent to 66 percent—in favor of a tax-financed national health insurance.

But it wasn't just the *New York Times*. A panel discussion of managed competition on PBS's *MacNeil/Lehrer NewsHour* included three government officials who were mainly supportive of managed competition and Dr. Steffie Woolhandler of Physicians for a National Health Care Plan, who supported a single-payer plan.

Near the end of the discussion, Robert MacNeil noted that Woolhandler was "in the minority"—to which she responded: "Robert, I'm not in a minority. Polls are showing two-thirds of the American people support government-funded national health insurance." MacNeil responded by insisting that single-payer was "considered impossible politically at the moment." Of course, that situation has plenty to do with the media's restricting debate on health care—even when the "unpopular" position is, contrary to elite wishes, quite popular.

Journalists Go to War

In times of war, the tendency to severely restrict the boundaries of media debate actually gets worse. When FAIR studied the over 900 sources appearing on the networks' newscasts during the first two weeks of the Gulf War in January 1991, only 1.5 percent of those appearing on the screen were antiwar protesters, and only one of those 900 sources quoted was a national antiwar leader. This proportion paled in comparison to other groups—for example, seven professional football players were asked about the war on the nightly newscasts.

In the lead up to the invasion of Iraq in 2003, those patterns were largely unchanged. During what was perhaps the most important moment of the pre-war debate—the week before and after Secretary of State Colin Powell's February 5 address to the United Nations—the media's discussion of Iraq was dominated by current and former government officials, who made up 76 percent of all sources. At a time when polls showed that 61 percent of Americans wanted more time for diplomacy or inspections, only 6 percent of United States sources on the networks could be reasonably considered "skeptics" of the Bush administration's drive to war. Of the 393 sources appearing during those two weeks, just 3 were affiliated with antiwar activism.

Given that the mainstream media are so overwhelmingly dominated by official sources, one might hope that public broadcasting could offer a healthy alternative, showcasing perspectives that fall outside this narrow consensus. In fact, that is the very purpose of public broadcasting. Unfortunately, FAIR's source studies have revealed that national news offerings on PBS and National Public Radio (NPR) often mimic the same patterns found in mainstream corporate media. While public radio and television might theoretically exist to provide a home for voices that may otherwise be unheard, in reality they often end up repeating the offerings of corporate, advertiser-supported media. Environmental advocates, labor spokes-people, and other public-interest voices find themselves at the same disadvantage in "public" media as they do in commercial media.

Consider FAIR's 1990 study of the guest list of the PBS show *MacNeil/Lehrer NewsHour*, which happened to coincide with the Exxon Valdez oil spill. Though the event was an absolute environmental catastrophe, the *NewsHour* decided that one group wouldn't need to be part of the discussion of the oil spill: environmentalists. MacNeil/Lehrer had seven segments on the spill, but not one included an environmental representative. Some segments were limited to Exxon officials and friendly government officials, including one discussion that featured Alaska's governor counseling Exxon's chairman that he'd been too hard on his own company.

The Big Question: Why?

If source studies like those conducted by FAIR offer a sense of who is appearing in the media, and which interests dominate the discourse, the obvious question is why things are this way. To answer that question, it makes sense to look at the ownership structure of the media and what pressures that structure might place on working reporters and editors.

In the past few decades, the news media have become big businesses, with media outlets becoming fully integrated into major corporations whose very existence relies on the ability to turn a profit for investors. Once subsumed into a corporation, a newspaper or television station is expected to serve that corporation's goals just like any other part of the company; to expect otherwise would be illogical.

This situation creates a journalistic environment in which "making waves" by challenging corporate power is discouraged. There are advertisers to placate, and corporate owners who would not look kindly on a journalistic investigation into other aspects of a company's affairs.

These are more than theoretical concerns for reporters. In 1997, FAIR published a survey of investigative reporters and editors at TV stations around the country. Nearly three-fourths of the respondents reported that advertisers had "tried to influence the content" of news stories. Of these, 60 percent claimed that advertisers had attempted to kill stories, while 56 percent had felt pressure from within the station to produce news stories to please advertisers. In other words, it might not take long for a young reporter to understand how the game works.

Other polls of journalists have reached similar conclusions about the influence of owners: a 2000 survey of reporters, editors, and news executives found that about one-third reported that news that would "hurt the financial interests" of the media organization or an advertiser goes unreported, while slightly more of the respondents (41 percent) responded that they have avoided stories, or softened their tone, to benefit their media company's interests.

For the past few years, FAIR has released an annual report titled "Fear & Favor: How Power Shapes the News." The report gathers some of the year's most egregious examples of owner, advertiser, and government influence on the news. From CNN's decision to carry live coverage of the open and close of the NASDAQ stock exchange—not because it was newsworthy, but because NASDAQ was a sponsor—to the *St. Louis Post-Dispatch*'s reversing its editorial line on a new stadium for the Cardinals baseball team after the paper's owner bought a stake in the team. These examples illustrate the increasing pressures on journalists to use something other than journalistic judgment in deciding what gets covered and what gets left out. Reporters have long acknowledged the existence of such pressures; "Fear & Favor" is an effort to provide concrete, specific examples of this pervasive problem.

Most of the anecdotes in "Fear & Favor" have been reported at least once, but the greater number of everyday pressures on reporters remains unseen and unheard by the public. However, there are also occasions where these trade-offs between sponsors and sponsored are acknowledged in the open, suggesting a discouraging lack of respect for the "firewall" traditionally supposed to separate editorial priorities from those of advertising. *Time* magazine's special Spring 2000 issue was the culmination of the magazine's "Heroes for the Planet" series. The concept was to publish profiles of environmental activists and advocates, but there was a catch: the series had an exclusive sponsor, the Ford Motor Company. As *Time*'s international editor explained, the series wasn't likely to profile environmentalists battling the polluting auto industry. As he put it, "We don't run airline ads next to stories about airline crashes."

And as journalists work for expanding corporations with ever more sprawling interests, the very notion of journalistic independence is threatened. "News" programming is now regularly turned over to self-promotion for a company's other interests: theme parks, films, or entertainment programming carried on the same network. Thus NBC devoted several hours of its news program *Dateline* to the NBC sitcoms *Friends* and *Frasier*.

There's very little shame left, too; network executives hardly feel the need to say sorry, or to pretend that journalists should be exempt from shilling for the networks that pay their salaries. NBC News chief Neal Shapiro recently dismissed criticisms of this blurring of the lines between news and entertainment as "asinine." Perhaps more to the point, a former executive producer of network morning shows explained that these promotional tie-ins are practically a job requirement: "You'd be a fool not to do it. It's a business."

How to Read the Media

This is not to suggest that all problems of modern journalism can be traced to who owns what, or even what the guest list of a given program or network looks like. Often, media analysis requires skillful critical thinking. When a skeptical reader or viewer is trying to make sense of a given story, here are some sensible questions to ask:

- Is the information in a given article accurate? Bad journalism doesn't necessarily have to be the byproduct of corporate ownership or advertiser pressure. But the most important media criticism should try to understand the difference between routine errors (misspelling, erroneous dates) and the errors that result from overreliance on official sources or the refusal to incorporate dissenting views.

For example, a *U.S. News & World Report* profile of Attorney General John Ashcroft attempted to dispel some of the "myths" about his tenure. "Derided as a religious zealot by some," the magazine explained, "Ashcroft has never invoked religion in policy or procedural discussions, say colleagues, who add that they have never even seen him pray." But shortly after he took office, a front-page article in *The Washington Post* described daily prayer meetings that Ashcroft was holding at the Justice Department, a move that, the *Post* reported, alienated some staff members who saw it as coercive.

Not all media outlets are created equal, of course. Some journalists and commentators have a long history of distortion and inaccuracy, and FAIR has seized opportunities to correct the public record when their misinformation hits the airwaves. FAIR's fact-checking of journalists such as ABC's John Stossel, talk-radio host Rush Limbaugh, and Fox News Channel's Bill O'Reilly has drawn serious attention to their dishonest reporting.

- Is there missing context that might undermine the premise of a given article or television segment? This possibility is closely related to journalism that relies on a narrow set of elite experts. In reporting about Saddam Hussein's supposed weapons of mass destruction, for example, how many articles discussed United States support for Hussein in the 1980s? After the United States-led coalition occupied Iraq in March 2003, did reports about the dismal state of the Iraqi infrastructure mention the effects of United Nations sanctions on that state of affairs? The ability to pose difficult questions at difficult times is essential to meaningful journalism.

- Which experts are quoted—and, in turn, who isn't allowed space to weigh in? Is there a political significance to these patterns? As noted above, these patterns do not often mirror the political debate in the country as a whole. The media debate is often a very different creature, excluding ideas that have not been embraced by the elite. As the conditions of the United States occupation of Iraq worsened for Americans and Iraqis, growing numbers of Americans called for a total withdrawal of United States troops from the country. That opinion hardly penetrated the media debate, where it was derided as a "cut and run" strategy.

- When TV news shows feature a point/counterpoint debate, what political spectrum is offered? For years, FAIR has critiqued the left-right debates that pit a bonafide conservative with a centrist or lukewarm liberal (prompting one of FAIR's favorite slogans: "I'm not a leftist, but I play one on TV."). Sometimes the playing field is tilted even further; FAIR staffers have participated in debates that pit three conservatives against FAIR's progressive perspective. The subject? "Liberal" media bias, of course.

- Are media simply reinforcing the establishment line on a given topic, even though there may be no reason to believe that it is correct? When the Democratic presidential contender Howard Dean noted that the capture of Saddam Hussein would not make Americans any safer from terrorism, the media and political establishment pounced on him for expressing such ideas out loud. Yet it would have been very difficult to argue that he was incorrect.

Asking these questions (and many others) while reading or watching television is likely to reveal some very interesting patterns. FAIR's work demonstrates that knowing how to read (and read through) media spin is often just a matter of knowing which questions to ask. The next step is giving people a way to do something about it.

Getting Active

Understanding the challenges to building a viable democratic media movement can be disheartening. When we're asked if FAIR's existence has made the media "better," the answer is difficult. Considering the rise of such conservative outlets as Fox News Channel, the dominance of right-wing voices on talk radio and on the nation's op-ed pages, and the tilt in favor of powerful business and economic interests in most news programming, the answer might appear to be no.

But FAIR understands that many of the problems with media are deeply entrenched and will change only with time and concerted effort. And FAIR's history, in fact, is filled with examples of successful media activism. From the start, FAIR's progressive critique of mainstream media penetrated into mainstream media discussions. FAIR's studies of *Nightline* and NPR elicited responses from those outlets. Even news organizations that might be considered ideologically hostile to FAIR's message sometimes agree with our research. After FAIR's 2001 study of the guest list of the Fox News Channel's *Special Report* newscast, the anchor Brit Hume conceded that we had a point, telling the *New York Times* that "if it is a reasonable question, and we find that there is some imbalance, then we'll correct it."

So what can citizens do when media misrepresent important information or events? We can act together to put pressure on a given outlet to correct the record. When the *New York Times* dramatically downplayed the size of the crowd at a major antiwar rally in Washington, D.C., in October 2002, FAIR activists called on the paper to do better. The result? Three days later, the paper revisited the event, with a more accurate accounting of turnout. While the paper did not print a formal "correction," it is clear that the second, more accurate report would not have happened without the input from FAIR activists.

When HBO turned the Gulf War book *Live from Baghdad* into a film, they portrayed a piece of wartime propaganda as if it were true. The film strongly suggested that a discredited anecdote—the story of Iraqi soldiers removing Kuwaiti babies from incubators—had actually happened. After FAIR activists contacted HBO, the company added a disclaimer to the film's release on DVD.

Many media analysts and writers think that one of the right wing's most successful strategies has been to complain about the bias of "liberal media." In truth, many conservatives don't actually believe in such a bias, but they do understand the political effectiveness of claiming that one exists. Over the course of two decades, they have forced media to internalize the "liberal bias" critique, and in some cases to overcompensate in order to try and prove the critics wrong. This strategy ("working the refs," as Republican National Committee chair Rich Bond once described it) has certainly contributed to some of the media successes of the conservative movement in recent years. In short, many reporters and editors know that someone out there is "watching." Part of FAIR's effectiveness is to act as a counterweight to conservative critics of the media—though, as distinct from most of those critics, FAIR's goal is not media representing only "our" progressive views, but inclusive and diverse media that reflects a wide range of opinions.

FAIR's activism also focuses on media policy. For example, for the last several years, FAIR has generated thousands of letters opposing the FCC's attempts to redraw media ownership rules in favor of corporate media owners. FAIR has also taken the media to task for its industry-friendly coverage of issues concerning ownership of media.

Challenging Hate Speech

FAIR has also challenged the hateful rhetoric of certain radio talk show hosts, exposing their bigotry and using activism to draw attention to their hate speech. In 1996, FAIR documented numerous instances of racism and bigotry on the *Bob Grant Show*, broadcast on Disney-owned talk radio station WABC in New York City. Grant frequently called African Americans names like "savages," a term he applied very widely: "I can't take these screaming savages, whether they're in that A.M.E. Church, the African Methodist church, or in the street, burning, robbing, looting" (4/30/93). Grant prayed for basketball star Magic Johnson to "go into full-blown AIDS" (10/1/92), and he said that the black victim killed by a white mob in Howard Beach, Brooklyn "got what was coming to him" (12/9/92). Grant's preferred response to a gay-pride march: "Ideally, it would have been nice to have a few phalanxes of policemen with machine guns and mow them down" (6/29/94).

FAIR's campaign focused on getting Grant and Disney to answer for the divisive and hateful rhetoric on the show. FAIR asked Disney to publish its policy regarding on-air racial slurs and to add anti-racist programming that would serve as a kind of counterweight to Grant. After FAIR succeeded in getting some mainstream media attention to Grant's bigotry, he was fired from the station. Though FAIR's goal was not to get Grant fired, the campaign focused attention on a very simple idea: unanswered racial slurs and calls for violence are not a healthy part of public discourse.

Of course, media bigotry did not end with Bob Grant. The San Francisco-based talk radio host Michael Savage promoted the same kind of hatred, referring to "turd world nations" and calling the Million Mom March in favor of gun control the Million Dyke March. Savage's racism and homophobia didn't seem to get him in trouble with the mainstream media. In February 2003, MSNBC hired Savage to host a weekend talk show. In announcing the hire, MSNBC president Erik Sorenson described Savage as "brash, passionate, and smart" and promised that Savage would provide "compelling opinion and analysis with an edge."

As with Grant, FAIR helped to publicize Savage's hate speech and encouraged activists to write to MSNBC about its programming decision. These activists made Savage's bigotry an issue for MSNBC executives. After he hired Savage, Sorenson told a newspaper that the statements cited by FAIR and other groups "are not appropriate for MSNBC . . . Those kinds of statements will not be permitted. And if they do happen, they won't happen more than once."

It didn't take long. That July, Savage was booted off the air for telling a caller, "You're one of the sodomites. You should only get AIDS and die, you pig." Because of activism, Sorenson had made a zero-tolerance pledge, and was forced to keep it.

For close to twenty years, FAIR has been dedicated to the notion that understanding patterns of media bias and exclusion could be popularized. Part of what motivated FAIR's founders was the hope that a genuine media movement could become an integral part of the larger progressive community for social justice. It has always been FAIR's contention that winning on the media front leads to larger victories. By that measure, we think the future looks bright. More and more citizens have joined the battle for media democracy. Despite the efforts of the media giants, low-power radio stations are springing up around the country. The Internet is now an effective activism tool. And, most importantly, people are becoming savvier about detecting media bias and spin. Citizens are speaking up and demanding a more aggressive and independent media, while at the same time supporting independent and alternative media.

As in most struggles, the odds are not in our favor. But that didn't stop those who came before us, and it will not stop us either.

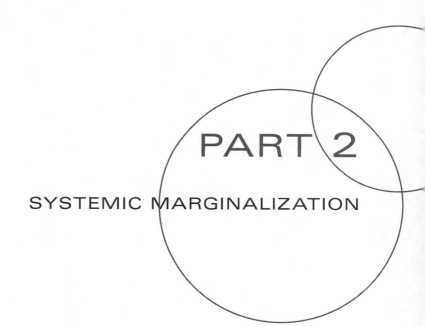

PART 2

SYSTEMIC MARGINALIZATION

WHY AMERICANS SHOULD
TAKE BACK THE MEDIA

CONGRESSMAN BERNIE SANDERS

For a number of years now, many of us have believed that the problem of corporate control over the media and consolidation of ownership had to be dealt with as a political issue. The recent public response to the Federal Communications Commission's attempts to loosen media ownership regulations—millions of people contacted legislators in Washington during 2003—shows us the very long way we have come in making that happen. It is high time that the American public woke up to the dismal public service our media system provides and started demanding better.

The reality now is that a handful of huge media conglomerates, such as Viacom, Time Warner, News Corporation, General Electric, Clear Channel, and Disney, with enormous conflicts of interest, largely determine the information the average American receives. In my view, this is a very dangerous trend. A vibrant democracy requires a full airing of all points of view. Increasingly, this is not the case. With few exceptions, the mass media now present to the American people the perspective of the wealthy and powerful, while largely ignoring the needs of the middle class, working families, and the poor.

The broad strokes of why media consolidation has occurred, the crisis in journalism it has produced, and the deeply antidemocratic forces at work to maintain monopoly control over public voices have been ably discussed at length by others in this book. What I want to focus on is how the media impacts those of us who are in day-to-day politics and the issues our constituents care about. This is something that I know about as a congressman of thirteen years and a mayor of eight years.

But before I do that, I want to briefly relate an incident that touches on everything this book is about, and that we can still learn from today. About thirty years ago, I had run for office in Vermont as a third-party candidate and received 1 or 2 percent of the vote. And then, having been a little bit involved in media production, I decided to produce a video biography on the life of Eugene V. Debs, one of my heroes—the great labor and socialist leader of the early part of the 20th century.

The video was sold mostly to universities around the country. In the process, however, in order to get additional exposure, I sent the video to Vermont Public Television, which, at that time, had a weekly slot available for independent productions. To make a very long story short, after months of delay, Vermont Public Television wrote me that they couldn't put the show on the air because it didn't present "both sides of the story," or some other such nonsense. In other words, it was kept off the air because of its political content.

How did I respond to that? First, I learned from some other independent filmmakers in the state that they too had not been able to get their work on Vermont Public Television, even when their productions were without political content. In a very significant way, Vermont Public Television was just not open to film producers in its own state. So it wasn't just me. Next, we all got together and began an unofficial media movement that focused on Vermont Public Television, which at that time was owned by the University of Vermont. Simply put, we raised hell.

In the course of our efforts, we broadened our concerns beyond our own narrow interests to the whole question of what public television in a small rural state was supposed to be about. What should its focus be? Who should it serve? How should programming decisions be made? We continued asking questions, organizing interested citizens, and drawing public attention until the broadcasters decided to meet with us. In the end, the university and Vermont Public Television were forced to hold a three-hour prime time Town Meeting on the Air, jointly produced by the university and our committee, to discuss the function of public television in Vermont.

That Town Meeting on the Air was an incredible experience. The antiestablishment group at the studio had about fifteen people, and the establishment side had an equal number. The Town Meeting, of course, welcomed phone calls to the studio—and did they come in. So many phone calls reached the station that the switchboard to the studio actually broke down. This kind of public outcry caused quite a stir. In short order, thanks to our efforts, the management of Vermont Public Television was replaced, our committee was given the right to produce six prime-time shows on issues of our choice, and the station became somewhat more responsive to the needs of Vermonters.

Thirty years ago, at that Town Meeting on the Air, I learned that the issue of the media was one that people felt strongly about. In my view, this is even more true today; at a time when Americans have been taken to war on false information; at a time when Americans have been hoodwinked on public healthcare, energy policy, and tax reform; at a time when fewer and fewer Americans know the first thing about the way the government works, much less where their voice can make a difference. These are crises in the media. We are all awakening to that crisis in dark times, and our hope lies in the speed and passion of people's organizing themselves to make change.

I am proud, looking back, that it was my own state of Vermont that held the first series of congressional town meetings in the country to discuss the problem of corporate control over the media. In my small state, we brought out over 1500 people to debate the issue and imagine a better media system and the paths to achieving it. The energy and emotion in all of those meetings brought me back to the lesson I had learned during the Town Meeting on the Air thirty years ago. Trust me: media *is* an issue that people are concerned about. That's true in Vermont, and it is true all over America.

In Congress in the last year or two, progressives, liberals, and conservatives have been working hard in a most unlikely coalition to stop the Bush administration from allowing even more media consolidation in our country, the exact opposite of the direction we should be going. Our demand is for more diversity, more competition of ideas, more localism. Not a situation in which an ever-smaller number of multinational corporations control what we see, hear, and read.

In September 2003, the Senate voted overwhelming to reverse the FCC and restore public-interest regulations over media consolidation. When the House Republican leadership refused to take up the issue despite enormous public pressure, we gathered a coalition of members to demand a vote. A total of 205 of us in the House of Representatives sent a letter to the Speaker of the House, Dennis Hastert, requesting a vote on this issue. The American people have a right to know where their elected representatives stand on an issue of such concern to so many citizens. "Mr. Speaker, respect democracy: Give us a vote!" Sadly, as has so often occurred in recent years, the Speaker refused to allow democracy to prevail in the House. We were forced to pursue a motion to discharge, which would allow the members to overrule the Speaker, force the bill out of committee, and bring it to the floor for a vote. It was a long, hard fight, shaping up to be even longer and harder. But we were quite confident that a large majority of citizens were behind us.

In June 2004, the efforts of the millions of Americans who contacted legislators and regulators and organized a full-scale media reform movement were completely vindicated. A federal appeals court heard arguments from a group of public-interest lawyers, led by the Media Access Project, challenging the FCC's attempts to loosen media ownership rules. The judges ruled decisively in their favor. This small group of attorneys, buoyed by principle, reason, and the overwhelming support of the American people, defeated the legal teams of the Bush administration, the largest broadcasting groups, the major television networks, and the largest newspaper chains. The thin arguments of the Republican majority at the FCC and its allies in the Congress were blown out of the water, and the truth was laid bare. The Commission's antipublic ruling was firmly rejected on the grounds that it was unsupported by reasonable evidence and ungrounded in the core principles of the public interest. The courts have given us an enormous opportunity to get the ball rolling back in the other direction—away from media consolidation and toward a more democratic system of public communication. The implications of such a movement are hard to overstate.

The main point I want to make is that if you are interested in addressing the major problems facing our country: an economy that works for all Americans rather than just the very rich; a nation in which all Americans are guaranteed health care through a national health care program; the need to break our dependence on fossil fuels and move to sustainable energy and protect our environment; a nation free of discrimination based on race, gender or sexual orientation; a nation in which we have a much fairer distribution of wealth and income; a nation in which all Americans have the opportunity to get the education they need regardless of social standing; and perhaps most importantly, a nation in which we have a vibrant democracy with a voter turnout not of 40 or 50 percent, but of 80 or 90 percent—if you are interested in these concerns, or a dozen others, you *must* be interested in the issue of corporate control over the media.

In my view, we will not be successful in creating social justice in this country, environmental sanity, and foreign policies that lead us to peace and not war, unless we make fundamental changes in the media. The media are intricately related to all these issues. One would be very naïve, indeed, to believe that we can have a substantial impact on any of those issues without changing how the American people receive information or, in fact, the very kind of culture that our media system helps to create.

Clearly, it is not difficult to understand that the large, multinational corporations that own much of our media are not "fair" in terms of their political or economic coverage. Why should that be otherwise? As large multinational conglomerates, owned by some of the wealthiest people in the country, they are sympathetic to tax breaks for the rich and corporate welfare from taxpayers. They are antiunion and support trade policies that allow them to throw American workers out on the street so that they can move their operations to China and other low-wage countries. They are prowar because in wartime viewing audiences substantially increase. Large media corporations help to create the "consumer culture" because, in fact, their main function is not to inform or entertain, but to sell the products their advertisers produce.

From a broad perspective, we can divide our major media outlets into at least two general areas. First, we have media outlets like Rupert Murdoch's Fox TV and *The New York Post*, the Reverend Moon's *Washington Times*, the editorial page of *The Wall Street Journal*, and the radical voices of talk radio like Rush Limbaugh. These right-wing outlets should simply be seen as an extension of the Republican National Committee. They are, pure and simple, the propaganda arm for right-wing Republicans and, as often as not, work closely with them.

On the question of the second category of mainstream media, I believe that an examination of their record on the question of "fairness" would show that, while clearly not as extreme as the right-wing media, they also lean to the right. Let me cite a few examples. Contrast the mainstream media coverage of President Bill Clinton, a moderate Democrat, with that of George Bush, a right-wing Republican. One was attacked mercilessly from before he took office until after he left. The other has, for the most part, been given a rather free ride even as he hacks away at our civil liberties, undermines our economy, and goes to war on flimsy pretexts. Another example is the presidential campaign of Gore versus Bush, where one candidate was berated constantly for items as small as the color of his shirts, while the other was never challenged about his corrupt business dealings, his dubious military record, and his oxymoronic policies of "compassionate conservatism." Further, and very importantly, there was the coverage of the mainstream media that took place leading up to and including the war in Iraq. The situation became so bad, so completely dominated by whatever point of view and spin the Bush administration wanted to push on the American people, that large numbers of Americans literally abandoned the national media's coverage of the war and turned to the BBC, the CBC, and the international media—now accessible over the Internet—for objective coverage.

While the issue of "fairness" of the corporate media on this or that political or economic issue is extremely interesting, that is not really what I want to focus on. The main point I want to make is that far more important than how the media cover a particular issue is the question of how the media determine what issues are important, or unimportant. In other words, what are the criteria that determine that some issues should appear on the front pages and receive widespread coverage, or as lead items on the television news, while other issues are ignored or deemphasized?

As a United States congressman, my major concern is the lack of emphasis, the lack of coverage, that is given to some of the most important issues facing the middle class and working families of our country, and the huge impact that media refusal to deal with these issues has on political participation in the United States and on the quality of American democracy.

Let me give some concrete examples.

Over the last thirty years, there has been an explosion of technology. Worker productivity has substantially increased, and corporate revenues have soared. Yet, the average American worker is now working longer hours for lower wages. From an economic point of view, reflecting the interests and the needs of tens of millions of American workers, *this is the major story of the last thirty years.* The middle class is shrinking. Two breadwinners in a family need to work in order to support a household, where thirty years ago one worker could do that. Americans now work, by far, the longest hours of any people in the industrialized world, and millions of them are exhausted and stressed out. We have just witnessed the greatest loss of jobs since the Great Depression. Our manufacturing sector—long a source of high wages and job security—has been decimated. The impact on working families has been extremely severe, unprecedented in the postwar era. And yet this story rates well below the latest celebrity trial in the list of the media's top items of attention.

Yes, we can read editorial after editorial from the largest newspapers in America giving us the Fortune 500 position on the virtues of the global economy and unfettered "free trade." But how many editorials do we read that tell us what happens to workers when two million decent-paying manufacturing jobs are lost in the last two years, as companies move their production to China, Mexico, and other low-wage countries?

In fact, that enormous story, in the broadest sense, has been virtually ignored by the corporate media. The result is that millions of working people who are hurting economically turn on the television and discover that their reality is not reflected in the media. They learn about crime and disasters, celebrities and sports, human-interest stories, the weather, and political attacks, but they don't learn much about why their standard of living and quality of life is declining. In other words, they learn about almost everything except what is happening in their lives. And they certainly don't get the kind of information they need to determine how they can improve their situation. Nor do they are given any evidence that political involvement in a democratic society is even an option for improving their lives. If people do not see the reality of their lives reflected in the media they see, hear, and read, should we really be surprised that in the last national election only 40 percent of Americans voted, and that voter turnout in this country is going down?

Another issue. We hear from our current political leadership about the importance of religion and morality. Well, the United States now has the greatest gap between rich and poor of any major nation, and that gap is growing. While the richest 1 percent own more wealth than the bottom 95 percent, the CEOs of large corporations earn 500 times the salaries of their employees. In the United States, today, there are children who go hungry, and many of our fellow Americans sleep out on the street. Is it fair, is it just, is it moral that a tiny handful of people enjoy incredible wealth while millions of their fellow citizens struggle to keep their heads above water and many, in fact, are simply not making it economically? Why has the media determined that gross disparity in wealth and income is not a moral or religious issue? What I can tell you is that in my twenty-one years as an elected official not one reporter, not one, has ever asked me, "Bernie, what are you going to do to end the national disgrace of the United States having the most unfair distribution of wealth and income in the industrialized world? Damn it. What are you going to do about that?" That question has never been asked of me or probably any other member of Congress. It's a nonissue.

When you turn on television today, you will see many shows analyzing today's football game and analyzing the last football game and analyzing the next football game. You will see shows, many shows, that talk about the ups and downs of the stock market and about the latest celebrity divorce or scandal. You will see shows about cooking, about shopping—there are whole networks made only for shopping—and about weather. Meanwhile, at a time when millions of Americans participate in trade unions, and with trade unionists earning 30 percent more than nonunion workers who do the same kind of jobs, how many programs have you ever seen that discuss why it is important for workers to be in a trade union? Or how workers can form a union? Or what positive things happen when a workplace is unionized and workers have a say in their job conditions? Millions of workers are in unions, millions more want to be organized, and the media are completely silent on that issue.

At a time when forty-three million Americans lack health insurance and some seventy-five million have gone without health insurance for some period in the last two years, there is little in-depth coverage from the media. This situation is inexcusable. The United States is the only nation in the industrialized world without a national health-care program that guarantees health care for all. Meanwhile, we spend twice as much per capita as any other country on health care, and we pay, by far, the highest prices in the world for prescription drugs. How much serious discussion have you seen in the media that compare our health-care (non)system with the health-care programs of other countries? How many Americans even know that there are alternatives to our failing, inefficient market-based system? How many Americans know that, for much of the world, health care is a right of citizenship?

The media report, over and over again, President Bush's views about how America stands for "freedom and democracy." Given that reality, one might expect that the media would pay some serious attention to the fact that the United States has the lowest voter turnout among major countries and that the rate of voter-participation is getting worse every election. Why do the overwhelming majority of low-income people and young people not vote? Why is political consciousness so low in our country? What can we do to achieve the same voter turnouts as Western Europe, Canada, or Scandinavia? Seen any good programming on that subject lately? Seen any major efforts on the part of the media to play a constructive role in increasing voter turnout?

In terms of the most important current foreign-policy issue, President Bush announces that he invaded Iraq in order to bring, among other things, democracy and prosperity to that country. Twenty years ago, when Ronald Reagan supported the Contras in Nicaragua, he said much the same thing. In order to a get a sense of how effective unilateral American military action has been from a historical context, and whether the stated goals have been accomplished, one might think that there would be widespread and serious media coverage of contemporary Nicaragua. The United States funded a war in Nicaragua, which killed and wounded many thousands of people there and resulted in the removal of the Sandinista government from power. What have been the results, and what might these tell us about the future of Iraq? With the defeat of the Sandinistas, how is democracy and prosperity doing in that small Central American country? What can we learn about Nicaragua that might be relevant to our current experience in Iraq?

Rather amazingly, there is almost no coverage of Nicaragua today. When the United States was attempting to overthrow the Sandinistas, there was constant and full-blown media attention and every problem in that country received extensive coverage. Today; nothing. Nicaragua no longer exists for the American media. It would take very little work to discover that fourteen years after the victory to bring "democracy and prosperity," Nicaragua's deteriorating economy has made it one of the poorest countries in the world. Unemployment in Nicaragua today is over 50 percent, basic social services are almost nonexistent, and there are reports that some children in that country have died of starvation. In terms of freedom and democracy, the last president of that country is being investigated for allegedly stealing over $100 million, an incredible sum for a country so small and poor. Could any lessons be learned from today's Nicaragua regarding American foreign policy in Iraq, unilateral intervention, and whether political rhetoric had anything to do with reality? Maybe? Any wisdom to be learned is silenced by the total media blackout that exists today with regard to Nicaragua.

And I could go on and on and on. As a general rule, the more important the issue is to the well-being of the American people and to our understanding of our place in the world, the more likely an honest debate and a general hearing of the facts would provoke sweeping change, the less coverage the issue receives. The situation is shamefully predictable. It is totally unacceptable for a society that aspires to democratic freedom and self-government.

As we fight for media reform, therefore, let us remember that our major concern should be not just fairness and objectivity on the issues that are covered. Those are important; but far more important is the need to end a media system in which a handful of corporations determine for us what, in fact, is covered, what is considered important, and what is considered unworthy of attention. What media reform really means is that the American people, to the greatest degree possible, should be making those determinations. When we accomplish that end, we'll have the kind of vibrant democracy that will make us proud.

LESSONS FOR REALISTIC RADICALS IN THE INFORMATION AGE

MARK LLOYD

For a very brief period of time, roughly the fifteen years between 1969 and 1984, local communities exercised real power over television, and the trends toward diversity in television were headed upward. I benefited directly from the hard work of civil-rights activists focused on media, and I have been working ever since to restore the media justice they fought for.

I took my initial steps into American journalism with a newspaper article for the *Westland Daily Eagle* in 1970, at the age of fifteen. At that time I began to understand the pull of storytelling as a vehicle for advocating social change, and nothing seemed more important to a young black man growing up in a race-torn society. The lesson about the power of journalism was reinforced by the drama of Watergate. The reporting of President Nixon's illegal activities by two relatively young reporters at *The Washington Post* created many young journalists and vindicated a profession then under attack by the soon-to-be convicted felons of the Republican Party. If you wanted to change the world, follow Woodward and Bernstein and write.

But what I had trouble reconciling was the Kerner Commission Report of a few years earlier. That look at the causes of the riots of the mid-1960s, including the riot in Detroit, my birthplace and still the home of many relatives, noted the failure of journalism to convey what it meant to be black in America. What I did not fully appreciate was that there were so few black and brown reporters working at the paper I once delivered, the *Detroit News*, or working alongside the Republican Woodward. While there were regular reports on the "Negro problem," somehow stories about bigotry in the media never made it to the front page or to newscasts.

Receiving little fame or attention, lawyers and activists in the civil-rights movement fought to make space for Americans like me in the all-white newspaper rooms and in radio and television stations. I would still face tremendous barriers and racism to get to that place, but lawyers and activists were changing the face of American journalism, just as journalism was taking credit for changing America.

After about four years working in radio in Ann Arbor, Michigan, in 1978 I was offered a job about thirty miles south, at WTOL-TV, a CBS affiliate in Toledo, Ohio. A large part of my job was to talk with all sorts of local leaders to find out what they believed to be the most important issues facing our community. One of the executives at WTOL, Law Epps, made it very clear to me that my work was important in helping the Cosmos Broadcasting Company keep its broadcast license. "We're in the public service business here," Epps liked to say. I also learned from members of the community that they had lobbied WTOL to hire more minorities. The fact that Cosmos hired me, and later promoted me to Public Affairs Director, was also an important part in helping Cosmos keep its license.

It would be many years before I understood that Epps' devotion to public service, and the protests of community leaders in Toledo was my connection to the lawyers and civil rights activists of the 1960s. It would be many years before I fully understood the relationship between law and community activism, between public policy and the journalism I would be encouraged to practice. On the road to that understanding I would write for other newspapers, report and produce programs at other local radio and television stations and national networks, and garner my share of awards now collecting dust on my shelves. My awareness sparked when, as a producer and reporter at CNN in Washington, I met one of journalism's heroes looking for work, Nelson Benton.

Benton was one of the brave white Southerners who reported on the Negro movement in the South. He was abruptly fired from his job as a producer at CBS when the tobacco and theater magnate Laurence Tisch took over the network and began shutting down CBS bureaus and firing senior staff. Nelson told me that the drive for profits was even influencing the previously sacred news division, and he warned that more major changes were on the way. I had a vague notion that somehow the FCC should prevent what was happening, and so I began to read some of the public documents published by the FCC under Mark Fowler. I was frankly shocked. The television is a toaster? The more I looked, the more it became clear that the laws put in place at the FCC in the early 1970s to promote workplace equality and programs to serve the public interest were being repealed right under my nose in Washington, D.C.

Under the Reagan administration, the National Association of Broadcasters Code of Conduct was deemed to be in violation of antitrust laws. The Fairness Doctrine's encouragement of discussion about local issues of controversy was said to hamper debate. Laws created to subject radio and TV stations to local scrutiny were determined to be unnecessary because of the marketplace. Laws meant to encourage the hiring and promotion of minorities were now said to discriminate against whites. And, somehow, I could not convince my colleagues at CNN that this major change qualified as news.

This essay is a brief synopsis of what I've learned about media from the inside out, inspired in part by "a pragmatic primer" Saul Alinsky wrote in the early 1970s on grassroots activism and coalition building called *Rules for Radicals*.[1] It remains a useful guide on how to effectively challenge the dominant interests in America. I offer here a modest and small addendum, Lessons for Realistic Radicals in the Information Age:

1. If you want to reform America, you must change America's communications policies. These policies no longer serve our democracy; they have been corrupted by the domination of one interest in our society—Corporate America.

2. The debate about a liberal media bias misses the point. Media with the most resources and power in the United States are alternately timid or in the service of Corporate America.

3. The battle over communications policy in a democracy is fundamentally a battle over political power.

4. Race matters. Despite the prevalence of some high-profile minorities in the civic sphere, 30 percent of the United States population continues to be badly underrepresented in public debate.

5. Independent, alternative, and niche media are important, but the battleground over public policy largely takes place on commercial television.

6. Who is in the White House does, in fact, matter.

The Role of Communications Policy in a Democracy

Communications policy is central to our unique republic. The great advance in statecraft established by the Founding Fathers in the Constitution was the check and balance of conflicting interests within the structure of governance. Central to this idea was a set of communications policies limiting the federal government's ability to prohibit speech, but more importantly, supporting equal communication among competing interest groups. This basic framework of our democracy has been destroyed, not by new technology or the invisible hand of the market, but by deliberate policy decisions that have allowed one segment of our society to dominate communication. Our republic has suffered much as a result.

Our government is supposed to be one where the lawmakers represent the people. As Lincoln famously put it, our republic is a "government of the people, by the people, and for the people." It is vital to the health of such a system that its citizens are informed and can share their views with each other on an equal basis. The Founders, particularly James Madison and Alexander Hamilton, understood that people divide along lines of interests, whether regional, religious, or economic.

Their first challenge was to balance these competing interests so that no one group could monopolize the national debate.[2]

Madison, one of the key architects of our Constitution, called our republic "a popular government" and sponsored legislation to finance the post office, understanding the central place of communication in the American republic.[3] As he argued, "A popular Government without popular information or the means of acquiring it, is but a Prologue to a Farce or a Tragedy or perhaps both. Knowledge will forever govern ignorance, and a people who mean to be their own Governors, must arm themselves with the power knowledge gives."[4] When Madison talked about popular information, he did not have our modern celebrity culture in mind. He was instead talking about information that citizens need for making intelligent judgments about the actions of their representatives.

The importance of the post office comes as something of a shock to many Americans. Even before they amended the Constitution to forbid the federal government from "abridging" speech and the press, the Founders established in Article One of the Constitution a mechanism that supported speech and the press in the form of the post office. Stretching from the wooded territory of Michigan to the coasts of Georgia and the territory of Arkansas, the postal service pulled together a geographic area at one time deemed too large to hold a republic. Here was our first communications policy in action.[5]

And who paid to subsidize the distribution of newspapers across this gigantic territory? Merchants were charged more to send items through the mail so that the highly partisan small newspapers from scores of small presses could distribute political information.[6] The health of the republic, even a highly restrictive republic, was deemed more important than the interests of merchants. What the Founders established was a mechanism ensuring that public debate would be largely free from government control, in such a way that neither merchants nor farmers nor church nor any other interest would dominate that debate.

This logic, so central to our republic, was lost on the Jacksonian Democrats. And so, along with the destruction of the national banks and other national projects such as canals,[7] these early Democrats forced the telegraph service out of the Post Office. This action set the stage for the first national monopoly controlled by merchants and financiers—Western Union.[8]

This reverse in public policy was the first, and perhaps most critical, break with the Founders' designs for the republic. The United States would be the only emerging industrial nation to make this mistake. Western Union came to power at the dawn of the Gilded Age, a time when ruthless early capitalists were defeating the independent farmer so beloved by Jefferson and Lincoln. The small independent presses that armed citizens with information would soon come under the power of these capitalists, as the monopoly of Western Union prompted the monopoly of the Associated Press.[9] Western Union also served as the model for the Bell

Company monopoly, American Telegraph & Telephone.[10] A.P. and Ma Bell were typical of the hated trusts of the early 1900s, and the inevitable reaction against them led directly to such entities as the Interstate Commerce Commission and the administrative state we know today. But the strategy of building large government bureaucracies to tame giant monopolies largely failed.

The regulatory bodies established by Theodore Roosevelt and Woodrow Wilson were no match for the communications trusts (not to mention the steel and railroad trusts) they were supposed to oversee.[11] Indeed, the administrative state only helped to further erode our republic by hiding policymaking from the public. Not only were citizens deprived of information about what their government was doing, they also had no real voice in determining what the unelected "independent" experts would do. So powerful was the embrace of monopoly that a raucous new medium of communication, the radio, would be wrestled from Marconi and scores of young inventors and entrepreneurs, and turned over to a government created monopoly, the Radio Corporation of America.[12] So, once again, unlike other industrial nations, the United States failed to ensure for its citizens access to sufficient information and the voice to self-govern. There would be no BBC in the United States.[13]

Radio, and soon television, would follow the lead of the major newspapers, coming to be dominated by monopoly capital administered by large corporations, reflecting one interest and one segment of our political and economic fabric. Under the modern American administrative state, communication would not be controlled by a republic of, by, and for the people. Even as the state would attempt, weakly and erratically, to regulate communications, the priorities, tendencies, strengths, and weaknesses of capital would determine how Americans communicated.

The Founders established a set of communications policies that put citizen engagement first. We now live in a society with a set of communications policies designed around the needs of market capitalism. The existence of other postindustrial societies (the United Kingdom, France, Sweden, to name a few) that have constructed communications policies to support democratic engagement argue against the notion that the Founders' core ideas cannot be applied in a modern United States. Nations with strong publicly funded communications services have better-informed and more engaged citizens and provide better for the citizens' health and welfare.[14] Our current public policies not only violate the intent of the Founders, they also harm the general welfare of all Americans, and most especially they harm our common interest in a strong democracy.

The Timidity or Republican Tilt of Dominant Media

With occasional exceptions, ever since the printing of newspapers became dependent upon the advertising dollar of corporate America, the dominant voices of the newspaper industry have been largely supportive of monopoly capital and the Republican Party that represents its interests. A simple count of supporters among the nations' newspaper publishers will reveal that Democratic leaders, from Franklin Roosevelt to Bill Clinton, have all suffered in comparison to Republican leaders, from Calvin Coolidge to George W. Bush. The former Governor of Vermont and presidential candidate Howard Dean's attack on the mainstream media (and vice versa) directly descends from the battles of Harry Truman.[15]

How then does one explain the persistence of the myth of the liberal press?

As Eric Alterman points out in the several hundred pages he devotes to the odd cobwebs spun by such propagandists as Bernard Goldberg and Ann Coulter, distortion is clearly a timeworn political technique.[16] I would only add that there is also a good bit of confusion about the term "liberal." I actually agree with Coulter and Goldberg that the papers such as *The Washington Post* and the *New York Times* and NBC, CBS, and ABC (the Big Five) tend to exhibit a bias toward opinions most popular in New York and Los Angeles. The public sentiment in major metropolitan areas tends to support racial equality, women's rights (including abortion), gun control, environmental protections, and a tolerance of the religious views and sexual behavior of private but not public citizens. And if these public opinions are what it means to be liberal, then the press is liberal. However, this support does not translate into more media support for Democrats than for Republicans.

The so-called liberal press—even the Big Five—was long supportive of such Republican right-wing causes as Nixon's execution of the Vietnam War and Reagan's adventures in South America. It took massive corruption and illegal tactics—such as the thefts and wiretapping at Watergate, and the arms and drug dealing of Iran-Contra—on the part of Republican administrations to wake these supposedly liberal bastions from their stupor. It took far less prompting for the Big Three to attack President Clinton for his affair with Monica Lewinsky. What, then, does it mean to be liberal? If being against burglary and illegal arms dealing is liberal, the press is liberal. If denouncing a married man for lying about adultery is liberal, the press is liberal. If being overtly skeptical of the use of military power is liberal, then the press is certainly not liberal.

Communications policies supported by the lawyers and lobbyists working for the Newspaper Association of America, the National Association of Broadcasters, and the National Cable and Telecommunications Association have tended to be against government regulation of the communications industry and in favor of policies concentrating ownership in their hands. If liberal is synonymous with laissez-faire, then the media is certainly liberal.

The problem with the media, especially the Big Three, is not that they are liberal, but rather that they are timid. Edward R. Murrow did not lose his nerve after a string of stirring reports on Joseph McCarthy and Robert Oppenheimer and migrant workers—he lost his sponsors.[17] The Beverly Hillbillies program is a much more comfortable environment for the car, soap, and pharmaceutical companies than is the sort of "popular information" James Madison had in mind.

I write this after the premiere cultural event in the United States—the 2004 Super Bowl. A group known for its Internet organizing, MoveOn.org, attempted to purchase commercial time on CBS to broadcast a rather tame criticism noting the future costs of President Bush's economic policies. They were not allowed to purchase the airtime because CBS deemed the advertisement too controversial. During the same program, CBS aired beer ads featuring horse flatulence and a dog biting a man in the crotch, old people tripping each other to get a bag of potato chips, and drugs for "erectile dysfunction." Put aside, if you can, Justin Timberlake revealing Janet Jackson's breast and the simple warlike brutality of the game of football, and the Super Bowl is a perfect example of the dominant characteristic of media in the United States today—politically timid, sexually suggestive, obscenely violent and commercially excessive.[18]

A Continuing Battle

While the antitrust, tariff, and licensing mechanisms were ineffective substitutes for the federal control of communications established by the Founders, the battle for power over the public arena did not go away. The battle simply shifted toward making these weak administrative tools more effective. In broadcasting, the battle centered on a regulatory framework designed to encourage the private broadcast licensee to act as if he were a trustee of public property. To some limited extent, particularly in the early days of broadcasting, this concept provided some minor balance against the understandable tendency in commercial media to air whatever sells while avoiding content that might stir political debate.

The public-trustee framework stated that, in exchange for a free federal license and protection to use designated frequencies over the publicly owned electromagnetic spectrum, broadcasters were supposed to act in the best interest of the public. This framework was buttressed by a set of rules known as the Fairness Doctrine. The core of the Fairness Doctrine was the concept that broadcasters were supposed to air a balanced presentation of controversial issues. Broadcasters liked the part about getting a free license. They did not like the part about airing programs that might not attract advertisers and might be contrary to their own views. But the public-trustee deal was tolerable as long as the public had no voice in determining what was in its own interest.[19]

The cozy relationship between the FCC and the broadcaster, a relationship that largely excluded the public, was what Dr. Everett Parker and his lawyer Earle Moore attacked in the mid-1960s at the height of the civil-rights movement. Their legal challenge eventually stripped away the license of WLBT, a racist television station in Jackson, Mississippi. After nearly forty years of broadcast regulation, the Republican moderate Warren Burger, presiding over the Court of Appeals in the District of Columbia, ruled that the public had a role in determining whether a local broadcaster was acting in the public interest.[20] During that same year, 1969, a case was brought by a conservative broadcaster, Red Lion, against the FCC's determination that the broadcaster had violated the Fairness Doctrine. The Supreme Court, led by a Republican liberal, Earl Warren (a Court that must be considered a noble oddity of American history), ruled that when the broadcaster's right to free speech is in conflict with the public's right to a fair expression of views, it is the public's right that is paramount.[21]

What followed these two cases was the promulgation of a clear set of rules (ascertainment and program reports) that laid out the ways broadcasters were to go about determining the kinds of local issues that should be discussed and the manner in which to report these efforts to the FCC. The golden age of public-interest broadcasting had begun.

I have read the writings of more than a few academics, lawyers, and economists who have argued that the ascertainment process was a pointless waste of a station's resources. But where I worked, the process led to substantive local discussion programs on a wide range of controversial issues, and not only on Sunday morning. I produced two weekly discussion programs, both of which aired around 7:00 PM, and I produced two quarterly documentary programs that aired around 8:00 PM. Some of these programs, such as the Baxter program on marital rape or the community discussion program I hosted on an antiabortion ballot measure, were quite risky.

Moreover, a newly tapped clamor for such public-affairs programming, and a regulation allowing relevant programs produced by the network to be listed by the local station as serving the local public interest and reported to the FCC, encouraged the networks to produce more of these programs. It was a time in broadcasting when local and national news operations were not expected to make money. Instead, news and public-affairs programs were good demonstrations of the seriousness with which the local broadcasters and the networks took their roles as public trustees. The programs I produced helped to justify the federal license granted to WTOL. The public-interest rules fought for by Parker and Moore and established by the FCC made those programs possible. The possibility of having a broadcast license taken away because of disgruntled members of the public made these sometimes boring, sometimes controversial, and sometimes exciting programs worth the broadcaster's risk.

That brief period in the history of broadcasting ended in 1984. The Reagan-Fowler FCC argued that the television was just a toaster with pictures and that the market was a sufficient mechanism to satisfy the public interest. And so the FCC eliminated the ascertainment rules, claiming that they were a burdensome intrusion on the industry.[22] The Reagan administration even determined that the industry's standards were a burden on the industry itself when the Department of Justice ruled that the National Association of Broadcasters' Code of Conduct was a violation of antitrust rules.[23]

To say that the Reagan assault on the public interest standard had an impact on public-affairs programming would be an understatement. During the "golden years" of the public-interest standard, between 1973 and 1979, the average amount of public affairs programming was 4.6 percent of total broadcast hours.[24] Professor Philip Napoli, of the Graduate School of Business at Fordham University, studied 142 commercial broadcast stations over a two-week period in January 2000. He found that of the total 47,712 broadcast hours, only 156.5 (or 0.3 percent) were devoted to local public-affairs programming. Local plus national public-affairs programs reached 1.09 percent of total broadcast hours studied.[25]

The Reagan administration also determined that the Fairness Doctrine was not necessary. Indeed, that administration's expensive "supply side" economists argued that the Fairness Doctrine actually worked to limit controversial speech. The decimation of the Fairness Doctrine did lead to an increase in talk radio—dominated not by balanced debate, but by right-wing haters like Rush Limbaugh, Michael Reagan, and Bob Grant, who were free to use the public airwaves to disparage others without having to be concerned that their lack of balance or facts would require rebuttal.

According to the Reagan-right, the relatively young *Red Lion* decision was made old law by cable TV and the abundance of VCRs. Under the facile declaration that somehow Jane Fonda's exercise tapes killed scarcity, many broadcast experts argued that the limited availability of free federal broadcast licenses should not create any special burden for broadcasters and that the public-trustee framework was unnecessary. And yet, in another twelve years, with the 1996 Telecommunications Act, the broadcasters would successfully lobby to continue to be treated as public trustees.[26] They took one look at the fees telecommunications companies were paying for licenses that gave them access to less valuable portions of the spectrum, and being a public trustee suddenly didn't seem so unattractive.

So we have returned to a version of the public-trustee framework established under Herbert Hoover. Yes, broadcasters are public trustees, but there are few rules to enforce and fewer opportunities for public oversight of what the trustees are doing. The result of this return to Hoover's vision of broadcasting has been the loss of local public-affairs discussion programs. It also has an odd affect on local and national news. News programs, which were the public-service ornaments of local and national news, now had to make money. And so the birth of happy talk and Dan Rather's sweaters. News "shows" moved away from local-beat coverage of city hall and toward a less expensive dish of local car crashes, video of distant natural disasters, "investigative" reports of petty criminals and rare illnesses, and consumer news about what products you can use. Some of us may doubt whether these programs are newscasts, but there are certainly more of them than ever before. And while two or three hours of local and national news programs may not provide more information about what your local representatives are doing than the brief newscasts of the late-1960s, they have become a much more comfortable environment for advertisers.

The point is not only that the broadcasters have won decisive battles to weaken the mechanisms of public-interest regulation, but also that broadcasters have understood that the battle was not lost in the 1960s to Parker and Moore. You can see that the telephone industry understands this point when watching its continuing battles against competition waged from the early 1900s to the present. The cable industry understands it as well, as evidenced in its battles to weaken the regulatory power of municipalities. Unfortunately, no sustained opposition to these corporate interests is working on behalf of the public good. This lack of sustained opposition over communications policy leaves most of us at a loss even to name minority, labor or religious groups as interests which might compete with corporate America.

The Continuing Problem of Race in Media

Michael Powell, the Chairman of the FCC during President Bush's first term is a black man. The Chief Executive Officer of TimeWarner, one of the most dominant media conglomerates in the world, is an African American, Richard J. Parsons. Robert Johnson, another black man, became a multimillionaire by developing a cable television channel devoted to blacks, Black Entertainment Television. Cathy Hughes has built a small empire of radio stations, Radio One, focused on black audiences. There are a half-dozen situation comedies on broadcast network television, particularly UPN, featuring casts that are almost entirely black. In addition, there are networks devoted to serving the large Latino audience in the United States, most notably Univision and Telemundo. So what could possibly justify the statement that race continues to be a problem in the American media?

As of 2000, the most recent year studied by the FCC and the National Telecommunications and Information Administration, while nonwhites, including Latinos, make up roughly 30 percent of the United States population, they are licensed to operate only 3.8 percent of all full-power commercial radio and television stations. Looking only at the most dominant media in the United States, broadcast television, all nonwhites combined are licensed to operate 23 of the nation's 1,288 full power TV stations—1.9 percent.[27] I use the term *nonwhite* rather than *minority*, because in some markets, nonwhites make up the majority of the population. I wrote about these shocking numbers in a memorandum to partners at my law firm, but got the usual reaction of mild sympathy until I reversed this usual presentation: white Americans own and control 98.1 percent of all full-power commercial television stations. The reaction I got to this statement was annoyance bordering on anger.

What about employment? A 2003 study by the Radio Television News Directors Association revealed that the total television-news workforce was 20.6 percent nonwhite in 2002. This was down from a high of 24.6 percent in 2001.[28]

The average number (not percentage) of nonwhites in any position on a news staff at a network affiliate was 5.1. The percentage of nonwhite news directors was 9.2 percent, and the percentage of nonwhite news directors working at network affiliates (the most-watched broadcast stations) was 4.1 percent.

NEWS DIRECTORS: TELEVISION

	2002 (in percentages)	2001 (in percentages)	1994 (in percentages)
White	90.8	92	92.1
Black	2	0.6	1.6
Hispanic	5.8	5.7	3.8
Asian American	0.4	1.1	1.5
Native American	1	0.6	1

NEWS DIRECTORS: RADIO

	2002 (in percentages)	2001 (in percentages)	1994 (in percentages)
White	94.9	95.6	91.4
Black	1.9	1.5	5.4
Hispanic	2.6	2.9	2.4
Asian American	0	<1	0
Native American	0.6	<1	0.8

The percentage of nonwhite general managers at network affiliates was 2.5 percent. Radio is not much better, and the trends are not improving.

As pitiful as they are, all of these numbers, including ownership, represent increases compared to my days in broadcasting from roughly 1976–1991. The number of conversations I have had where whites suggest that, just as blacks dominate basketball, whites dominate broadcasting, are too depressing to count. Perhaps, this argument goes, minorities are simply not interested in owning broadcast stations, or even more racist, perhaps minorities simply do not possess the requisite talent to own broadcast stations. What these numbers do not represent is a lack of interest among nonwhite Americans in having broadcast licenses.

In the era of Colin and Michael Powell, it is all too easy to forget that America was not only a deeply segregated nation, but also deeply racist just thirty years ago. This racism, as practiced by lending institutions, the federal government, and the broadcast industry, had a direct and long-term impact on the opportunities available to nonwhite Americans. After forty years of licensing broadcasters, racial minorities were licensed to only 10 (yes, ten) of the approximately 7,500 radio stations and held no (yes, zero) licenses to operate the 1,000 television stations in the United States in 1971.[29] The early attempts to correct this problem, inspired by the 1968 Kerner Commission Report and the work of Parker, focused on establishing guidelines to promote and monitor equal hiring practices in the broadcast industry.[30] This approach had little effect.

In 1978, under the leadership of President Jimmy Carter, the FCC adopted a Statement of Policy on Minority Ownership of Broadcasting Facilities. That statement noted that, despite its policies discouraging employment discrimination among broadcast licensees, "the views of racial minorities continue to be inadequately represented in the broadcast media. This situation is detrimental not only to the minority audience but to all of the viewing and listening public." The Commission proposed two sets of policies: (1) to consider minority participation as a factor in comparative license proceedings; and (2) to encourage broadcast licensees to sell to minority buyers through a distress sale (a broadcaster whose license may not be transferred because he is in jeopardy of losing it may transfer it to a minority applicant) or a tax certificate (a broadcaster may sell to a minority and defer any gain realized from the sale).[31] That year, minority broadcast ownership climbed to nearly one hundred—still less than 1 percent of the nation's broadcast licensees.[32]

By 1986, all minorities combined were licensed to just 2.1 percent of the more than 11,000 radio and television stations in the United States.[33] This was progress, but by 1990, the backlash against the civil-rights movement reached broadcasting. The Supreme Court, still dominated by New Deal and Great Society appointees, ruled in *Metro Broadcasting, Inc.* v. *FCC*,[34] that the FCC minority ownership programs mandated by Congress were constitutional because they serve the important governmental objective of promoting program diversity. The Reagan appointees on that court, William Rehnquist, Antonia Scalia, Sandra O'Connor, and Anthony Kennedy dissented. But with the help of the black arch-conservative Clarence Thomas, appointed by President George H. W. Bush, the *Metro Broadcasting* dissenters have dominated the Court since 1990. Presidents Reagan and Bush packed not only the Supreme Court but appellate and lower courts as well.

By 1994, in response to the Reagan-Bush court ruling questioning the inclusion of a government preference for minority applicants, the FCC froze its comparative hearings process.[35] And by 1998, citing a decision by the Reagan-Bush majority on the Supreme Court overturning a federal affirmative-action program,[36] the Reagan appointees on the Court of Appeals in the District of Columbia declared that the FCC's Equal Employment Opportunity rules were unconstitutional. The FCC EEO rules never made much of a difference in licensing, merely encouraging broadcasters to inform women and minorities when employment opportunities were available and to report on the number of women and minorities employed.[37]

The Reagan backlash against the civil rights of black Americans was apparent not only in the courts; it also created an antiaffirmative action frenzy in both the press and the Republican-dominated Congress. In their book, *The Black Image in the White Mind*, Robert Entman and Andrew Rojecki report on a framework used by print and broadcast journalists that distorts the issue of affirmative action (calling the complex set of programs either quotas or racial preferences, while ignoring white women as beneficiaries) and exaggerates the conflict over the issue between blacks and whites:

> The most comprehensive review of survey data concludes that Whites' attitudes on affirmative action remained virtually unchanged between 1965 and 1995, despite journalists' and politicians' frequent claims of a massive shift in the mid-1990s. . . . The failure of the issue to catch on in the 1996 election campaign despite the expectations of many pundits and politicians suggests White Americans were much less exercised over the issue than the news media depicted.[38]

Concerned about the political backlash of a tax policy tarred by the black brush of "affirmative action" (which meant black preferences in the press),[39] Congress voted to eliminate (and President Clinton did not veto) section 1071 of the tax code in 1995.[40] While this move effectively killed the tax certificate used to promote minority ownership in the communications industry, it also eliminated the use of the tax certificate for a wide variety of purposes to which it had been applied since 1943.[41] Two years after the tax certificate was eliminated, the number of minority broadcast licensees began to drop.[42]

Well, why does it matter who owns and controls stations? Isn't the news always just the news? Roughly thirty years after the Kerner Commission reported that the white press failed to communicate to white audiences "a sense of the degradation, misery, and hopelessness of life in the ghetto,"[43] *The Washington Post* reported:

> Whether out of hostility, indifference or simple lack of knowledge, large numbers of white Americans incorrectly believe that blacks are as well off as whites in terms of their jobs, incomes, schooling and health care . . . 40 to 60 percent of all whites say that the average black American is faring about as well and perhaps even better than the average white in

these areas. In fact, government statistics show that blacks have narrowed the gap, but continue to lag significantly behind whites.[44]

Whatever progress that was achieved toward integrating society has been lost. A variety of factors have resegregated America into the two unequal nations, one black and one white, about which the Kerner Commission warned.[45] Not enough whites and blacks know each other personally. Given the resegregation of America, where do the perceptions of white Americans about black Americans come from? Television. More particularly, the dominant source of information about others in our society today comes from local television news. And local television news tells a tale of black violence.[46] As Entman and Rojecki wrote: "Television news often portrays an urban America nearly out of control: night after night the news overflows with victims and perpetrators of violence." And while the news shows victims who are most likely white, the criminals are disproportionately black. Moreover, unlike whites, blacks tend not to be portrayed as individuals, are more often portrayed in handcuffs and chains, and are not seen as helpers or police officers.[47]

The ugly portrayal of black Americans on local television occurs despite the ever present black anchor or reporter. As a former television reporter and producer, I can personally attest to the lack of influence an anchor person has on news stories and to the difficulty of including nonwhite perspectives. Aside from the simple resistance to go beyond stock footage, or the "perp walk" offered by police stations, there remains the not too subtle pressure to conform to the status quo.

In 2001, the veteran broadcast journalist Av Westin wrote an article decrying the impact of the ratings chase on television news. One of the victims of the overt commercialization of television news, of the chase for ratings, was a decrease in whites' understanding of nonwhite America. Just as the push for hiring people of color was beginning to have some minor impact, the public-interest standard was being destroyed. Television news, an odd commercial product once expected to lose money, was now being forced to justify its existence to the gods of the market. Westin quoted a president of news at a major station group:

> I think what's happened over the last five or ten years is that certain ratings information, research information that was never shared beneath a certain level, started being shared. So you ended up getting young producers . . . worrying to a great degree about ratings. . . . And so, when you walk into certain newsrooms . . . you hear producers talking about their quarter-hour strategy, how they're going to get the meter, get the audience over to get the credit for the quarter hour.

In other words, they're not thinking about journalism: Demographics, and minute-by-minute Nielsen analyses, have influenced story selection. And that, in turn, has prompted my project's most sobering discovery:

Every week—every day stories about African-Americans, Hispanics, and Asians are kept off their air.[48]

As Westin wrote, race was often an uncomfortable subtext in news decisions: blacks and Latinos were simply bad demographic segments of the audience. The stories of these "demos" were killed by the subjective judgments of white editors using vague phrases, such as "It's not a good story for us." I remember these sorts of conversations at every news operation where I served as one of the few nonwhites and, usually, one of the only nonwhite news producers. I became a producer, rather than a reporter or an anchor, because it was clear that anchors have little impact on newscasts. And those few black anchors who fought to be more than well-paid role models did not last very long. Indeed, rather than convey the challenges nonwhites face in America, the black anchor's role is to comfort the audience. As Entman and Rojecki suggest, while black anchor persons have no real impact on the stories they tell, their "very presence suggests that if Blacks just keep quiet and work hard, the system will indeed allow them to progress." Whites are able to retain negative stereotypes about blacks while being comforted by black performers that they are really without racial animosities.[49]

While network news is not as important a source of information about blacks as local news, it is still relied upon more than cable news, newspapers, or other sources of information. And while crime is not as prevalent, the experts so relied upon by news shows are overwhelmingly white and male. A recent study of the network news programs showed that 92 percent of United States sources were white and 7 percent were black.[50]

The combination of exaggerating both black violence and white expertise leads to the quite understandable set of warped perceptions the *Washington Post* article revealed. It also leads to a lack of support for policies that might create conditions of equality.[51] The presence of token exceptions, such as Parsons and Powell, Telemundo, or the occasional minority anchor person, does not alter the place held by most people of color in and outside the communications industry.

What I've tried to describe here is a circle, perhaps a spiral, from which there seems no escape. Black Americans, as second-class citizens during most of the history of radio and television, had little opportunity to participate as licensees. The inability to participate effectively in the arena where the dominant discourse takes place amounts to an inability to correct stereotypes and the warped perception a majority of white Americans hold regarding blacks. Black economic and political advance continues to be held hostage to what Cornel West calls "the structural dynamics of corporate market institutions that affect all Americans."[52]

The Marginalization of Dissent

Much of the focus of this essay has been on mainstream media, especially local commercial television. What about alternative media, such as public broadcasting, public-access cable, and the Internet?

Alternative media in the United States are important and vital. When we see alternative media, whether independent press, community radio, low-power television, public-access cable, or personal web sites, we can only be impressed with the vast range of opinion and access to popular information possible in the United States. The black press, for example, with a long and noble history dating back to Frederick Douglass and the *North Star*, was and remains an important alternative to mainstream media. But small newspapers distributed by mail, along with community radio, personal web sites, low-power television, and so on, are not a vital part of the public debate. The reasons are not, I think, the quality of these small alternatives or their potential to push the public's buttons. The reasons alternative media remain alternative and not mainstream have to do with the enormous power of promotion held by major media forces, combined to some extent with the power of these forces to influence distribution mechanisms. This power is not very different from the power wielded by the great trusts that arose in America in the late 1800s. It is the power to thwart real competition. It is the power to determine who benefits from federal regulation and contracts. It is the power, in the communications industry, to determine who gets heard above the roar. The problem in the United States is not free expression; the problem is equal access to those places where the public debate is held.

In the United States today, people do not go to the local tavern or the town meeting to get the latest information, they do not wait for the mail to bring news from the state capital or halls of Congress. Today the public debate is held in an increasingly complex media environment, which includes the local tavern and the town hall, as well as newspapers, talk radio, Internet web sites, and more. Alternative media remain an excellent place for groups to discuss among themselves their own particular concerns. It is a place to prepare to engage in the larger, wider public debate. But it is not where the larger public debate is held. In the United States today, the public conversation takes place on television.

In a survey by *Harris Interactive* the day after the attacks on the World Trade Center and the Pentagon, television was "the primary source of information for 78 percent of Americans *with online access* in the 24 hours immediately following the attacks, followed by radio at 15 percent and the Internet at 3 percent" (Emphasis added.) Three weeks later, the group reported that the Internet was the primary source for 8 percent of the online population, while there was no statistically significant change in the figures for television (76 percent).[53] In January 2004, the Pew Research Center for the People and the Press reported that 42 percent of Americans report that they regularly learned something about the presidential campaign from local television news. Cable TV news networks followed with 38 percent, network TV news was a source for 35 percent, daily newspapers accounted for 31 percent, while talk radio stood at 17 percent, and the Internet was a source for 13 percent.[54] In the course of a year, people spend an average of 1,661 hours with television, more than with any other medium. Radio ranks second, with 983 hours.[55] Advertisers understand that if you want to participate effectively in the public arena, you must be on TV.

ADVERTISING REVENUE 2001		TELEVISION COMPONENTS 2001[56]	
Television	$54,423,000,000	Station TV	$21,479,000,000
Newspapers	$44,255,000,000	Network/	
Direct Mail	$44,725,000,000	Syndicated TV	$17,408,000,000
Radio	$17,861,000,000	Cable TV	$15,536,000,000
Yellow Pages	$13,228,000,000		
Magazines	$11,095,000,000		

Any group wishing to communicate to the public (even the Internet phenomenon MoveOn.org) understands that the media environment is increasingly complex and that while the Internet is gaining in importance, reliance upon the Internet alone to get a message out would be a fool's errand. Advertisers, politicians, and serious public-interest campaigns understand that TV is the dominant public arena now. And just as cable is viewed as another extension of TV, in the future the Internet will perhaps also be considered as just another device of TV.

The result of the dominance of television is that alternative views, particularly those that are not endeared to the controllers and funders of the timid, if not conservative, medium of commercial television, tend to be relegated to the margins of public debate. The corollary to this situation is that, no matter how irrelevant to the public interest, no matter how illogical or ugly the display, information can make its appearance on the public stage if it can pay the fare and manage not to offend the political interest of the stage managers.

Who is in the White House Matters

The failure of antitrust and public-interest regulations over the telephone, broadcast, and cable industries bear the hallmark of the probusiness laissez-faire tendencies of Republican administrations dating back to Warren Harding and Calvin Coolidge.

But the Democrats are not without blame either. For example, while the Carter administration restored a little of the funding, independence, and integrity to the public-broadcasting system nearly wrecked by Nixon and initiated the first serious set of regulations that addressed the appalling underrepresentation of "minorities" in federal broadcast licensing, Carter's FCC appointee, Charles Ferris, can take the credit for beginning the destruction of public-interest regulation by reducing federal oversight of radio. Ferris gave the radical-right agenda of Reagan's FCC Chairman Mark Fowler a running start. If the record of Democrats is mixed, the record of Republicans, at least since Theodore Roosevelt, is clearly pro-big business.

Whether it is the appointment of federal judges, FCC Commissioners, antitrust lawyers in the Department of Justice, policymakers in the National Telecommunications and Information Administration at the Commerce Department, or board members at the Corporation for Public Broadcasting, who is in the White House matters in defining the debate over communications policy. I learned this lesson through painful first-hand experience.

In 1997, I was the executive director of the Civil Rights Forum on Communications Policy. One of the initiatives we began in 1998 was a coalition effort to support certain liberal or progressive members of the President's Advisory Committee on the Public Interest Obligations of Digital Television Broadcasters (also known as the Gore Committee). The Gore Committee was created as a response to Congress's decision in the 1996 Telecommunications Act, giving existing broadcasters licenses to use the public spectrum for free. As stated earlier, the broadcasters argued that they should be given these free licenses because they operated in the public interest. The Gore Committee was set up to determine just what it meant for digital broadcasters to operate in the public interest.

This work ultimately led to the formation of a large national coalition dedicated to getting the FCC to promulgate public-interest guidelines called People for Better TV (PBTV). With over a hundred members and with chapters in a dozen communities, PBTV was driven by a steering committee that included my organization, the American Academy of Pediatrics, the Communications Workers of America, the Consumer Federation of America, the League of United Latin American Citizens, the NAACP, the National Association of the Deaf, the National Council of Churches, the National Organization for Women, and the Project on Media Ownership. I served as its national coordinator and lead attorney.[57]

On June 3, 1999, PBTV submitted to the FCC a Petition for Rule Making and for a Notice of Inquiry into the public-interest obligations of digital television broadcasters. When we submitted our petition, we knew that we had support from both the White House and the majority of votes at the FCC. We also knew that the National Association of Broadcasters had tremendous support in the Republican-controlled Congress. And so on December 15, 1999, when Congress was on its Christmas recess, the FCC announced the Notice of Inquiry, prominently referring to People for Better

TV.[58] Ralph Neas led our efforts in developing relations not only with the White House and the FCC, but also with a bipartisan coalition in Congress, including Senators John McCain, Joseph Lieberman, Robert Byrd, and Sam Brownback.

By September 2000, the FCC proposed a set of public-interest rules, quoting heavily from our submitted comments. The core of those rules focused on making the local broadcaster more accountable to the local community. The first step was "to replace the issues/programs list with a standardized form and to enhance the public's ability to access information on a station's fulfillment of public interest obligations by requiring broadcasters to make their public inspection files available on the Internet."[59] But it was clear as early as October 2000, at a speech FCC Chairman William Kennard gave in New York, that our coalition efforts were having an impact that was just beginning.

> I want to cut the Gordian knot of public interest vs. financial interests, and outline clear, tangible public interest obligations that broadcasters can commit to. I want to ensure that the American people are suitably compensated for the use of their valuable spectrum, and that underutilized portions of this precious resource are returned to them as soon as possible. And I want to see that the awesome power and remarkable ubiquity of television is put to the service of our democracy, rather than at the expense of it. We are the strongest, most vibrant democracy this world has ever seen. But we owe it to ourselves and to the nations who view us as a role model of democratic governance to realize the enormous promise of communications technologies old and new in serving and enhancing democracy.[60]

Chairman Kennard repeated his concerns and recommendations in a letter responding to the senators referred to earlier.[61] All in all, this was tremendous progress, but by the time Chairman Kennard issued his Report to Congress, it was clear that our two-year effort would be snuffed out. As the world looked on in astonishment, by a 5:4 vote the Supreme Court reversed the Supreme Court of Florida and stopped a count of votes that would have confirmed that Vice President Al Gore had won Florida and the 2000 presidential election. Within a matter of weeks, all of our supporters at the FCC were gone, and our most consistent detractor at the FCC, Michael Powell, would be named FCC chairman.

Powell had no patience for talk of the public interest. I was present at the breakfast meeting during the NAB Convention in Las Vegas in 1998, when Powell said, "The night after I was sworn in, I waited for a visit from the angel of the public interest, I waited all night, but she did not come. And, in fact, five months into this job, I still have had no divine awakening."[62]

What a difference a president makes.

Conclusion

The fact that the dominant mechanism of deliberating, acquiring, and conveying popular information in the American republic is controlled by one set of interests, corporate America, is one of the most important causes of our democracy's dysfunction. If all "factions" in America—labor, independent farmers, the church, and other interests—had an equal ability to participate in the public sphere as the Founders intended, no one interest would be able to dominate. Despite our access to satellite radio, the latest shampoo, the ability to purchase stock online, and even the right to vote, factions are not checked and balanced against each other, and the average citizen is not an equal participant in her own governance.

Time Warner, Viacom, Comcast, and the News Corporation are members of one faction—corporate America. That faction controls society through its dominance in communications. Until reformers understand that the battle over communications policy is a never-ending struggle for the equal right of self-governance in any society, we will continue to operate at the margins, and all our victories will slip through our fingers. And yet, history also teaches us that when the monopolization of communication becomes too concentrated, the silenced majority finds a way to alter the equation.

Notes

1. Saul D. Alinsky, *Rules for Radicals, A Pragmatic Primer for Realistic Radicals* (New York: Vintage, 1972).
2. Alexander Hamilton, et al., *The Federalists Papers* (Mentor: New York, 1961), pp. 301–303.
3. Richard R. John, *Spreading the News: The American Postal System from Franklin to Morse* (Cambridge: Harvard University Press, 1995), p. 61.
4. James Madison, letter to W.T. Barry, August 4, 1822.
5. John, pp. 3–5.
6. Ibid, pp. 39–40.
7. Gareth Davis, *The Destruction of the Second Bank of the United States, Rationale and Effects*, http://www.maths.tcd.ie/local/JUNK/econrev/ser/html/destruction.html.
8. Richard B. Du Boff, "Business Demand and the Development of the Telegraph in the United States, 1844–1860," *Business History Review*, 54 (Winter 1980), pp. 469–71.
9. Erik Barnouw, *A Tower in Babel, A History of Broadcasting in the United States, Volume I—To 1933* (New York: Oxford University Press, 1966), p. 254.
10. Amy Friedlander, *Natural Monopoly and Universal Service, Telephones and Telegraphs in the U.S. Communications Infrastructure, 1837–1940* (Reston, Va: Corporation for National Research Initiatives, 1995), pp. 15–16.
11. See John Milton Cooper, Jr., *Pivotal Decades, The United States, 1900–1920* (New York: Norton, 1990) for a fairly good presentation of Roosevelt's and Wilson's efforts to manage the Trusts.
12. Barnouw, *A Tower in Babel*, pp. 57–73.

13. See Erik Barnouw, *The Golden Web, A History of Broadcasting in the United States, Volume II—1933-1953* (New York: Oxford University Press, 1966).

14. Henry Milner, *Civic Literacy: How Informed Citizens Make Democracy Work* (Hanover: Tufts, 2002), pp. 95–98.

15. "Even the segments of the press and radio which were not directly controlled by anti-administration interests depended to a great extent upon the advertising revenue which came from the wealthy, and often selfish, private groups . . . As far as I was concerned, they had sold out to the special interests, and that is why I referred to them in my campaign speeches as the 'kept press and paid radio.'" Harry S. Truman, *Memoirs, Years of Trial and Hope, Vol. Two* (Doubleday: New York, 1956), pp. 175–176.

16. Eric Alterman, *What Liberal Media? The Truth About Bias and the News* (New York: Basic Books, 2003).

17. Alexander Kendrick, *Prime Time, The Life of Edward R. Murrow* (New York: Avon, 1970), pp. 421–440.

18. Frank Rich, "My Hero, Janet Jackson," *New York Times*, February 15, 2004, available at http://www.nytimes.com/2004/02/15/arts/15RICH.html.

19. For an excellent discussion of the public-interest framework see, David Bollier, "Advisory Committee on Public Interest Obligations of Digital Broadcasters," *The Public Interest Standard in Television Broadcasting*, available at: http://www.benton.org/publibrary/piac/sec2.html.

20. *Office of Communication of the United Church of Christ* v. FCC, 359 F.2d 994 (D.C. Cir. 1966); *Office of Communication of the United Church of Christ* v. FCC, 425 F.2d 543 (D.C. Cir. 1969).

21. *Red Lion Broadcasting* v. FCC, 395 U.S. 367, 390 (1969).

22. *Revision of Programming and Commercialization Policies, Ascertainment Requirements, and Program Log Requirements for Commercial Television Stations*, 98 FCC 2d 1076 (1984) [hereafter *Revision of Programming*].

23. *U.S.* v. NAB, 536 F. Supp. 149 (1982).

24. See *Revision of Programming*, 98 FCC 2d at 1080 (1984).

25. Philip Napoli, "Market Conditions and Public Affairs Programming: Implications for Digital Television Policy," March 2000, available at: http://www.benton.org/publibrary/television/lpa.pdf.

26. "Channeling Influence, The Broadcast Lobby and the 70-Billion Dollar Free Ride," Common Cause, http://216.147.192.101/publications/040297_rpt3.htm.

27. "Changes, Challenges, and Charting New Courses: Minority Commercial Broadcast Ownership in the United States," MTDP Minority Ownership Statistics Reports, 2000 Report, available at: http://search.ntia.doc.gov/pdf/mtdpreportv2.pdf.

28. "Mixed Results," 2002 Women & Minorities Survey, RTNDA/F Research, available at: http://www.rtndf.org/research/womin.shtml.

29. See TV 9, Inc. v. FCC, 161 U.S. App. D.C. 349, 357, n.28, 495 F. 2d 929, 937, n.28 (1973), cert. denied, 419 U.S. 986 (1974); see also 1 U.S. Commission on Civil Rights, Federal Civil Rights Enforcement Effort 1974, (November 1974), p. 49.

30. See *Newhouse Broadcasting Corp.*, 37 Rad. Reg. 2d 141, decided April 21, 1976.

31. *Statement of Policy on Minority Ownership of Broadcasting Facilities*, 68 FCC 2d 979 (1978).

32. FCC Minority Ownership Task Force, *Report on Minority Ownership in Broadcasting* (1978).

33. *Metro Broadcasting, Inc.* v. FCC, 497 U.S. 547 (1990).

34. Ibid.

35. See "FCC Freezes Comparative Proceedings in Response to Court Integration Ruling," *Communications Daily*, February 28, 1994, p. 3.

36. *Adarand Constructors, Inc.* v. *Pena*, 515 U.S. 200 (1995).

37. *Lutheran Church-Missouri Synod* v. *FCC*, 141 F. 3d 344 (1998).

38. Robert Entman and Andrew Rojecki, *The Black Image in the White Mind* (Chicago: University of Chicago Press, 2000), pp. 113–114.

39. See Mark Robichaux, "A Cable Empire That Was Built On a Tax Break," *The Wall Street Journal*, January 12, 1995, p. B1.

40. To amend the Internal Revenue Code of 1986 to permanently extend the deduction for the health-insurance costs of self-employed individuals, to repeal the provision permitting nonrecognition of gain on sales and exchanges effectuating policies of the Federal Communications Commission, and for other purposes. Public Law No: 104–7.

41. Mark Lloyd and Kofi Ofori, "The Value of the Tax Certificate," *Federal Communications Law Journal* (May 1999).

42. See "Minority Commercial Broadcast Ownership in the United States," Report of the Minority Telecommunications Development Program, National Telecommunications and Information Administration, U.S. Department of Commerce, available at: http://www.ntia.doc.gov/reports/97minority/.

43. *Report of the National Advisory Commission on Civil Disorders* ("Kerner Commission Report") (Washington, D.C.: U.S. Government Printing Office, 1968).

44. Richard Morin, "Misperceptions Cloud Whites' View of Blacks," *Washington Post*, July 11, 2001, p. 1.

45. See E. J. Bienenstock, P. Bonacich, and M. Oliver, "The Effect of Network Density and Homogeneity on Attitude Polarization," *Social Networks*, 12 (1990), pp. 153–172.

46. F. D. Gilliam, Jr., S. Iyengar, A. Simon, and O. Wright, "Crime in Black and White: The Scary World of Local News," *Harvard International Journal of Press/Politics*, 1 (1996), pp. 6–23; see also F. D. Gilliam, Jr., and S. Iyengar, "Prime Suspects: The Influence of Local Television News on the Viewing Public," *American Journal of Political Science*, 44, no. 3 (July 2000), pp. 560–573; and Frank Gilliam, "Moral Literacy: Virtue and the Renewal of Civil Society," National Funding Collaborative on Violence Prevention, available at: http://www.peacebeyondviolence.org/res_mono_gil_hero.html.

47. Entman and Rojecki, p. 81.

48. Av Westin, "The Color of Ratings," *Brill's Content*, April 2001, pp. 83–84.

49. Entman and Rojecki, p. 87.

50. *Who's On the News? Study Shows Network News Sources Skew White, Male & Elite*, Fairness and Accuracy in Reporting, June 2002, http://www.fair.org/press-releases/power-sources-release.html.

51. See Gilliam and Iyengar, *Prime Suspects*.

52. Cornell West, *Race Matters* (New York: Vintage Books, 1993), p. 27.

53. See "Survey Shows Internet's Growth as Primary Source of News and Information in Weeks Following September 11 Attacks," *Harris Interactive*, October 5, 2001, http://www.harrisinteractive.com/news/allnewsbydate.asp?NewsID=%20371.

54. See "Cable and Internet Loom Large in Fragmented Political News Universe," Pew Research Center for the People and the Press, January 11, 2004, http://people-press.org/reports/.

55. TV Basics, Consumer Media Use, available at: http://www.tvb.org/rcentral/mediatrendstrack/tvbasics/17_Consumer_Media_Usage.asp.

56. TV Basic, TV-Top Ad Medium, available at: http://www.tvb.org/rcentral/mediatrendstrack/tvbasics/18_TV_Top_Ad_Medium_Component.asp.
57. See Mike Snider, "FCC Urged to Make Broadcasters do Better," USA Today, May 3, 1999.
58. "FCC Begins Proceeding to Seek Comment on Public Interest Obligations of Television Broadcasters as they Transition to Digital Transmission Technology," December 15, 1999, http://ftp.fcc.gov/Bureaus/Mass_Media/News_Releases/1999/nrmm9030.html.
59. Notice of Proposed Rule Making, *In the Matter of Standardized and Enhanced Disclosure Requirements for Television Broadcast Licensee Public Interest Obligations*, MM Docket No. 00–168, adopted September 14, 2000, Federal Communications Commission, http://www.fcc.gov/Bureaus/Mass_Media/Notices/2000/fcc00345.txt.
60. Remarks By FCC Chairman William E. Kennard, "What Does $70 Billion Buy You Anyway? Rethinking Public Interest Requirements at the Dawn of the Digital Age," October 5, 2000, http://ftp.fcc.gov/Speeches/Kennard/2000/spwek023.html.
61. "Report to Congress on the Public Interest Obligations of Television Broadcasters as They Transition to Digital Television," January 18, 2001, http://ftp.fcc.gov/Speeches/Kennard/Statements/2001/stwek106.doc.
62. Gal Beckerman, "Tripping Up Big Media," (November/December 2003), http://www.cjr.org/issues/2003/6/media-beckerman.asp.

MEDIA AND MARGINALIZATION

MALKIA A. CYRIL

Media justice is more than an oppositional framework or simple effort at political contrast. It is a multi-layered, emerging analysis that draws on civil and human rights, globalization struggles, corporate accountability and cultural studies. It starts with a structural analysis but it doesn't stop there because media doesn't stop there. Who owns it, what's on it, and how it makes us feel are all spheres we must address simultaneously. Where we go from here has to take into account where we've been and who has been advantaged and who has been hurt. And it is this analysis that separates media justice from the fight for media democracy, because without a vision that seeks to repair the impact of the past and the privilege, we'll have the same old oppression with better, high-speed resolution.
—Makani Themba-Nixon, media critic and author

When my mother was my age, the civil-rights movements of people of color, the poor, lesbian/gay/bisexual/transgender (LGBTQ) communities, and the women's movement had all achieved outstanding victories. The dislocated and excluded bodies of hundreds of thousands of people, flanked by national guardsmen, had faced-off against water hoses and lynch mobs as tangible testament to the theory of nonviolent noncooperation. These same bodies were lynched in the 1950s, jailed and shot in the 1960s. When these victories could not stop the war against Vietnam and the marginalization here at home, this movement took a more oppositional stance and demanded not just policy change, but also power.

For my mother's generation, racial justice was tied inextricably to internationalism and the equitable distribution of capital, and it was best fought for with the analytical tool of a broad black nationalism that exposed the deep divide between the first-class citizenship of middle- and upper-class whites and the bottom-rung citizenship of everyone else.

As a queer, black, butch woman, I would not have known where to stand. Racial justice for me at that time would have been what it is now—the restructuring of a complex web of power defined by a polarized economic world order that remains controlled by corporate interests and political gain. My childhood in Brooklyn was characterized by the age of crack, debilitating economic policies, declining social services, and booming war and prison budgets. My teenage years were tattooed with anti-youth policies—like prosecuting minors as adults, curfews, "zero tolerance" legislation, abstinence-only sex education, and a battery of measures to contain "out-of-control" youth impelled by the War on Drugs. The dangerous stereotypes behind these policies were reflected back to me through television, radio, and newspapers in the ransomed language of personal responsibility, individual choice, superpredators, and the undeserving poor. Then, as now, even as racism colors the rhetoric of war and deepens the cavern separating rich and poor, the progressive movement could not find the language to prove through the media or to itself that racism even exists.

But some of us know better.

Coding Racism

Two-thirds of the people claim that they make decisions about important policy issues based primarily on information from news and entertainment media. Dominated by the right, influenced by corporate interests, and deregulated by the FCC, mainstream media excludes and misrepresents young people and people of color. As a result, the conditions in which we live, the policies that create those conditions, and the struggles to change them are erased from media content—leading to an uninformed public that supports punitive social policies instead of opportunity, peace, and justice for vulnerable communities. In the media, the term "youth" has become a coded mechanism to talk about race, and youth policy has become a way to legislate racism while using colorblind language.

Like immigrants and prisoners, youth sees its citizenship rights abridged—young people cannot vote or participate fully in democratic processes. Yet their role as policy *scapegoats* for social problems, *scarecrows* to generate fear-driven public discourse, and *sex symbols* to sell corporate agendas, have all gone unabated. Founded in 2001 to address these biases in media representation, the Youth Media Council (YMC) is building a new vision as a leading member of the growing Media Justice movement. Using a strong race, class, and gender-conscious lens, the Youth Media Council strengthens mechanisms for communities to understand and act on issues of ownership, control, access, content, and structure of media.

Media Justice is a change model for media content, ownership, and policy. It is a vision and strategy that prioritizes self-determination and structural change while developing the leadership of marginalized constituencies of media change-makers *both* as producers and consumers. It is founded on the principle of communication as a human right, not as a civil liberty. Over the past ten years, a new generation of young visionaries has emerged in the San Francisco Bay Area to lead community organizations tackling police misconduct and brutality, criminalization and incarceration, and the economic and educational policies that put youth in a qualitatively worse situation than that of a generation earlier. As part of their growing sophistication, these organizations have learned that strategic media communication is crucial to their campaigns. Through the context of Media Justice, these organizations are shifting the dynamics of media access and accountability, advancing racial justice and representation in media content, and working toward socially responsible media policy. Their goal is to protect the human rights of marginalized communities and, ultimately, to change the terms of debate by reframing public dialogue for progressive social change.

"Build a People's Station" Campaign

As the nation was reeling from the attacks of September 11 and preparing for the wars against Afghanistan and Iraq, local Clear Channel radio stations were also pitching their own battles. The media conglomerate was marshaling its more than twelve hundred stations nationwide to push its jingoistic brand of patriotism. Radio stations made headlines with sensational actions like bulldozing CDs by musicians opposing the war, the most famous of whom were the Dixie Chicks.

One of the ten Clear Channel stations in the San Francisco Bay Area had a somewhat different political tradition. With its tagline, "The People's Station," 106.1 KMEL was a hip-hop and R&B radio station with more than 600,000 listeners and home of the popular grassroots program *Street Knowledge* and its equally popular host Davey D. Prior to its acquisition by Clear Channel in 1999, the station boasted the most extensive community-affairs lineup of any privately owned radio outlet in the market area. After the Clear Channel takeover, community-affairs programming and community access were dramatically reduced. When Davey D was fired in October 2001 after airing antiwar sentiments by local Congresswoman Barbara Lee and hip-hop artist Boots Riley of The Coup, this action was the last straw for local listeners.

Davey D's show was known to the progressive community as one of the few points of access for community members, activists, and youth. Though Clear Channel officials denied that the basis of his firing was his antiwar position, many youth and progressive activists saw clearly that given the show's top ratings and strong popular base, there was no other explanation. Further, they saw Davey's dismissal and the shrinking community-affairs programming as part of a trend to narrow access for progressive young voices on a show whose primary audience was young, of color, and working class.

Youth organizing groups, local artist collectives, human-rights and media-reform organizations together called on the Youth Media Council, a unique movement center for constituency-led media justice led by young working class activists and people of color, to monitor the content at 106.1 KMEL.

Their suspicions about bias and lack of accountability at KMEL were confirmed. The month of YMC monitoring revealed that KMEL routinely excludes the voices of youth organizers and local artists, sensationalizes policy debates affecting youth and people of color, focuses disproportionately on crime, violence, and punishment, and has no clear avenue for listeners to hold the station accountable for this bias.

These organizations began to mobilize, claiming that as Clear Channel supported prowar rallies, donated hundreds of billboards carrying pictures of the American flag, pulled radio ads critical of GOP candidates, and hosted right-wing conservative websites, the *People's Station* had begun to act more like the *Right-Wing Patriot's Station*. Listeners and the organized progressive movement in the Bay Area decided that enough was enough, and together they formed the Community Coalition for Media Accountability (CCMA).

Unlike our allies in the media-reform sector, we didn't have money, attorneys, lobbyists, policymakers, or insiders to pressure Clear Channel's KMEL. As a result, we could not use the primary strategies and change methods of the media-reform movement. Instead, we had the support of a community angry at a corporate media outlet and a coalition of constituency-based organizations representing the primary listenership of the station. This was a coalition that wanted to do more than change media content, create access, or increase accountability. We wanted an outlet that would contribute to the process of building racial, economic, and gender justice. We needed more than reform. We needed systemic, institutional change.

The Youth Media Council understood, for example, that a purely legal strategy without mass participation would not work, nor would demands focused primarily on increasing choice and "diversity" without shifting decision-making power. In a society stratified by race, class, and gender, marginalized communities do not benefit from simply increasing the diversity of perspectives and voices if there is no simultaneous radical shift in the power dynamics of information and communication. With plentiful stereotypes of young people of color in media content, and having virtually no influence over those images, we found that we could not fight for increased access without working to change the power dynamic. In strategy sessions and coalition meetings, we clamored for a movement that spoke beyond increasing rights and choices for some, instead offering a vision of fundamental change and victory for all.

What We Did

We decided to organize against Clear Channel by focusing on 106.1 KMEL as a way to make the commodification of culture and information relevant to marginalized stakeholders. We began by monitoring KMEL, and produced an analysis of its content.[1] We brought social-justice, youth, and arts organizations together in the regional Community Coalition for Media Accountability. Collectively, these leaders planned and implemented a series of delegation visits and actions that resulted in a two-hour live broadcast on KMEL, hosted by youth organizations discussing violence prevention and the impact of war at home. We used art and culture in our outreach to pressure targets and consolidate a base of support. We worked to educate this base by organizing parties and writing songs and poems about media justice and policy, developing popular education workshops for students. We used these low-level cultural actions to highlight the lack of accountability at KMEL, exposing the station's right-wing agenda through coverage in opinion-leading and alternative media outlets, such as the *San Francisco Bay Guardian*, *Asian Week*, and the *San Francisco Chronicle*.

After emerging from a broad-based gathering at the Highlander Retreat Center, a group of progressives dedicated to making media reform a more expansive movement emerged, incorporating the experiences and leadership of multiple communities into a unified force. This group, comprised of the Youth Media Council, Media Alliance, Praxis Project, Third World Majority, and others, founded a national Media Justice Network to connect individuals and organizations interested in pushing this progressive framework. It would build a movement of reform activism, grassroots organizing, influential lobbying, using the tools of policy and legal expertise. Through this Network and the ongoing work of the Community Coalition for Media Accountability, the YMC is engaging marginalized youth as a new constituency fighting for media justice with a new vision.

Grounding Our Work: What Media Justice Is, What it Means, What it Does

Like the power movements that grew out of the civil-rights movement, Media Justice challenges and expands the basic positions of media reform. It prioritizes building collective power over media production and simply increasing the individual choices of media consumers. It posits organizing and direct action as key change strategies for marginalized communities instead of relying solely on legislative advocacy and lobbying. It focuses on transforming media content, not just increasing media access. This power-building strategy is based fundamentally on the subordinated experiences of marginalized people, and for that reason requires organizations dedicated to building their media skills, increasing the media capacity of their movements, and developing and centralizing their leadership. In this model, we build new constituencies by shifting the lens of media-making, looking at marginalized communities both as media consumers and producers.

A Media Justice Analysis

Media Justice suggests that:

- The media was racist before consolidation became a trend, though race is not the sole axis of power on which communication is balanced. All forms of marginalization contribute to a communications industry that is owned, produced, managed, and profited from, by and for a select few. The terms "public interest" and "public debate" indicate a framework of inclusion. *Media Justice exposes the myth of media inclusion and highlights the systematic exclusion of a majority audience.*

- All people of color and other marginalized groups experience the media as those who both function inside and outside of democracy, in multiple tiers of citizenship. This is reflected by media content, in which marginalized people appear frequently as objectified buffoons, criminals, apathetic slackers, or out-of-control kids. *Content, not access alone, must be central to our fight for Media Justice.*

- The dynamics of media ownership reflect the dynamics of capital in a racially stratified and patriarchal, capitalist society. As we fight for fair stories, media accountability, and wider debate, we must also demand that media ownership reflect a transformative standard of racial and economic justice, acknowledging that current media reform strategies increase influence for some, but not justice for all. *We must increase public control over the infrastructure of media to build power.*

Tactics and Strategy

The tactics and strategy of Media Justice express the duality of our experience with the media.

- Transforming Media Production: As we shift the dynamics of access, we must transform how we understand the dynamics of production. In media, there are multiple points of production, as people develop art, culture, news, and information. The media package life events and political moments into a product they sell back to us, and we are seen as consumers of that product. What if we saw ourselves as media producers? Through Media Justice, we seek to understand the dynamics of media production in innovative ways, identifying new constituencies that can be mobilized for action. Where are ideas, culture, and information produced, if not in the lives, minds and experiences of people? We must reclaim control of the media, not simply as consumers, but as those who are denied ownership and influence over the information created by our lives.

- Speaking for Ourselves in Our Own Voices: When Afrikaans was instituted as the national language of South Africa, black children refused to speak it, using languages of resistance instead. Media Justice pressure tactics use culture to help form a relevant language of resistance, articulating the impact of this media system on our lives. When Act Up staged die-ins and took over news rooms, when hip-hop artists Jay-Z and Mary J. Blige joined thousands of New York students fighting to fund schools instead of jails, when Freedom Uprising, a group of antiwar activists of color, stepped into San Francisco streets recalling the speeches of Malcolm X, Martin Luther King, and Angela Davis—these were examples of home-grown culture being used as a medium of resistance.

- Facing Off for Justice: Direct action is another principle held by the YMC. Confronting media outlets and policymakers is one way communities can build power and influence. We designed a system of mobilization, whereby effective responses can be rapidly instituted against pressing media concerns. Media changes quickly, and communities must be able to hold outlets accountable for bias and policymakers responsible to those they are sworn to protect at the pace of that change.

- Organizing: Activism works, but not without organization. Organizing roots activism in local communities for concrete change that structurally alters the dynamics of power. We need organized battles for media justice with the capacity to link the issues of racial justice, capitalism, and gender to the fight for ideological power, communications infrastructure, and media policy. This is why the Youth Media Council works to build rapid response networks of membership-based community institutions, conducts campaigns on media policy engaging marginalized people, and builds the media activist skills of new leaders.

Conclusion

Over the past decade, we have discovered that there must be goals, strategies, tactics and organizations that go beyond reforming a media that has, since its inception, helped perpetuate power dynamics that keep communities of color and other marginalized folks outside the public debate that shapes and defines our lives. Since the days of American slavery, this public debate has been a central institution of power and control. There must, therefore, be structural analysis, strategy, change model, and vision that fundamentally alter these relations of power while making concrete changes in the relationship of communities to media outlets.

We need a communications system that allows us the chance to fight for our livelihoods. Marginalized constituencies need the tools, resources, tactics, and strategies to make media the watchdog and portal for civic engagement that it should be. We must reinvent communications so that we may reinvent justice.

Note

1. Youth Media Council, "*Is KMEL The People's Station?*," Fall 2002, available at http://www.youthmediacouncil.org/pdfs/BuildAPeoplesStation.pdf.

RESISTING THE
CONQUISTA OF WORDS

BÁRBARA RENAUD GONZÁLEZ
(AND LA BUENA GENTE OF THE ESPERANZA CENTER)

"I'm a teacher here at a high school on the south side of town, which is predominantly Hispanic kids, and it hurts me every day to hear these kids saying they don't care about school, they don't care about getting their degree and they don't—they don't know what's out there for them. I hear young girls saying that their boyfriends are going to support them. They don't care about school. In my opinion, these kids don't have anything to relate to on TV. They love TV, they love radio, but they're not seeing programs that they can relate to. They're not seeing people of their ethnicity that are successful lawyers, doctors, dentists, CEO's, and that's what we need, and that's why local programming—you guys really need to reflect our community." [Applause]
—Manuel Peña, testifying before the FCC Regional Hearings
in San Antonio, Texas on January 28, 2004

"They want our beauty and they want our food and they want our music. But they don't want us."
—Marina Renaud, my mother,
who always told me not to believe what I saw on television

The Media Don't Respect Us

Some years ago, Henry Cisneros, then CEO of the nation's largest Spanish-speaking network, complained about his job at Univision. "Those advertisers!" he criticized, "They sell us hamburgers, cars, beer." But raising money for public-service campaigns encouraging people to vote proved to be much more difficult.

Respeto—that's the word he used that night, and I have learned the hard way that his sentiment was right. The media, English or Spanish-language, no longer serve us. The democracy enshrined in our Constitution gives brown and poor people what the rest of the world envies: the freedom of speech; yet we have been betrayed by media that are supposed to protect our right to speak out.

The combination of democracy and open media helped to give this country the right of women to vote; the right of people of color to be treated equally (which affected people like my father, a World War II veteran, who was prohibited from eating at certain restaurants in the 1960s); the Voting Rights Act, which allowed people of color to get representation in our cities and in Congress; the right to get a loan and buy a home in any neighborhood; minimum-wage laws; employment compensation in case of injury or illness; disability laws; sexual harassment protection for women at work. Many more rights have been won that we take for granted. But the first right is the one that has made all the others possible: the guaranteed right to free speech.

Without the ability to speak freely, the people in a democracy lack the ability to debate issues of utmost importance. Without free speech, we cannot educate each other about who we are, what we've seen and what we want. And without free speech in the media, we risk losing the democracy that has taken us this far—as difficult, hard-won, and messy as it is.

Our government has entrusted radio and television stations with our very democracy. Just like the Grand Canyon, the Sangria Mountains, and the Rio Grande, the airwaves belong to us all. And we, the people, entrusted with broadcast licenses those who own or want to buy radio and television stations with this precious commodity.

But they have betrayed us. Let me tell you what television, radio, and newspapers should be, and what can be done to take back the media. If we don't reclaim what is rightfully ours, future generations will grow up without knowing the stories of their communities—unless they deal with an accident, riot, scandal, or tragedy. They will hear their stories told by people who respond only to advertisers, not public audiences. And when the media tell us that we should go to war, we won't ask why. Is that what we want?

From the simplistic voices of newspapers to the seductiveness of television, we are being trained to desire the lifestyles, appearances, and riches of beauty while glamorizing the ugliest of stereotypes, in the name of advertisers who have lost all semblance of responsibility to the people who own the airwaves. We consume ideas from people who don't know us, people who want only that we will make them even richer still.

Respeto.

How We Are Silenced By The Media

According to columnist Juan Gonzalez, past president of the National Association of Hispanic Journalists, there are 1,400 newspapers, 1,700 television stations,
12,000 radio stations, 17,000 magazines, and hundreds of channels to choose
from, thanks to cable. And yet, he notes, there's almost nothing worth watching.
How did this happen? Simply put, media deregulation led to media consolidation,
driven by the lure of power and money. According to the National Telecommunications and Information Administration, as of 2001 (the last time the statistic
was measured) people of color owned only 1.9 percent of the 1,288 full-power
commercial television stations in the United States, while we account for a third
of the country's population.

As a result of the consolidation of media markets, many TV and radio stations and
newspapers fell into the hands of just a few companies, preventing us from knowing the truth about what's going on in our communities and around the world. For
example, how does coverage of the United States war and occupation of Iraq change
when one of our major news networks—NBC—is owned by General Electric? Keep
in mind that General Electric is one of the world's top producers of weapons.

Univision, though Spanish-speaking, is not any better than the English-language
stations, with its fixation on telenovelas and copycat programming. Its chairman is
Jerry Perenchio, an Italian American who was formerly a Hollywood talent agent.
Thanks to deregulation, Perenchio, who doesn't speak Spanish, purchased five
Univision stations in 1992 and began assembling his media empire. A billionaire
and staunch Republican, Perenchio gave $400,000 to California Governor Pete
Wilson while he was campaigning for the passage of Proposition 187, which sought
to deny public schooling to the children of illegal immigrants.

Univision now controls 70 percent of the Spanish-language market, including
television, cable, music, and radio. For singers and musicians already signed to Univision, this situation can be a blessing, but it is disastrous for independent labels and
artists. Cultural commentators point out that the homogenized music promoted by
radio stations has marginalized the most original musicians and their passionate
audiences. The lone place where upcoming talent can be heard in San Antonio is on
Radio Jalapeño, KEDA-1540 AM, the only independent radio station left in town.

In this city, known as the mecca of *tejano* culture, and, some say, the northern-
most city in Mexico, Univision owns five radio stations and four television stations,
including both the first Spanish-language radio station established in the country
(KCOR 1350 AM, est. 1946) and the first Spanish-language television station (KCOR-41
TV, est. 1955). In a city with a brown majority—80 percent of the children born in
Bexar County are *color café*—all the top radio stations are corporate-owned by
Clear Channel, Univision, and Cox. So it should be no surprise that only 4 percent

of the 12,000 radio stations in the United States are owned by minorities. While independent minority voices bring diverse perspectives to the debates of the day, "radio news has almost disappeared," says NAHJ's Gonzalez. "There are virtually no Latinos doing news on radio today."

There is a conservative slice of this country that is afraid of the brown faces of immigrants. The corporate media, responding to advertisers and not to readers, listeners, or viewers, rarely tell the story of the immigrants' suffering and aspirations. The effect is to maintain the segregation between rich and poor, denying the children of immigrants a decent education and the opportunity to actively participate in the democratic processes and ideals on which this country was founded.

San Antonio! The Media Attacked Us And We Fought Back—And Won

> "By far, the most direct impact on the everyday lives of ordinary citizens is the news information and right of our voices and viewpoints to be heard via our airwaves. And as such, we must ensure that the broadcast media is held to the highest standards via improved renewal and licensing evaluations. The public trust that has been given to them for safeguarding is not an entitlement program. It must be earned every day by viable engagement of ideas, management and governance within their corporate structures, or that trust will be lost in the very near future."
> —Oscar Moran, LULAC, panelist testifying before the
> FCC Regional Hearings in San Antonio, January 28, 2004

The Esperanza Center, a vanguard nonprofit organization that employs art and culture to promote political and social justice, went to federal court to defend itself against the media in the summer of 1997. Adam McManus ("voted the #1 talk show host in San Antonio!") attacked the Esperanza center for its lesbian and gay film festival, the first of its kind in the city. His station, KSLR AM 630, is a conservative radio station owned by Salem Communication Corporation, which operates ninety-two radio stations nationwide, all targeted at Christians. McManus found a receptive audience in San Antonio, given its five military bases and its conservative Catholic and Baptist institutions. Thanks to media deregulation, Salem Communications now operates 1,500 syndicated programs in twenty-three of the nation's twenty-five radio markets.

After McManus asked his audience to protest at City Hall, Leo Garza, a conservative cartoonist at the *San Antonio Express-News* (owned by the Hearst Corporation), also weighed in on the matter. From August 22–26, 2000, Garza (aka Nacho Guarache) derided Esperanza Center's popular grassroots campaign in his cartoon strip.

Nacho Guarache by Leo Garza

As a result of the concerted drumbeat of homophobia launched against the Esperanza, the City Council defunded the Center. It became the only organization to lose their entire city funding in an ensuing budget rollback.

The Esperanza decided to sue the city on First Amendment grounds. The City Council defunded the Esperanza to "appease public animus," claimed Amy Kastely, lead counsel for the Center, citing the media for irresponsible and prejudiced viewpoints that distort public debate. In a stunning upset for the local media's negative coverage, the federal judge Orlando Garcia agreed with the Esperanza.

The Esperanza learned that the media would not be held accountable unless they were pressured, and we decided to begin to learn about their organization, monitoring coverage and other stories affecting our community. As we began to understand the local media and their ignorance of our issues, we realized how our grassroots campaign—our bumper stickers, yard signs, street banners, with slogans that spoke to the people (*Respeto es Basico*, *Arte Es Vida*, and finally, *Todos Somos Esperanza*)—was having an influence on the journalists and editors who didn't know us. Our signs were appearing all over the city, and our political organizing forced the editors and reporters to confront us.

After we won the lawsuit, Larry Walker, the publisher of the *San Antonio Express-News*, visited the Esperanza himself to see what his reporters were writing about.

We Made the Media Listen to Us

In early September 2003, Araceli Herrera walked into our offices. She was a forty-three-year-old *mexicana* and ad-hoc leader of a group of housekeepers who had lost their bus route to work after it was canceled by the local service, VIA Metropolitan Transit. Araceli and dozens of other housekeepers had to slog through heat and brush, walking in the hottest part of the Texas summer, just to reach their jobs in the richest and northernmost neighborhoods of the city. Their new route, requiring more transfers and inaccessible bus stops, took two hours longer than the previous one.

Araceli had heard that the Esperanza could help. She and the other women had been attending the VIA board meetings, but to no avail. We knew that the only way to force the VIA to pay attention was to publicize its harmful actions, and the housekeepers' political activism gave us the impetus to try.

We first had to find out who was in charge of VIA coverage at the *San Antonio Express-News*. In this case, contacting the English-language media was the most effective method of broadcasting the story. The English-speaking media had the audience that votes on VIA taxes and reached those most likely to contact VIA board members. It's important to know whom you want to reach, so that you can communicate with the appropriate media; when we called the editor in charge of VIA coverage at the *San Antonio Express-News*, we were able to "sell" the story to the paper by noting that the newspaper is supposed to tell the "whole" story.

In due course, the editor sent a reporter to the Esperanza offices to meet the affected women. By that time, we had already contacted alternative media outlets as well, since it is important to tell the story through as many channels as possible, ensuring that it will be written up in a more complete fashion and publicized to the widest possible audience.

Following the meeting, the *San Antonio Express-News* editor agreed that the VIA story was being told "top-down" instead of as a "people's story," and he promised to meet with us again about other transportation issues. We scored a major victory when the paper published Araceli's story in an article headlined, "The Long Way Home." After the stories ran in multiple papers, television stations began to call Araceli and extensively covered the story. Ultimately, Araceli and the other women got their route back.

Orale! The FCC Regional Hearings Come To San Antonio: Making Washington Listen!

Thanks to the millions of emails and letters protesting the Federal Communications Commission's 2003 approval of media deregulation, then-FCC Chairman, Michael

Powell, attempted to save face by holding a series of unprecedented "town hall" meetings across the country. These FCC Localism Hearings were ostensibly to hear citizens' views on local ownership, relevancy, and diversity of media, to determine whether they were meeting standards of local accountability.

San Antonio was a unique city to host a Localism Hearing, and as a Latino-majority city and home of the Clear Channel conglomerate, we were in the perfect setting to make our voices heard.

We knew that all the local media organizations would be out in force to cover the event, and accordingly we organized as quickly as possible, contacting communications professors, student leaders, activists, and even panelists who were invited to speak at the hearing who might be of help. We were lucky to receive assistance from the Prometheus Radio Project, which connected us with other national media watchdog groups. They helped guide us through the politics of the FCC, providing the information we needed to understand the context of media ownership in San Antonio. We had to explain to our community about the role of FCC in media history and advocacy to underscore the importance of the hearing.

After our initial organizing sessions, we made press releases (like the one below) and sent out email blasts to a growing Listserv, utilizing technology to the best of our ability. We welcomed the participation of student media majors and filmmakers who wanted to help, while interviewing on every radio program that we could find and distributing public-service announcements widely. We knew that it was incredibly important to testify before the FCC, but we also realized that the hearing had to be defined on our terms.

TAKE BACK THE AIRWAVES! THEY BELONG TO US!!!

Teach-In

Thursday, Jan. 22, 2004
7–9 pm
Fuerza Unida
710 New Laredo
Hwy.
927.2294

San Antonio's Top 10 Radio Stations
Everyone Else 30%
CLEAR CHANNEL 70%

Get Your
Learn On/Baile

Saturday, Jan. 24, 2004
3–5 pm
Café Revolución
527 El Paso
223.9293

DID YOU KNOW?

THAT THE MOST POWERFUL RADIO AND TELEVISION STATIONS IN TOWN ARE OWNED BY CLEARCHANNEL AND UNIVISION?

THAT THIS MEANS THAT THE MOST IMPORTANT LOCAL STORIES ARE IGNORED OR INTERPRETED BY CORPORATIONS THAT ONLY WANT TO MAKE PROFIT?

THAT YOU HAVE A CHANCE TO PROTEST AND TESTIFY AGAINST THE MEDIA MONOPOLIES AND DEMAND LOCALISM WHEN THE FCC HAS A HEARING HERE ON WEDNESDAY, JANUARY 28TH, 2004, 5:30 –9:30 PM AT CITY COUNCIL CHAMBERS!!!!

For more information, please call the Esperanza at 228.0201
This non-commercial message brought to you by
Centro Esperanza, Food Not Bombs, Fuerza Unida, Madmedia,
peaceCENTER, y otros más

What We Deserve

The media must become a place where all voices are heard, and national news needs to connect more appropriately with local communities. What happens during a typical newscast reporting on a NAFTA meeting in Mexico, for example? Sound bites from various officials and a few seconds devoted to the inevitable protest? What the media never does is relate international problems of trade to the local community, to the *barrio* level.

If Levi-Strauss is taking its operations to Mexico or Central America, then how does that move affect laid-off workers in San Antonio? This is a story that affects many people, but clocking the typical newscast, we are lucky to have ninety seconds devoted to news that truly affects our lives. There is so much we need and deserve from our media, and getting quality programming on the air is essential for promoting healthy and relevant discourse.

How Can We Get These Programs on the Air?

- Organize!
- Bring together other community leaders who share your concerns, and set up a meeting with a newspaper editor, television, or radio station manager.
- Prepare a petition drive regarding your concerns. A journalist once told me that a hundred newspaper subscription cancellations for six months was all it would take to get the newspapers' attention.
- If the media don't respond: Write to the Federal Communications Commission (www.fcc.gov) and copy the station managers and ask them to place your letter in the FCC file. Their broadcast licenses aren't permanent, and they can be revoked with enough public pressure.
- Get help from the national organizations dedicated to media reform. Such lists can be found at www.freepress.net.
- Use the web to organize—with student groups, with women's organizations, with union members, and others. Enlist a savvy student leader to set up a web page with links.
- Boycott print, radio, or television outlets that ignore your requests without good reason.
- Hold a press conference and have community leaders and activists present.
- Find out how to get your own low-power radio station. The Prometheus Radio Project is a useful resource (www.prometheusradio.org).
- Finally, tell your community that we all have a moral responsibility to take control of our own stories, by investing in and supporting progressive media.

PART 3

MEDIA REGULATION
IN THE PUBLIC INTEREST

WHERE IS THE PUBLIC INTEREST IN MEDIA CONSOLIDATION?

The Honorable Michael J. Copps

On June 2, 2003, the Federal Communications Commission, of which I am a member, cast its most important vote during my tenure. On that day, the FCC weakened its protections against excessive media concentration and empowered America's media conglomerates with unprecedented levels of influence over the media on which our society and our democracy so heavily depend.

On that day, the FCC found itself at a crossroads. Down one road was a reaffirmation of America's commitment to local control of our media, diversity in news and editorial viewpoint, and the importance of competition. This path beckoned us to update our rules to account for technological and marketplace changes, but without abandoning core values going to the heart of what the media mean in our country. On this path we also would reaffirm that FCC broadcast licensees have been given very special privileges and that they have very special responsibilities to serve the public interest.

Down the other road was more media control by ever fewer corporate giants. This path would surrender to a handful of corporations awesome powers over our news, information, and entertainment. Here we would treat the media like any other big business, trusting that in the unforgiving environment of the market, the public interest would somehow magically trump the urge to build power and profit for a privileged few. On this path we would endanger time-honored safeguards and time-proven values that have strengthened the country as well as the media.

At issue in that huge vote on June 2 was how America's TV, radio, newspapers, and even the Internet are going to look for many years to come. Who is going to control the media? How many—or, rather, how few—companies? For what purposes? Will we still be able to get real local news and clashing points of view so we can make up our own minds on the issues of the day? And how do we assure quality TV and music instead of being so often fed a diet of precanned and nationalized fare aimed primarily at selling products? I think I exaggerate not at all in saying that the issue is whether a few large conglomerates will be ceded content control over our music, entertainment, and information; gatekeeper control over the civil dialogue of our country; and veto power over the majority of what we and our families watch, hear, and read. So the stakes are high.

With the vote, the majority of the Commission, over my dissent, took the wrong road. The decision would have allowed the big media companies to exert more pervasive influence by wielding up to three TV stations, eight radio stations, the already monopolistic newspaper, the cable system, cable channels, and the dominant Internet provider in the larger markets. It would have allowed each television network to buy up even more local TV stations to cover up to 45 percent of the national television audience—and, if those were UHF stations, potentially up to 90 percent. Newspaper-broadcast cross-ownership was henceforth to be acceptable in 179 of the country's 210 markets, and television duopolies got the green light in up to 162 of them. One broadcaster who was trying to figure out exactly what our new rules meant told me his numbers indicated one owner could hold up to 370 stations in 208 of the 210 markets. Where were the blessings of localism, diversity, and competition in that? *I saw centralization, not localism; I saw uniformity, not diversity; I saw monopoly and oligopoly, not competition.*

What I saw at this particular commission was a tectonic shift in policymaking across the whole wide range of media and telecommunications issues that are under our jurisdiction. It was a shift in decidedly the wrong direction. And in the process, the FCC was short-changing its responsibility to protect the public interest. The public interest—some claim it's unworkable, even unknowable. Yet there it is, appearing some 110 times in our enabling telecommunications statute, put there to be our lodestar. To fulfill our public-interest obligation, for decades we have promoted the goals of localism, diversity and competition—all building blocks for a healthy and dynamic media environment. These things aren't luxuries, nice things to have if we can afford them. They are necessities for a thriving American society, and we can't afford *not* to have them. And we need them across our entire media landscape.

The Commission's decision, now sent back to use for further study by the courts, would enable new waves of mergers and acquisitions and would guarantee that big-media companies exert even more pervasive influence. When is "big media" big enough? We have already opened the door to totally unanticipated levels of consolidation, and yet all the talk from the analysts and pundits is yet another Gold Rush of wheeling and dealing if the new rules eventually get the green flag.

Let's remember that when we talk about media concentration, we're not talking just about future threats. We're talking present reality. Fewer people own more properties. Big companies own radio, television, newspapers *and* cable—cable systems and cable channels. They own the production of programming, as you know all too well. They own the distribution. Increasingly, they own the creativity.

Radio deregulation gives us powerful lessons. The loosening of ownership caps and limits eight years ago created real problems in radio, most experts agree. Now, arguably, consolidation also created some economies and efficiencies that allowed broadcast media companies to operate more profitably and may even have kept some stations from going dark and depriving communities of service. And that's fine. That's why many congressmen and senators voted as they did. But the consolidation that ensued went far beyond what anyone expected, leading to outrageous concentrations of social, cultural and political influence. Conglomerates now own dozens, even hundreds—in one case, more than a thousand—stations all across the country. Nearly every market is an oligopoly at best. Competition in many towns has become nonexistent as a few companies—in some cases, a single company—bought up virtually every station in the market. More and more programming seems to originate hundreds of miles removed from listeners and their communities. And we know there are one-third fewer radio station owners than there were before these protections were eliminated.

Respected media watchers argue that this concentration has led to less coverage of local news and public-interest programming. When it comes to entertainment, the Future of Music Coalition in its multiyear study found a homogenization of music crowding out local and regional talent. Others point out that radio now serves more to advertise the products of vertically integrated conglomerates than to entertain Americans with the best and most original programming.

Rather than learn the lessons of radio concentration, the FCC plunged ahead and voted to visit this "Clear Channelization" on the rest of our media. What we are seeing now is the closing off of distribution channels. And nowhere is this more evident than in television. Already, the big media conglomerates that own the networks control approximately three-quarters of the primetime audience—broadcasting and cable together. That audience share of households is approaching—and could soon surpass, according to the analysts—the share the three networks had during the 1960s and 1970s. And today, these conglomerates are more vertically integrated, controlling the production of most of the programs as well as the distribution. It was by adding distribution to production that monopolists like John D. Rockefeller amassed their power. History never repeats itself exactly, but sometimes there are enough similarities to indicate that we ought to pay more attention than we do. This is one of those times. By the way, in contrasting network power now with, say, thirty or forty years ago, remember that back then they didn't have their own stable of "owned-and-operated" stations, and we also had financial syndication rules as a check against market power.

Back then, when some expressed their concern about growing network power, they were told not to worry, that the rapidly expanding multichannel universe of cable TV would save us. What happened? Well, 90 percent of the top cable channels are owned by the same giants that own the TV networks and the cable distribution systems. More channels are great, but when they are all owned by the same people, cable doesn't really nourish diversity, localism, or competition. So that didn't quite pan out. And now we're being told not to worry because the Internet will forever ensure the openness and diversity we crave. Well, guess who owns the top twenty Internet news sites. The same Big Media folks.

What we have to keep in mind is that this is only the latest, most radical step in a twenty-year history of undermining the public interest. Step by step, rule by rule, bit by bit, we have allowed the dismantling of public interest protections and given a green light to the forces of consolidation, until now a handful of giant conglomerates are in the saddle. Fundamental protections of the public interest have been allowed to wither and die. Vertical safeguards, such as the financial syndication rules, are long since gone. Horizontal protections were whittled down significantly long before June 2, 2003. Requirements like ascertaining the needs of the local audience, the Fairness Doctrine, teeing up controversial issues, and providing demonstrated diversity in programming have long since been abandoned. And rigorous public interest scrutiny is more a quaint relic of the past than an effective safeguard to protect against excessive concentration.

Over the years, the Commission has relied more and more on marketplace forces as a proxy for serving the public interest. Don't get me wrong—I don't have anything against folks making a buck from their media investments. We decided long ago in this country that the media would be part and parcel of our great system of capitalist enterprise, and that's fine. But our licensees, in return for the privilege of using airwaves that belong to somebody else—they belong to the people—undertook and pledged to serve the public interest. It's a very different and very special industry. And when its foundation stones begin to crack and things like diversity and localism and competition are imperiled, then it's past time that we do something about it. I think the heart and soul are going out of much of our media. And by neglecting to do justice to proposals that could supplement our ownership rules, such as requiring more independently produced programs and enforcing real public-interest performance standards on our stations, we are skirting perilously close to taking the "public" out of the public airwaves.

During the more than a dozen hearings and forums on media concentration that my colleague, Commissioner Jonathan Adelstein, and I attended from coast to coast, I saw and heard first-hand the stories of hundreds of citizens about the detrimental impact that consolidation has already had on their local media and their fears about where still more concentration will lead. We heard from people laid off from the newsroom when local news got the ax from the new owner. We heard from creative artists who couldn't get air time for their music because they weren't on the centralized, homogenized playlists. We heard from independent programmers who couldn't find outlets for their programming because the networks and the studios had a lock on so much of what is produced.

This popular outcry was one consequence of the June 2 vote that the Commission majority did not count on. Its determination to loosen the rules and its reluctance to share draft rules with the American people—or the Congress—before we voted awoke a sleeping giant: the people. Citizens across this land of ours let their voices be heard. They were downright angry that far-reaching changes were being plotted and planned behind closed agency doors. They didn't like the Commission messing around with their airwaves that way. And they made up their minds to make a difference.

In these times, when many issues divide us, an unprecedented coalition has taken shape—a coalition of left and right, liberals and conservatives, Democrats and Republicans, who understand the dangers of too much concentration and who went to work to do something about it. Concerned parents, creative artists, religious leaders, civil-rights activists, labor organizations, and broadcasters have all united on this issue. As Brent Bozell of the Parents Television Council so aptly put it one afternoon when this motley collection of folks was gathered around one table, "When all of us are united on an issue, then one of two things has happened. Either the Earth has spun off its axis and we have all lost our minds, or there is universal support for a concept." Well, it's the concept—a transcending, nationwide concept. It is an all-American, grassroots issue.

And then there was the "Tell Us the Truth Tour!" Several incredibly busy recording artists gave up their time and resources to raise awareness of this issue. They weren't doing it for money or because it would advance their careers. No—they volunteered because they wanted to awaken the country to an issue that affected not only them and their fellow artists, but each of us as citizens. Everywhere the tour went, they held press conferences, they discussed media concentration, and they performed a tremendous public service.

It took a lot of people to bring this issue to the forefront of the nation's consciousness. It took people raising their voices in song, in protest, in books and pamphlets, in whatever media and forums they could manage to penetrate, to get this issue front and center and to force the issue of media concentration outside the pages of *The Federal Register* and into the mainstream of America.

A lot of the so-called experts said that the coalition would have no staying power; that it would splinter and die right after the vote. It didn't. It stayed together. It went to court together. It went to Congress together. And it is getting results. Part of that difference is to be seen over at the FCC. The Commission now faces a far more informed and involved citizenry than it did just a year ago. The obscurity of this issue, which some relied on in the past, is gone forever. Part of the difference can be seen up on Capitol Hill, where long-time champions of good media policy found themselves joined by many more colleagues than they ever expected. The United States Senate has already voted to overturn the FCC decision in its entirety, and over 200 members of the House of Representatives have asked the house leadership for permission to vote on the same resolution of disapproval. Part of the difference can be seen in the courts, because a united coalition took one look at those awful rules that the Commission majority passed on June 2 and marched them right to court.

The court has now responded. On June 24, 2004, the Third Circuit overturned virtually all of the FCC's attempts to unleash more media concentration, ruling that the FCC's 2003 media concentration plan was legally and procedurally flawed.

The good news is that we have an opportunity to start over and come up with a set of rules that encourages localism, diversity, and competition in the media. But this is not a complete victory. It is merely a second chance to protect the people's interest in the people's airwaves, if we decide to do so.

So now is demonstrably *not* the time to slow down. This is the best opportunity this country will have, perhaps for years, to do something about media concentration and to make sure the public's airwaves serve the public's interest. This problem needs to be fixed now. And if it's not fixed now, the consolidation genie will be out of the bottle with an energy the likes of which we have never seen, and hungry to complete every kind of merger, acquisition, and swap imaginable.

There were so many questions that should have been addressed in the ownership proceeding that were not. Let me mention a few.

What might be the effects of further concentration on America's minorities in terms of providing Hispanic Americans and African Americans and Asian-Pacific Americans and Native Americans and other groups the kinds of programs and access and viewpoint diversity and career opportunities and even advertising information about products and services that they need? America's strength is, after all, its diversity. Diversity is not a problem to be overcome. It is our greatest strength. *Our media need to reflect this diversity and to nourish it.* Yet, the number of minority owners of licensed television stations has dropped to a shocking, and nationally embarrassing, 1.9 percent. And there has been an even greater drop in minority station managers and newsroom employees. Why not ask these questions *before* we change the rules instead of creating the potential for even more harm?

What is the impact on small, local broadcasters? Increasing consolidation threatens the very survival of independent broadcasters. Media analysts expect that the only option for local broadcasters will now be to sell. They conclude that those that want to remain will face an extremely tough road. They will find themselves less and less captains of their own fate and more and more captives of Wall Street and Madison Avenue manipulators. During our hearings, we heard from small broadcasters that had already been squeezed out of the market. These rule changes can only accelerate this trend. And many of these broadcasters are uniquely local stations that serve an important role in their communities.

How about the effects on our kids? Again, we failed the test. When this ownership proceeding was launched last September, we searched in vain for even a mention of the word "children" in the text. We should have examined the impact of consolidation on increasing sex and violence on the airwaves before we allowed further consolidation to take place. We should also have considered to a greater extent the relationship between concentration and children's programming. A recent study analyzed the market in Los Angeles and found that the number of broadcast TV programs for children dropped sharply after independent local stations were swallowed up in media mergers. The study found a 47-percent drop in children's programming, with duopolies accounting for the largest decreases. Another recent survey found that 80 percent of parents think the FCC is doing only a poor to fair job of protecting families and children. That's a sad indictment.

And then there is the question of local artists getting airtime on local stations. In our hearings across the country, we have heard time and again that with increasing consolidation, if you do not have a major label contract with promotional money behind it, you do not get airtime. We even heard from such recording artists as Tift Merritt who have major label contracts, but can't get airtime in their home states. Does local music no longer have a place on local commercial radio? Is that in the best interests of our citizens?

And there was the question of the impact on independent programming. Should we require a set amount of independent programming, so that a few conglomerates don't get a complete hammerlock on the creative entertainment that we see? Network ownership of the full range of prime-time programming constrains competition, consigns independent production to second-class roles, and cripples the production of diverse programming. It also entails serious job losses for thousands of workers, including creative artists, technicians, and many, many others.

There were many other questions that went unasked. What about the impact on advertisers, particularly small advertisers, trying to get their message out in a market where somebody controls most of the outlets? How does technology change the debate? We are transitioning toward the era of digital television, wherein broadcasters will be able to multicast six different channels. Does having one company control eighteen channels in a market not alter the ability of others to compete? These strike me as the kind of questions we should have vetted before we voted.

So the issue of media consolidation is now back before the Commission as a result of the appellate court ruling in June of 2004. The story is far from over. At the FCC, we are now considering other issues related to the public interest and our media. One area is in the public-interest obligations of local broadcasters. As we make the transition to digital, there is a crying need to update our rules on the public-interest obligations of those who are given the right to use spectrum, particularly those who will multicast additional program streams. The potential of digital television and radio is enormous, and I believe the rewards, for everyone, can be enormous, too. But while we have been very attentive to expediting the mechanics of the digital transition—things like DTV tuners and the like—and we've made progress there, on the central questions of what the digital transition means for the public interest, we have a bad case of lockjaw. The result is a great big digital gap. We actually started having a discussion about digital television and the public interest a few years ago, and it was a pretty good one. The Commission even initiated a couple of specific proceedings.

I want us to finalize action on these rulemakings and then go beyond that with a more comprehensive proceeding on the public-interest obligations of digital television broadcasters. I am pleased to see that a coalition—the Public Interest, Public Airwaves Coalition—is forming on this issue to press for such things as more local civic and electoral affairs programming and more independent programming. I also want to see us expand the public-interest discussion to include radio. We have an opportunity in radio to avoid the experience we have had so far with digital television and accord the public interest the high priority it deserves. The additional program streams that are becoming digital reality could be a real boost for localism, competition, and diversity. I hope we will not miss this opportunity to make sure that the American people realize the full benefits of the digital transition.

Another area that merits attention in our effort to increase localism, competition, and diversity is low-power FM stations. These community-based stations are licensed to local organizations and can help meet the needs of underrepresented communities. They can benefit recording artists by providing more outlets for airplay, especially on a local or regional level. We need to get serious about licensing more low-power FM stations.

Finally, let me mention one additional area—license renewals. I want the Commission to start taking this seriously again, like it used to do. Every three years, the FCC would look rather rigorously at what a station was doing to serve its community, working from a fairly specific checklist. That process has degenerated to the point that now, once every *eight* years, we go through a process that is pretty accurately defined as "postcard renewal." Unless a citizen of a community files a petition to deny the renewal, or unless there is a major complaint pending against a station, its license is almost automatically renewed. And, even though stations are required to keep a public inspection file, we don't generally even look at that file unless we hear from members of the community.

As big media gobbles up more local stations, we need a process to ensure that licensees are serving their local communities, your communities. Until we put such a process in place, we will rely on public input on how stations are living up to, or not living up to, their public interest obligations. Are stations adding to the civic dialogue? Are they covering issues of importance to the community? Are they responding to the community's needs?

I see a lot of challenges ahead. Am I worried? Of course, we should all be worried. Powerful economic forces that favor consolidation are converging with regulatory policies that pave the way. They could yet carry the day. But I also see opportunity and the good news is that we still have a chance to avoid all this. I believe, after traveling the length and breadth of this country, that our citizens want, deserve, and are demanding a renewed discussion of how their airwaves are being used and how to ensure they are serving the public interest.

If we roll up our sleeves, if we continue to work together now, all of us—business people, artists, workers, regulators, consumers, citizens everywhere—we can win the battle, we need to win the battle. We have a chance to settle this issue of who will control our media and for what purposes, and to resolve it in favor of public airwaves of, by, and for the people of this great country. Let's make it happen.

WHO IS WATCHING THE WATCHDOG?

JOHN DUNBAR

The Center for Public Integrity has been investigating the federal government for nearly fifteen years. We have made public all manners of corporate and other special-interest influence on Congress and the White House. In January 1996, we released the first *The Buying of the President*, which identified the major presidential candidates' career patrons—their most generous lifetime political donors—and documented what favors they had gotten in return. In September 1998, we released *The Buying of the Congress*, which scrutinized the top political donors to incumbents and to the House and Senate leadership. We have studied the all-too-often decisive influence of money on politics.

In August 2002, we decided to extend our reach beyond elected officials and into the sometimes mysterious workings of a federal agency, beginning a three-year investigation of the Federal Communications Commission. With the same leave-no-stone-unturned approach we had taken to money in politics, we likewise studied the FCC, filing dozens of Freedom of Information Act requests, compiling tens of thousands of records in databases, analyzing them, and presenting our findings on our Web site, www.publicintegrity.org.

We found that the basic data that is critical for the FCC to do its regulatory duty is usually supplied by private sources reliant on the industry, making it virtually impossible to perform a truly independent analysis of whether the agency is acting in the public interest. We discovered that, while every government agency suffers from the "revolving door" syndrome, the traffic of top FCC officials working in the industry is extraordinary. The door is not revolving, it is spinning. We showed that for years, FCC commissioners and top staff accepted millions of dollars in free travel and entertainment from the same companies the agency is supposed to be keeping an eye on. We were able to document that while public participation in FCC decisions is rare, the Commission has an open-door policy for top industry executives. Such ex parte meetings take place out of the public view, usually without public knowledge, and are entirely legal. In short, we found an agency so thoroughly beholden to the industry it regulates that the goals of governance and the goals of business were at times nearly inseparable.

The Unknown Agency

The FCC is often described as an insulated agency. Even its offices, tucked away in the concrete canyons of Southwest Washington, seem secluded. Commissioners are appointed by the president and confirmed by the Senate. Once they are in office, they all but disappear from public view. The Commission relies heavily on staff to make recommendations on telecommunications issues. Most rules are decided on before the commissioners even meet to vote.

The agency receives little coverage from the traditional media. Although some critics say that the lack of coverage reflects a conspiracy of silence—that broadcasters are unwilling to cover their own industry—a more likely explanation is that the FCC's work is by nature highly technical and often deathly dull. It does not make for good television.

There is also the issue of what to do with the news itself.

Because FCC decisions can make the difference between profit and loss for multibillion-dollar companies, their deliberations are often covered on the financial pages. But business reporters have a very different agenda from those who cover Congress, and all too frequently issues like openness, public accountability, and industry influence are overshadowed by the economic consequences of FCC decisions.

Of course, we were not aware of any of this when we first began looking into the agency. Our first challenge was to define the telecommunications industry itself, which was no small task. To help us focus, we opted to look at all FCC-regulated companies. We took a pipeline approach: Any company that controlled the conduits of information and communication would be fair game for our investigation.

Given that the agency was soon to make a pivotal decision on ownership rules, we were especially interested in radio and television stations. We also wanted to find out more about the cable television industry, local- and long-distance telephone providers, and wireless companies. It took us months to gather the most basic information. Much of it came from FCC reports, which in turn attributed the data to private companies. In some instances, the data came from industry associations that also lobbied the FCC. When we constructed our searchable geographic database of media companies (www.openairwaves.org), FCC staff repeatedly referred us to private companies for basic information on ownership and audience reach. Getting market-share information, which is key when reviewing whether broadcasters are within existing FCC regulations limiting the number of households any one owner can reach, was all but impossible without going outside the agency.

The problem is that such data is systemically protected. You can get it, but it costs a lot, and once it is obtained, there are severe restrictions on how it can be used. (For example, making it available for free on our Web site for anyone to see is not allowed.) To get the data we needed for our project, the Center had to go through an inordinate number of hoops. More significantly, the FCC's heavy reliance on industry-provided information has serious public-policy implications, a point that was hammered home when we looked at how the agency researched the issue of the concentration of media ownership.

When the FCC was created in 1934, its primary responsibility was to keep fledgling broadcasters from stepping on one another's radio signals. They did that by setting up a licensing system. Each broadcaster got its own piece of the spectrum, which would remain public property. In return, the broadcasters would use their slice of the airwaves to broadcast programs that would serve "the public interest, convenience and necessity." While the definition of "the public interest" is subject to interpretation and considerable controversy, over the ensuing decades a key function of the FCC was to prevent a single broadcast company from gaining too much control over the public airwaves. Rules prevented television broadcasters from reaching too large an audience nationally and in individual markets. Radio broadcasters were limited in how many stations they could own, both nationally and in a single market. Broadcasters were banned from owning newspapers and broadcast stations in the same cities.

Things began to change in the 1980s. The Reagan administration, under the rubric of deregulation, began rolling back some of these rules. License renewals for broadcasters, an event that gives the government and the public an opportunity to see how well the public's interest is being served, became less frequent and less involved. Rules on ownership were loosened, though modestly so by today's standards.

In 1996, Congress passed a rewrite of the 1934 Communications Act. The Telecommunications Act of 1996 was an enormous and extraordinarily complex piece of legislation. Virtually every communications lobbyist in Washington worked Capitol Hill in advance of its passage in the hope that their industry would benefit. The lobbying was intense and expensive.

While the main selling point of the Act was to provide a way for telephone companies to compete for local phone business, it also made serious changes in how the media are regulated. Among the key changes were the removal of a national cap on radio station ownership and a mandate that the FCC examine ownership rules every two years. The radio rule gave rise to such broadcast giants as Clear Channel Communications Inc., and its 1,200-plus stations. The biennial review gave broadcasters a guaranteed opportunity every two years at convincing the FCC to loosen media concentration rules.

And here is where the trouble of relying on privately produced data arises. In November 2001, FCC Chairman Michael Powell created the Media Ownership

Working Group to help Commissioners in their review of broadcast rules. The group commissioned twelve studies examining the media marketplace, and these were released on October 1, 2002. Watchdog groups claimed that some of the studies were biased in favor of deregulation, and they asked that data used in them to reach conclusions about the marketplace be released. Four of those studies used proprietary data—produced by private companies that sold the data at a profit—to reach their conclusions. Unlike numbers generated by, say, the Census Bureau or the Bureau of Labor Statistics, the FCC was relying on numbers that it had not generated, that it, in fact, did not own and could not release to the public.

On November 4, 2002, the Commission's Media Bureau Chief Kenneth Ferree agreed to make the data available to the studies' critics, but only if those who viewed it agreed to an agency-prepared "protective order." The FCC made the data sets available only to "authorized representatives" of the viewing parties, or to anyone "designated by the Commission in the public interest." To see the data, the viewing party had to swear, in writing, not to share it with any unauthorized persons. Viewers were allowed to look at the data only at FCC headquarters and were prohibited from making copies.

"The protective order business is truly bizarre," said Andy Schwartzman of the Media Access Project, one of the groups that requested to review the FCC's numbers. "We ultimately got to see everything we needed to see and got access to data sets and everything, although there were a lot of controls placed on how we could do it."

He estimated that it took about six weeks from the time the order was issued until his organization was actually able to review the information. This was a critical lag for public-interest groups, as time was limited for them and other concerned parties to make their case on whether the rules should be revised before a comment deadline.

Commissioner Michael Copps at the time released a statement criticizing the Commission's handling of the information. "The FCC is required to seek public participation before it eliminates these rules," he wrote. "The Commission recently released a dozen studies for the public to review as part of this process. It withheld the data used in these studies, however, until releasing parts of it today." Public commentators complained that the comment period allowed by the FCC denied them the ability to participate meaningfully. Just as unreasonable, according to these commentators, is the fact that "the clock on the comment period has been running even while the underlying data was unavailable."

An FCC analyst told the Center that protective orders are not unusual with federal agencies, especially in proceedings dealing with large mergers.

Despite the lack of publicly available government data, the Center was able to construct a database of radio and television stations as well as cable and telephone companies. But the process took months, and the information gleaned from FCC documents was often out of date and incomplete. To make the information useful required hundreds of hours of additional research.

Consider, for example, the way the FCC tracks information on cable television systems. The FCC's Media Bureau makes cable information available to the public through its Cable Operations and Licensing System, known as COALS. The data is available for download via the FCC's Web site and is updated nightly, according to the site. Among the most useful statistics tracked by the agency is a count of cable subscribers by community. After our research team downloaded a number of tables, linked them together, and totaled the subscribers, we discovered that the total was about 7.5 million fewer than the national number of subscribers the FCC lists in its most current cable-industry report. (That report, incidentally, is produced by Kagan World Media Inc., a private research firm.) In other words, after adding up all the cable subscribers the FCC claims live in Philadelphia, Boston, Wichita, and every other community in the United States, we found we were some 7.5 million subscribers short of the national figure that the FCC issues in its own cable-industry report.

An analyst in the Media Bureau told the Center that she did not know much about COALS or why total subscribers in that database were so much lower than the total cited in the most current FCC report. She referred the Center to Kagan (and provided a contact person). A programmer there said the subscriber information was not supposed to be in the COALS database and told Center researchers that the FCC stopped collecting it after "deregulation" of the industry in 1996. In short, the agency was posting nine-year-old data on its site and listing it as current.

And that is on par for the course of the FCC. Schwartzman notes that the Commission is collecting a lot fewer data now than it ever did, and he and some public-interest groups worry that with the increase in deregulation and the decrease in information available, the public will find it that much harder to have access to the information it needs.

"When the agency deregulates, and stops collecting data, they say we're going to rely on marketplace forces and public complaints to make us aware of problems," Schwartzman said. "Then the Commission takes away the means of members of the public to do that monitoring."

The Spinning Door

The FCC's reliance on industry to make its decisions may have surprised us, but once we started digging deeper, that reliance began to make some sense. We soon discovered that the agency itself was full of former industry executives and lawyers, and vice versa. We took a closer look at the revolving-door syndrome in early 2003.

We learned, for example, that SBC Communications Inc., the giant local-tele-phone-service provider, had hired the former chief of local telephone regulation at the FCC. Dorothy Attwood, former chief of the FCC's Wireline Competition Bureau, quit the agency on September 15, 2002, and joined SBC barely six weeks later as senior vice president for federal regulatory strategy. Attwood joined SBC just in time for the company to make its case in advance of a crucial FCC vote that could potentially make it more difficult for companies to compete with "Baby Bells" like SBC on local phone service.

"The stakes are enormous," Consumers Union's Gene Kimmelman told the Center at the time. "What the Commission decides . . . could be a dagger in the heart of potential telecommunications competition—or it could help keep fledgling competitors alive to fight another battle."

Prior to the vote, Attwood met with senior FCC officials a total of four times. Three of those meetings were with FCC Chairman Powell's senior legal adviser to discuss competition-related issues, FCC records showed. The former bureau chief was a favorite of the chairman's. Upon her departure from the FCC, Powell praised her for playing an "integral role in the FCC's implementation of the Telecom-munications Act of 1996, and in shaping our policies in the transition to a more competitive telecommunications environment."

While job-hopping from government to industry is not illegal, it is certainly troublesome in some cases—especially when the one doing the hopping is in a senior position at an agency that regulates an industry and if the break between jobs is extremely brief. One concern is that the former government employee may use inside information, gained while on the public payroll, to benefit a new employer. Even more troublesome is the possibility that the employee could be tempted to rule favorably on industry matters in the hope of getting a lucrative private sector job.

According to the federal Office of Government Ethics, "A former employee is forever barred from representing another person or organization before a Federal Department, agency, or court on certain matters in which the former employee participated personally and substantially while working for the Government."

That's the harshest restriction. A lesser rule stipulates a two-year ban. "The post-employment statute provides that, for two years after terminating Gov-ernment employment, a former employee may not represent another person or organization before a Federal department, agency, or court on certain matters which were pending under the employee's supervision during the last year of his Government service."

There is also a one-year "cooling-off period" for the most senior government officials. Attwood did not fall under the cooling-off rule because she was not senior enough. As for the lifetime and two-year bans, those prohibitions are for party-specific activity, usually related to some form of judicial or quasi-judicial proceeding. Attwood's representation of SBC before the FCC does not qualify because the rule that was under consideration affected an entire sector of industry, and not just her employer.

Attwood told the Center that she was careful about meeting with FCC personnel, even though she is not legally required to restrict her visits. "I can recall three times going back, one in the nature of just saying hello to a new Commissioner," she stated, apparently referring to the meeting with Adelstein. Attwood assured us that she restrained herself from visiting the FCC and could have gone there "200 times" under the letter of the law.

We still felt this was an issue worth raising so that our report might spark some sort of reaction. We were wrong. The media, which frequently picks up Center reports, ignored it.

When the Center reached Attwood for comment, she seemed insulted that anyone would ask whether the job switch could be viewed negatively by the average citizen. She told us that when she left the agency, she was careful to ensure that she would not violate federal "revolving door" laws and sought the opinion of the FCC general counsel's office on post-employment rules. "I've been very careful in the approach I've taken," she said.

An SBC public-relations representative called the Center (unsolicited) to sing Attwood's praises. "For what it's worth, she is a person of utmost integrity. She goes out of her way to make sure there is not any problem in terms of her roles and that she is working within the letter of the law," he said. He went on the say that Attwood is "the breadwinner" for her family and that it would be a "shame" for her to be "tarred by living within the law."

The SBC caller's indignant tone began to make more sense when we dug further into the employment background of other FCC officials. The truth is that such moves from government to industry and back again are utterly routine at the FCC—standard operating procedure. While Attwood's case was a bit more blatant than some, dozens of examples can be found just by reading the FCC's own website and industry press releases. This is especially true in the pro-industry office of the chairman.

On Feb. 25, 2004, Powell's former senior legal adviser, Susan Eid, joined Hughes Electronics Corp., operator of television satellite broadcaster DIRECTV. She was hired as vice president of government relations. Hughes, which has sold a 34-percent stake in the company to the global media giant News Corp., left no doubt about the reason why Eid was hired. "Her vast public policy expertise and in-depth knowledge of the Beltway undoubtedly will serve Hughes well in our nation's capital," said company President and CEO Chase Carey. Eid was hired to oversee "all regulatory and legislative affairs for Hughes and its operating companies," a company release reads.

This was not the first time Eid had ducked through the revolving door. Prior to her FCC service, she was vice president of federal relations for Media One Group, one of the country's largest cable companies at that time.

Powell's former Chief of Staff, Marsha J. MacBride, left the FCC to become executive VP of the National Association of Broadcasters' legal and regulatory affairs division, overseeing the NAB legal team. The division represents broadcasters before the FCC and the courts. Prior to her job as Powell's top staffer, she served a stint as vice president of government relations for the Walt Disney Co. Before joining Disney, MacBride held several top staff positions within the FCC. She originally joined the FCC in 1991, after a six-year career as a communications lawyer in Washington.

John Muleta, chief of the agency's Wireless Telecommunications Bureau, came directly from Source 1 Technologies LLC, where he was president and CEO. Muleta previously worked at the FCC from 1994 to 1998, serving in the Common Carrier Bureau and the Office of Plans and Policy. He served as deputy bureau chief there and was chief of the Enforcement Division. After leaving the FCC, Muleta worked at PSINet, Inc.

Before being named a commissioner in 2001, Kathleen Abernathy was vice president of public policy at BroadBand Office Communications, Inc., a start-up telecommunications venture. Before that, she was a partner at Wilkinson Barker Knauer, a leading telecommunications law firm. She also served stints as vice president for regulatory affairs at U.S. West Inc. and as vice president for federal regulatory issues at AirTouch Communications Inc. In addition to her experience in the private sector, Abernathy held several positions at the FCC at various times. She was a telecommunications legal adviser to former FCC Chairman James H. Quello, legal adviser to former Commissioner Sherrie P. Marshall, and special assistant to the FCC's general counsel. Most of Abernathy's legal advisers also came directly from the private sector.

Hiring former FCC officials is no guarantee of a successful policy outcome. For example, Attwood's old connections at the FCC did not help SBC. A renegade commissioner, Kevin Martin, defied his fellow Republicans and voted with the two Democrats on the commission to keep in place the rules that SBC objected to. (That decision was recently reversed in a federal appeals court. The issue is far from settled.)

The FCC, meanwhile, found another revolver to replace Attwood. Washington attorney William Maher came to the FCC from the telecommunications law firm of Halprin, Temple, Goodman & Maher. Before that, he was at the U.S. Department of Commerce assisting on telecommunications issues. Prior to that job, he was at the FCC as a special counsel for competitive issues.

Frequent Flyers

Although the revolving-door report failed to draw much attention, another Center study that examined the cozy relationship between the agency and the industry certainly did. "On the Road Again—and Again" was released two weeks before the FCC was to vote on relaxing limits imposed on broadcasters about ownership concentration. At the time of the release, the commission, especially then-Chairman Powell, was under an unusual amount of scrutiny. Powell has been an unabashed proponent of deregulation throughout his tenure with the Commission and has called for doing away with most or all of the current ownership restrictions, pointing out they were put in place before the advent of the Internet, cable, and satellite broadcasting.

The media consolidation issue had struck a common chord across the nation. The FCC, after conducting only a single public hearing, was widely expected to vote in favor of allowing big media companies to become much bigger. As is often the case with the agency, most of the work was done behind the scenes, and the final vote was virtually a foregone conclusion. But the fear of a corporate broadcast "Big Brother" galvanized groups as disparate as the National Rifle Association and the National Organization for Women. Regardless of party or ideology, interest groups were concerned that a media landscape dominated by only a few players would keep them from getting out their message. More than 750,000 messages from irate Americans were received by the FCC following the decision. And the "On the Road" report added fuel to the fire.

The study showed that the FCC had accepted nearly $2.8 million from outside sources in travel and entertainment over eight years, most of it from the telecommunications and broadcast industries the agency regulates. The $2.8 million paid for FCC commissioners and agency staffers to attend hundreds of conventions, conferences and other events in locations all over the world, including Paris, Hong Kong, and Rio de Janeiro.

The biggest industry sponsor was the National Association of Broadcasters, whose members had a tremendous financial stake in the FCC's June 2 vote. Records showed that the broadcast lobbying group paid $191,472 to bring 206 FCC officials to its events. For example, the NAB spent $24,601 to bring 14 FCC officials to its annual convention in Las Vegas in 2002, including Chairman Powell and Commissioners Copps and Martin. Not far behind was the National Cable and Telecommunications Association, which spent $172,635 to bring 125 FCC officials to its events, including the $21,147 it spent to bring 13 FCC officials to its annual convention in Chicago in 2003. Coming in third was the Consumer Electronics Manufacturers Association, which spent $149,285 to bring 103 FCC officials to its events, primarily its glitzy annual Consumer Electronics Show held in Las Vegas each year. CEMA heavily lobbies Congress and the FCC on a variety of issues including digital television, broadband deployment, consumer home recording rights and spectrum management.

Among the top sponsors were companies that lobbied heavily for a relaxation of the ownership rules. Viacom, which owns CBS, sponsored seven trips on its own, costing $9,581. Viacom spent $6,901 to bring FCC Media Bureau Chief Ferree and Eid to a company management conference in March 2002. Ferree, the chief architect of the proposal to relax the media-ownership rules, did not respond to an interview request from the Center.

While the vast majority of the trips were sponsored by the telecommunications and broadcast industries, some were paid for by universities and international organizations. Still others were sponsored by companies that put together trade shows and conferences for a variety of industries.

The top traveling commissioner, according to the study, was Powell. He chalked up 44 trips costing $84,921. Powell almost always flies first class because of an injury to his pelvis, which he suffered in a vehicle accident while serving in the U.S. Army. (The Commission Chairman has never responded to any request by the Center for comment on any issue.)

All told, agency officials took more than 2,500 such industry-sponsored trips from May 1995 to February 2003. The Center report analyzed any trips costing more than $250 that were paid for by sources other than the FCC. FCC officials took 330 such trips to Las Vegas during the period, 173 to New Orleans, 102 to New York and 98 to London. Other popular destinations included Orlando, San Francisco, Miami, Anchorage, Palm Springs, Buenos Aires and Beijing.

The officials often served as speakers or panelists at the events, but many times they went only as attendees. They often stayed for the entire event at glitzy hotels, such as the Bellagio in Las Vegas, even though they may have been scheduled to give only a single speech or serve on a single panel, FCC travel records showed.

FCC commissioners went on dozens of trips each, often staying at posh hotels or resorts on the industry tab. Some of the sponsors had special dinners or other events to honor the FCC officials in attendance. They were sometimes provided with cars and drivers. Two top FCC policy advisers took more than 100 trips each during the period.

Michael Copps, a commissioner since June 2001, took 14 trips costing $15,410. Kevin Martin, a Commissioner since July 2001, has taken 12 trips valued at $14,857. He took another 7 trips valued at $8,966 while working in a previous capacity as a legal adviser at the agency. Jonathan Adelstein, who joined the commission in December 2002, took three trips costing $2,998. And Abernathy, a commissioner since June 2001, took 14 trips costing $16,185.

Like most FCC officials the Center contacted, Abernathy declined to be interviewed about her travel but issued a statement noting that at times, she accepts reimbursement from outside groups for travel expenses in order to conserve FCC resources. "The Commissioner believes that meeting with a diverse range of groups, including industry, consumer groups, and other interested parties, serves a crucial information-gathering purpose that is necessary to effective decision making," read the statement. "The Commissioner occasionally travels to meet with interested parties for this purpose, particularly where parties seek to provide a tour or demonstration that cannot be provided in Washington, D.C."

Abernathy's take on the "benefits" of accepting industry-sponsored travel is not unique. Telecommunication industry representatives and some FCC officials defend the trips by arguing that they help to educate regulators on important issues and provide a voice to small companies and individuals who cannot afford to travel to Washington or hire a lobbyist. "We need to understand what the industry is doing and the industry needs to understand what we are doing," said Robert Pepper, chief of the FCC's Office of Plans and Policy, who took 104 trips costing $149,595 during the period studied, second highest among agency officials. "We need to get outside the Beltway in order to do that."

Pepper indicated that the FCC should pay for such trips in an ideal world, but that this procedure is not possible in an age of tight agency budgets. "I'm not crazy about having the industry pick up the tab, but I think it is the second-best option we have in tight fiscal times like now," he noted. "The other option is for us to just stay home. That does not benefit anyone."

But consumer advocates had a darker view of the practice. They told the Center that the trips are unseemly and represent an improper coziness between FCC officials and the businesses they regulate. "It is silly to say they [FCC officials] don't lose some of their objectivity when they are being wined and dined like they are at these industry events," said Mark Cooper, director of research at the Consumer Federation of America. "You would have to be superhuman not to."

Other critics worry that the trips could dull the objectivity of FCC officials and make the agency too chummy with the huge and politically powerful industry it is supposed to regulate. What is more, they point out, the industry enjoys much better access to FCC officials because of the trips, access that is not available to the public. "The problem for me is the access and the personal face time the industry gets with these top officials they bring out to their events," explained Schwartzman of the Media Access Project. "It's impossible for the public to get the same kind of access with those officials."

Roy Stewart, chief of the Office of Broadcast License Policy in the FCC's Media Bureau, took 107 trips, more than any other FCC employee. Stewart had been head of the agency's Mass Media Bureau since 1989. He lost that job in a restructuring ordered by Powell in March 2002. That restructuring put Stewart under new Media Bureau Chief Ferree, a former communications lawyer who first met Powell in college at Georgetown. Stewart says he considers travel to industry events a major part of his job.

"It is important for a government official like me to sit in a room with the industry and hear their concerns," noted Stewart. "Then it is my job to come back and relate those concerns to the Chairman and the Commissioners."

Some members of Congress clearly did not see it that way. Shortly after the Center's report was released, Senator John McCain offered legislation to outlaw the practice; it did not see the light of day. Other such attempts to stop the trips met a similar fate. But the pressure from Congress prompted Powell to substantially limit the practice, if not end it altogether.

On July 25, 2003, Virginia Republican Congressman Frank Wolf, chairman of the House appropriations subcommittee that oversees the FCC's budget, wrote Powell to ask that his agency stop accepting such travel. On Aug. 18, 2003, Powell wrote Wolf back, promising to request a $500,000 funding increase to cover necessary travel. "Even while this effort is underway, I have commenced a further review of our travel program to substantially reduce section 1353 [i.e., non-agency-funded] travel and to guarantee that all travel is necessary to advance the agency's mission."

While the Commission dramatically reduced such trips, the Center gathered documents showing that in the seven months following Powell's letter, FCC staff had accepted $90,000 worth of travel. While trips by commissioners and bureau chiefs had all but stopped, other managers and lawyers were still taking advantage of such benefits.

For example, the January 2004 International Consumer Electronics Show in Las Vegas was attended by five FCC employees, including three deputy chiefs and the chief of the Policy and Rules Division in the Office of Engineering and Technology. The trips totaled $6,355 and were funded by the Consumer Electronics Association, an industry trade group. But that was a dramatic decrease compared with the previous year, when twenty-seven FCC workers, including Powell and Commissioners Kathleen Abernathy and Jonathan Adelstein, attended. The total cost to the association was $45,736.

Wolf, while pleased that the agency had changed its travel policy, told Powell at the subcommittee hearing that he would prefer to see the trips cease altogether except when funded by charitable organizations. "I think our goal should be to get down to zero, with the exception being again on a charitable institution," he said. "And maybe the committee and your staff, we can work together to see if we can do that."

No mention was made of Powell's earlier intention to ask for a $500,000 increase in travel funds.

Behind Closed Doors

When they are not hobnobbing with industry officials in Las Vegas or New Orleans, the top decision-makers at the FCC often rub elbows with those they regulate at the

FCC's headquarters in Washington. Three days before the FCC voted 3:2 to loosen the media ownership rules, the Center released another report illuminating the chumminess between commissioners and top industry executives.

The Center reported that the nation's top broadcasters had met behind closed doors with Federal Communications Commission officials more than seventy times to discuss relaxing the media ownership rules. Media moguls Rupert Murdoch of News Corp., which owns Fox, and Mel Karmazin of Viacom, which owns CBS, virtually dashed from one FCC office to another for a series of private meetings with Commissioners and top staff in late January and early February, as the agency was crafting the controversial proposals.

All told, the five FCC Commissioners and thirty-one other top officials participated in such meetings from September 2002, when the new media rules were proposed, to June 2, when the FCC voted on them. A total of sixty-three executives and representatives of the nation's top ten television and radio broadcasters participated in the meetings.

One particularly busy day was March 11, when eighteen FCC officials met with executives and representatives of ABC and its parent company, Disney, in six different sessions. Some of the sessions included several commissioners and top staff, all gathered in one room to discuss the proposed rule changes with broadcasters. At some of the sessions, executives from the nation's top broadcasters, such as News Corp/Fox, General Electric/NBC, Viacom/CBS, and Disney/ABC, teamed together to lobby for the proposed changes. Among some of the more notable meetings:

- On January 30, Powell and legal adviser Susan Eid met with News Corp.'s Murdoch and two other company officials.

- On February 20, Powell and legal adviser Susan Eid met with Viacom's Karmazin and two other company executives.

- On April 1, Powell, Eid, and his chief of staff, Marsha MacBride, met with NBC President Robert Wright and other network brass. Commissioner Kevin Martin and Media Bureau Chief Ferree, the chief architect of the proposed rule changes, also attended that session.

- On May 1, Powell and MacBride met with Gannett President and CEO Doug McCorkindale and three other executives from the company.

The closed-door sessions, which are officially called ex parte meetings, are allowed under FCC rules. The meetings are not recorded, nor are the participants required to keep detailed minutes of the sessions. Non-FCC people who participate in the meetings are supposed to file a notice of the session by the end of the following day. The notice is meant to include a summary of what was discussed.

Some critics charge that the ex parte process simply allows broadcasters and other industries the FCC regulates to conduct their meetings out of the public eye. "Traditionally, these things have been done by the FCC without any sort of meaningful public involvement," remarked Robert McChesney, author of *Rich Media, Poor Democracy* (1999) and research professor in the Institute of Communications Research at the University of Illinois at Urbana-Champaign. "This is just par for the course with the FCC. They are much more interested in protecting business than looking out for the public."

And that is precisely what George Stigler, a conservative economist at the University of Chicago, whose economics department is synonymous with free-market advocacy, suggested would happen to government regulatory agencies. Stigler coined the phrase "captive regulator" and argued that, given enough time, a regulatory agency will end up beholden to, and even a defender of, the very industry it is supposed to oversee in the public interest.

Even Powell, the deregulation proponent, suggested in an interview with CNBC that industry influence over the commission may have gone too far. Powell stated that he believes the FCC to be the second-most heavily lobbied institution in the federal government, trailing only Congress. "I do think that—that sometimes it gets out of hand," admitted Powell. "I often think that we need time to do our work rather than hear pitches."

Does Powell's almost wistful expression of hoped-for change point to a new direction for the FCC? No one knows for sure, though long-time observers of the agency may be forgiven for expressing some skepticism. But whether Powell gets his wish or not, one thing has become clear: an agency too long noted for its seclusion and below-the-radar pronouncements and decisions can only benefit from the continued spotlight organizations like the Center for Public Integrity shine on it. At least the citizens on whose behalf the FCC is supposed to work may get clearer glimpses of exactly how it goes about doing its work.

THE MEDIA AND CAMPAIGN REFORM

Vidya Krishnamurthy

"Follow the money"—that's the mantra of campaign-finance reformers. And most of the time, they're talking about following the money in politics back to its source, the special interests that use campaign cash to win policy favors. But if you keep following the money, the trail will lead straight to the nation's media.

The skyrocketing costs of the paid political ads that dominate our television sets every even-numbered year represent the biggest expense in competitive federal races, according to the Committee for the Study of the American Electorate. And while the money-drenched campaign system serves the purposes of a whole gamut of special interests, none profits so richly as the media industry. In 2004, television stations raked in more than $1.6 billion from political ads aired by candidates, issue groups, and parties, according to the Alliance for Better Campaigns. In fact, in election years, television stations regularly take in more money from political ads than they do from automotive and fast food ads. As former New Jersey Senator and onetime presidential candidate Bill Bradley once remarked, "Today's political campaigns function as collection agencies for broadcasters. You simply transfer the money from contributors to television stations."

Meanwhile, station managers and network heads are pulling back from substantive coverage of campaigns, opting for ratings-friendly entertainment and focusing on the horse-race nature of campaigns when they cover them at all. This spurs an even greater need for candidates to rely on paid media, leaving fewer citizens with the information they need to cast an educated vote. The result, in former Federal Communications Commission chairman Newton Minow's words, is a colossal irony: "Politicians sell access to something we own: our government. Broadcasters sell access to something we own: our public airwaves. . . . By creating this system of selling and buying access, we have a campaign that makes good people do bad things and bad people do worse things."

Many campaign-finance laws, such as contribution limits and disclosure requirements, focus on the supply of campaign cash. However, the solution to the ubiquity of money in politics, and to a marked decline in civic engagement,

141

must address the *demand* for all that campaign cash: the need to pay for airtime on commercial media to communicate with citizens. It seems clear that the goals of media reformers and campaign finance reformers are inextricably linked: To fix what ails United States democracy, you have to reform the media's role in campaigns and public affairs.

PROFITING FROM THE MONEY CHASE:
POLITICAL SPENDING ON TELEVISION (IN MILLIONS)
Sources: Television Bureau of Advertising, PaineWebber, Harris Nesbit (2004, projected)

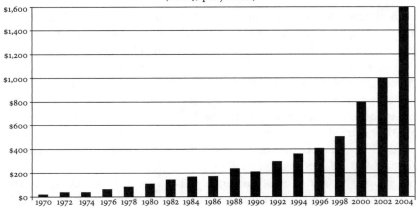

Politics on Television

California, launch pad for many a political trend, served up a new offering in 1998: the all-ad, no-news campaign. It was an open-seat race for the governorship of the nation's most populous state, widely believed to be the most important contest that year. But for most local television stations, the political unit may as well have been synonymous with the sales department. That's because the race, which opened with a fiercely contested Democratic primary, was virtually ignored by local television news—even while local television stations aired an eye-popping $100 million worth of advertising. According to a study by the University of Southern California, stations in the state's top five major markets devoted *less than 1 percent* of news coverage to the race.

The 2000 election cycle brought more of the same across the country: ads dominated news coverage, particularly for races below the presidential level. Across the board, the campaign coverage that actually aired on broadcast television featured little more than the usual horse race and sound bites. And even the sound bites were getting clipped shorter and shorter: The average length of a sound bite by a presidential candidate on the network evening news went from forty-three seconds in 1968 to less than eight seconds in 2000. The incredible shrinking sound bite was just one of the horror stories that illustrated the state of politics on television that year. Broadcast news coverage was markedly down at the presidential level as well; the three main nightly newscasts devoted 28 percent less time to coverage of the 2000 campaign than they had given to the 1988 campaign, the last open-seat presidential race, according to the Center for Media and Public Affairs; nearly three-quarters of this coverage focused on the horse race of the campaign rather than substantive issue positions. In fact, the group's head, Robert Lichter, found that when candidate George W. Bush went on David Letterman's late-night talk show, he received more airtime in a single block than he received during all of October on the three major networks combined. The forums where viewers have a chance to hear more than just eight seconds out of a candidate's mouth, such as debates, also received short shrift from broadcast television. During the most tightly fought presidential election in history, for the first time ever, two of the major networks—Fox and NBC—decided against carrying all of the general-election presidential debates, choosing to run entertainment and baseball instead. This decision followed a primary season that featured twenty-two presidential debates, but just two on broadcast television. Coverage of the parties' nomination conventions was also sharply reduced; the three big networks cut back coverage by two-thirds compared to 1988.

Broadcasters justified this cutback by pointing to cable news channels. As veteran political correspondent Sam Donaldson told the *Dallas Morning News* during the 2000 primaries, "Outside of *Nightline* and our Sunday show, ABC News, in my view, has simply forfeited the field." He went on, "For us to run long programs in prime time as a public service doesn't make a lot of sense anymore to our bosses. All you have to do is tune to CNN, MSNBC, or the Fox News Channel." The decision to cede campaign coverage to cable sparked much hand-wringing within academic circles because of the loss of the "inadvertent audience"—those individuals who stumble across coverage. A 2000 poll by the Pew Research Center found that about 83 percent of people "bump into" campaign news, while just 15 percent actively seek it out. "For political junkies, it's the best of times," argued Princeton political science professor Larry Bartels. "For ordinary citizens, it's the worst of times." While cable news channels may be available in millions of homes just like the networks, their actual audiences are routinely dwarfed by nightly network newscasts. The migration of presidential coverage to cable in 2000 meant that fewer people were likely to stumble onto the information necessary for casting an informed vote.

On local television news, the picture is even grimmer. Down-ballot races aren't likely to be picked up by the CNNs and Fox News Channels of the world, so it isn't a question of ceding coverage to cable. All too often, the decision to shy away from political reporting comes from the advice of news consultants who do market research, helping to guide local television news staffs in building a broader audience. Among these hired guns, it is accepted wisdom that politics is a ratings loser.

Even though only a handful of congressional races and Senate races are competitive in most election years, local television stations are withdrawing from covering these contests. Not surprisingly, these races attract the lion's share of campaign dollars. With campaign coffers brimming with money to spend on television ads, station sales departments champ at the bit to sell candidates airtime, even as their counterparts in the news department opt against covering the campaigns for free in news reports. In 2000, for example, viewers tuning into the top-rated stations in New York and Philadelphia—host to two hot Senate elections as well as a gubernatorial contest in Pennsylvania—were ten times more likely to see a campaign ad than a campaign story during the evenings in the last two weeks before election, according to a study by the Alliance for Better Campaigns.

The trend has continued: In 2004, voters in presidential battleground states saw twice as much in the form of advertising as campaign news on their local evening news, according to the Lear Center, and races below the presidential level received short shrift. Viewers were hit by $1.6 billion worth of political advertising—the highest figure yet, and more than *fifteen* times the total spent thirty years ago, even adjusting for inflation. These dollars are hugely important to broadcasters' bottom lines. Political ads account for most of the projected growth in the year's spot advertising market, according to the research firm Competitive Media Reporting. Fueling the skyrocketing figures is the rise of political ad buying by outside groups, from issue groups such as NARAL Pro-Choice America and the Club for Growth, as well as from shadowy groups like Republicans for Clean Air, which served as cover for a few prominent individuals in the 2000 election, and so-called 527 organizations such as the Media Fund, active in the 2004 campaign. During the height of the campaign season, the additional demand from all of these players causes the price of airtime to spike, even as the additional clutter makes each individual ad even less effective.

What's more, this out-of-control demand for advertising time, and the resulting price spike, renders ineffectual the one policy that was originally intended to offer an affordable playing field to federal candidates. The "lowest unit charge" rule, passed in 1971, calls for stations that hold publicly granted licenses of the broadcast spectrum to offer their best rates on ad time to federal candidates in the closing weeks of an election. However, this rate is essentially a discount from whatever the going rate for ad time is on a station; as prices across the board skyrocketed during the final weeks of campaigns in 2000 and 2002, candidates saw their so-called discounted rate double and sometimes triple. Senator Dick Durbin [D-IL] compared the ad prices at a network affiliate in St. Louis before and after Election

Day in 2000: "On the early morning weekday news shows, the rate that this station charged after the political campaign was over went down 55 percent from the political campaign time. During noon weekday news, the rate went down 66 percent in the weeks after the election campaign."

Critics claim that the dominance of attack ads and sound bites has an impact on democracy and civic engagement in general, albeit a less measurable one than the colossal expense of political advertising and the resulting reliance of politicians on wealthy special interests. However, the deluge of ads in 2004 was part of an election that captured more interest than recent campaigns: 54 percent of registered voters responded that they were following election news "very closely" in the closing weeks of the campaign, 14 percentage points more than in 2000, according to the Pew Research Center for the People and the Press. More people paid attention, and more came out to cast ballots. At the same time, voters across the board noted that it was a banner year for mudslinging. 72 percent of voters thought that there was more negative campaigning in 2004 than in previous elections—more than double the percentage who expressed that opinion in 2000, according to the Pew pollsters. Arguably, viewers exhausted by the flood of political ads can become disaffected, uninformed citizens. In 1998, another year that saw a particularly high peak in advertising because of the rise of soft-money-funded issue ads, Democratic consultant Raymond Strother declared, "The most notable thing to me is how difficult it is this year to penetrate the public mind, how cynical they are and how they are skeptical of anything anybody says." Democratic media consultant Bob Shrum—adviser to both the Gore campaign in 2000 and the Kerry campaign in 2004—defended political ads: "The average sound bite in a news broadcast is now eight seconds. It makes a political ad look like *War and Peace*."

Only two groups benefit from this system of skyrocketing ad rates, waning coverage, and reliance on paid media. One group is composed of the candidates who can buy their way into office by saturating the media with political ads. This group includes those who are willing and able to raise immense amounts of campaign cash and look past the conflicts of interest in quid pro quo donations, as well as the millionaire candidates who can finance their own bids at high office. The second group that benefits handily, of course, is the broadcast industry. Its members pocket the cash from the ads and continue to enjoy their status as a very special interest.

The Impact on Policy and Politics

Former *Washington Post* political reporter Paul Taylor, who has advocated that broadcasters must give candidates free air time as a condition of their publicly granted license, calls the relationship between incumbent broadcasters and incumbent politicians "the most profitable, exclusive, and mutually beneficial relationship in the new Gilded Age of politics." For a quick example of what that relationship means, consider Dick Durbin's story of the St. Louis station. He recounted the tale in spring of 2001, as the Senate debated campaign-finance reform and considered how to make the cost of communication cheaper to candidates. A measure to fix the lowest-unit-charge rule passed in the Senate, supported by everyone from campaign finance reformer-in-chief Sen. John McCain [R-AZ], to reform's most ardent opponent, Sen. Mitch McConnell [R-KY]. But in the House, the measure died under an onslaught of lobbying from the broadcasters and compliant legislators. Broadcasters could continue cashing in on politics; House incumbents, who later enjoyed an almost 800-percent edge in campaign cash over their challengers in the 2002 campaign, wouldn't have to worry about their opponents getting more air time.

"No one has more sway with members of Congress than the local broadcaster," boasted the National Association of Broadcasters president Edward Fritts in 1995. Lawmakers and political observers seem to agree. The industry has scored repeated wins in Washington because of its lobbying power, its ability to contribute large sums of campaign cash, and its uniquely important role as the means of communication vital to virtually every politician's bid for reelection. McCain, who as chairman of the Senate Commerce Committee used to oversee telecommunications matters, calls them the most powerful lobby in Washington, noting, "My record with the broadcasters is unblemished by victory." Neil Hickey of the *Columbia Journalism Review*, who has written about the lobby group for years, remarks, "The NAB has chalked up a virtually unbroken series of triumphs against any enemy that would dare impose unwanted obligations on the broadcast industry." And during the tussle over the 1996 Telecommunications Act, conservative columnist William Safire wrote in the *New York Times* that the broadcasters showed lobbying muscle that "the vaunted gun lobby wishes it could generate." During that battle, the industry succeeded in receiving billions of dollars worth of additional spectrum from the public, free of charge—a move that was roundly criticized as a massive allocation of corporate welfare at the expense of the public good.

The industry has worked hard to preserve the current system of campaign financing. In the words of Paul Taylor, an advocate of free airtime, the broadcasters "profiteer on democracy." Such a lucrative set-up is hard to defeat. Between 1996 and 1998, the National Association of Broadcasters and five media companies owning local television stations spent nearly $11 million in lobbying to defeat campaign-finance reform, according to the Center for Public Integrity, a nonpartisan watchdog group. Killing the effort to close a loophole in existing law with the lowest-unit-charge rule in 2001 was just the latest example of their success. But as Taylor later wrote, the lowest-unit-charge provision is "more bandage than cure," a mechanism that is too easy for stations to evade, even if it could be repaired. "For a more market-friendly and sustainable way to lower the cost of campaign communication on the broadcast airwaves . . . vouchers for free political ads . . . would work far better," Taylor argued. Many advocates have adopted this more aggressive perspective, which argues that there ought to be a law mandating free airtime for electoral speech in America, as there is in virtually every other industrialized nation. Countering the entrenched interests of profit-hungry broadcasters and reform-wary politicians will require a radical shift in the financing and mediation of public elections.

Civic Discourse and the Public Interest Standard

In 2004, media reformers came together under the rallying cry of "Our Democracy, Our Airwaves," to fight for new mandates that would ensure citizens have access to more and better election information. Reformers note that since the early years of broadcasting, the government has required that those who receive licenses to the public airwaves free of charge must serve the public interest. Courts have said repeatedly that civic discourse is at the heart of that standard. As the Supreme Court said in its *Red Lion* decision, broadcasters' status as public trustees means that they are "given the privilege of using scarce radio frequencies as proxies for the entire community [and] obligated to give suitable time and attention to matters of great public concern." Congress has also made it clear that electoral discourse is part of the public-interest standard. That concept is apparent in the equal-time requirement on broadcasters—by which licensees that sell air time to one candidate must offer equal air time to other candidates—as well as the aforementioned lowest-unit-charge provision and the requirement that broadcasters offer federal candidates "reasonable access" to purchase airtime.

A host of public-interest groups, media reformers, and academics agree that some system of free airtime ought to be made a mandatory part of broadcasters' public interest obligations. These could take the shape of vouchers for free ads, which would allow a floor for spending so that even candidates who aren't movie stars or millionaires will have a fighting chance against a well-funded incumbent. That provision might help bring back a little competition and give voters a sense that they have real choices. Instead, in 2002, 98 percent of House incumbents running for reelection and 83 percent of senators running for reelection were successful. What's more, experiments with voluntary donations of free airtime, in which stations required candidates to appear on air for a few minutes to address a particular issue, have shown that such formats can improve the level of political discourse on television. A study by the Annenberg Public Policy Center of the University of Pennsylvania of such an alternative that aired in the 1997 New Jersey governor's race found that these segments were less negative, more specific, and more accurate than other candidate's advertising.

Advocates for good government—and good journalism—recognize that several reforms by the nation's media would help to resuscitate electoral discourse in the United States. More debates, televised by a single station or all of the stations in a market at a time when people are actually watching, could help the processes of reform. So would a commitment to actually covering issues and framing campaign stories as matters that have an impact on people's lives, instead of as spectacles made up of strategy, tactics, fund raising, and poll numbers. After every election, round tables of political journalists, consultants, and academics wring their hands and promise to do better next time. Citizens can certainly play a role in demanding that journalists live up to these promises. But they can also demand that their elected representatives take some concrete action to change the way politics and elections happen on television. As public trustees, the licenses broadcasters hold over the public airwaves are immensely profitable. Asking them to give a little time so that citizens can hear from candidates ought to be the least that broadcasters can do to serve the public interest.

Reforming the nation's media isn't the silver-bullet solution to all that ails American elections. Even if free time was granted, political coverage was robust, and debates were aired and watched by all, wealthy interests would still be able to influence politicians. There would still be critics who would agree with Jerry Nachman, former editor of the *New York Post*, who once complained, "The problem is that today's politicians who have all the money in the world to spend on commercials have nothing to say." But if broadcasters used their control over the public airwaves to offer meaningful, engaging programming, and if candidates didn't have to rely on raising mountains of cash to have a fighting chance at the ballot box, more citizens would get real choices and better information. They would be better able to hold candidates and parties accountable. And on election day, maybe more Americans would actually show up ready to cast a truly informed vote. The fact is that the media are part of the problem. They have to be a part of the solution.

THE LEGAL CASE FOR DIVERSITY
IN BROADCAST OWNERSHIP

ANDREW JAY SCHWARTZMAN, CHERYL A. LEANZA,
AND HAROLD FELD

Broadcast ownership regulation dates to the Radio Act of 1927, yet it was not until 2003 that media concentration became an issue of broad general concern. FCC Chairman Michael Powell's effort to lift many of the FCC's broadcast ownership limitations sparked an extraordinary bipartisan grassroots reaction that was unprecedented in size, duration and impact. [1]

The Powell FCC was repudiated in the Courts as well. An appeal challenging the decision was filed under the case name *Prometheus Radio Project* v. FCC. [2] On September 3, 2003, a panel of the United States Court of Appeals for the Third Circuit in Philadelphia issued an order blocking the new ownership rules from going into effect. On June 24, 2004, the Court reversed the FCC's ownership decision, sending the case back to the FCC for a top-to-bottom revision.

As of this writing, it is impossible to predict what will happen next. Supreme Court review is possible, but congressional legislation to block the FCC's decision may supercede further judicial or FCC action. What is more certain is this: there is now broad public opposition to increased media ownership consolidation, and future FCC chairpersons are likely to wish to follow a far less deregulatory course of action.

What the FCC Did

The 1996 Telecommunications Act was a product of the Republican takeover of Congress in 1994. Although congressional Democrats and the Clinton administration were able to blunt some of the worst aspects of the bill, the multipart legislation is highly deregulatory in nature. Enactment of the 1996 law led to the greatest wave of media consolidation in history. The worst provision of the new law lifted all limits on how many radio stations one company could own. Within five years, Clear Channel Communications, Inc., grew from about forty stations nationally to about twelve hundred. Television chains bulked up to the new maximums as well, and TV "duopolies" (ownership of two stations in one community) became common.

Having received slightly less than what they wished, big broadcasters left a time bomb buried in the new law. Section 202(h) directed the FCC to review all its ownership rules every two years and to consider eliminating any provisions which might become outdated. While this review requirement appears to be a relatively benign measure which calls for little more than reporting to Congress, Rupert Murdoch's News Corporation (whose lobbyist was reported to have had a major hand in drafting this part of the law) convinced a panel of the Reagan-Bush dominated Court of Appeals in Washington, D.C., to turn Section 202(h) into a powerful instrument for deregulation. In its February 2002 decision, *Fox Television Stations, Inc.* v. *FCC*, the Court ruled that Section 202(h) "upended" traditional legal principles so that the FCC was expected to apply a "presumption in favor of deregulation."

FCC Chairman Powell and his Republican colleagues enthusiastically accepted their new mission. In the fall of 2002, they started a new proceeding intended to apply the Court of Appeals' "presumption" to all existing broadcast ownership rules. Their request for written comments signaled a desire to repeal or relax almost all of these rules. Spurning calls for public hearings and pressing for rapid action, they voted on June 2, 2003, to adopt an order drastically cutting back existing restrictions. The two Democratic Commissioners voiced powerful dissent; Commissioner Michael Copps said:

> The majority . . . chooses radical deregulation . . . . This decision allows a corporation to control three television stations in a single city. Why does any corporate interest need to own three stations in *any* city, other than to enjoy the 40-50 percent profit margins most consolidated stations are racking up? What public interest, what diversity, does that serve? This decision also allows the giant media companies to buy up the remaining local newspaper and exert massive influence over some communities by wielding three TV stations, eight radio stations, the cable operator, and the already monopolistic newspaper. What public interest, what new competition, is enabled by encouraging the newspaper monopoly and the broadcasting oligopoly to combine? This decision further allows the already massive television networks to buy up even more local TV stations, so that they control up to an unbelievable 80 or 90 percent of the national television audience. Where are the blessings of localism, diversity and competition here? I see centralization, not localism; I see uniformity, not diversity; *I see monopoly and oligopoly, not competition.* [Emphasis in the original]

The intensity of negative public reaction to the FCC's decision stunned observers on all sides. Several measures to overrule all or part of the new scheme were introduced in Congress, receiving favorable votes despite efforts of the Republican leadership to derail them. Backing down on a veto threat, President Bush signed one such measure that was attached to an appropriations bill in January 2004. This measure rolled back the limit on national TV ownership to a 39-percent share. (Under the 1996 deregulation, TV broadcasters were allowed to own stations reaching no more than 35 percent of the nation's TV homes; the FCC had raised that limit to 45 percent. Loopholes continue to exist. According to an outdated regulation, UHF stations' audience is "discounted" by 50 percent, so that an all-UHF broadcaster can now reach 78 percent of the nation's homes.) The measure also cut back the review required under Section 202(h) to a quadrennial rather than biennial schedule.

What the Court Did

The Court of Appeals majority decision reversing the FCC's ownership deregulation action is 121 pages in length; one judge, who disagreed with substantial portions of the opinion, wrote another 92 pages in dissent. A complete summary is neither possible nor necessary to show how decisively the Court repudiated Chairman Powell. The Court was even more forceful in unanimously rejecting some broadcasters' claims that the FCC's deregulation had not gone far enough and that ownership rules were unconstitutional.

It is difficult to overstate the political significance of the Court's ruling. The decision rejects the legal premise of the FCC majority's action, the FCC's application of the facts to the law and even the fact-finding itself, criticizing its failure to obtain meaningful public participation in the decision-making process. These actions, combined with the extraordinarily negative reaction of a Congress controlled by the FCC Chairman's own party, will have a lasting impact on how broadcast ownership will be addressed in the future by any FCC.

From a technical standpoint, the most important part of the Court of Appeals decision is the holding that Section 202(h) of the 1996 Communications Act does *not* contain within it a "presumption in favor of deregulation." This means that the next quadrennial review (in 2006), will be conducted without the built-in bias that infused the 2003 decision.

From a practical standpoint, the most important aspect of the decision was the Court's rejection of Chairman Powell's elaborate "diversity index" mechanism, which purported to substitute a single formula to guide decisions on ownership of TV-radio and newspaper-broadcast combinations in a single community. While the majority left room for the FCC to adopt a different replacement formula, any further FCC action will likely make few if any changes to these rules. (This includes newspaper/TV combinations; although the Court ruled that the FCC could properly end the previous rule which nominally banned newspaper owners from buying broadcast properties, the practical effect of the Court's decision is that such combinations probably will not be permitted in the future.)

One especially interesting aspect of the Court of Appeals action is its clear awareness of the increased public concern about media concentration. This is not to say that the Court was simply acceding to the public will, but its understanding of the importance attached to this question clearly affected its decision to stay the FCC's decision as well as its assessment of the way that the FCC compiled and analyzed the factual record on which it acted.

Why Broadcast Ownership Matters

One can fairly ask why progressives have devoted so much effort to preserving diversity in ownership of over-the-air broadcasting. After all, over-the-air broadcasting (which is today more accurately referred to as "terrestrial" broadcasting) is a very mature industry. Commercial radio broadcasting is more than eighty years old, while television service has been available to most of the nation for almost sixty years.

Satellite technology has decreased dependence on terrestrial broadcasting by bringing vastly increased choice to the public over the last three decades. While about half the programming viewed by cable TV and direct broadcast satellite (DBS) subscribers on an average night remains available through over-the-air channels, this situation is a far cry from the state of affairs twenty-five years ago, when ABC, CBS, and NBC typically shared nearly 90 percent of the prime-time TV audience. Satellite-delivered radio service is just beginning to come to market, but many people believe that commercial radio has become fat and lazy since deregulation began under the Reagan administration and that it will rapidly lose much of its audience in the coming years.

Another reason that broadcasting seems less important to activists is the growth of the Internet. The open architecture of the Internet offers unlimited content choice, unless and until policymakers impose restraints upon it. Broadband technology will eventually permit audio and video programming to be available on demand, thus greatly vitiating the importance of whatever remains of broadcasting's power and influence.

All of that is true enough, but it does not really change the need to address broadcast ownership as one of the most important influences on democratic self-governance in America. Here is why progressives should continue to regard consolidation in broadcast ownership as one of the greatest challenges to democratic self-governance.

First, however insignificant broadcasting may become some day, it remains for the foreseeable future the most powerful political, social, and cultural force shaping American thought. Cable news networks are increasingly important for those motivated to follow news and public affairs issues, but the vast majority of Americans get most of their news, information, and culture from over the air TV and radio channels, including local and network newscasts and talk radio. (Most consumers now receive this broadcast video programming through cable or satellite systems, but that does not change its influence.)

Second, television and radio form the centerpiece of most major media empires. Broadcasting is the cash cow which has funded the expansion of NBC, Disney, Fox, Viacom, and Clear Channel into new media. Cable giant Time Warner is the only major content provider for which broadcasting is a minor component. (As evidenced by its unsuccessful attempt to acquire Disney, Comcast owns a vast distribution system but produces very little of its own content.)

Third, the political and financial muscle of television broadcasters has assured them important future roles. In what was perhaps its greatest legislative accomplishment since its founding, the National Association of Broadcasters inserted into the 1996 Communications Act an extraordinary provision giving existing TV licensees exclusive use, free of charge, of a huge swath of prime spectrum for digital TV transmission. Access to this spectrum assures placement on cable TV systems from the "must-carry" and "retransmission" rights granted in the 1992 Cable Act. Thus, however vestigial over-the-air TV technology may become in the future, over-the-air TV stations will have top billing on the nation's cable TV systems. The same is essentially true for radio; the FCC has authorized a "digital audio" technology that locks in the rights of existing broadcasters and makes it almost impossible for new commercial competitors to obtain spectrum.

None of this is to say that cable television ownership, newspaper dominance of local markets, the supremacy of a few companies in the music industry, and the threat of content control over the Internet are unimportant now, or in the future. But those who say that broadcasting is a dead industry, and that the fight over broadcast ownership is best left to the last century, are very wrong.

Why the Public Needs Competitive, Diverse Media

The Supreme Court of the United States has stated that "the widest possible dissemination of information from diverse and antagonistic sources is essential to the welfare of the public." The Court has applied this principle of diversity of views as a necessary stimulus of democracy and vigorous public debate to entertainment as well as news production.

Many citizens fear a world in which a few media gatekeepers control access to the mass media. At best, these multimedia conglomerates will homogenize news and entertainment into a single "infotainment" package leveraged across multimedia platforms and targeted primarily at advertiser-coveted demographics. At worst, the few media gatekeepers may suppress news or perspectives that run counter to their economic or ideological interests, or they will do so to curry favor with the government.

These problems are not new. However, the threat they pose is more palpable today. Indeed, the public's perception that this already began appearing earlier probably accounts for the public's visceral reaction against further relaxation of the rules.

Contrary to the assertions of those favoring deregulation, the media marketplace is not open and competitive. The government prohibition on broadcasting without a license, together with the economic structure of the cable industry, has created a highly concentrated market with effectively impenetrable barriers to entry. Moreover, even if the media marketplace were competitive, legal principles as old as this country state that the news and information deserve treatment as something more than mere commodities. Democracy depends upon a competitive marketplace of ideas; it is a compelling governmental purpose "of the highest order" to take prophylactic steps to ensure that market does not fail.

Ownership restrictions offer a far more effective means of achieving the needed diversity to ensure a robust democracy with less damage to the First Amendment. Because the connections that allow large corporate interests to influence content are complex and subtle, structural rules that protect diversity by fragmenting ownership are essential. Indeed, if media ownership restrictions were removed, the only way to ensure diversity would be to impose explicit content mandates and access rules.

Media Concentration Will Exacerbate Existing Market Failures

Contrary to the arguments of those favoring deregulation, the current "market" in news and entertainment is not characterized by competitive entry or abundance. Further, the majority of media owners are vertically integrated, multinational conglomerates with diverse economic interests. Accordingly, the economic incentives of media content suppliers do not necessarily align with the interests of viewers and citizens.

Critically, broadcasting remains a government-controlled monopoly, and only those with a government license can broadcast. No matter how much money one wants to invest to develop better or more popular television or radio programming, these productions will not reach potential audiences unless someone with a federal license agrees to carry them. When these local broadcast licenses become concentrated in a few hands, those few hands decide what is aired. Cable television operators are monopolies in virtually every market, and they are typically vertically integrated. Thus, cable viewers who want a different type of programming have no competitive options if they do not like the selections available on their cable systems. They cannot pick and choose to pay for only one or two channels; they must pay for a whole package in order to receive most channels.

The development of the Internet does not change this calculus. Because of the economics of news production, only a handful of websites control the bulk of news generation and distribution over the Internet. Although anyone remains free to set up a website and post or send information to the rest of the world, this freedom does not equate with an ability to effectively compete with existing media companies. The question is not whether news is somehow discoverable, but whether it enters into the public's awareness. Finally, fights over access to content and technological limitations have prevented streaming media from emerging as serious competitors to either radio or television. In addition, as even supporters of deregulation agree, neither cable networks nor the Internet provide local news.

Although consumers display a considerable interest in local news, and local news remains critical to maintaining an informed local electorate, increased concentration harms, rather than enhances, the production of local news. An independent study from the Pew Foundation's Project for Excellence in Journalism (PEJ) found that stations owned by small companies (three stations or less) were more than twice as likely than the largest owners to receive the PEJ's highest news quality score.

The structure of the industry bears this out. Local stations generate local news from local revenues. Because typical margins on a well-run television station in a top market are 60 percent (and even weak performers earn between 50 and 55 percent), owners of large groups of stations view them as cash cows and absorb the local revenue for other corporate purposes, such as servicing debt.

As a result, deregulation and increased concentration result in failures in local news markets. Even on a national level, economic incentives lead to market failure in news production. Several PEJ studies support the conclusion that major networks prefer to produce soft news about the entertainment industry or "infotainment" stories dwelling on the misdeeds of celebrities than report hard news on significant public policy issues.

Even where broadcasters or other providers of programming rely solely on their interests in the broadcast markets, the results can still be detrimental to the broader concerns of democracy and civic discourse. Two recent cases—ABC-Disney's attempt to replace the popular news show *Nightline* with *Late Show with David Letterman* because of the desirability of the latter's perceived viewer demographic, and CBS-Viacom's attempt to interview former Iraqi prisoner of war Jessica Lynch—demonstrate the fallacy of relying on economic incentives to ensure a mass media market that produces accurate, unbiased, and detailed news programming, even when such news programming is both popular and profitable.

First, in 2002, ABC attempted to replace Ted Koppel's news program *Nightline* with *Late Show with David Letterman*. Although more people watch Koppel than Letterman, Letterman draws a younger demographic that is more desirable to advertisers, which will pay a premium for shows that are less popular overall but that concentrate on that desirable demographic.

By the same token, a cable company has a greater incentive to air its own programming than to give access to another company's product. In the second, more disturbing, example, there is a demonstration of how economic incentives of vertically integrated media conglomerates can warp news coverage, as in the recent attempt by CBS, a subsidiary of Viacom, to secure an interview with U.S. Army Private First Class Jessica Lynch. PFC Lynch attracted public attention during the Iraq war when a squad of Marines apparently rescued her after her capture by Iraqis. To land the first interview, CBS offered to leverage PFC Lynch across Viacom's media properties. In addition to a news interview promoting Lynch, Viacom offered to provide a two-hour CBS news documentary, a reunion with her rescuers, and a publicity campaign. The latter would feature segments on several CBS news programs including the CBS *Evening News*, an MTV appearance, a Country Music Television concert in her hometown, a two-hour made-for-TV movie produced by CBS Entertainment, and book publication with the imprimatur of Viacom's Simon & Schuster.

Although this proposed deal made economic sense for Viacom, it represents a serious breakdown in the ability of the public to receive news with confidence that it meets high standards of journalistic integrity (rather than simply being a cross-promotional advertisement). The same incentives problem exists in the production of entertainment. Because media conglomerates have multiple platforms, the industry has increasingly come to rely on "repurposing," i.e., reusing entertainment developed on one property for another.

Although this practice saves costs, it severely undercuts the argument that greater concentration leads to an increase in original programming, or that more outlets without ownership limitations guarantee more programming variety. In one case study of the Los Angeles market, where television stations increasingly have come under common ownership, the quantity of children's programming in the market decreased (as stations stopped competing with each other and segmented the market), and the quantity of original children's programming declined precipitously (as commonly owned stations repurposed children's programming from their sister stations and affiliated cable networks).

Indeed, a company may prefer to air a show of poorer quality that the company produces itself than to air a higher-quality, independent show. The same company may continue to air its own show despite low ratings, solely because it can reuse the programming. Programming in such situations does not have to be the best to succeed, as would be necessary in a competitive market. It merely has to be good enough to prevent viewers from abandoning television altogether. Finally, as illustrated by the Letterman-Koppel example, relying on market forces will leave underserved those markets that advertisers see as less desirable from a demographic standpoint. Society should not have to tolerate a media market in which programming is aimed almost exclusively at eighteen- to thirty-five-year old white males. Increasing the diversity of owners by limiting horizontal and vertical integration creates a greater likelihood that minority demographics will be served. Studies show that minority owners are more likely to program for minorities and that local owners are more likely to program for the local community than the national demographic.

Accordingly, the Supreme Court has consistently recognized that the broadcast and cable markets are not functioning free markets; rather, they are a system of government broadcast monopolies and "natural" cable monopolies. A privileged few are free to make programming decisions based not on free market principles and genuine audience interest, but on the ability to control captive customers.

We Must Distinguish Between Toasters and Information

Ronald Reagan's FCC chairman, Mark Fowler, famously said that television was "simply another appliance . . . a toaster with pictures." While Chairman Fowler can be complimented for having a direct and clear philosophy, he was utterly wrong in his belief.

Why do the American people have an interest in maintaining a competitive and diverse mass media? Antitrust law applies to the media, so why does the public need more protection? Since the founding of the nation, believers in our democratic form of government have argued that the public must remain informed of the news and stimulated with debate. No less a figure than James Madison, who regarded deliberative debate as a necessary element of democracy, articulated the principle that the government has an obligation to protect the marketplace of ideas when private interests threaten it.

In the words of the Supreme Court, "[a]t the heart of the First Amendment lies the principle that each person should decide for him or herself the ideas and beliefs deserving of expression, consideration and adherence. Our political system and cultural life rest upon this ideal." As a result, Congress and the Supreme Court have identified the maintenance of a competitive media marketplace as a "government purpose of the highest order."

Because the broadcast media remain the primary means by which the public receives information and entertainment, the government has a vital interest in maintaining competition and diverse ownership in this sector. Proponents of deregulation respond that competition has replaced the need for regulation. When these ownership rules were made, they argue, three networks were broadcasting and most Americans had access to only a handful of local channels. Now anyone can subscribe to systems that provide access to hundreds of channels. This argument misses the mark for several reasons. As discussed above, Americans depend on their local broadcasters and newspapers for local news. To allow local news to become dominated by a single provider would undermine democracy as much as a monopoly on national news would. Even without an owner consciously slanting the news, the deterioration of local news coverage from concentration justifies ownership limits that preserve multiple local outlets. More important, the First Amendment command that the government ensure a robust marketplace of ideas is, like the world of communication itself, an expanding ideal, not a minimum threshold. The continued availability of newspapers did not negate the need to ensure diversity in broadcasting, nor did the continuation of broadcasting negate the need to preserve diversity in cable. Rather, as the Supreme Court has stressed, the government has a duty to preserve more than a "rump" information market, and should instead promote "the widest possible dissemination of information from diverse and antagonistic sources."

The Threat Is Real, If Subtle

Proponents of deregulation make their argument in a *reductio ad absurdum*. Because information cannot be completely suppressed, it follows that fears of media concentration are unfounded. At the FCC hearing adopting the deregulation order, GOP Commissioner Kathleen Abernathy mocked "speculation about hypothetical media monopolies intent on exercising some type of Vulcan mind control over the American people."

This demand for absolute proof that news outlets will be influenced in all cases by the economic interests of the news outlets' parent companies creates a diversion, as Commissioner Abernathy failed to confront the realities of public debate served by the First Amendment. The question is not whether information is somehow discoverable, but whether the public at large has sufficient information to stimulate debate on public affairs and to ensure an informed and active electorate.

As a practical matter, because the public generally relies on daily newspapers and broadcast media for its news and entertainment, these outlets generally set the public agenda. As for irrefutable evidence, rarely do corporate heads send notices directing their staffs to cover only one side of a story or to omit coverage of an issue. As with all social-policy issues, the question of cause and effect is subtle, and it is not always easy to measure it empirically. Further, the impact on our news and culture from large media owners is many-layered. Nevertheless, the Supreme Court has found that the FCC can, and indeed must, consider the effects of concentration on public discourse.

Moreover, there is powerful evidence that ownership influences media coverage in both gross and surreptitious ways. A survey by the Pew Research Center and the *Columbia Journalism Review* (CJR) demonstrated that 25 percent of local and national journalists have intentionally avoided newsworthy stories, the same number have softened the tone of stories to benefit the interests of their news organizations, and 41 percent have done both. Of those surveyed, "one-third (35 percent) say news that would hurt the financial interests of a news organization often or sometimes goes unreported, while slightly fewer (29 percent) say the same about stories that could adversely affect advertisers."

Indicative of the subterranean nature of the problem, 26 percent of local reporters in the Pew-CJR study believed that a directive to avoid a story for other reasons was really a pretext to protect the financial interests of the corporate owner. Anecdotal examples abound to support the link between the size and identity of a station's owner with that station's content and quality. For example, newspapers' and cable news' coverage of the broadcast provisions of the 1996 Telecommunications Act directly correlated with whether the corporate parent derived significant income from broadcasting properties. Those that derived significant income from broadcasting properties supported the measure; those that did not opposed it. Similarly, local radio-station managers sponsored prowar rallies when they suspected that their efforts would be greeted with welcoming telephone calls from corporate headquarters that invested mightily in shoring up links with the current administration.

Furthermore, although they may be rare, centralized decisions do occur, and the instances that become public should raise concerns about what happens behind closed doors. For example, at one talk-radio station, a corporate policy prohibits airing any callers who sound "old" in order to better target the more profitable twenty-five- to fifty-four-year-old age group. There is also strong evidence that General Electric exercised corporate influence over its subsidiary, NBC, not to cover governmental investigations of GE's pollution of the Hudson River.

Owners may also make central decisions to support government policy as a means of currying favor, further compromising the critical role of the media in democracy. For example, Clear Channel management sent a list of 160 songs to its stations that were deemed inappropriate for air time after 9/11, among them antiviolence songs such as John Lennon's "Imagine" and Bob Dylan's "Blowin' in the Wind." After a member of the Dixie Chicks criticized the Bush administration's Iraq policy at a concert, radio stations owned by Cumulus and Clear Channel banned the group from airplay. Although the Dixie Chicks have survived (after lead singer Natalie Maines apologized for her remarks), the chilling message to less popular musicians was quite clear: "toe the corporate party line, or else."

Examples of other Western democracies that do not have ownership limitations provide lessons of the danger of concentrated ownership to democratic discourse.

In Canada, for example, CanWest, which owns more than 14 metropolitan daily newspapers, 120 community newspapers, 16 television stations, 7 networks, and an Internet news portal, ordered all its daily newspapers to carry the same national editorials as of December 2001 and prohibited editorials or letters to the editors that contradicted an approved editorial on Palestinian-Israeli relations. In Italy, Prime Minister Silvio Berlusconi's ownership of the three commercial Italian broadcast networks (as well as his influence over the content of the three government-owned networks) gives him effective control over news programs, which inevitably support the position of the government.

Finally, politicians who set national and local policy believe that broadcasters are in a unique position to control their access to constituents. They therefore will rarely oppose policies favored by the broadcast industry. Consider again the TV spectrum giveaway in the 1996 Telecommunications Act, which gave broadcasters $70 billion in spectrum for free. Bob Dole, then a candidate for the Republican nomination for president, opposed the giveaway. On the eve of the Iowa caucus, Dole received a letter from the owner of several Iowa television stations threatening to support other candidates if he did not change his stand. A few days later, Dole withdrew his opposition.

As broadcast outlets concentrate in the hands of fewer interests, these few owners wield a proportionately greater influence. When these owners are not merely broadcasters, but multinational, vertically integrated corporations with a multiplicity of interests, the ability of these few media giants to shape national policy through their direct influence on legislators (at both the national and the local level) becomes frightening indeed. Decentralizing ownership defuses the threat to democracy. Maximizing the number of media owners does not eliminate the influence of economic interests, but at least multiple owners will have different interests. In a world with many media owners, if one refuses to cover a newsworthy story, rivals will do so instead, and the public will ultimately be informed. If a news manager is fired for certain practices, he or she may be able to find a job elsewhere. But if a few owners with similar economic interests dominate the media, stories will go uncovered and will essentially be suppressed.

Structural Rules Facilitate the First Amendment

Those who oppose ownership restrictions accuse opponents of attempting to control content. If a station owner supports the Iraq war and therefore chooses to ban the Dixie Chicks from having airtime, the First Amendment protects this choice; no one has claimed otherwise. Rather, what the U.S. Supreme Court and supporters of ownership regulation have pointed out is that the First Amendment also requires that no one person or oligarchy can act as censor for the rest of the country. Ownership restrictions thus protect the rights, assured under the First Amendment, of broadcasters to make independent editorial choices and of the public to have a diversity of views.

Media ownership rules are like a breakwater or anchor that keeps some boundaries on the decision-making process. They preserve a minimum level of competition sufficient to encourage the production of quality news and entertainment, serving diverse segments of our society without imposing content mandates. More important, they protect our society from corporate censorship as inimical to our democratic society as government censorship. At a minimum, if one corporation has a conflict of interest with respect to a story, at least another outlet is available to investigate it. As a result, media ownership rules free those who depend upon the media—not merely performers like the Dixie Chicks or others in the entertainment industry, but politicians as well—to speak their minds. First Amendment analysis recognizes that even small threats to speech can have a chilling effect on speech.

This effect is no less powerful when the private sector is doing the threatening.

Notes

1. A portion of this chapter appeared in *Communications Lawyer*, Fall 2003, at pp. 12, 18–22 under the title: "More Than 'A Toaster With Pictures': Defending Media Ownership Limits," by Cheryl A. Leanza and Harold Feld.
2. The authors served as counsel to the Prometheus Radio Project.

RECLAIMING THE FIRST AMENDMENT: LEGAL, FACTUAL, AND ANALYTIC SUPPORT FOR LIMITS ON MEDIA OWNERSHIP

MARK COOPER

Michael Powell, Chairman of the Federal Communications Commission (FCC), has complained about the firestorm of criticism and the political movement aimed at overturning the new media ownership rules,[1] remarking: "The issue is very complex; have you heard the opposition express their criticism in a complex way? No. It's a lot easier to blast the messenger than deal with the substance of the issue."[2] He defends his Commission's broadcast ownership Rule and Order of June 2, 2003, by claiming that they are a modest "recalibration"[3] or "surgery,"[4] made necessary by the Courts and justified by the evidence.[5] Throughout, Powell remained boldly unconcerned about upholding the public interest.[6]

This chapter shows that the Chairman is wrong on all counts. His complaint ignores almost 1,000 pages of detailed, complex legal and empirical analysis filed in the proceeding by citizen interveners[7] that show the Commission's order misinterpreted the law, ignored the facts, and came up with an analytic scheme that produces absurd results.

Notwithstanding Chairman Powell's desire to treat the media ownership rules as a narrow legal and economic matter inside the Washington beltway, for two years he struggled to build a record on which to implement his agenda. This chapter shows that he failed. A federal agency is supposed to implement the law as Congress intended by applying reasoned analysis to the facts before it. The FCC's rewrite of the media ownership rules did none of the above. Demonstrating the legal, factual and analytic flaws in the Commission's order provides the basis for conceiving alternative public policies to promote the public interest in the media markets subject to the commission's jurisdiction.

The Law

For almost sixty years, since the landmark ruling in *Associated Press*, the Supreme Court has expressed a bold aspiration for the First Amendment in the electronic age. The Court has declared that "the widest possible dissemination of information from diverse and antagonistic sources is essential to the welfare of the public."[8] The Court has drawn on the principles of the Founders, holding that diversity and antagonism are fundamental forces that support democracy.[9] Moreover, the First Amendment is not limited to preventing government from impeding the free flow of ideas. As Justice Hugo Black wrote, "[s]urely a command that the government itself shall not im-pede the free flow of ideas does not afford non-governmental combinations a ref-uge if they impose restraints upon that constitutionally guaranteed freedom."[10]

While *Associated Press* was an antitrust, newspaper case, the Court has applied it to every form of electronic media involving regulatory law. The statement with respect to television broadcast media can be found in *Red Lion*. "It is the purpose of the First Amendment to preserve an uninhibited marketplace of ideas in which truth will ultimately prevail, rather than to countenance monopolization of that market, whether it be by the government itself or a private licensee."[11] In *Red Lion*, the Court elaborated that "the 'public interest' in broadcasting clearly encompasses the presentation of vigorous debate of controversial issues of importance and concern to the public"[12] and "the right of the public to receive suitable access to social, political, esthetic, moral and other ideas and experiences."[13]

In its June 2003 ruling on media ownership, the FCC abandoned this bold aspiration for the First Amendment. In its place, we are given a "leak out" theory of the First Amendment (an idea articulated by the broadcasters that I will take up shortly). The Order in the broadcast ownership proceeding states: "In the context evaluating viewpoint diversity, this approach reflects a measure of the likelihood that some particular viewpoint might be censored or foreclosed, i.e. blocked from transmission to the public."[14] This limited defense of First Amendment freedoms marks a stark contrast with the Supreme Court rulings. Gone is the proposition that "the greater the diversity of ownership in a particular area, the less chance there is that a single person or group can have an inordinate effect, in a political, editorial, or similar programming sense, on public opinion at the regional level."[15] Gone with it is the obligation to promote diversity "on the theory that diversification of mass media ownership serves the public interest by promoting diversity of programs and service viewpoints, as well as by preventing undue concentration of economic power."[16]

The narrow, unbalanced discourse that is likely to result is of no concern to the FCC. The Commission states unequivocally: "Nor is it particularly troubling that media properties do not always, or even frequently, avail themselves to others who may hold contrary opinions. Nothing requires them to do so, nor is it necessarily healthy for public debate to pretend as though all ideas are of equal value entitled to equal airing."[17]

For the FCC, public freedoms of speech will be subjected purely to market forces. Gone is the recognition that "Truth and understanding are not wares like peanuts and potatoes and so, the incidence of restrains upon the promotion of truth through the denial of access to the basis for understanding calls into play considerations very different from comparable restraints in a cooperative enterprise having *merely, a commercial aspect.*"[18] With it goes the observation that "Congress may, in the regulation of broadcasting, constitutionally pursue values other than efficiency—including in particular diversity in programming, for which diversity of ownership is perhaps an aspirational but surely not an irrational proxy—and therefore not unconstitutional—for the Congress to prefer having in the aggregate more voices heard."[19] The FCC would have none of this. Each of the existing limits on the concentration of media ownership was overturned because it impeded the efficiency gained from greater concentration of ownership. The FCC refused to bring back serious limits on ownership in pursuit of these noneconomic goals. In short, the FCC abandoned analysis from the position of a citizen speaker in which "public discussion is a political duty"[20] and "speech concerning public affairs is more than self-expression; it is the essence of self-government."[21]

The courts have long held that public rights to broadcast speech must be protected because of constraints on the capacity of the airwaves. Starting with a 1943 radio case, the Supreme Court found that "its facilities are limited; they are not available to all who may wish to use them; the radio spectrum simply is not large enough to accommodate everybody."[22] Thirty-five years later, the Court again pointed to the disproportionate relationship between potential speakers and electronic voices. "Because of the problem of interference between broadcast signals, a finite number of frequencies can be used productively; *this number is far exceeded by the number of persons wishing to broadcast to the public.*"[23]

Here we must not fall into the trap of narrowing the First Amendment to spectrum scarcity, however. Opponents of a bold aspiration for the First Amendment would like to see spectrum scarcity as the sole basis for public policy, so that they can declare that an abundance of cable and satellite channels are available and thus escape their public-interest obligations. The claim is wrong because this is a listener/viewer analysis, not a speaker analysis. Even if hundreds of channels are available to citizens as listeners, this situation does not empower them as speakers. In fact, because cable and satellite owners control almost all of the channels on the system, they are a single powerful voice that may do more to distort discourse than enrich it. It is not the scarcity of spectrum that matters, but the scarcity of voices. In a nation of almost three hundred million people, the number of channels is still far exceeded by the number of persons wishing to broadcast to the public. Never once did the Commission present an analysis that looks at the population as potential speakers.

The Commission's radical redefinition of the First Amendment adopts a view of the public interest under the Communications Act that the broadcasters' have unsuccessfully pressed for decades. The only new thing in the broadcasters' argument is its extreme nature and the fact that the FCC bought it hook, line, and sinker. The expert witness for the broadcasters who authored a dozen studies for the major networks, declared, "What really matters with ideas from a political point of view is whether they can be suppressed. But given the importance of interpersonal communications, it is extremely difficult to suppress ideas—they can "leak out" even through small or economically minor media outlets."[24]

For the broadcasters, the First Amendment is reduced to simple economics. They reject the notion that Congress can pursue public policies that the courts have upheld. The only expert proffered by the broadcasters asks, "Why should the government seek to promote local content as opposed to, and especially at the expense of, any other category of idea?"[25] From this perspective, citizens engaging in political debate disappear, having been devoured by consumers enjoying entertainment. "[T]he Commission's sometime preoccupation with news and public affairs, as distinct from entertainment programming . . . makes even less sense than localism. First, broadcast news is entertainment—it has to be, at least in part, in order to attract audiences that can be sold to advertisers." By this logic, the Communications Act disappears and the Commission becomes superfluous, having been devoured by economics interests and antitrust. "Whether ownership concentration poses harm to competition or to consumers is precisely the question on which the Commission should focus, and it is exactly the question upon which the antitrust laws and their enforcers focus."[26]

In response to the FCC's actions and the logic of its thinking, we have a grassroots rebellion because this "leak out," elitist, "economics-above-all" view of the First Amendment offends the sense and sensibility of the American people on the left and right. The groups on the left and the right may not believe that all ideas are of equal value, but they sure as heck believe their "social, political, esthetic, moral and other ideas" should have an equal opportunity to be aired.

The Facts

Mass Media and Democracy

The evidentiary record before the Commission presents a strong case for a bold aspiration for the First Amendment and consequently limits on media ownership.

The objective of promoting diversity is vital for a number of reasons. First, diversity promotes democracy by exposing citizens to a broader range of views. Second, the mass media influence the agenda of public-policy issues and the public's perception of those issues.[27] Third, the agenda setting and influence of perception that takes place during election campaigns frames issues and influences voter behavior.[28] The special role of television in providing information and influencing elections is well documented.[29]

It has long been recognized that print and broadcast media have unique economic characteristics.[30] To the extent that economics is a consideration, economic competition in commercial mass-media markets cannot assure diversity and antagonism.[31] The dictates of mass audiences create a largest market-share/lowest-common-denominator ethic that undercuts the ability to deliver culturally diverse programming, locally oriented programming, and public interest programming.[32] The tendency to avoid controversy and seek a lowest common denominator is augmented by the presence of advertisers who express their preferences in the market. News and public-affairs programming are particularly vulnerable to these economic pressures, because concentration drains resources from journalistic endeavors and compromises the quality of the programming.[33]

Given the profit-maximizing incentive to recover high fixed costs from the largest audiences, media target the majority. Minorities are underserved and suffer from a form of tyranny of the majority in media markets.[34] Greater concentration results in less diversity of ownership and diversity of ownership across geographic, ethnic and gender lines is correlated with diversity of programming. To put the matter simply, minority owners are more likely to present minority points of view[35] just as females are more likely to present female points of view,[36] in the speakers, formats and content they put forward. Other empirical evidence clearly suggests that concentration—fewer independent owners—in media markets has a negative effect on diversity.[37] The tyranny of the majority in media markets is linked to the tyranny of the majority in politics because the media are the primary means of political communication.

One of the central benefits of promoting decentralized and diverse media markets is to provide a self-checking function on the media. The media need to be accountable to the public, but, in our political system that function cannot, as a general matter, be provided by government action. It can best be provided by the media itself, as long as there is vigorous antagonism between sources of news and information. Concentration of ownership undermines the watchdog function.[38] The market tends to produce too little, from the societal point of view.[39] Abuses are less likely to be uncovered and more likely to occur because the deterrent of the threat of exposure will be diminished.[40] Further, conglomeration reduces institutional diversity, undermining vigorous investigative journalism.[41] The ongoing trend of economic integration and cross-media ownership in the industry and the potential for a substantial increase in these developments raises a qualitatively new type of problem—the potential for institutional conflicts of interest arises.[42]

The central fact that all of these discussions share is that market forces provide neither adequate incentives to produce the high quality media product, nor adequate incentive to distribute enough diverse content to meet consumer and citizen needs.[43] The weak competition that results from the economic structure of media markets allows owners to use excess profits to pursue their personal agendas. The claim that ownership of the media does not matter to the selection and presentation of content is not plausible. The empirical evidence on news coverage of events,[44] the ongoing battle between the networks over bias in reporting, and the use of political advertising[45] reinforces the longstanding opinion of the courts that ownership matters a great deal[46] and is a good proxy for diversity.[47]

The specific concern with localism in mass-media policy also finds support in the research literature. In order for the media to meet the needs of these groups, it must inform and mobilize them. That these needs have traditionally been centered in localism is understandable, since the primary referent for identity and community has traditionally been and remains significantly local. Concentration of national and local markets into national chains reinforces the tendencies of media owners to ignore local needs.[48]

The Current State of Media Markets

While many in the debate over limits on media ownership asserted that market structure analysis based on economic concepts could not be used for diversity analysis purposes, the FCC has two grounds on which it could argue that this type of analysis is necessary. First, it has an obligation to conduct competition analysis under the statute. Second, the Court has accepted a voice-count approach but wanted it to be more rigorous. Citizen interveners argued that market-structure analysis within the antitrust tradition is a starting point for the unified analytic framework the Court demanded. The problem is not in the concept of market structure analysis but in the fact that the FCC butchered the implementation.

To the extent that communications policy chooses to rely on the analysis of commercial media markets, especially if different types of media are combined, caution is necessary and should be expressed in the form of rigorous analysis and high standards. Public policy should err in favor of more voices, which translates into greater diversity, to reflect the unique importance and role of media in promoting the robust exchange of views on which democratic dialogue and debate depends.

For the purposes of assessing media markets, industrial-organization analysis focuses on the number and size of firms in the market. For media, market-structure analysis must start with the audience that each of the media outlets retains. Just as market power is grounded in the size of the market an individual firm gains, so, too, media influence and the ability to be heard, is a function of the audience.

The evidentiary record before the FCC shows that the mass media have not experienced an Internet or broadband revolution. Most people still get their news and information from TV and newspapers. Further, there is no simple common "currency" by which TV viewing and newspaper reading can be measured. In other words, is a half-hour of TV worth an inch of newspaper space? Citizens do not easily substitute between these media, making it even more difficult to compare them. Rigorous analysis must recognize the distinct product markets and the importance of newspapers and television.

We should not be surprised to find that people use different media in different ways to meet different needs. The media rely on different senses and mental faculties to different degrees. People spend vastly different amounts of time in different media environments, consume services under different circumstances, and pay for them in different ways. They have different content, offered by different means, and they differ widely in their impact and effect. Similarly, the various media are based on different business models and address different advertising markets.

Television provides high impact announcements of news and events. Newspapers supply in-depth analysis of local news. Radio regurgitates wire stories in extremely short sound bites, primarily when people are driving to and from work. The Internet has not changed this pattern substantially. Different media have different mixes of news and information. The traditional electronic mass media, radio and television, are used for both news and entertainment in equal measures. In contrast, newspapers are predominantly a source of news and information and much less a source of entertainment. Four times as many people say that they use newspapers for information as say that they look to newspapers for entertainment. The Internet falls between the two extremes; just under twice as many people say they use it for information rather than entertainment.

Claims that Americans are turning away from TV for news are not supported by the evidence. For national news, TV is dominant, with 55 to 60 percent of the respondents citing it as their primary source of news. Newspapers are second, with 25–30 percent. Radio is third, with 10 percent. The Internet is a distant fourth with only 5–10 percent citing it. These percentages have been stable since 1996, when the Internet began its major penetration of American homes. When it comes to local news, however, newspapers play a much larger role, while television (particularly cable TV) and the Internet decline in importance.[49]

Econometric studies show little substitution between the media. Much of the FCC's previous analysis has focused on entertainment and advertising markets, but even here it did not find a great deal of substitutability between the media. Thus the evidence before the Commission now shows that news and information is a distinct product market and that each of the media is a distinct product.[50]

It is also critical to recognize that different media deliver their products in different markets. Broadcast stations and newspapers are predominantly local sources.

Certainly, when it comes to issues like elections for local and congressional offices and public-policy issues like school board elections, first responder services (fire, policy, emergency), and similar policies, like local economic growth, newspapers and TV are dominant local sources.

Using standard antitrust market definitions and analytic principles, we find that lax First Amendment policy implementation and weak antitrust enforcement have resulted in local media markets in America that are shockingly concentrated. Market shares of the firms are used to calculate an index called the HHI (Hirxhman-Herfindahl Index). If there were ten equal-sized firms in a market, the HHI would be 1,000, and the market would be considered unconcentrated. Any HHI above 1,000 is considered concentrated. If the HHI is above 1,800, with the equivalent of fewer than six equal-sized firms, the market is considered highly concentrated.

By these standards, every local television, radio, and newspaper market in the country is already concentrated. Approximately 95 percent are highly concentrated. The average HHI index falls well up into the highly concentrated range. Because only half of all local TV stations provide news and only about one-third of local radio stations provide news, the concentration of the production of local news is likely to be substantially greater than the concentration of entertainment. Newspaper markets, now often near-monopolies in most cities, are even more highly concentrated.

In 1980, the average United States city had fewer than four TV stations producing news and two newspapers. Today, the average is still fewer than four TV stations and fewer than two newspapers. The total number of newspapers in the country has declined. Plus, the number of radio stations providing news has declined.

These trends become even more pronounced if we look at the availability of media on a per capita (or per household) basis. This is much closer to a speaker's analysis. Describing the availability of electronic voices on a per capita basis gives an indication of the opportunity that an individual has to be heard and to influence the opinions of his or her fellow citizens through electronic media. At best, counting the number of owners, there has been slow growth in the past forty years, but most of that occurred between 1960 and 1980. Since 1980, the number of media owners per household declined in all ten radio markets and in seven of the ten television markets. It has certainly dropped for newspapers as well.

In an opinion piece on the FCC's new rules, FCC Chairman Michael Powell identified seventeen cable and satellite networks that, he believes, compete with the broadcast networks.[51] He failed to notice that thirteen of these are owned by the same corporations that own the networks and two are owned by a firm with a substantial ownership interest in one of the major network owners. The FCC *Order* is riddled with similar observations that fail to recognize the nature of the media market.

All the national broadcast networks are owned by five vertically integrated video conglomerates. As Bernstein Research recently put it, "a study of the December ratings from Neilsen Media suggests that we are beginning to see a rebuilding of the old programming oligopoly when cable and broadcast network station viewing are combined . . . . Together, the five companies controlled about a 75% share of prime time viewing, not including their nonconsolidated partnerships like A&E, Court TV and Comedy Central."[52] The February 2004 effort by Comcast to acquire ABC/Disney only underscores how potent the drive for vertical integration is.

The domination of the television marketplace by these five corporations does not stop with just these broadcast and cable networks. The suggestion that "by setting a slightly revised national television ownership limit, the FCC will help the networks attract and maintain quality programming"[53] does not jibe with viewing the statistics. Using their rights to carriage, the parent corporations of the broadcasters have been able to capture approximately two-thirds of the cable prime-time audience.[54] *They are not losing viewers to cable; they are shifting their delivery of programming from over-the-air to through-the-wire.*

The corporations that would be strengthened by the new rules already account for three-quarters of America's viewing. The FCC's own statistics show that they own all of prime time's twenty most popular cable programming services[55] and nineteen of the top twenty most widely available cable networks.[56] We arrive at a similar conclusion when we examine writing budgets and program expenditures. These are already thoroughly dominated by the network owners. The five network owners already account for about three-quarters of the television market by any measure.

In light of these facts, the claim that "producers and creators of television shows are often lured to the greater creative freedom of pay TV" misrepresents the programming decision-making process. The decision to create and place programs on free or pay TV is a business decision controlled by a handful of large corporations that dominate both pay and free TV. The choice is made by the network owners to generate the maximum revenues.

The courts have suggested that the FCC should adopt a consistent methodology for voice counts for all of the rules. The case can be made that TV and newspapers play such important and unique roles in civic discourse that they should be kept separate. Even adding together television, newspaper and radio outlets, and taking into account lesser outlets, I find that 95 percent of local markets are concentrated and 50 percent are highly concentrated. There are only a handful of markets in which a merger between the leading newspaper and, as discussed below, a large television station would not drive the market into the highly concentrated range.

The FCC Analysis

In its proceedings on the ownership rules, the FCC failed to conduct rigorous analysis or to set high standards. It did not look at the actual market shares of the media outlets and set standards far below even the antitrust guidelines. The narrow interpretation of the First Amendment played a key part in this outcome. By adopting the "leak out" theory of the First Amendment, the FCC refused to consider the audience of an outlet. It assumed, contrary to fact, that each outlet within a medium is equal to every other outlet in that medium. It counted all outlets, regardless of whether they actually provide news and information. It weighted the outlets in a manner that gives radio an importance it has not had in a quarter of a century and that the Internet might not achieve in the next quarter-century. The result is a surreal map of media space.

The analytic framework that underlies the relaxation of the rules includes the following types of absurd assumptions. In the New York City market, for example,

- Shop at Home Incorporated TV and the Dutchess Community College TV are each 50 percent more important than the *New York Times*.

- Multicultural Radio Broadcasting Inc. (with three radio stations) also has more weight than the *New York Times*.

- Shop at Home Incorporated TV and the Dutchess Community College TV are each equal to ABC in weight.

- Univision TV has more weight than ABC Inc., NBC/GE, Viacom or News Corp., even when Viacom's and News Corp.'s radio stations and newspapers are included. Univision is three times as important as the *New York Times*.

- The Internet counts more than the top eight TV stations.

- Radio and weekly newspapers are equal to television in importance.

Having botched the market structural analysis by assuming markets were vastly less concentrated than they actually are, the FCC then proceeded to adopt a ridiculously low standard for concentration. In over half the scenarios for broadcast-newspaper mergers, the FCC has offered blanket approval to mergers that would violate the Merger Guidelines by a substantial margin. The result, had it become law, would have been a virtual repeal of the media ownership limits.

- *A near total ban on the cross-ownership* of TV stations and newspapers in the same market is replaced with a rule that grants blanket approval to TV-newspaper cross-ownership in all market with more than four TV stations and allows waivers for mergers in markets with fewer than three TV stations. Over 97 percent of all Americans live in cities where *blanket approval* of newspaper-TV cross-ownership will be granted.

- The old duopoly rule that would have allowed about a hundred duopolies in markets serving 50 percent of the country was replaced by a rule that allows triopolies in markets serving about a quarter of the nation and several hundred duopolies in markets serving another 50 percent of the nation.

- Broadcast networks would be allowed to increase their ownership of local stations from the current limit of stations reaching 35 percent of the national total to 45 percent (39 percent pursuant to subsequent congressional action).

The media market structure in many of these localities would become greatly distorted because of a lack of diversity. On average, the number-one newspaper has a 65 percent market share, which is generally enough that monopoly power is deemed possible under antitrust laws. The second newspaper has an average share of 19 percent. Television markets are somewhat less concentrated in these markets, but still highly concentrated. The leading station has a market share of 44 percent, the number-two station a market share of 25 percent. Thus, the dominant player would have over half the combined TV-newspaper market; the number two would have less than a quarter of the combined market.

The absurdity of the results and the clear violation of the jurisprudence should make the new rules difficult to justify as reasoned analysis. The FCC stumbles badly when it tries to put forward an analytic rationale for the rules. The most interesting contradiction comes in the schizophrenic treatment of audiences. The reality of media markets that the Commission denies in its new rules breaks through in its discussion of why it must abandon the old rules. The FCC justifies getting rid of the ban on cross-ownership on the basis of a discussion of the market share and "influence" of the various media. Yet, when it comes to writing the new rule, it declares that market share and influence do not matter.

For example, in a paragraph labeled "Benefits of Common-Ownership," the FCC claims that cross ownership yields diversity benefits, stating the following: "A recent study, for example, determined that, on average "grandfathered" newspaper-owned television stations, during earlier news day parts, led the market and delivered 43% more audience share than the second ranked station in the market and 193% more audience than the third ranked station in the market."[57]

In a paragraph labeled "Harm to Diversity Caused by the Rule," the Commission claims that the newspaper cross-ownership ban harmed diversity. It again made direct reference to market shares: "Newspapers and local over-the-air television broadcasters alike have suffered audience declines in recent years. In the broadcast area, commenters have reported declines in the ratings of existing outlets as more media enter the marketplace. . . . Broadcast groups owned by GE, Disney, Gannett, Hearst-Argyle and Belo have lost 10 to 15% of their aggregate audience in the past five years."[58]

It is not the number of stations that matters most, but the loss of market share or audience that is the driving force in the argument. "We must consider the impact of our rules on the strength of media outlets, particularly those that are primary sources of local news and information, as well as on the number of independently owned outlets."[59] How does one measure the strength of media outlets, but by their audience size, which determines the earning capacity of the outlet? The FCC goes on to assert that "Given the growth in available media outlets, the influence of any single viewpoint source is sharply attenuated."[60] How does one measure the influence of an outlet, but by its audience size? The FCC presents no measure of influence or evidence of its "sharp attenuation" other than market share and audience data.

Yet, when it came to writing the new rule, the Commission refused to consider the audience or market share of the media outlet.

The FCC also tries to justify abandoning market shares with an economic argument. The audience shares of the dominant mass media do not matter, we are told, because entry into the market is easy and the production of news can be expanded at little marginal cost. This claim is simply wrong, contradicted by the evidence before the Commission and even by the Commission's own words.

The Order states that "This point has particular force when dealing with competition in the marketplace of ideas because media outlets can rapidly expand their distribution of content (including local news and current affairs) at very low marginal cost." Yet, in the discussion of the need to relax the duopoly rule, the Commission reaches exactly the opposite conclusion, stating, "Moreover, rising news production costs and other factors may cause broadcasters to turn to less costly programming options."[61]

The FCC might claim that it is addressing the marginal cost of expanding news production for stations already doing news, which it deems to be low. At least for these stations the marginal cost of expanding output, although not low, would not involve starting a whole news department. If this were the argument on which the FCC was relying, it should have counted only broadcast stations that currently provide news in its index and not those stations that do not. It did not make this distinction. However, the actual language used by the FCC to describe the cost of news production will not allow it to get away with this dodge. There is no doubt that the difficulty and expense of news production stems from its variable costs, not its fixed costs.[62]

The failure to conduct a rational market-structure analysis for purposes of the cross ownership rule draws the FCC into a broad range of contradictions with the other rules at the level of policy. Based on sound market-structure analysis of the local and national television markets, the FCC concludes that the dominant firms—the top four local stations and the four major national networks—should not be allowed to merge with each other. The FCC identifies a host of dangers in such mergers and little potential public interest benefit from them.

According to the FCC, such mergers would increase economic market power,[63] create dominant firms that are much larger than their nearest rivals[64] who could distort the market for inputs available to other distributors of content,[65] and diminish the incentive to compete.[66] Furthermore, there is likely to be little public-interest benefit from dominant firm mergers, because the merging parties are likely to be healthy and already engaged in the production of news and information products.[67]

Each and every one of these reasons given for banning mergers between dominant entities in TV markets is a valid reason to ban a merger between dominant TV stations and newspapers in the local media market. A merger between a dominant TV station and a dominant newspaper results in an entity that dwarfs its nearest competitors in terms of control of news production. The dominant firm would control a large percentage of the reporters in the market. It would also have a sufficiently large cross-media presence to diminish the antagonism between print and video media, thereby reducing competition. It would have a diminished incentive to compete (especially across media types), an increased incentive to withhold product, and it would be able to leverage its market power in cross promotion. The public interest benefit is likely to be small because these are the most profitable entities in their local market and not likely to add product that promotes the public interest. Indeed, the synergies sought are likely to diminish the total resources available for news production.

The Commission concludes that news and information are the proper objects of public policy,[68] but then it fails to base its rules on an analysis of that programming. Virtually all of its qualitative analysis deals with entertainment. When the Commission conducted quantitative analysis, it included all outlets, regardless of whether the outlet distributed news and information programming. Implementing its conclusion that news and information are the focal point of analysis would have corrected many of the problems in its empirical work.

As noted, the FCC can insist that if it is to offer a coherent analytic framework, it must combine outlets and audiences of different media types in some manner. It must find a way to weight the various media. Unfortunately, the FCC got the media weights wrong. The agency failed to ask the proper questions in its survey and chose not to conduct a second survey.[69] It then combines questions that distort the weights. It cites other surveys to support some of its analytic conclusions, but does not notice that those same surveys contradicted its much more important assumptions and choices.

The FCC attributes an importance to radio that it has not had in decades. It over-weights the Internet and weekly newspapers. The weights produce results that defy common sense because the FCC conducted sloppy research and selective analysis of the data it consulted. It asked the wrong questions and failed to correct the mistakes.

Conclusion

Contrary to the claims of the FCC, the FCC should have upheld the existing rules. The Court did not invite the Commission to reinterpret the First Amendment; it asked it to do a better job at justifying its rules. The "empirical gap" to which the D.C. Appeals Court referred in the *Sinclair* decision has been closed.[70] The hard data and evidence on the record does not support the rules the FCC has proposed. A set of rules that restricts merger activity to a small number of mergers in a small number of markets is well justified on the basis of the empirical data analyzed within the frame work of a rigorous approach to market structure analysis informed by high First Amendment standards.

For example, in the case of *Sinclair v. Federal Communications Commission*, the D.C. Appeals Court held "that the Commission had failed to demonstrate that its exclusion of non-broadcast media from the eight voices exception 'is necessary in the public interest.'"[71] Why didn't the FCC include newspapers and radios in its voice count for the rule that limited the number of markets in which one owner could hold licenses to more than one TV station (the duopoly rule)? The answer it could have given is now clear and supported overwhelmingly by the empirical evidence in the record:

- TV is the dominant source of news and information, while radio, newspapers, and the Internet are not good substitutes for TV.
- These other products do not belong in a TV voice-count analysis, and TV markets are already highly concentrated.
- The limits on TV mergers are well justified.

Similarly, the question posed by the review of the newspaper broadcast cross-ownership ban can be answered with a strong empirical statement. The Commission "seeks comments on whether and to what extent we should revise our cross-ownership rule that bars common ownership of a broadcast station and daily newspaper in the same market."

- Newspapers are the second-most important source of information and play a unique watchdog role, providing in-depth and investigative reporting.
- All newspaper markets are highly concentrated, and virtually all newspaper-TV markets are already concentrated.
- Newspaper-TV combinations should not be allowed in all but a handful of media markets because they would drive media concentration above already unacceptably high levels and would allow excessive control over the production of news content in local media markets.
- There would be neither balanced competition between combinations nor sufficient competition between newspapers to ensure the critical role that print journalism plays in civic discourse.

Postscript

The ruling by the United States Court of Appeals for the 3rd Circuit overturning the FCC's media ownership order closely follows the outline offered in this article. It constitutes a massive victory for opponents of media concentration, but it leaves critical issues unresolved.

The Court rejected the claims of the media corporations that ownership limits violate their First Amendment rights. It brushed aside their effort to replace the public interest standard for the First Amendment under the Communications Act with the much weaker antitrust principles of the Sherman Act.

The Court embraced the bold aspiration for the First Amendment, citing the most aggressive statements by the Supreme Court on preventing undue economic concentration. It defended ownership limits with a speaker, not a listener, analysis, reminding the broadcasters that the number of citizens who would like an electronic voice vastly exceeds the number of such voices available.

It reinforced this reasoning with a careful discussion of the nature of the media, focusing on the independent production of local news and public affairs, not national news or local restaurant reviews. It found that repackaging of news from one source for distribution through different media does not contribute to diversity. It differentiated the functions of media outlets—aggregation, distillations, depth, and accuracy—from the mere dissemination of individual, organizational, or governmental information or points of view or information. The Court found that the FCC lost touch with reality and abandoned all logic in assessing the importance of different types of media and sources of local news and information.

But, the Court accepted the approach of market-structure analysis and the concept of a diversity index to combine media that many progressives declared should not be used. It also rejected the position that a ban on mergers is necessary to protect the public interest. Indeed, the Court all but demanded that the FCC do market-structure analysis right—fix the media weights, count the eyeballs, and do the math. The Court retained control of the case, which means that this is the framework that will govern media ownership rules in the near future. Thus, the battle for rigorous market structure analysis is won.

The battle for high First Amendment standards has not yet been fought. The FCC adopted a "six equal-sized firms" standard for television markets and a "five equal-sized firms" standard for radio, and then the Commission assumed that all firms are equal, when they are not. The Court was properly outraged, but it took no position on the level at which the thresholds should be set. By recognizing the difference between the antitrust laws and the Communications Act, the Court opens the door to arguments on remand that the standard for the media should be higher.

Moreover, because it found that the FCC had failed to give the public adequate opportunity to comment on the market structure analysis, the Court instructed the FCC to properly notice the next diversity index before it presented its new rule to the Court. This ruling guarantees the public the opportunity to demand a higher standard and ensures the grassroots movement will have a highly visible target on which to focus its attention.

Notes

1. Federal Communications Commission, "Report and Order," *In the Matter of 2002 Biennial Regulatory Review—Review of the Commission's Broadcast Ownership Rules and Other Rules Adopted Pursuant to Section 202 of the Telecommunications Act of 1996, Cross Ownership of Broadcast Stations and Newspapers, Rules and Policies Concerning Multiple Ownership of Radio Broadcast Stations in Local Markets, Definition of Radio Markets*, MB Docket No. 02–277, MM Dockets 02–235, 01–317, 00–244, July 2, 2003[hereafter, *Order*].
2. Frank Ahrens, "'Soldier's Ethic' Guides Powell at the FCC," *Washington Post*, October 15, 2003, E-4.
3. *Order*, para. 9.
4. "Press Statement of Chairman Michael Powell," June 2, 2003.
5. Chairman Powell's claim that Court rulings in *Fox Television Stations, Inc.*, v. FCC, 280 F.3d 1027 [hereafter *Fox v. FCC*] and *Sinclair Broadcasting, Inc.* v. FCC, 284 F.3d 148 (D.C. Circ. 2002) [hereafter *Sinclair*] had the effect of "placing a high hurdle before the Commission for maintaining a given regulation," is particularly bothersome, since, as demonstrated in the *Brief for Citizen Petitioners and Interveners, Prometheus Radio Project, et al.*, v. FCC, October 21, 2003, at 18–27, the Commission had actually convinced the Court to not adopt the high hurdle to which the Chairman referred and had itself applied a lower hurdle in at least four instances.
6. Chairman Powell has very publicly expressed distaste for the public interest standard of the Communications Act, stating, "The night after I was sworn in, I waited for a visit from the angel of the public interest. I waited all night, but she did not come. And, in fact, five months into this job, I still have had no divine awakening and no one has issued me my public interest crystal ball" (Michael K. Powell, "The Public Interest Standard: A New Regulator's Search for Enlightenment," 17th Annual Legal Forum on Communications Law, American Bar Association, April 5, 1998), http://www.fcc.gov/Speeches/Powell/spmkp806.doc.
7. See "Comments," "Reply Comments," and Ex Parte Filings of Consumers Union, Consumer Federation of America, in FCC MM Docket Nos. 01–235, 96–197, 02–277, 01–317, 00–244, 92–264, 94–150, 92–51, 87–154, CS Dockets 98–82, 96–85.
8. *Associated Press v. United States*, 326 U.S. 1, 20 (1945) [hereafter *Associated Press*].
9. Ronald J. Krotoszynski, Jr., and A. Richard M. Blaiklock, "Enhancing the Spectrum: Media Power, Democracy, and the Marketplace of Ideas, *University of Illinois Law Review*, 2000, p. 867; Cass Sunstein, *Republic.com* (Princeton: Princeton University Press, 2001), p. 40.
10. *Associated Press*.
11. *Red Lion Broadcasting* v. FCC, 395 US 367 (1969) [hereafter Red Lion].
12. *Red Lion*.
13. *Turner Broadcasting System, Inc.* v. FCC, 512 U.S. 622, 638–39 (1994) [hereafter *Turner I*];

Time Warner Entertainment Co., L.P. v. FCC, 240 F.3d 1126 (D.C. Cir. 2001) [hereafter *Time Warner III*].

14. *Order*, para. 420.

15. *Sinclair.*

16. FCC v. *National Citizens Committee for Broadcasting*, 436 U.S. 775, 780–81 (1978).

17. *Order*, para. 353.

18. *Associated Press*, italics added.

19. *Fox* v. FCC.

20. *Whitney* v. *California*, 274 U.S. 357 (1927).

21. *Red Lion.*

22. NBC v. *U.S.*, 319 U.S. 190 (1943)

23. FCC v. *National Citizens Committee for Broadcasting*, 436 U.S. 775 (1978), italics added.

24. Bruce M. Owen, "Statement on Media Ownership Rules," Attachment to *Comments of Fox Entertainment Group and Fox Television Stations, Inc., National Broadcasting Company, Inc. and Telemundo Group, Inc., and Viacom,* In the Matter of 2002 Biennial Regulatory Review—Review of the Commission's Broadcast Ownership Rules, January 2, 2003.

25. Owen, "Statement on Media Ownership Rules."

26. Ibid.

27. Sei-Hill Kim, Dietram A. Scheufele and James Shanahan, "Think About It This Way: Attribute Agenda Setting Function of the Press and the Public's Evaluation of a Local Issue," *Journalism and Mass Communications Quarterly*, 79 (2002), p. 7; Steven Chaffee and Stacy Frank, "How Americans Get Their Political Information: Print versus Broadcast News," *The Annals of the American Academy of Political and Social Science*, 546 (1996); Jack M. McLeod, Dietram A. Scheufele, and Patricia Moy, "Community, Communications, and Participation: The Role of Mass Media and Interpersonal Discussion in Local Political Participation," *Political Communication*, 16 (1999).

28. Nicholas A. Valentino, Vincent L. Hutchings, and Ismail K. White, "Cues that Matter: How Political Ads Prime Racial Issues During Campaigns," American Political Science Review, 96, 2002, p. 75; Kathleen Hall Jamieson, *Dirty Politics: Deception, Distraction and Democracy* (Oxford University Press, New York: 1992); David L. Paletz, *The Media in American Politics: Contents and Consequences* (New York: Longman, 1999).

29. See, for example, David Domke, David Perlmutter, and Meg Spratt, "The Primes of Our Times? An Examination of the 'Power' of Visual Images," *Journalism*, 3 (2002), p. 131; LeAnn M. Brazeal and William L. Benoit, "A Functional Analysis of Congressional Television Spots," *Communications Quarterly*, 49 (2001), pp. 346–437.

30. Yochai Benkler, "Intellectual Property and the Organization of Information Production," 22 International Review of Law and Economics, 22: 81 (2002), available at http://www.law.nyu.edu/benklery/IP&Organization.pdf; Carl Shapiro and Hal R. Varian, *Information Rules: A Strategic Guide to the Network Economy* (Cambridge: Harvard Business School Press, 1999), pp. 22–23.

31. Steven T. Berry and Joel Waldfogel, "Public Radio in the United States: Does it Correct Market Failure or Cannibalize Commercial Stations?" *Journal of Public Economics*, 71 (1999).

32. See, for example, V. A. Stone, "Deregulation Felt Mainly in Large-Market Radio and Independent TV," *Communicator*, April (1987), p. 12; P. Aufderheide, "After the Fairness Doctrine: Controversial Broadcast Programming and the Public Interest," *Journal of Communication* (1990), pp. 50–51; K. L. Slattery and E. A. Kakanen, "Sensationalism Versus Public Affairs Content of Local TV News: Pennsylvania Revisited," *Journal of Broadcasting and Electronic Media*, 1994.

33. See, for example, J. H. McManus, "What Kind of a Commodity is News?" *Communications Research*, 1992; Bagdakian, pp. 220–221; D. L. Paletz and R. M. Entmen, *Media, Power, Politics* (New York: Free Press, 1981); N. Postman, *Amusing Ourselves to Death* (New York: Penguin Press, 1985).

34. Joel Waldfogel, *Who Benefits Whom in Local Television Markets?* November 2001, http://rider.wharton.upenn.edu/~waldfogj/tv.pdf; Joel Waldfogel and Peter Siegelman, *Race and Radio: Preference Externalities, Minority Ownership and the Provision of Programming to Minorities*, October 2001, http://www.fcc.gov/ownership/roundtable_docs/waldfogel-c.pdf; Joel Waldfogel and Lisa George, *Who Benefits Whom in Daily Newspaper Markets?* October 2000, http://www.fcc.gov/ownership/roundtable_docs/waldfogel-a.pdf.

35. M. Fife, *The Impact of Minority Ownership on Broadcast Program Content: A Multi-Market Study* (Washington: National Association of Broadcasters, 1986); Akousa Barthewell Evans, "Are Minority Preferences Necessary? Another Look at the Radio Broadcasting Industry," *Yale Law and Policy Review*, 8 (1990); Christine Bachen, Allen Hammond, Laurie Mason, and Stephanie Craft, *Diversity of Programming in the Broadcast Spectrum: Is there a Link Between Owner Race or Ethnicity and News and Public Affairs Programming?* (Santa Clara University, December 1999).

36. L. A. Collins-Jarvis, "Gender Representation in an Electronic City Hall: Female Adoption of Santa Monica's PEN System," *Journal of Broadcasting and Electronic Media* (1993); Martha M. Lauzen and David Dozier, "Making a Difference in Prime Time: Women on Screen and Behind the Scenes in 1995–1996 Television Season, *Journal of Broadcasting and Electronic Media* (Winter 1999).

37. W. R. Davie and J. S. Lee, "Television News Technology: Do More Sources Mean Less Diversity," *Journal of Broadcasting and Electronic Media* (1993), p. 455; D. C. Coulson, "Impact of Ownership on Newspaper Quality," *Journalism Quarterly* (1994).

38. Krotoszynski and Blaiklock, pp. 867–868, C. Edwin Baker, *Media, Markets, and Democracy* (New York: Cambridge University Press, 2002), p. 64.

39. Baker, *Media, Markets, and Democracy*, p. 64.

40. Baker, *Media, Markets, and Democracy*, p. 64; Cass Sunstein, "Television and the Public Interest," *California Law Review*, 8 (2002), p. 517; Neil Netanal, *Is the Commercial Mass Media Necessary, or Even Desirable, for Liberal Democracy*, TPRC, October 2001, pp. 20–24, http://arxiv.org/abs/cs.CY/0109092.

41. Baker, *Media, Markets, and Democracy*, p. 120; Rajiv Shah and J. Kesan, *The Role of Institutions in the Design of Communications Technologies*, TPRC, October 2001, http://arxiv.org/abs/cs.CY/0109109.

42. Charles Davis and Stephanie Craft, "New Media Synergy: Emergence of Institutional Conflict of Interest," *Journal of Mass Media Ethics*, 15 (2000), pp. 222–223.

43. Robert H. Frank and Phillip J. Cook, *The Winner Take All Society* (1999), p. 191; Pierre Bourdieu, On Television (New York: The New Press, 1998); C. Edwin Baker, "Giving the Audience What it Wants," Ohio State Law Journal 58 (1997).

44. See, for example, Sue Carter, Frederick Fico, and Joycelyn A. McCabe, "Partisan and Structural Balance in Local Television Election Coverage," *Journalism and Mass Communications Quarterly*, 79 (2002), p. 50; Kim Kahn and Patrick J. Kenny, "The Slant of News: How Editorial Endorsements Influence Campaign Coverage and Citizens' Views of Candidates," *American Political Science Review*, 96 (2002), p. 381; James H. Snider, and Benjamin I. Page, "Does Media Ownership Affect Media Stands? The Case of the Telecommunications Act of 1996," April 1997, http://www.newamerica.net/Download_Docs/pdfs/Pub_File_1237_1.pdf.

45. See, for example, J. Hansen Glenn and William Benoit, "Presidential Television Advertising and Public Policy Priorities, 1952–2002," *Communications Studies*, 53 (2002), p. 285; Gregory W. Gwiasda, "Network News Coverage of Campaign Advertisements: Media's Ability to Reinforce Campaign Messages," *American Politics Research*, 29 (2001), p. 461; C.L. Brians and M. P. Wattenberg, "Campaigns Issue Knowledge and Salience: Comparing Reception for TV Commercials, TV News, and Newspapers," *American Journal of Political Science* 40 (1996).

46. W. L. Bennett, *News, The Politics of Illusion* (New York: Longmans, 1988); J. C. Busterna, "Television Ownership Effects on Programming and Idea Diversity: Baseline Data," Journal of Media Economics (1988); E. Herman and N. Chomsky, *Manufacturing Consent* (New York: Pantheon, 1988); Theodore L. Glasser, David S. Allen, and S. Elizabeth Banks, "The Influence of Chain Ownership on News Play: A case Study," *Journalism Quarterly*, 66 (1989).

47. *Fox v. FCC*, pp. 12–13.

48. Krotoszynski and Blaiklock, pp. 871–876; Joel Waldfogel, *Who Benefits Whom in Local Television Markets?* November 2001, http://rider.wharton.upenn.edu/~waldfogj/tv.pdf.

49. See: Mark Cooper, "ABRACADABRA! HOCUS-POCUS! Making Media Market Power Disappear with the FCC's Diversity Index," July 2003, http://www.consumersunion.org/abrafinal721.PDF, 18.

50. The FCC accepts this and states that it should be analyzing news and information, although it devotes the overwhelming majority of its attention to entertainment.

51. Michael K. Powell, "And That's the Way It Is," *The Wall Street Journal*, September 11, 2003, available at http://www.fcc.gov/commissioners/powell/wsj_0911030ped.html.

52. Tom Wolzien and Mark McKenzie, *Returning Oligopoly of Media Threatens Cable's Power*, Bernstein Research, Sanford C. Bernstein & Co., February 7, 2003, p. 3.

53. Ibid.

54. Based on *Comments of Sinclair*, In the Matter of 2002 Biennial Regulatory Review, January 2, 2003, pp. 31–33.

55. Federal Communications Commission, Ninth Annual Report, *In the Matter of Annual Assessment of the Status of Competition in the Market for the Delivery of Video Programming*, MB docket No. 02–145 (December 31, 2002), Table C-7; Comments of the Writers Guild of America Regarding Harmful Vertical and Horizontal Integration in the Television Industry, Appendix A. Federal Communications Commission, *In the Matter of Implementation of Section 11 of the Cable Television Consumer Protection and Competition Act of 1992 Implementation of Cable Act Reform Provisions of the Telecommunications Act of 1996 The Commission's Cable Horizontal and Vertical Ownership Limits and Attribution Rules Review of the Commission's Regulations Governing Attribution Of Broadcast and Cable/MDS Interests Review of the Commission's Regulations and Policies Affecting Investment In the Broadcast Industry Reexamination of the Commission's Cross-Interest Policy*, CS Docket No. 98–82, CS Docket No. 96–85, MM Docket No. 92–264, MM Docket No. 94–150, MM Docket No. 92–51, MM Docket No. 87–154, January 4, 2002 (hereafter, Writers Guild).

56. Id., Table C-8; Writers Guild.

57. *Order*, para. 357.

58. *Order*, para. 359.

59. *Order*, para. 360.

60. *Order*, para. 366.

61. *Order*, para. 167.

62. *Order*, para. 167.
63. *Order*, para. 604.
64. *Order*, para. 195, 608.
65. *Order*, para. 602, 605.
66. *Order*, para. 196, 200, 608.
67. *Order*, para. 197, 198, 611.
68. *Order*, para. 32, 78.
69. *Order*, para. 410, "Unfortunately, we do not have data on this question specifically with regard to local news and current affairs."
70. *Sinclair*.
71. *Sinclair*.

PART 4

TOWARD A NEW MEDIA AGE: THE POLITICS OF CONVERGENCE, NEW MEDIA, AND INNOVATION

SHARING THE WEALTH:
AN ONLINE COMMONS FOR
THE NONPROFIT SECTOR

JEFF CHESTER AND GARY O. LARSON,
CENTER FOR DIGITAL DEMOCRACY

The twenty-first century is awash in alphanumeric technoglyphs—802.11x, IPV5, and DOCSIS 2.0 among them, each heralding the promise of the broadband future. But there's another, nontechnical, standard from an earlier era—501(c)(3)—that we neglect at our peril. That's the designation, of course, for nonprofit, tax-exempt organizations, common enough in the analog world of education and culture, religion and social welfare, but of uncertain status in the digital universe. On the one hand, certainly, even with the indiscriminate use of the ".org" domain by all manner of enterprises, the presence of nonprofit organizations on the Web has been justly celebrated.[1] On the other hand, even a cursory glance at the traffic patterns of the Web, dominated by the online "properties" of Yahoo, Time Warner, and Microsoft, reveals the extent to which the nonprofit sector must endure the same slender "market share" in the new media that it does in the old.[2]

The difference is that in the old media, at least, we generally know where to find the noncommercial content. Fully one-fifth of the radio and television spectrum is dedicated to noncommercial broadcasts, for example (although the ratings share for such programming is closer to one-*fiftieth* than to one-fifth). While mainstream print publications' coverage of the nonprofit culture has declined in recent years, it is still possible to find niche periodicals devoted to one or more aspects of education, science, civic affairs, arts, and the humanities.[3] The major institutions of the nonprofit sector, moreover, the schools and libraries, churches and hospitals, museums and orchestras, continue to loom large in our society. And, thanks to public and private funding alike (more than $12 billion in private philanthropy for the arts and humanities alone), a robust culture of much smaller organizations—from storefront churches and neighborhood community centers to dance companies and literary magazines—has flourished. These may not be the corporate powerhouses that dominate a local economy, but collectively the nonprofit sector's economic clout is considerable: 1.2 million nonprofit organizations generate $664.8 billion in revenues, employing 7.1 percent of the United States workforce.[4]

The online universe, in contrast, lacking the set-asides and signposts that demarcate the nonprofit sector in the real world, seems scarcely to distinguish between for-profit and noncommercial. The two main entry points for Web-based travels, portals such as AOL and the Microsoft Network, and such search sites as Google and Yahoo, are completely agnostic on this score (when they aren't favoring affiliated and sponsored programming, that is). Nor has the nonprofit sector itself (with the partial exceptions of scattered community-based networks and the "branded" empires of PBS, NPR, the Smithsonian, *et al.*) succeeded in establishing the online on-ramps that fully honor the high standards, deep resources, and long traditions of nonprofit culture. The 501(c)(3) label has real meaning in the analog world, in short, conferring not only tax-exempt status, but a certain "seal of approval" as well. We have yet to find a way to map these values onto the virtual world, where style often triumphs over substance and where marketing and cross-promotion often exert the same tyranny-of-the-majority pressure on new media that Nielsen ratings and box-office receipts exert on the old.

At first glance, it is true, the Internet appears to be the most democratic of media systems, offering a virtual solution to A. J. Liebling's famous dictum, "Freedom of the press is guaranteed only to those who own one." With millions of websites and billions of pages, almost everyone has access to a printing press. Upon closer inspection, however, the limits of this new publishing platform become all too apparent. In an article entitled "More News, Less Diversity," Matthew Hindman and Kenneth Neil Cukier of the National Center for Digital Government at Harvard University argue that the Internet, contrary to appearances, does not really increase the number of information sources that Americans actually use. Despite the vast range of sites available online, the reality, according to Hindman and Cukier, is that "almost all this diversity is ignored."

> Users may be able to choose from millions of sites, but most go to only a few. This isn't an accident or the result of savvy branding. It's because Internet traffic follows a winner-take-all pattern that is much more ruthless than people realize. Relying on links and search engines, most people are directed to a few very successful sites; the rest remain invisible to the majority of users. The result is that there's an even greater media concentration online than in the offline world.[5]

Large, well-connected sites, not surprisingly, have more links to one another than to smaller sites. Unfortunately, these smaller sites tend *also* to have more links to larger sites than to their own peers.[6] In the absence of any recognition of the need for a more coordinated approach to online programming among such

sites—a collaborative, noncommercial corollary, in effect, to the mergers and strategic alliances that have made the media conglomerates such potent forces in our
society—independent and alternative voices will continue to suffer from a lack of
critical mass online. Freedom of the online press, it seems, is guaranteed only to
those who enjoy large circulations. Put another way, freedom of speech means little
if no one can hear you, and on the Web, unfortunately, noncommercial expression
can seldom be heard over the din of conglomerate culture.

If this "supply side" of the noncommercial online content equation needs attention (with more collaboration among libraries, public broadcasters, and educational
institutions nationally and community-based organizations locally, for example, in
order to aggregate larger audiences and to build a keener sense of "alternative" culture),
the *demand* side also needs some work. Search engines, the unofficial "gatekeepers
of the Web" that are themselves subject to its rich-get-richer dynamic, play a key role
in this regard, contributing mightily to the consolidation of power in the Internet's
marketplace of ideas.[7] While any number of techniques (some less scrupulous than
others) have been developed to influence the output of search engines, no one has
ever figured out a reliable way to influence the *input* of those who use them.[8] As the
annual lists of most popular search terms tabulated by the major search engines suggest (Yahoo's top ten featured seven pop-culture staples along with queries related to
professional wrestling, automobile racing, and MP3 file sharing), our quest for a more
civic, democratic Web faces a three-fold challenge: coordinating efforts to share noncommercial resources online, creating spaces for civic participation, and convincing
the public to avail themselves of these services and applications.[9]

Fortunately, a number of efforts to realize the full democratic potential of the
Internet are already underway, seeking both to expand the range and depth of
noncommercial programming online and to foster an awareness of the *need* for
such resources.[10] Especially as the Web grows increasingly commercialized (and
increasingly becomes the domain of media giants), the digital incarnation of the
"civic sector"—the loose collection of organizations and projects, online and off,
that encompass democratic values, social services, educational opportunities, and
cultural traditions—becomes all-the-more important. In envisioning this more
diverse, participatory media system for the future, it is instructive to recall an earlier
era online, when options for data retrieval were far fewer but when opportunities
for sharing resources were plentiful and the overall character of the online world
was decidedly noncommercial.

"Usenet Represents Democracy"

Just over a decade ago, with the World Wide Web only beginning to emerge, a
study of the civic sector online would have focused on an entirely different set

of actors. Some activity would have been found in Usenet groups, such as soc.
human-nets or talk.politics.misc, two of the online roundtables of the day, and in
community networks such as the Cleveland Freenet or the Santa Monica Public
Education Network, where the seeds of an online civic sector first bore fruit.[11]
There were also over 100,000 electronic bulletin-board systems (BBS) operating worldwide at the time, isolated electronic enclaves that served a variety of
interests at the local level.[12] Other civic activity might have been found in such
nearly forgotten e-phemera as Fidonet (a store-and-forward message-exchange
protocol that linked thousands of BBSs), ToasterNets (cooperative networks
that brought low-cost Internet connectivity to communities in the early 1990s)
and gopher spaces (a point-and-click Internet navigation protocol developed at
the University of Minnesota in 1991).[13] There might even have been some civic
activity among the closed, commercial systems of the time, led by CompuServe
and America Online, although until the early 1990s, the commercial sector's
online influence was modest.[14]

One of the distinguishing features of the early Internet, before the National
Science Foundation decided to privatize the major backbone carriers of network
traffic, was that it was almost wholly noncommercial in character. Concerning
the Internet's original main thoroughfare, for example, the NSF's "Acceptable Use
Policy" made clear that "NSFNET Backbone services are provided to support open
research and education in and among United States research and instructional
institutions, plus research arms of for-profit firms when engaged in open scholarly
communication and research. Use for other purposes is not acceptable." Among
those forbidden "other purposes," the NSF policy made clear, was "use for for-profit
activities (consulting for pay, sales or administration of campus stores, sale of
tickets to sports events, and so on) or use by for-profit institutions unless covered
by the General Principle or as a specifically acceptable use."[15]

With the NSF's decision to "privatize" the Net, however, turning over the operation of the basic network infrastructure to corporate control, the Acceptable Use
Policy was soon a distant memory.[16] And with the arrival of Web-based technology in the early 1990s and the debut of graphical browsers in 1993, the Internet's
version of the Oklahoma Land Rush was soon under way.[17] Ironically, while the
dust of that digital juggernaut is still settling (along with the ashes of the many
dot-com ventures that crashed and burned during the period), one of the corporate heavyweights now endeavoring to make the Internet safe for commerce has
invoked the NSF's ancient noncommercial principle. In its effort to stamp out the
sharing of music files on high-speed college networks, the Recording Industry
Association of America sued four students at three universities in April 2003 for
having "taken a network created for higher learning and academic pursuits and
converted it into an emporium of music piracy."[18] For one opportunistic moment,
at least, the original spirit of the Internet as a noncommercial refuge held center

stage, if only as a means of protecting the recording industry's right to *sell* its wares online and offline.

Still, this fundamental part of the Internet's DNA—that it was established for noncommercial purposes, and that the underlying architecture is essentially neutral to the nature of the traffic it carries—remains important. It both informs many of the current experiments in civic networking and comprises a strong argument for devoting a portion of the emerging broadband infrastructure for noncommercial, civic purposes. Unfortunately, much of the history of the Internet (admittedly, a system that reached only a tiny fraction of the population during its first two decades of existence) has been almost wholly obscured by more recent and more spectacular events in the online economy. For better or worse, it was not until the Internet became thoroughly commercialized that it became relevant to most people's lives. Before that, the academics, scientists, and other online trailblazers were too busy exploring cyberspace to be too conscious of its potential social, civic, and cultural significance. In the absence of Googlelike searches of the early Net's disparate resources, moreover, any attempted reckoning of the interplay of technology, civil society, and nonprofit culture would have been both fragmented and incomplete—not unlike the online civic sector itself.[19]

Today, in contrast, it is rather the sheer size of the World Wide Web—estimated to comprise more than 3 billion pages on some 20 million websites—that proves to be so daunting to surveys of online activity. But at least all of these resources, however varied in quality and content, in style and substance, can be found underneath one digital roof. It was not so long ago that the online world was still a remarkably disjointed affair, with specialized research networks (initially Arpanet and later BITNET and CSNET, for example), self-contained commercial enclaves (initially The Source and CompuServe and later America Online), and literally thousands of dial-up Bulletin Board Systems serving those who, lacking the necessary institutional affiliations or costly commercial accounts, sought access to online communications.[20]

If there was a common thread running through these several systems (and one of the hallmarks of the "pre-Internet" era is that such a common thread was conspicuously absent), it was the Usenet discussion groups that made it possible to exchange ideas and information worldwide. Developed by two graduate students at Duke University in the late 1970s as a way "to give every UNIX system the opportunity to join and benefit from a computer network (a poor man's ARPANET, if you will)," Usenet newsgroups covered a broad range of topics, from the questions about the UNIX operating system that spawned the message-exchange system in the first place, to almost any topic that could be wedged into one its several categories: comp (computers), misc (miscellaneous), news (for announcements concerning Usenet itself), rec (recreation), sci (science), soc (social), talk (discussions, including controversial subjects), and alt (alternative).[21] By 1995, some

330,000 sites around the world exchanged over 131,000 posts every day in more than 10,000 newsgroups.[22]

It was a decidedly democratic, collaborative function that Usenet fulfilled (and continues to fulfill), initially extending Arpanet expertise and networking services to a far larger group of users. "In its simplest form," observes Usenet historian Michael Hauben, "Usenet represents democracy."

> The basic element of Usenet is a post. Each individual post consists of a unique contribution from some user placed in a subject area, called a newsgroup . . . . Usenet is controlled by its audience. Usenet should be seen as a promising successor to other people's presses, such as broadsides at the time of the American Revolution and the Penny Presses in England at the turn of the 19th Century . . . . Usenet is an uncensored forum for debate—where many sides of an issue come into view. Instead of being force-fed by an uncontrollable source of information, the participants set the tone and emphasis on Usenet. People control what happens on Usenet.[23]

"On the Net," adds Ronda Hauben, "participants gain from being active and from helping each other. People who post or send e-mail are contributors to the culture and all gain from each other's efforts. A vibrant and informative bottom up, interactive grassroots culture has been created and a broad, worldwide, informative and functioning telecommunications network is the product of their labors."[24]

With its collaborative, resource-sharing philosophy, moreover, Usenet helped to establish the interconnected, self-propagating nature of online culture, in which a specialized network like Arpanet reached beyond its closed borders through widely disseminated newsgroup discussions, while otherwise isolated BBSs similarly joined ranks through Fidonet discussion groups, and civic free-nets arose to extend the reach of the Internet still further.[25] Eventually, these several electronic tributaries all contributed to a critical mass of participants and a body of literature that, however evanescent, finally forced the increasingly popular commercial systems of the early 1990s (e.g., CompuServe and America Online) to join the Internet community as well.[26] In time, of course, these commercial ventures came to dominate the online world, and even if AOL's star faded somewhat in its ill-fated merger with Time Warner and in the transition from dial-up to broadband (having lost some 2.2 million dial-up subscribers in 2003 alone), the Internet remains a thoroughly commercialized medium.[27]

The Information Commons

Despite the dominance of such commercial sites as Yahoo and Google, Usenet continues to this day to serve as a global online roundtable. Although overshadowed by the Web and its much more colorful offerings, some 30,000 newsgroups still exist, and even if many are abandoned shells, Usenet traffic remains brisk, with over 150 million messages posted in 2001 alone. Equally important, perhaps, the original *spirit* of Usenet survives in various efforts to establish an "information commons."[28] Usenet itself represents one such commons, especially now that a "Google group" devoted to the system permits online searching of over two decades of Usenet archives comprising some 700 million posts.[29] Given the sprawling nature of these forums, the results of such queries can be overwhelming—some 65,000 entries were returned in a recent search of Usenet's coverage of "information commons," for example—but the results are fascinating: notice of an article on commercial threats to the information commons in misc.activism.progressive, a reference to a 2001 conference on "Nurturing the CyberCommons" in soc.org. nonprofit, and an announcement of an upcoming conference on libraries and the information commons in bit.listerv.mla-l.[30]

There is renewed interest in recapturing the Net's heritage of collaboration and sharing—strengthening both its archival and its deliberative aspects—and many of these civic networking projects invoke images of the commons. In the words of David Bollier and Tim Watts, for example, "the Internet has given rise to an entirely new sort of public and democratic cultural space—the information commons—that now coexists alongside the mass media" and "deals with non-commercial dimensions of American life that are not key priorities for market-driven enterprises, but which nonetheless are vital to our society." The problem, as Bollier and Watts point out, "is that we do not conceptualize and celebrate this remarkable effusion of non-commercial content as a preeminent public interest achievement."[31] Nor, it should be added, have we fully come to terms with the false cornucopia of commercial content that the mass media spew forth—the seeming explosion of new delivery platforms (for example, direct broadcast satellite and digital cable), new recording formats (DVDs and MP3s), and new gadgets (such as TiVo and digital-hub home entertainment systems) that mask the concentration of power in the handful of conglomerates that dominate these markets. And the two issues are related: once we become more aware of the constriction of cultural choice exercised by the media giants (where whole classes of independently produced music and literature, for example, are excluded from the shelves of Wal-Mart and Waldenbooks, and where television news and public-affairs programming is limited largely to the networks' mainstream fare), interest in alternative sources of programming will only grow. But much work remains to be done in this regard.

At the moment, evocations of the commons tend toward one of two extremes—anguish over the loss of these shared resources and rapture over their sudden reappearance in various digital incarnations. Benjamin Barber, for example, speaking from the perspective of "Paradise Lost," laments that "Citizens are homeless:

suspended between big bureaucratic governments which they no longer trust . . . and private markets they cannot depend on for moral and civic values. . . . They are without a place to express their commonality. The 'commons' vanishes, and where the public square once stood, there are only shopping malls and theme parks and not a single place that welcomes the 'us' that we might hope to gather from all the private you's and me's."[32] Howard Rheingold, in contrast, who has done as much as anyone to promote the idea of "virtual communities" and the power of the Internet to promote social and political change, speaks rather of the Internet's capacity to permit all of those "private you's and me's" to act in a public, cooperative capacity. "In the many-to-many environment of the Net," observes Rheingold, "every desktop is a printing press, a broadcasting station, and place of assembly. Mass-media will continue to exist, and so will journalism, but these institutions will no longer monopolize attention and access to the attention of others."[33]

While such declarations as Barber's and Rheingold's are useful in stimulating debate over the sad fate or the bright prospects of the commons, that concept is neither so tenuous as to be swept aside by shopping malls, as Barber would have it, nor so readily available as Rheingold's desktop democracy. "Historically and conceptually," as Lew Friedland and Harry Boyte point out, "the public commons is better understood as a civic site and a stimulus to civic action—a place where people gather, discuss things, and work on common problems. Around such settings, public cultures also form. The commons, understood in this sense, often expresses the culture, traditions, and common work of particular places. It is something people help to create."[34] Viewed in this light, it is clear that the information commons is much more of an abstraction—an organizing principle, even a rallying cry—than a specific, tangible space. It is neither a fenced-off portion of cyberspace (a hypothetical .civ domain to shield civilization from the commercial excesses of .com) nor a dedicated portal or search engine (an AOL for political activists, say, or a Google for civic gadflies). Examples of the commons concept online abound, in the distributed expertise of the Open Directory Project, for example, or the archival function of the Public Library of Science, or in the efforts to expand the public domain through Creative Commons licenses.[35]

This is the glue, in other words—the complementary interests, mutual benefits, shared space—that binds those efforts, public and private, that are designed to achieve social or cultural rather than personal or profitable ends. And it is the spirit that informs much of the work of the nonprofit sector, especially in its efforts to cushion the often harsh impact of market forces and to compensate for the shrinkage in government social programs. It is also the missing ingredient, as David Bollier has pointed out, in so much of online content today. "The commons comprises not just marketable assets," he observes, "but social institutions and cultural traditions that help define our common life as Americans. In virtually every case, the market *price* for a resource does not begin to capture its actual *value* to the larger community. But generally we have no rigorous way to speak about such shared assets, or about the costs of enclosing them."[36]

Nor, it should be noted, have we found a way to *pay* for the online civic, educational, and cultural materials that comprise the digital incarnation of the commons, although such proposals as the Spectrum Commons and Digital Dividends Act of 2003 and the Digital Opportunity Investment Trust Act envision public support for such material.[37] Even former Congressman Thomas Bliley, a staunch defender of marketplace solutions during his tenure as chairman of the House Commerce Committee in the late 1990s, has recognized the need for enhanced civic and educational content online. "Compared to the colossal strides in hardware, software and broadband," Bliley observed in offering his support of the Digital Opportunity Investment Trust in 2003,

> when it comes to content—the material that's actually transmitted—we've taken only baby steps. When one envisions the possibilities, what could be made of today's technology, one realizes how far we really have to go . . . . Despite all our wealth and military strength, all our technological supremacy, if we are to remain competitive in the new century, we must fulfill our potential in the area of telecommunications—not just in entertainment, but in lifelong learning and content development.[38]

While the passage of legislation to create a noncommercial trust fund could be years away, the stage has been set for a movement that will do for the digital era what educational broadcast set-asides and arts and humanities funding did for the analog age.[39]

Clearly, finding the proper balance in the online environment between the role of government and the play of market forces, between the imperatives of e-commerce and the needs of e-citizenship, will not come easily. And in prescribing a role for the nonprofit sector to act more aggressively in this regard, the power of the entertainment and media industries in asserting their own narrow interests should not be underestimated. The source of millions of dollars in campaign contributions every year, and equipped with elaborate state and federal lobbying apparatuses, the conglomerates' influence over elected officials (who are doubly beholden to the media for the exposure they receive in broadcast and in print) is enormous. But with the backlash against the excesses of the Digital Millennium Copyright Act and the growing opposition to the FCC's relaxation of media ownership limits, the possibilities for genuine media reform are greater now than they have been in years.[40]

Independents' Day

For the BBC's Bill Thompson, "The real fight here is political." Using the Big Five record labels as a proxy for the entertainment industry generally, Thompson believes that "[t]he record industry wants complete control over what people do with the songs it publishes; the people want some freedom to decide for themselves. Until we can resolve this difference we will continue to see more court cases, threatening letters, and new releases of file-sharing tools. We need to rethink what copyright means in a digital world, rather than wasting so much time, effort and money on this conflict."[41]

In the meantime, quite apart from the legal implications of the new technologies, and distinct from the corporate sector's exploitation of their power, the benefits of the digital age for smaller, grassroots projects should not be overlooked. With the costs of mass-market entertainment spiraling to unprecedented levels ($400,000–$500,000 per song in promotional costs alone, over $100 million per Hollywood movie, and minimum press runs for major publications of 500,000 and above), the field for smaller-scale, niche-market productions is suddenly wide open.[42] As Dan Gillmor has observed in his "eJournal" blog for the San Jose Mercury News, "Personal technology is undermining the broadcast culture of the late 20th century. It's putting tools that were once the preserve of Big Media into the hands of the many."[43] From the well-chronicled desktop publishing revolution to more recent developments in desktop audio and video, never have the tools of media production been so readily available. And while the term "independent" has lost much of its meaning in the current media environment, covering everything from self-produced CDs to multi-million-dollar movies, it is undeniable that there are more examples of small presses, record labels, and video projects than ever before.

As a low-cost distribution platform, moreover, the Internet excels at making such works more widely available, and has rejuvenated the notion of the public domain. Project Gutenberg (http://promo.net/pg/), for example, the volunteer-driven project that dates back to the early 1970s, makes nearly 9,000 books freely available for downloading. And roughly seven books a minute are downloaded from the 1,600 e-books available free from the University of Virginia's Electronic Text Center (http://etext.lib.virginia.edu/). The broadband revolution will only accelerate the pace at which more demanding online applications, including streaming audio and video, will become a viable alternative for nonprofit organizations and individuals alike. Projects such as Live Music Archive and the Movie Archive, both associated with the Internet Archive (itself a notable online commons), are pointing the way toward an information commons that extends far beyond purely informational resources to include all manner of expressive works.[44]

"We're not that far from a time when artists and writers can distribute their own work and make a living doing so," suggests PBS commentator Robert X. Cringely, "which makes the current literary and music establishments a lot less necessary. . . . So we will have little movies and little records and little magazines on the Internet because the Internet is made up of so many different interest groups. For the larger population, there will still be Britney Spears and Stephen King singing and writing for big labels."[45]

The Regulatory Challenge

But whether it is pop divas and best-selling authors or performance artists and political scribes, the digital content of the twenty-first century will invariably find its way to our homes over commercial networks. If current trends continue, most of these networks will be those of cable companies (roughly two-thirds of all homes connected to the high-speed Internet), with the remaining one-third most likely to be controlled by one of the four Baby Bell phone companies.[46] And if the current regulatory structure that governs these networks prevails, we may well find ourselves at the mercy of private corporations for accessing all digital content online—public domain and private enterprise alike. Here, then, is the *other* side of the new-media copyright coin—*not* the ownership and control of the digital artifacts themselves (which is worrisome enough), but the ownership and control of the *networks* over which that material will be transmitted. In this context, even works in the public domain are at risk, since the thoroughly commercialized and privatized broadband networks that the cable monopolies and Baby Bells are introducing will likely serve civic expression and nonprofit culture as poorly as the entertainment industry does today.

But it is not the nonprofit sector alone that feels threatened by the new broadband hegemony. In his testimony before the House Subcommittee on Telecommunications and the Internet on July 21, 2003, for example, Paul Misener, Amazon.com's vice president for global public policy, assessed the change that the closed broadband networks might soon represent:

> Although perhaps subtle at first, the resulting change to the fundamental character of the Internet would be nothing short of radical and tragic. No longer would Americans be able to obtain for free or purchase all the myriad content they have grown accustomed to receiving at home. The Internet would metamorphose from being the ultimate "pull" medium, in which consumer choice is paramount, to being yet another cable TV-style "push" medium, where gate-keeping service providers decide what content Americans are allowed to obtain. By destroying unimpeded connectivity, the anti-competitive exercise

of market power by a handful of broadband service providers would do to the Internet what even a nuclear strike could not.[47]

Misener's remarks may seem a little melodramatic, but most observers agree that the battle over "open access" as we've traditionally known that term—in which, literally, thousands of Internet service providers (ISPs) were allowed to ply their trade using dial-up connections—has been lost. The danger now is that the FCC, in pursuing its decidedly market-driven goals—"the development and deployment of broadband infrastructure is the central communications policy of the day," it claims—will effectively render content diversity as endangered a concept as ISP diversity.[48]

The analysts at Legg Mason have dubbed the debate surrounding such diversity "Open Access II," a cluster of issues involving "the extent to which the network provider can restrict the customers' use of the network.

> Some have raised the fear that the Bell and cable companies could use their network control to undermine competitive offerings. In responding to such concerns, the government may have to address whether network providers can (1) restrict access to any Internet content, (2) restrict the user from running an application even if it does not harm the network and stays within bandwidth limits, (3) use routers to improve the performance of affiliated services (or undermine the performance of unaffiliated services), or (4) prohibit the attachment of devices to their Internet connection for reasons other than harm to the network or theft of service.[49]

The FCC is still in the process of crafting the ground rules for broadband Internet, but all indications suggest that Chairman Michael Powell's regime favors a deregulatory approach that raises the possibility of cable and Baby Bell ISPs becoming "last mile" gatekeepers of broadband content.[50]

Traditionally, of course, the Internet's response to such gatekeepers and the bottlenecks they create was simply to "route around them," finding the next-best path in transmitting a packet from point A to point B. While such "best-effort" techniques may continue to hold through large portions of the Internet, at the present there simply aren't many alternatives to cable or DSL broadband connections to the home. There still may be a way to "route around" even these wired obstructions, however, via wireless networks on the horizon. As James H. Johnston and J.H. Snider point out in their working paper for the New America Foundation, "The current debate over last-mile broadband policy is all too often a sterile debate focused on the wired infrastructure. The debate needs to shift to spectrum policy. Spectrum is not just a third last-mile broadband platform to compete with cable modems and DSL. It is the platform of choice. The wired infrastructure belongs in the backbone, not in the consumers home, lawn, or neighborhood."[51]

Strategies for Broadband Democracy at the Local Level

For better or worse, however, the potential of wireless broadband is also tied to federal policy—the way in which we organize and manage the radio spectrum—and the resolution of this issue could take years.[52] In the meantime, it is not too early to begin thinking more expansively about the "ecology of bandwidth" (drawing on both public and private network capacity across a variety of platforms, including broadband cable and digital television) that will be needed to ensure the full democratic potential of the broadband revolution. That revolution, clearly, is still in its infancy but the *promise* of a new, more open and diverse media system has arrived. Roughly 40 percent of all United States homes connected to the Internet now enjoy high-speed access, and that number is growing daily. So, too, are the speeds at which users connect to the Internet increasing, although we have yet to see the kinds of robust residential networks (operating at ten megabits per second and above) that will readily permit multimedia material to flow in *both* directions. In order for that potential to be realized, however, community leaders, media activists, and representatives of the nonprofit sector will have to become more actively engaged in the broadband build-out process. Without question, the new high-speed networks are headed our way, but whether they simply deliver more-of-the-same conglomerate culture, or whether they open new opportunities for civic discourse and cultural expression, will depend on the actions that communities take today.

Given the tight control over broadband networks wielded by cable and phone company monopolies, unfortunately, there is no guarantee that any of the new online resources will extend beyond the usual market-driven fare. However dazzling on-demand entertainment, sports, and gaming might be, we need to ensure the availability of public-interest online programming as well, including content produced by individuals and community groups themselves. Just as we have set aside space in the natural environment for public parks and beaches, and just as we have designated portions of the broadcast spectrum for noncommercial and educational use, so must we ensure that the new broadband infrastructure similarly accommodates applications and content designed to meet civic, social, and cultural needs. Communities must be informed of the public-interest options they should have in the new broadband marketplace, and encouraged to take part in the decision-making process surrounding the deployment of broadband and digital television platforms.[53]

A multifaceted approach such as this one must look first at the social, civic, and cultural assets that help define a particular community. These include the cultural institutions, churches, schools, libraries, parks and recreational facilities, the nonprofit organizations and social service agencies, the community-based groups and volunteer associations—all of the community resources, in short, that are neither beholden to market forces nor derived from the powers of the state. These are the components of civil society that tend to be overlooked in the media's twin preoccupation with Wall Street and Pennsylvania Avenue. But despite the obvious attractions of those two dominant thoroughfares, we mustn't lose sight of another important part of the cultural landscape, the town square—"our shared assets and civic inheritance," in Bollier's words—that will prove so vital to the future health of our democracy.[54]

Second, if we are to realize the full democratic potential of the broadband revolution, we need to determine the capacity of our local telecommunication infrastructure to serve *civic* as well as purely commercial ends. Will the new cable broadband networks, for example, ensure open access to, and nondiscriminatory transport of, *all* programming? Will the more sophisticated set-top boxes, which are just now being introduced, operate in an open, non-proprietary fashion? Are the cable system's public-, educational-, and government-access (PEG) channels being upgraded for full, two-way digital communications? Is there a high-speed institutional network (I-net) through which municipal and civic resources can be linked? Are there other opportunities for community networking that take full advantage of the new broadband networks? Such is the community broadband assessment that will hold private telecommunications providers and municipal governments alike up to public scrutiny, to determine if they measure up to the civic networking standards that must be met for our democracy to flourish in the digital age.

Third, there must be a concerted effort, drawing on public and private resources alike, to bring these two forces—our community assets and the broadband infrastructure—together in a meaningful fashion, *not* as an afterthought, as a mere add-on, to a market-driven delivery system for entertainment, sports, and endless sales pitches. Instead, the digital commons must be built into the new broadband networks at the outset, with common-carriage regulations, updated PEG commitments, and the necessary funding in place to ensure the ready availability of public-interest programming to all interested citizens.

With the widespread deployment of high-speed networks, the broadband revolution is well under way. In the process, there will be any number of efforts to exploit the commercial potential of the high-speed Internet. Our task is to ensure that broadband *serves* as effectively as it *sells*, fostering two-way, interactive applications. By working together at the local level, assessing the broadband infrastructure for its potential to serve the public interest, and building new alliances to ensure such service, we have the opportunity to develop the local online resources that will contribute to a larger information commons.

In the process, we will invariably confront a series of basic civic networking issues:

- In the context of a World Wide Web that grows more commercial every day, what are the prospects for a meaningful online civic sector? How do we strike the proper balance between local needs and national interests?

- Is such an electronic commons destined to be merely a collection of laudable URLS, or can it become something more dynamic and useful, drawing together the shared expertise of the nonprofit sector, while addressing local issues as well?

- Can a movement be fashioned around the virtual civic sector that will adequately serve both the production and the distribution needs of nonprofit organizations (needs that will surely escalate as the online environment itself evolves toward richer, more complex, high-bandwidth applications)?

- Can we ensure, even as we make progress in bridging the Digital Divide that separates the *haves* from the *have-nots*, that we also overcome a new range of "digital divisions" separating the haves from the have-mores, placing premium services (including such increasingly vital services as streaming media and video conferencing) beyond the means of community and other nonprofit organizations?

- Will the information commons be truly inclusive, featuring not only the well recognized riches of nonprofit culture, but also information and services addressing the needs of "those with low incomes, limited-literacy or English skills, or one or more disabilities"?[55]

And even if these several needs are met, can anything be done to aid citizens in finding these vital online resources? This is the crucial process of *discovery* that is likely to become even more perplexing in a highly commercialized broadband environment that favors big business over small, e-commerce over e-democracy, and public relations over public service. Even if there are meritorious sites out there amidst the billions of Web pages, what guarantees are there that anyone will be able to locate them? And once found can we build in interactive elements to help create a genuinely two-way, participatory media system?

If such questions as these remain to be answered, one thing seems certain: that a more organized, coordinated movement, built around the theme of an electronic commons, will yield the kind of critical mass that is sorely lacking today. The civic sector, of course, both online and off, will always remain a work in progress. But given the changes that are taking place today, especially as the broadband revolution brings to growing numbers of the public the riches of the Internet (or, more likely, a streamlined, branded facsimile thereof), the time to redouble our efforts on behalf of an online commons for nonprofit culture has arrived.

Notes

1. David F. Gallagher, "Internet Labels Lose Meaning in Rush for Popular Addresses," *New York Times*, November 29, 1999. In perhaps their biggest oversight of the digital era, media

watchdog groups failed to secure an exclusive top-level domain (TLD) for the nonprofit sector (assuming, apparently, that the "miscellaneous" .org TLD would suffice). Use of the .org (the fifth-largest domain, with 2.4 million registered domain names worldwide) soon became open and unrestricted, however, and the nonprofit sector still lacks a TLD of its own (although the ".museum" domain, administered by the Museum Domain Management Association, was established in 2001). Even with the new management of the .org TLD by a nonprofit group (the Internet Society's Public Interest Registry), .org will still lack the exclusivity of such TLDs as .edu (limited to educational institutions) or .gov (limited to federal government agencies). Todd R. Weiss, "Nonprofit Group Takes Over Management of the .org Domain," *Computerworld*, January 2, 2003, http://www.computerworld.com/developmenttopics/websitemgmt/story/0,10801,77211,00.html.

2. "comScore Media Metrix Announces Top 50 U.S. Internet Property Rankings for February 2004," press release, March 19, 2004, http://www.comscore.com/press/release.asp?press=443. As an indication of the concentration of power on the Web, the top three online properties in comScore's February 2004 survey (Yahoo sites, Time Warner Network, and MSN-Microsoft sites) attracted more unique visitors (326 million) than the rest of the top ten combined (a group that includes Ebay, Google, Amazon, and Disney). The top ten, in turn, attracted more visitors than the rest of the top fifty combined. None of the top fifty was a nonprofit, and only one was a government site (IRS, whose popularity, based on the proximity of the April tax filing deadline, is decidedly seasonal).

3. In 2002, there were 13,846 different periodicals in circulation, a 35 percent increase over the number available in 1980. US Census Bureau, *Statistical Abstract of the United States: 2003* (Washington, D.C.: Census Bureau, 2004), p. 722.

4. These figures, for 1997–1998, are the latest available from the Independent Sector, *The New Nonprofit Almanac in Brief* (Washington, D.C.: Independent Sector, 2001).

5. Matthew Hindman and Kenneth Neil Cukier, "More News, Less Diversity," *New York Times*, June 4, 2003, http://www.ksg.harvard.edu/news/opeds/2003/hindman_cukier_nyt_060403. Other scholars, including Clay Shirky, have described this "power law distribution" of incoming links to any given site. Clay Shirky, "Power Laws, Weblogs, and Inequality," http://www.shirky.com/writings/powerlaw_weblog.html. "The formation of links," observe Boris Galitsky and Mark Levene, " is explained through the process of 'preferential attachment,' where sites having more incoming links are more likely to be linked to than sites having less incoming links, leading to the 'rich get richer' phenomenon." Boris Galitsky and Mark Levene, "On the Economy of Web Links: Simulating the Exchange Process," *First Monday*, 9, no. 1 (January 15, 2004), http://www.firstmonday.dk/issues/current_issue/galitsky/index.html.

6. Shi Zhou and Raul J. Mondragon, "Analyzing and Modelling the AS-level Internet Topology," Computing Research Repository, http://arxiv.org/ftp/cs/papers/0303/0303030.pdf. See also Shirky, "Power Laws, Weblogs, and Inequality."

7. As Galitsky and Levene explain, "Google and other Web search engines interpret a link to a Web site as a vote for that Web site by the author of the link, so the more votes a Web site has the more important it is considered. Google also takes into account the importance of the source of a link, so a link from a more prominent site is worth more than a link from a less prominent one. Since Web search engines have become the gatekeepers of the Web, visibility of a site through Web searches has become an essential ingredient for the survival of the site." Galitsky and Levene, "On the Economy of Web Links."

8. For search engine "optimization" schemes, see, for example, Web CEO (http://www.webceo.com/), which promises to "move your site to the top."

9. Chris Sherman, "2003's Most Wanted Search Terms," *SearchEngineWatch.com*, January 7, 2004, http://searchenginewatch.com/searchday/article.php/3296341. Even in the presumably loftier realm of online political communities, the subject of the aforementioned study by Hindman and Cukier, the Web's predictable traffic patterns prevail. Analyzing three million Web pages covering such issues as abortion and capital punishment, Hindman and Cukier found that each website's traffic correlates directly with the number of links to that website. Popular sites, they explain, are linked-to more frequently the more they grow in popularity. As an example, the authors note that "although there are more than 13,000 Web pages on the subject of gun control, two-thirds of all hyperlinks point to the 10 most popular sites. In the case of capital punishment, the top 10 sites receive 63 percent of the total number of links on the topic. In every category of content we examined, more than half the Web sites have only a single link to them." The effect in this civic realm as in all others online, according to the study, is one of "a staggering degree of consolidation." Hindman and Cukier, "More News, Less Diversity."

10. For an overview of civic applications on the Internet, see Center for Digital Democracy, "The Dot-Commons: A Virtual Tour of the Online Civic Sector," http://www.democraticmedia.org/issues/digitalcommons/dotcommonstour.html. See also David Bollier and Tim Watts, *Saving the Information Commons: A New Public Interest Agenda in Digital Media* (Washington, D.C.: New America Foundation, 2002), pp. 71–78, and the American Library Association's Information Commons (http://www.info-commons.org/).

11. For a history of USENET, see Ronda and Michael Hauben, *Netizens: An Anthology*, http://www.columbia.edu/~rh120/; Douglas Schuler, *New Community Networks: Wired for Change* (New York: ACM Press, 1996) discusses the Cleveland Free-Net, Santa Monica PEN, and other examples of civic networking.

12. Bernard Aboba, *The Online User's Encyclopedia: Bulletin Boards and Beyond* (Reading, MA: Addison-Wesley Pub. Co., 1994) offers a fascinating and comprehensive overview of the early-1990s telecommunications environment.

13. Aboba, pp. 264–271, 315, 377–384. Gopher continues to exist, actually, with over 250 servers still in use and with efforts to adapt its simplified interface for PDA and cell-phone Web browsing. Lore Sjöberg, "Gopher: Underground Technology," *Wired News*, April 12, 2004, http://www.wired.com/news/technology/0,1282,62988,00.html.

14. Writing in 1993, for example, when AOL, Prodigy, and CompuServe combined had 3.9 million subscribers, Aboba reflected the view of many online veterans in finding fault with all three commercial services: CompuServe was "definitely overpriced," according to Aboba, noting its $39.95 start-up fee, $2.50 monthly maintenance fee, and $22.50 per hour for 9600 bps access, while AOL's Internet "gateway is unreliable and the message size limitations are so severe as to preclude use of the gateway for anything other than mail." Prodigy, meanwhile, which still lacked an Internet gateway, was dismissed as "the McDonald's of online services: It has served the most customers, but it's not exactly filet mignon." Aboba, pp. 598–600.

15. NSF's Acceptable Use Policy can still be found online, especially on campus websites that either haven't bothered to update their files or that still subscribe (in theory, anyway) to the noncommercial tenets of the AUP. See, for example, Creighton University's web site, http://www.creighton.edu/nsfnet-aup.html.

16. "Starting in 1990," notes Bill Stewart's Living Internet project, "over the next few years

the NSF conducted a series of workshops and studies to plan for transition of the NSFNET to private industry. The vehicle that evolved to support this new architecture was a set of Network Access Points that acted as connection points for the commercial backbones so that the network would remain connected at the top level once the NSFNET was retired. In February, 1994, the NSF awarded contracts for establishment of four NAPs operating at 155 Mbps—one in New York operated by Sprint, one in Washington, D.C., operated by MFS, one in Chicago operated by Ameritech, and one in California operated by Pacific Bell." "The Living Internet: Internet/History/NSFNET," http://livinginternet.com/.

17. Aboba, pp. 274–276. The arrival of Mosaic in 1993 helped spawn a whopping 341,634 percent increase in network traffic. A number of articles look back at the broader impact of the Web browser from the vantage point of its tenth anniversary. See, for example, Stephen Levy, "The Killer Browser," *Newsweek*, April 21, 2003, http://www.creighton.edu/nsfnet-aup.html; and Mike Yamamoto, "A Brave New World Wide Web," CNET News. com, April 14, 2003, http://news.com.com/2009-1032-995680.html.

18. Amy Harmon, "Recording Industry Goes After Students Over Music Sharing," *New York Times*, April 23, 2003. At $150,000 per copyright violation, the potentially billion-dollar case was clearly one of legal intimidation and was quickly settled out of court (although similar suits followed, as the RIAA pursued private citizens as well as college students in its quest to stamp out illegal downloading). John Borland, "Recording Industry Settles Student Copyright Suits," zDNet, May 2, 2003, http://www.zdnet.com.au/newstech/ebusiness/story/0,2000048590,20274153,00.htm. The initial response from the academic community to the suit was mixed. "It's been very difficult," conceded Penn State President Graham Spanier, "because students have grown up viewing the Internet as a place where you go to get lots of free access to things. As we have tried to educate our students, half of them understand it's like going into a store and putting a CD in your pocket and the other half just can't see it that way." Princeton General Counsel Peter McDonough, on the other hand, stressed that the RIAA suit must be seen as an effort to protect corporate interests in copyright rather than an indictment of the hardware or software that facilitates peer-to-peer file exchanges. "If this becomes more about a challenge to the technology than about downloading music for recreational purposes," he observes, "that is a serious concern for us. Because we emphatically believe the technologies themselves are not illegal." Quoted in Harmon, "Recording Industry Goes After Students."

19. In the early 1990s, the colorfully named Archie and Veronica facilitated searches of file-transfer sites and gopher spaces, respectively, while Wide Area Information Servers facilitated database document retrieval. Aboba, pp. 212–16, 255–63, 265. But online civic experiments at the time were more likely to be localized affairs, on a BBS system (which date back to 1978) or a city-wide free-net (a movement that began in 1986 under the auspices of the Society for Public Access Computing and later the National Public Telecomputing Network until fading before the onslaught of such heavily marketed commercial services as CompuServe, Prodigy, and America Online). Schuler, pp. 333–375.

20. Katie Hafner and Matthew Lyon, *Where Wizards Stay Up Late: The Origins of the Internet* (New York: Simon & Schuster, 1996); Jack Rickard, "Home Grown BB$," *Wired*, September/October 1993, http://www.wired.com/wired/archive/1.04/bbs.html.

21. Ronda and Michael Hauben, *Netizens: An Anthology*, http://www.columbia.edu/~rh120/.

22. The searchable Usenet archives maintained by Google provide a fascinating glimpse into the culture of Usenet, covering over two decades and more than 700 million postings. http://www.google.com/googlegroups/archive_announce_20.html.

23. Michael Hauben, "The Social Forces Behind the Development of Usenet," in Ronda and Michael Hauben, *Netizens: An Anthology.*

24. Ronda Hauben, "The World of Usenet," in Ronda and Michael Hauben, *Netizens: An Anthology.*

25. The most authoritative and detailed picture of networking activity *before* all of the component parts were connected to the Internet is John S. Quarterman, *The Matrix: Computer Networks and Conferencing Systems Worldwide* (Bedford, MA: Digital Press, 1990). Quarterman has continued his work under the aegis of Matrix NetSystems, http://www.mids.org/.

26. Kara Swisher, *AOL.com* (New York: Random House, 1998), pp. 112–114. By 1995, the major commercial online services all offered their subscribers access to the Internet.

27. Jim Hu, "AOL Subscribers, Sales Keep Sliding," *CNET News.com*, March 16, 2004, http://news.com.com/2100-1038_3-5173484.html.

28. Unfortunately, we are less apt to enjoy such archival access to two other centers of online civic activity, the early BBS communities and their latter-day web-based counterparts, neither of which has been adequately recorded. "The early bulletin boards," explains Katharine Mieszkowski of *Salon.com*, "were essentially separate dial-up islands, which eventually became able to share files through a system called FidoNet. The preservation of this slice of digital culture depends on whether tens of thousands of one-time BBS operators happened to keep backups, and whether those old-timers can be bothered to contribute them to an archive." Katharine Mieszkowski, "Relics of the Lost Bulletin-board Tribes," *Salon.com*, January 22, 2002, http://www.salon.com/tech/feature/2002/01/22/bbs_archives/. Efforts to capture early BBS and Web culture include Jason Scott's textfiles.com (http://www.textfiles.com/) and Brewster Kahle's Internet Archive (http://www.archive.org/). See Katharine Mieszkowski, "Dumpster Diving on the Web," *Salon.com*, November 2, 2001, http://dir.salon.com/tech/feature/2001/11/02/wayback/index.html.

29. Katharine Mieszkowski, "The Geeks who Saved Usenet," *Salon.com*, January 7, 2002, http://www.salon.com/tech/feature/2002/01/07/saving_usenet/.

30. These three references were among the first 10 results of "about 65,000 . . . sorted by relevance" at the Google Usenet search site (http://groups.google.com/).

31. Bollier and Watts, *Saving the Information Commons*, pp. 2, 3.

32. Benjamin Barber, *A Place for Us: How to Make Society Civil and Democracy Strong* (New York, Hill & Wang, 1998), p. 45.

33. Howard Rheingold, "Community Development in the Cybersociety of the Future," June 1999, http://www.partnerships.org.uk/bol/howard.htm.

34. "Understood in this way," Friedland and Boyte add, "the commons has taken many forms in American history. Newspapers, schools, libraries, settlement houses, business centers, union hiring halls, community festivals and fairs, bands and sports teams, local political parties and other groups with wide civic participation could be seen as forms of commons in which people participated, around which they gathered, and through which they developed a collective public signature for the larger world." Lew Friedland and Harry Boyte, "The New Information Commons: Community Information Partnerships and Civic Change," January 2000, http://www.publicwork.org/pdf/workingpapers/New%20information%20commons.pdf.

35. The Open Directory Project (http://www.dmoz.org/) describes itself as "the largest, most comprehensive human-edited directory of the Web . . . , constructed and maintained by a vast, global community of volunteer editors." The Public Library of Science

(http://www.publiclibraryofscience.org/) "is a non-profit organization of scientists and physicians committed to making the world's scientific and medical literature a freely available public resource." The Creative Commons (http://creativecommons.org/), which includes sections for musicians, photographers and illustrators, writers and bloggers, filmmakers, and educators and scholars, "is devoted to expanding the range of creative work available for others to build upon and share."

36. David Bollier, "Reclaiming the Commons," *Boston Review*, 27, nos. 3–4 (Summer 2002), http://www.bostonreview.net/BR27.3/bollier.html.

37. The Spectrum Commons and Digital Dividends Act of 2003 (H.R. 1396), introduced by Rep. Edward J. Markey (D-MA), proposes to create a permanent trust fund using the proceeds of the auction of public airwaves to fund public-interest telecommunications initiatives. The Digital Opportunity Investment Trust Act (S. 1854), co-sponsored by Sen. Christopher J. Dodd (D-CT), Sen. Olympia Snowe (R-ME), and Sen. Dick Durbin (D-IL), would fulfill the vision first put forward by former FCC Chairman Newton Minow and former NBC News and PBS President Lawrence Grossman, as described in their Digital Promise website (http://www.digitalpromise.org/index.asp).

38. Thomas J. Bliley, "Seeking to Fulfill the Promise of Telecommunications," *The Hill*, July 9, 2003, http://www.thehill.com/op_ed/070903.aspx.

39. Although the Digital Opportunity Investment Trust has not yet been created, $750,000 was appropriated in 2003 for the Federation of American Scientists to study the project. Kay Howell, "Progress Towards a National Initiative for Information Technology to Improve Learning and Teaching," FAS Public Interest Report 56, no. 1 (Spring 2003), http://www.fas.org/faspir/2003/v56n1/learning.htm.

40. For information on opposition to the Digital Millennium Copyright Act, see the Electronic Frontier Foundation's DMCA Archive (http://www.eff.org/IP/DRM/DMCA/). On the issue of media ownership and deregulation, see Journalism.org (http://www.journalism.org/resources/research/reports/ownership/deregulation2.asp).

41. Bill Thompson, "Copyright Controls 'Out of Tune,'" *BBC News*, http://news.bbc.co.uk/1/hi/technology/2968216.stm.

42. See, for example, Lynne Margolis, "Independents' Day," *Christian Science Monitor*, April 11, 2003, http//www.csmonitor.com/2003/0411/p13s02-almp.html.

43. Dan Gillmor, "Democratizing the Media, and More," *eJournal*, January 11, 2004, http://weblog.siliconvalley.com/column/dangillmor/archives/001654.shtml#001654.

44. The Internet Archive (http://www.archive.org) was "founded to build an 'Internet library,' with the purpose of offering permanent access for researchers, historians, and scholars to historical collections that exist in digital format."

45. Robert X. Cringely, "Resistance is Futile: How Peer-to-Peer File Sharing Is Likely to Change Big Media," I, Cringely/The Pulpit, http://www.pbs.org/cringely/pulpit/pulpit20021128.html.

46. In time, various forms of wireless transmission may add new options to the cable and telco broadband "duopoly," but for the immediate future, cable and DSL networks will dominate.

47. Testimony of Paul Misener, vice president for global public policy, Amazon.com, before the House Subcommittee on Telecommunications and the Internet, July 21, 2003, http://energycommerce.house.gov/108/Hearings/07212003hearing1024/Misener1610.htm.

48. Testimony of Robert Pepper, chief, Policy Development Office of Strategic Planning and Policy Analysis, Federal Communications Commission, before the House Subcommittee on Telecommunications and the Internet, July 21, 2003, http://energycommerce.house.gov/108/Hearings/07212003hearing1024/Pepper1602.htm.

49. Legg Mason, "Beyond UNE-P: The Edge vs. the Network—a/k/a 'Open Access II,'" December 5, 2002. In response to these concerns over anticompetitive and discriminatory behavior, Ken Ferree, chief of the Media Bureau at the FCC, claims that existing antitrust laws will offer sufficient protection: "The irony of course is that, if the kinds of commercial arrangements that the proponents of openness regulation fear actually come about—and if they are as pernicious as suggested—no regulatory check should be necessary. The kinds of conduct that have been posited are precisely what the antitrust laws were intended to combat. If distributors actually start using whatever market power they have at the distribution level to eliminate rivals or favor some vertically integrated enterprise in an anticompetitive way, we would expect the antitrust authorities to have more than a little interest." W. Kenneth Ferree, chief, Media Bureau, Federal Communications Commission, Speech delivered at the Progress & Freedom Foundation Conference on "Net Neutrality," June 27, 2003, available for download at http://www.fcc.gov/mb/.

50. Jeffrey Benner, "Getting a Lock on Broadband," *Salon.com*, June 7, 2002, http://www.salon.com/tech/feature/2002/06/07/broadband/.

51. James H. Johnston and J.H. Snider, "Breaking the Chains: Unlicensed Spectrum as a Last-Mile Broadband Solution," Spectrum Series Working Paper #7, June 2003, New America Foundation, http://www.newamerica.net/index.cfm?pg=article&pubID=1250.

52. For the clearest expression of the public interest perspective in the spectrum management debate, see the New America Foundation's Spectrum Policy Program (http://www.newamerica.net/index.cfm?pg=program&ProgID=3).

53. In an effort to foster a collective envisioning of a new, more participatory communications environment, one that accommodates a full range of civic, educational, and cultural expression, the Center for Digital Democracy launched its "Digital Destiny Campaign" (http://www.democraticmedia.org/ddc/index.php). Combining activism at the local level with a range of informative online resources, the campaign provides the tools that communities need to harness the power of broadband—via cable, DSL, or wireless networks, and including digital television—with content, applications, and services that reflect the diversity of our culture rather than the marketing formulas of a handful of conglomerates. The Digital Destiny project addresses this need in six interrelated areas of activity: Broadband Assessment, Citizen Access, Policy Engagement, Collaboration, Support Structures, and Diversity of Viewpoint.

54. David Bollier, "Reclaiming the Commons."

55. For information on this "content gap," see The Children's Partnership, "The Search for High-Quality Content for Low-Income and Underserved Communities," October 2003, http://www.contentbank.org/research/QualityContent.pdf.

RECLAIMING THE PUBLIC AIRWAVES

MICHAEL CALABRESE AND MATT BARRANCA

The media ownership battle of 2003 raised citizens' awareness about the quality, diversity, and localism of our media choices, yet the ensuing debate did little to challenge the fundamental source of TV broadcasters' power—their exclusive rights to large swaths of public airwaves. However, thanks to the rise of "smart radio" technologies and "unlicensed" (open access) spectrum, the major networks and 1,400 local stations are facing a reallocation of TV frequencies from broadcasting to broadband. Community wireless networking over wasted TV frequencies could make high-speed broadband ubiquitous and affordable.

Each economic era has a resource that drives wealth creation. In the agricultural era it was land; in the industrial era, it was energy. Today the American people collectively own the most valuable resource of the information economy: the airwaves, also known as the radio frequency spectrum. For a number of industries—from broadcast and satellite TV to cellular telephone providers to consumer electronics and computer manufacturers—the electromagnetic spectrum is the most important yet least understood resource of the information economy. The economic importance of spectrum access to emerging technologies is comparable to that of the world's oceans to the global fishing industries. Just as companies lease license rights to mine such publicly owned resources as trees or oil, today's communications industries mine spectrum for the technologies and services that will drive our increasingly wireless world for generations to come.

The role of the spectrum to future economic growth is obvious. It is obvious that cell-phone use has exploded, as there were already 60 million more cellular subscribers than residential telephone lines in the United States as of mid-2004. Wireless Internet access is fast becoming ubiquitous with WiFi "hotspots" mushrooming in coffee shops, at airports, on college campuses and even now in rural communities. The rapid trend toward wireless communication has made access to the public airwaves the most crucial issue concerning communications policy of the knowledge economy, pitting industry stakeholders against each other in intense debates within the walls of the Federal Communications Commission

(FCC) and in Congress. Economists estimate the commercial value of access to the airwaves in the United States alone at over $750 billion. But often forgotten in these lobbying battles are the voices of United States citizens who are the actual owners of this immensely valuable public resource.

The electromagnetic spectrum is more than just an economic input for industry productivity. Economic valuations for spectrum, as staggering as they may be, rarely account for the great social and democratic benefits inherent in wireless communication. As new wireless technologies are developed and new opportunities for individual and political expression emerge, the public airwaves will become the essential medium supporting the First Amendment rights of future generations.

The opportunity costs of poorly managed spectrum resource go well beyond lost government revenues from spectrum sales. A poorly managed spectrum resource will jeopardize the ability of future generations to shape political discourse and create new means of expression. A free and open spectrum will foster democratic freedoms just as access to unregulated, private printing presses did in the era of Thomas Paine and Benjamin Franklin, as mimeograph and Xerox machines did for student activists of the 1960s and 1970s, and as the open, end-to-end architecture of the Internet has empowered current legions of civic-minded bloggers and netizens. Public airwaves that are exclusively licensed and sold off to the highest industry bidder—or worse, given away without commanding any sort of compensation for their use—represent an immense waste of human and civic potential far beyond any economic calculation. Yet, this is precisely the sort of privatization of the public airwaves that the Bush administration's FCC has been attempting to push through since 2001.

Spectrum policy is rife with baffling contradictions. On one level, the spectrum policy debate can be understood as a First Amendment issue, with access to the airwaves seen as the basic infrastructure for wireless communications. On another level, spectrum can be seen as a publicly owned natural resource (one with a profound capacity to enable democratic processes), making the allocation and cost of licenses an industrial-policy issue demanding a fair return to the public. With such a wide range of corporate, government, and civic stakeholders, spectrum reform is a uniquely complex public policy issue with far-reaching implications.

Unfortunately, spectrum policy is barely comprehended even at its most basic levels. As the exclusive intellectual property of radio-frequency engineers and communications lawyers, the intricacies of spectrum policy are often beyond the reach of ordinary citizens. Typically, most spectrum policy battles are fought over access rights (licenses) to specific frequencies of the spectrum and the technical engineering rules for using those bands. Effective participation in the FCC's "public" rulemakings demands a lobbyist's knowledge of the FCC's multilayered bureaucracy and an engineer's keen eye for how slight amendments to technical rules can impact entire industries. And with the boundaries of spectrum policy encompassing such diverse issues as media ownership and censorship, the delivery of broadband Internet services to underserved communities, promoting competition with duopoly cable and DSL services, the future of digital TV, and the convergence of the Internet with traditional telecommunications services, even most members of Congress sitting on the influential Commerce Committees have barely come to grips with the issue's complexities. But it need not be this way.

Spectrum 101

The spectrum, once called *aether*, is nothing more tangible than the electromagnetic properties of the earth's atmosphere. It is the collection of frequencies useful for transmitting radio signals. At the onset of wireless communications in the early twentieth century, the government (drawing on assumptions for 1920s radio technology) divided the spectrum into bands of frequencies, measured in hertz (Hz); the wider the band, the greater its capacity for carrying information. The prime lower-frequency bands are below 3 GHz (3 million hertz), where the most familiar consumer services, such as broadcasting and cell phones, are clustered. The higher frequency bands are much less useful and are allocated to applications with lower economic value, such as radar systems, security alarms, and other mostly short-distance applications. (For a diagram of the spectrum and how it's used—and misused—see the New America Foundation's "Citizen's Guide to the Airwaves," available free at www.spectrumpolicy.org.)

Like the atmosphere and navigable waterways, the spectrum is managed as a publicly owned asset—hence, the moniker "public" airwaves. The Communications Act of 1934 plainly prohibits private ownership of spectrum and authorizes the FCC to allocate frequencies to various services and to grant temporary licenses consistent with the "public interest, convenience, and necessity." The FCC, based on the limits of fifty-year-old analog radio technologies, rigidly zones the airwaves for specific purposes (radio, TV, cell phones) and then assigns slices of these bands to particular companies (Clear Channel, ABC, Verizon). For example, in 1945 the FCC allocated the frequencies between 174 and 216 MHz for TV channels 7 to 13 and more recently reallocated frequencies between 824 and 849 MHz to mobile telephone companies.

Like any other natural resource open to industry exploitation—such as livestock grazing or oil exploration on public lands—the economic value of the rights to "harvest" individual spectrum bands varies, based on the frequency of the spectrum and external market conditions, such as demand for service and the availability of technologies to operate on specific bands. Signals transmitted on the low-frequency spectrum bands have longer wavelengths and superior propagation characteristics, qualities that allow them to pass more easily through dense obstacles (such as walls or trees) and to carry more data. The rights to these lower-frequency bands are highly valuable, as their signals travel farther at lower power levels and reach more receivers with less chance of interference. The "beachfront" spectrum bands below 1 GHZ are especially sought-after and closely guarded by their incumbents. For example, a leading Wall Street analyst estimated the economic value of the 402 MHZ of low-frequency spectrum allocated to the exclusive use of TV broadcasters at over $350 billion. Beyond the value of this spectrum for its current allocated use, the potential economic benefits to broadcasters of the expanded license rights they have received for offering digital television (DTV)—including the right to sell or lease this spectrum to other industries—will generate new revenues for the industry and make TV broadcasters even more profitable and powerful than they are today.

Artificial Scarcity

With such a range of industries competing for airwave access, one might think that spectrum is a finite resource. The fact that cell-phone companies have been willing to pay tens of billions of dollars for spectrum licenses here and in Europe suggests that the airwaves are very scarce. In reality, the spectrum's capacity is hardly exercised at all. Using sophisticated spectrum-analysis equipment, the New America Foundation recently measured the use of spectrum over downtown Washington, D.C., near the White House, and found that during peak hours, between 60 and 80 percent of the prime frequencies are barely in use. (Notable exceptions include the frequencies used by a handful of local TV stations, cell-phone companies, and "unlicensed" consumer devices, such as cordless phones and wireless computer networks.) In more rural areas, the spectrum is even more vacant and could be particularly useful for advanced services, such as high-speed wireless Internet delivery to underserved communities. In both urban and rural America, the overwhelming capacity of the spectrum resource is barely tapped.

What's scarce is access to the airwaves. The prime low frequencies that allow signals to penetrate buildings and bad weather conditions have all been allocated on an exclusive basis to television and radio broadcasters, the military, and a host of other industries and services. The majority of the most useful and valuable frequencies are allocated permanently to the federal government for undisclosed military, intelligence, and federal-agency uses. The National Telecommunications and Information Administration (NTIA), an office of the United States Commerce Department, oversees spectrum allocations to the federal government. Federal spectrum uses are kept confidential, so that frequencies reserved for intelligence communications cannot be easily determined. Thus, although many of the most useful frequencies are used only around military facilities—or lie fallow most of the time—citizens are not even allowed to know what empty spectrum might be productively shared by using new technologies that can avoid interference with critical systems.

The second-largest allocation, in terms of economic value, goes to the television broadcasters, who have enjoyed a privileged, fifty-year free ride on the low-frequency bands below 1 GHz. This "beachfront" spectrum (so-called because of its high bandwidth capacity and propagation characteristics) is loaned to broadcasters, free of charge, by the federal government in the form of renewable eight-year licenses. In exchange for this grant, broadcasters have been asked to fulfill a number of vaguely defined "Public Interest Obligations" (PIOs), which have been steadily eroded or strategically amended to benefit broadcasters and their ability to attract audiences and extend their rights to the airwaves. The PIOs for commercial broadcast TV set the standard for other TV platforms (cable and satellite), but because over-the-air broadcasters use public airwaves granted to them at no cost, their obligations are intended to be more stringent. The current list of PIOs include: requiring a minimum of three hours of children's educational programming per week, with limits on the amount of advertising directed at children; setting standards for "indecency and obscenity," especially during the viewing hours between 6:00 AM and 10:00 PM; providing reasonable access and equal airtime to political candidates during election campaigns; and requirements for content accessibility to hearing and visually impaired audiences, prohibition of tobacco advertising, and encouraging broadcasters to provide program ratings to enable V-chip, or parental-choice, alerts. Given the value of the spectrum used by broadcasters over the past fifty years, this list of public-interest obligations is remarkably short and gives citizens scant opportunity to determine the terms by which broadcasters continue to use their airwaves.

After the government and broadcast TV incumbents, the cellular phone providers occupy the rights to a range of higher-frequency allocations, which were mostly purchased in high-stakes auctions held in the 1990s.

"Unlicensed" (Citizens' Access) Spectrum

Further up the spectrum are a few frequencies known as the unlicensed bands, which do not require an FCC permit. These frequencies (900 MHZ, 2.4 GHZ, and 5.7 and 5.8 GHZ) were once commonly referred to as "junk bands" because they are shared by roughly 400 million low-power household devices, from microwave ovens and garage door openers to cordless phones, baby monitors, and WiFi computer networking devices. Unlike licensed bands, where users have exclusive rights, unlicensed spectrum is managed like a public highway. It is subject to certain "rules of the road," but access is open, free, and shared. The unlicensed bands offer a unique space for innovation because their access is not restricted to the exclusive use of one particular industry or individual licensee. As long as technology developers adhere to FCC rules for low-power transmissions and receive proper authorization to market new unlicensed devices, individuals or industries are free to invent new applications for these bands.

The most recent unlicensed success is WiFi, short for Wireless Fidelity, or the suite of wireless networking technologies known to engineers as the 802.11, IEEE standard. WiFi is the unlicensed spectrum access that allows coffee drinkers at Starbucks and students almost anywhere on major university campuses to enjoy wireless, high-speed Internet connections on laptops and soon on Internet telephone devices. The WiFi technologies of 802.11 "a," "b," and "g" have been integrated into a host of affordable consumer products, such as wireless access points, WiFi laptop cards, and microprocessing chips—which, together, enable local-area wireless networking and Internet access at speeds as high as 54 megabits per second.

These WiFi technologies are, in fact, the first generation of a larger category of devices called "smart" or "cognitive radios"; they combine computer-processing power with advanced radio frequency receiver capabilities. WiFi and subsequent unlicensed technologies, such as WiMAX (an emerging commercial-grade smart radio standard designed for long-distance, wide-area networking) communicate using "spread spectrum" technologies, which divide data into packets and transmit and receive signals on multiple-frequency channels. Spread spectrum technology operates in a manner similar in principle to how the Internet works, by relying on the intelligence of end-user devices to receive data sent on multiple channels and reassemble the transmissions into coherent information.

The value of these smart radios is that they both conserve and actually create spectrum capacity by allowing multiple users to share frequency bands in ways that were previously impossible with such older receivers as those in TV sets or traditional radios. Because of these spectrum-sharing technologies, a growing chorus of engineers and Internet pioneers are advocating expanding unlicensed access to the airwaves, beyond the limited capacity of the existing unlicensed bands. They argue that in the near future, computer technology will usher in an era of smart broadband devices that will make sharing the electromagnetic spectrum as practical as sharing the acoustic spectrum, or sound waves.

To better understand how smart radios operate, it's useful to think of how the human ear and brain work during conversation—for example, at a cocktail party. Imagine a room filled with people organized into small groups, where a number of discrete conversations are occurring at once. While these separate conversations create background noise, the human ear, guided by the processing power of the brain, is able to easily tune out the ambient noise and listen discriminately to the desired speaker, or transmitter. Smart radios, enabled by their computer processors and enhanced with sensitive directional antennas, are able to discern intended signals from background noise, allowing them to share occupied frequencies without creating interference for less sophisticated tuners. In fact, many smart radios can "listen before they talk," modulating their signals to select unoccupied frequencies to avoid licensed broadcasters. This is the technology that persuaded the government in 2003 to open the military radar band at 5 GHz for sharing on a secondary basis by WiFi networks.

In a world of unlicensed, smart-radio communication, the government no more needs to regulate electromagnetic speech among cognitive radios than it does acoustic speech at a cocktail party. Whereas "dumb" analog receivers justified government grants of exclusive rights to narrow bands of frequencies, digital and smart technologies are making it feasible for any device to dynamically share wide ranges of underutilized spectrum without imposing harmful interference on other users. (For a detailed discussion of unlicensed spectrum and emerging smart radios, see "Radio Revolution: The Coming Age of Unlicensed Wireless"; and see "The Cartoon Guide to Federal Spectrum Policy" for a satirical perspective of how current spectrum regulation could impact the unlicensed wireless future. Both of these New America Foundation publications are available free at www. spectrumpolicy.org.)

The Stalled DTV Transition

In addition to unlicensed technologies, the continuing migration from analog to digital technology is providing other opportunities for more efficient and equitable spectrum management. Because of the poor receiver capabilities of analog tuners, over-the-air (OTA) analog TV can operate only on certain channels in each market area, with many empty spectrum channels separating broadcasters both within markets and between nearby markets. As a result, on average, 80 percent of the sixty-seven broadcast TV channels in each local market remain unassigned. These guard bands and unassigned TV channels create a vast wasteland of empty "white space."

Digital broadcasting reduces this waste somewhat, as it compresses data and allows frequencies to carry more information using less bandwidth, with less chance of interference. Since 1987, the United States Congress and the FCC have been attempting to transition broadcasters and the TV viewing public from analog to digital TV. While nearly 90 percent of United States households receive their signals from a video subscriber service (either cable or direct broadcast satellite), TV broadcasters have delayed making the transition—in large part because it means returning spectrum licenses worth tens of billions of dollars to the public. And even though freeing up broadcast analog spectrum will open up these bands for more affordable wireless broadband services, members of Congress have been unable to muster the political will to turn off analog for fear of alienating the remaining OTA viewers. The long and continued epic of the DTV transition is further evidence that licensed spectrum users actually need only a fraction of the frequencies they license—but reclaiming that spectrum is almost entirely impossible.

The problem is that the FCC's seventy-five-year-old allocation system—based on rigid spectrum "zoning" and perpetual, zero-cost licensing—gives incumbent users no incentive to give up spectrum or to use it more efficiently. Access to the airwaves is allocated service-by-service through elaborate rulemakings. Regulators rigidly define—and freeze in place, often for decades—the precise frequencies an industry can use and for what purpose. Although cell-phone companies are desperate for additional spectrum, it is not available at any price. Congress mandated auctions in 1994 to assign new licenses, but it has not given the FCC authority to auction or charge rent for prime spectrum previously licensed. To the contrary, pressured by the broadcasting lobby, Congress in 1996 effectively doubled the share of the airwaves held by local TV stations—a giveaway then valued by the FCC at up to $70 billion, but now worth far more.

But now, smart radio technology and the innovative deployments of thousands of independent, unlicensed wireless networks across the country are changing the terms of the debate. While industry and policymakers may be aware that the fastest growing telecommunications service in recent years has been WiFi, only the observant have noticed that the unlicensed technology has matured beyond its intended usage as a local area networking tool.

From "Hotspots" to Closing the Digital Divide

The first generation WiFi deployments (known as hotspots) targeted yuppies camped out at Starbucks, hotel lobbies, and airports. But in recent years, thousands of college campuses, community organizations, municipal governments, and scores of wireless ISPs (WISPs) have scaled-up WiFi to create wide-area hot zones, reaching more diverse users. If the first WiFi boom was about short-range mobility inside the home or office, the current growth in unlicensed spectrum is in fixed wireless networking—connecting homes and entire communities to affordable, high-speed Internet access. In a manner similar to the way cellular phone networks are built, more than 2,500 WISPs have built substantial, unlicensed wireless broadband networks offering high-speed Internet connections at distances as far as thirty miles from the wired Internet. By using the full range of unlicensed spectrum (900 MHZ, 2.4 GHZ, and 5.7 and 5.8 GHZ) and radio technologies developed within the open-access protocol of these bands, unlicensed wireless providers are bridging the "last mile" of the digital divide, bringing broadband to rural areas where high-speed wired connections are unavailable or unaffordable. An estimated

300,000 United States households receive broadband Internet connections from unlicensed WISP networks.

The success of these deployments has not merely been limited to the commercial WISP sector. A number of novel community networking models have also emerged from the WiFi boom and are attracting the attention of spectrum policymakers. Among these are growing ad-hoc metropolitan area networks comprised of independently built and managed free hotspots. Groups such as NYCwireless.net, SeattleWireless.net, and the Bay Area Research Wireless Network (BARWN.org) provide technical and organizational support, encouraging neighborhoods to build and expand open-access hotspots to make their communities more connected. NYCwireless, for example, has been leading a grassroots movement to bring free WiFi to every public space in Manhattan, beating pay-per-service providers to the punch with free networks built by volunteers, often funded by local businesses that benefit from the increased foot traffic attracted to these hotspots. In the San Francisco Bay Area, the BARWN project has raised access points on the San Bruno Mountain, Potrero Hill and Yerba Buena Island, providing high-speed Internet access to any household within the 6-mile, line-of-site range of the transmitters. These access points, connected with donated DSL lines, are proving that inexpensive unlicensed technologies, when properly deployed, can leverage existing wired bandwidth and serve as a last-mile, to-the-home competitor against cable modem and DSL.

In another promising trend, dozens of United States municipalities long ignored by wireline providers because their markets were considered too small to justify laying cable or DSL, have deployed unlicensed wireless networks that provide businesses and residents with high-speed connections. Municipal Electrical Utilities (MEUs) or local governments become wireless broadband providers by investing in commercial-grade fixed-wireless networking equipment and building expansive networks using municipal infrastructure, like water towers, town hall spires, and city lamp posts. Dozens of MEUs from across the country have built unlicensed networks in the past two years with rapid returns on their investment, including Owensboro, Kentucky; Buffalo, Minnesota; Dickenson County, Virginia; Sun Prairie and Waupaca, Wisconsin; Franklin County, Washington, and others.

A number of public safety organizations have also built unlicensed WiFi mesh networks, in which small, bread-box-sized transmitters, mounted on municipal street and traffic lights, communicate with each other over short distances, creating multipath networks that are easily expandable and allow police, fire, and emergency personnel to have unfettered, fast, and secure high-speed access. Unlicensed mesh networking manufacturers, like Tropos Networks and MeshNetworks, are building affordable networks in small and medium-sized cities across the country for both internal government purposes and for residential and business access.

The townwide mesh network in Cerritos, California, offers all residents both home and mobile Internet access over unlicensed spectrum at $30 per month. Mesh-networking technology is also being deployed by inspired community organizations. The Champaign-Urbana Community Wireless Network (CUWiN) in Illinois has developed open-source, "home-brew" mesh network nodes, made from recycled computers and WiFi antennas that can be placed in residential attics to create affordable community mesh networks for underserved populations.

With all of this innovation in unlicensed airwaves, community media activists, WiFi freenet builders, and groups representing the public interest have begun to question whether licensed spectrum incumbents should have rightful claim to exclusive use of the frequencies allocated to them. If unlicensed spectrum sharing has been able to flourish in the crowded, higher-frequency junk bands at 2.4 and 5 GHz, surely the higher bandwidth, low-frequency bands would be fertile ground for both licensed and low-powered unlicensed sharing. The success of 2,500 WISPs and scores of community networks have made the once radical and seemingly impossible idea of sharing adjacent and cochannel frequencies with local TV broadcasters a technological possibility and a demonstrable public good.

Even the FCC sees the logic in the proposal. To the surprise of many in the spectrum policy community, the FCC has opened a proposed rulemaking to allow smart radio receivers operating at low-power levels to share unoccupied TV channels in the VHF and UHF bands with the high-powered TV broadcasters. If the FCC rule passes, community broadband activists and entrepreneurial WISPs could have a fighting chance to bring an affordable and ubiquitous broadband option to millions of homes currently off the high-speed grid. But incumbent licensees are already lining up to oppose opening prime spectrum for shared access, since it would increase competition and reduce the value of their licenses.

Privatizing the Public Airwaves

While the unlicensed movement has created opportunities for more direct citizen access to spectrum, other threats have surfaced to privatize the airwaves and force consumers into paying licensed incumbents for access of the publicly owned resource. In the past few years, through a series of rule changes, the FCC has begun to implement a radical shift in the nation's spectrum-allocation policy that is contrary to both the policies codified in the Communications Act and to the obvious technological trend toward spectrum-sharing smart radio systems. In 2003, the Commission adopted rules to facilitate secondary markets for spectrum by allowing licensees—whether or not they paid the public for their license—to sell or rent unused capacity to other firms. FCC staff proposed a new rule permitting universities and other institutions that hold valuable free licenses for nonprofit educational purposes to sell their spectrum to private firms, encouraging these hard-pressed nonprofit institutions to abandon their educational use of the air-waves in return for a quick buck on new private spectrum markets. Although the Commission's June 2004 Final Order does not permit the permanent transfer of education licenses to private firms, it allows those institutions to raise money by leasing their spectrum.

The blueprint for this ongoing privatization of the public airwaves is a pair of FCC staff reports released in November 2002. The FCC's Spectrum Policy Task Force proposed that incumbent licensees should be granted permanent, private property-like rights in the frequencies they currently borrow. The Task Force also recommended that future licenses grant firms "maximum possible autonomy" to decide what services to offer, what technical standards to adopt, or whether instead to sell or sublease their frequency assignments to other firms. If the Task Force's recommendations were to be adopted, access to the airwaves would become a commodity traded on secondary markets and free of all public interest obligations except to avoid harmful interference with other licensed services.

This is not all bad news. The FCC's outdated command-and-control approach—based on rigidly zoning the airwaves by service and assigning exclusive licenses at zero cost—has exacerbated the scarcity of wireless bandwidth, stifling com-petition, slowing innovation, and restricting citizen access to the airwaves. The problem is not the stated goals of the Task Force but its means of achieving them. The Commission's senior economists added a proposal that these new and valu-able rights to sell and sublease frequencies be given away to incumbent licensees at no charge. The proposal is dressed up as an "auction," but one in which any incumbent opting to sell its license would be entitled to keep 100 percent of the revenue—money that, under current law, would flow into the public treasury. The logic of the proposal is that broadcasters and other spectrum incumbents have so much political clout that the only practical way to reduce scarcity involves bribing them to bring their spectrum to market.

There are three problems with this approach. First, it confers a massive and undeserved financial windfall—as much as $500 billion—on a few lucky indus-tries, taking revenues from the public during a time of ballooning deficits and shrinking revenues. Companies that never paid a nickel for scarce licenses will now be able to become absentee landlords and collect rents while paying nothing back to the public.

Second, freezing the old zoning system into permanent private property rights would forestall new smart-radio technologies that can dynamically share today's underutilized spectrum space. Intel and other technology companies are planning for a world in which unlicensed devices could cost as little as pen-nies, with thousands of them scattered around houses in beehive-like wireless networks. Anticipated uses include monitoring temperature, bacteria, mold, maintenance needs for appliances, food inventory, electricity usage, and potential crime. Unfortunately, if frequencies are privatized in the way the FCC proposes, it would turn such uses into "trespassing," allowing licensees to demand payment for access to their airwaves.

Finally, the move to grant licensees expanded rights to lease spectrum without asking them to pay for this right would foreclose more sensible and fairer approaches to spectrum reform. Making spectrum allocation more market-based can be achieved without a massive giveaway. One approach would be to rent for fixed terms the flexible new licenses proposed by the FCC Task Force, with the rental revenues going to the public's coffers for the public interest. Such an approach would put all companies on a level playing field, permit property-like rights for limited periods, protect capital investment by incumbents, and internalize incentives to use spectrum efficiently, all while giving taxpayers something tangible in return for the use of a public resource.

A substantial share of any revenue from licensing the airwaves should be earmarked to fulfill the public interest obligations that justified giving broadcasters free monopoly access to the airwaves in the first place. There are many unmet public-interest needs, including quality children's and educational programming, an expansion of civic discourse, and free media time for political candidates. One specific proposal would earmark $5 billion in federal revenue from the auction of analog TV channels to create a permanent endowment that funds the digital future of public broadcasting. Some of the revenue could also go into a proposed Digital Opportunity Investment Trust (DO IT), which would invest in the educational content and innovative software needed to make meaningful the federal E-Rate program that has been wiring the nation's public schools and libraries to the Internet.

Getting spectrum policy right will require a new politics. Congress and the FCC have been able to give away tens of billions of dollars' worth of spectrum rights without any discernible public outrage. They have also been able to favor incumbents at the expense of competition, innovation, and efficient spectrum use. The good news is that as wireless communication has become so popular and important to the economy, the White House, Congress, and the press are paying closer attention to the spectrum-management choices previously left largely to an opaque FCC regulatory process dominated by lobbyists for industry license holders. And, increasingly, important industries that lack FCC licenses—including the companies that make computer chips, software and wireless devices—are joining the effort to encourage a reallocation of prime spectrum frequencies for unlicensed citizen access.

One thing is for certain: as the Information Age goes wireless, getting spectrum policy right will have an enormous impact on our nation's economy—and on our democracy.

WIRELESSING THE WORLD:
THE BATTLE OVER (COMMUNITY)
WIRELESS NETWORKS

SASCHA D. MEINRATH

Halfway through the first decade of the twenty-first century, wireless technologies have become a common feature throughout United States cities. Cell phones are ubiquitous; wireless laptops are a common site in airports and cafes; and remote-control TVs, VCRs, stereos, and cordless phones appear in nearly every American home. According to *Business Week*, by mid-2004, "these technologies attracted $4.5 billion in venture investments [since 1999]."[1] Unfortunately, unbeknownst to most consumers of these technologies, control over wireless technologies is quickly and covertly being consolidated under the oversight of a few enormous corporations whose main interest is bolstering their profit margins, not building telecommunications systems for the public good. Quietly, a historic opportunity to build a public-interest communication system is being sacrificed before the altar of the marketplace.

The telecom corporations calling the shots feign competition, but they are actually very tightly integrated. For example, in 2004, it was announced that Cingular Wireless (co-owned by SBC Communications and BellSouth) would buy AT&T Wireless for $41 billion, creating the largest wireless company in the United States, with 47 million subscribers.[2] In a truly brazen feat of obfuscation, AT&T (which had spun off AT&T Wireless in 2001) then made plans to offer wireless service using Sprint Corporation's infrastructure. As the *Chicago Tribune* notes, "If you find that confusing, it is part of the plan."[3] Put simply, right after AT&T Wireless is bought (meaning AT&T Wireless customers will start paying money to Cingular), AT&T will begin offering the same services to new customers—who will buy service from AT&T, which will then pay Sprint for use of its network. According to Michael Grossi, an industry consultant, "Confusion is absolutely the cornerstone of AT&T's strategy."[4] Consumers, in the meantime, will find it difficult to know whose service they are buying or even which corporation's network they are using. When the sources of rising prices and poor service are obscured, it makes it harder to protest against them.

By 2004, many of the "success stories," the companies that had managed to grab market share in wireless technologies, were already being consolidated under the aegis of the largest telecommunications and computer technology firms in the United States. According to the *Washington Post*, "Through May [2004], $121.7 billion of telecom mergers were completed, compared with $140.5 million in all of 2003."[5] Behemoth wireless telecommunications companies invested in new technologies before they had even entered the mainstream consumer market; often paying an enormous premium to protect themselves from possible future competition (and passing these costs on to consumers). For example, in 2003, Motorola bought XtremeSpectrum, an Ultra-Wideband (UWB) pioneer, before UWB standards had even been set, much less tested, in order to bolster its position in the fight over UWB protocol standards.

As an additional example, the venture capitalist Craig McCaw (who had made his initial fortune selling his wireless cell-phone network to AT&T) bought Clearwire Holdings Inc. in March 2004 and NextNet Wireless Incorporated in April 2004 and invested $36 million in Microtell Communications in May 2004.[6] In doing so, Mr. McCaw has created a conglomerate with both infrastructure (spectrum) and manufacturing arms. In June 2004, Mr. McCaw announced a new wireless communications initiative with the goal of providing Internet connectivity in major cities across the United States. Major telecommunications giants were similarly buying up the assets of companies that had gone bankrupt (for example, T-Mobile's acquisition of MobileStar's infrastructure in 2001), often for pennies on the dollar. The end result has been a steady march toward fewer and fewer companies controlling more and more wireless market share.

Within this complex, rapidly evolving wireless context, it was critical that consumers fight to balance the profit-motive-driven decision-making processes tailored to these telecommunications giants. Without this counterweight, end users of wireless technologies would be forced to pay far more for worse services. By 2004, consumers were organizing to fight against the behind-the-scenes machinations of big business, demanding a say at every level of decision-making and insisting that the public airwaves serve, first and foremost, the public good, not the bottom line of a handful of asset- and lobbyist-rich corporations.

This chapter explores the behind-the-scenes battle over the future of wireless communications, using twin foci. First, the analysis explains the social-historical context surrounding the contemporary effort by major business interests to wrest control over the public airwaves. Second, the study examines the technological antecedents (often developed by the use of public funding, then given away to private interests for private gain) and the technological standards (often set by industry groups to ensure their own profitability rather than establishing the best option for the public) of these technologies. The first decade of the twenty-first century is a critical moment in wireless communications development that will determine the direction of wireless technologies for many years to come. This chapter illuminates the contemporary problems that have arisen from wireless-system development driven by the profit motive instead of the public good. As the American populace has become educated to the premeditated robbing of its wealth—the thieving of the public's airwaves and the pilfering of our intellectual property; and the abuses carried out by companies who, unbeknownst to most people, attempt to sell substandard services for far more than people in other countries pay—consumers have begun organizing for better alternatives.

The general public and consumers, in particular, are being actively misled by major businesses. These corporations use public ignorance to sell inferior products, maintain control over vast swaths of electromagnetic spectrum (and thus prevent both other uses for this resource and competition from gaining a foothold), and overcharge for their services when less expensive alternatives exist for consumers. The popular Centrino-based notebooks are a good case in point. According to Intel Corporation's website, "The Intel® Pentium® M processor, in conjunction with the Intel® 855 Chipset Family and the Intel® PRO/Wireless network connection family, is a key component of Intel® CentrinoTM mobile technology."[7] Without the marketing jargon, this means that a Centrino notebook is a "bundled" product. Like most bundled products (for example, the add-on services that phone companies always try to sell their customers), this is a bum deal for the end user. Contrary to popular opinion, there is no such thing as a "Centrino Processor"—the processor itself is a Pentium M Processor—but this fact has been purposefully obfuscated from most people buying notebook computers. According to Atheros, a major manufacturer of wireless cards, but also documented by multiple industry watchdog organizations and supported by empirical research,

> In a nutshell, Centrino is Intel's attempt to leverage the advantages of its new Pentium M microprocessor to help sell other components, by implying that you must buy the entire bundle from Intel to get the advantages. In reality, many Pentium M-branded laptops will include superior wireless functionality, provided by third parties, while still offering the power-savings processor capabilities attributed to Centrino.[8]

Thus, if you buy a "Centrino notebook," you may be paying a premium for the brand while at the same time paying for worse wireless connectivity than if you bought the *same* processor with a different company's "non-Centrino" wireless card.

The Hazardous Wireless Topography

Wireless communications encompass both voice and data networks. While wireless telephones have been widely offered since the late 1980s, Internet connectivity via this medium has been available only since the turn of the millennium. Wireless industry consultant Karen Spring defines three major eras in wireless telephone technologies.

> When it comes to the world of wireless, first generation (1G) refers to analog wireless phone services, while second generation (2G) refers to today's digital wireless communication services. The next generation of wireless services is referred to as third generation (3G), which will enable high-speed mobile access to information. It will bring computer functionality—streaming video, downloadable music, graphic presentations of data, video e-mail, location specific services, and high-speed access to the Internet—to wireless devices.[9]

Understanding the contemporary wireless topography necessitates taking into account the beleaguered social history of earlier communications systems and their corporatization over intervening decades. The battles fought for control over computer communications systems parallel the battles fought over other communications technologies in preceding eras (such as telegraph, telephone, radio). Unless the present outcomes differ from their historical counterparts, the main losers will continue to be the general populace, small businesses, and local communities.

Predictably, the major contenders building current wireless telephone networks in the United States are a who's who of the major telecommunications industry, with many familiar faces from previous generations: AT&T and AT&T Wireless; Cingular Wireless; Nextel Communications (which works with Motorola); Sprint PCS; T-Mobile USA (formerly VoiceStream Wireless); and Verizon Wireless. According to IEEE Wireless Communications Editor-in-Chief Michele Zorzi, "All major players in the wireless telecom arena have recognized the potential of WLANs [Wireless Local Area Networks], and the relevant standardization bodies are working on providing the necessary advancements in order to solve the remaining technical issues."[10]

Most of these companies (as well as Intel and Atheros) are members of a trade group called the WiMax Forum. This innocuously named organization has a stated mission, "to promote deployment of broadband wireless access networks by using a global standard and certifying interoperability of products and technologies." The forum is composed of "industry leaders who are committed to the open interoperability of all products used for broadband wireless access" by supporting IEEE 802.16 standard; proposing and promoting access profiles for the IEEE 802.16 standard; certifying interoperability levels both in network and the cell; achieving global acceptance; and promoting the use of broadband wireless access overall.[11]

According to the group's website, "WIMAX intends to foster a more competitive BWA [Broadband Wireless Access] marketplace by specifying minimum air-interface performance between various vendors' products and certifying products that meet those performance benchmarks." The goals of this industry coalition are directly stated: "for network operators this means interoperability between equipment vendors; for equipment vendors this means fewer product variants; for component vendors this means larger series; [and] for end users this means faster and cheaper access which is more widely available."[12] However, given the historical precedents by many of the corporations involved in this group, the potential impact of the WiMax Forum must be viewed with skepticism. As a trade-group, of course, the Forum's interest lies in maximizing profit for those involved. However, inveigled by the friendly talk about "interoperability" is the assumption that all competing standards (which potentially serve the public interest better than WiMax) must be pushed aside. More to the point, the WiMax Forum wants industry and government policies to eliminate all competing standards before the public has any idea what is at stake or what the alternatives might be.

Primary among the technologies feeling the squeeze from WiMax is "WiFi." WiFi or "Wireless Fidelity" 802.11 technologies (available off-the-shelf from almost any "big box" computer store) are widely available to consumers, who can use these devices to set up their own home, office, and community wireless networks (CWNs). WiMax or "Worldwide Interoperability for Microwave Access" 802.16 technologies are being marketed as a technology that will be regulated and certified by the very industries that control the major WiMax networks—allowing only large institutions and corporations to build systems that are only then rented to end users. Such a system creates a standards-compliance structure that puts smaller-scale, nonprofit, and community-based networks at a heavy disadvantage. Membership in the WiMax Forum, which was established by the Nokia Corporation in 2001, is carefully controlled.[13] Wielding a decision-making vote in this group requires paying $10,000 per year in membership fees. Even obtaining a nonvoting "seat at the table" costs $3,500 each year. In other words, community organizations, nonprofits, citizen's groups, and other forms of local, regional, and national interests are kept out, not explicitly but rather though a structure by which only the "heavy rollers" can afford to apply. The same tactic was utilized in 1999 in setting up the WiFi Alliance (a similar industry group focusing on WiFi technologies)—entrance to this industry group costs $25,000 dollars yearly.

WiFi was originally intended to simply refer to the 802.11b protocol,[14] but has since expanded in popular discourse to include 802.11a and 802.11g technologies. 802.11b and 802.11g both operate in the 2.4GHZ range—the same frequency used by many home radio phones to communicate with their base stations and that microwave ovens use to cook food. On the other hand, 802.11a operates in the 5GHZ range.[15] WiMax was originally envisioned to cover networks that utilized frequencies of between 10 and 66GHZ. Thus, WiFi and WiMax were conceptualized to be complementary technologies, allowing end users to choose the networking solution that best fit their own communications' needs.

However, in March 2003, an amendment to the WiMax standard was passed that allowed WiMax to be used in frequencies from 2 to 66 GHZ. This amendment conveniently covers the entire spectrum used by 802.11x technologies, making it legal for major corporations to both set up networks in these frequencies as well as control the "certifying interoperability" for WiMax equipment within this frequency range. According to industry consultant Karen Spring, "In early 2003, the IEEE agreed on another standard, 802.16a, which is considered a backbone wireless standard. This new standard can reach a 31-mile range and a speed up to 70Mbps and may eventually replace 802.11b altogether."[16] In other words, within the industry itself, there is acknowledgment that local-area networks (LANs) and personal-area networks (PANs) could be completely replaced by for-pay services such as metropolitan-area networks (MANs), with the local systems we use freely today becoming paid services within a few years' time.

The United States has one of the most advanced *wired* communications networks in the world (and certainly the most expensive). In no other country has private industry—with tens of billions of dollars in public backing—made such a tremendous outlay of capital to (over)build a highly redundant, massively underused, extremely expensive, and increasingly obsolete network. Om Malik's tale of corporate greed and the bilking of millions of small-time investors by telecom giants, *Broadbandits: Inside the $750 billion Telecom Heist*, documents many of the abuses carried out by the builders of these wired networks. With WiMax, new telecommunications giants (and in some cases, the same companies reconstituted) are posed to reinstitute the same abuses, redundancies, and swindles that transpired during the late 1990s. Meanwhile, consumers will end up with service that is both more expensive and reaches fewer people than in countries where market excesses have been controlled or where government itself has stepped in to ensure that communications systems serve the public good.

For example, South Korea's wireless infrastructure is years ahead of the United States. In Korea, "the government funded the development of a countrywide broadband network in the late 1990s, and now, broadband penetration is about 71 percent. . . . Broadband customers pay about $20 a month for an 8-megabit connection, which is both less expensive and faster than service in the United States. WiFi can be added for as little as $9 a month."[17] Because WiFi is cheap, nearly ubiquitous, and broadband, the need for WiMax technologies is greatly lessened: "While South Korea has become something of a testing ground for new wireless technologies, [Korea Telecommunications Assistant Vice President Won-Sic] Hahn speculated that WiMax . . . won't be a hit there." While United States industry would like consumers to see the overbuilt wired infrastructure as an asset, this infrastructure has, in fact, retarded the growth of wireless technologies.

The battle lines are thus being drawn between the enormous telecommunications firms who are highly invested in wired systems and new telecommunications firms who are utilizing wireless technologies to provide communications services for much cheaper. By 2004, Cisco, Symbol, 3Com, and Proxim were the four largest Wireless Local Area Network (WLAN) equipment manufacturers, while Linksys, D-Link, NETGEAR, and Buffalo were the four major home WLAN suppliers.[18] Intel, Siemens, Alcatel, and Motorola, to name just a few major manufacturers, have already declared their intention to build WiMax gear. According to *Business Week*, these corporations "are betting they can spur demand and quickly drive down modem prices. Intel plans to have embedded WiMax chips in laptops by 2006."[19] The end result has been that many "dinosaur" companies, which are heavily invested in obsolete wired infrastructures, are buying up newer companies and technologies and leveraging their branding to lock consumers into systems of lesser quality, and then passing the cost of these business practices on to end users. As Karen Spring states, "Service providers may try to lock customers into multi-year agreements that look attractive with steep discounts on equipment. But as new services and products are introduced at a fairly rapid pace, there is the danger of locking yourself out of better deals that come along later."[20] This practice does not help consumers, it simply lessens possible competition through costly buyouts while passing on these costs to end users; the only winners are the stockholders in the companies who get bought out. Finally, because business interests control the systems that set wireless standards, an objective analysis cannot help but note that this process is a way for industry to keep new technology deployment on a timeline that allows for planned obsolescence (that is, once people buy WiFi and the market is saturated, *then* roll out WiMax in 2007; once WiMax saturates the consumer market, current estimates call for 4G devices to be rolled out in 2010).

With the ground continually shifting and major consolidations being announced almost weekly, it is difficult to know what the terrain will look like for end users in coming years. For consumers, these battlegrounds create a treacherous buying climate, in which independent and critical information is difficult to compile and honest comparisons among available options are difficult to find. The massive industry consolidations affecting wireless communications since the turn of the millennium, and especially beginning in 2004, have had far-reaching effects, shaping the consumer terrain to the detriment of users. As illustrated, with WiMax poised to enter the market in 2007, a major shuffling has been taking place—computer and mobile phone communications are literally merging to form enormous communications giants that will enjoy monopoly control over multiple communications mediums. Within this context, a vibrant countermovement of entrepreneurs, programmers, researchers, and activists has begun organizing alternative, community-controlled communications systems. At the time of writing, the future of these alternatives is very much up in the air. The problem is not in the technological development but rather in the barriers to market entry formulated by major telecommunications firms to protect their monopolies and ensure that better, cheaper alternatives are not allowed to compete in the first place.

For example, today, most end users buy DSL and cable modems but use them only a few minutes of the day. Even when a user is online, the time spent utilizing the Internet connection is a small percent of computer time. For example, when a webpage is loaded, the connection downloads the content in a few seconds; computer users spend the vast majority of their time reading through content, not taxing their bandwidth. This phenomenon means that multiple users can, in fact, share Internet connections (and realize tremendous cost savings) without noticing any lessening in service quality. Most Internet Service Providers (ISPs) know this, and it is regular business practice to oversell bandwidth (that is, if everyone used the bandwidth they were paying for at the same time, the ISPs would not have enough bandwidth to meet the demand). This practice not only makes sense for businesses, it also makes sense for consumers. Following the same practice as the service providers, friends, neighbors, communities, and entire towns and cities could buy bandwidth in bulk and share their connections. The price savings of this arrangement are so great that broadband connectivity would cost the average consumer one-tenth (or less) of what they are currently paying.

Most businesses know that if consumers engaged in the same practices as they did, they would earn less, but having communities buy bandwidth in bulk to distribute throughout a geographic area also saves companies a tremendous amount of money. In the end, having local communities solving the "last mile" problem presents an opportunity for cost-savings for both consumers and corporations. Unfortunately, most ISPs are afraid of losing end-to-end control over their networks.

In many service contracts, ISPs claim that end users cannot share their Internet connection with others. This is particularly perplexing, since these same companies often provide equipment like Wireless Access Points (WAPs) whose only purpose is to allow end users to share their connections. Other companies explicitly allow the sharing of DSL lines in their service agreements yet continue to publicly state that they do not. For example, the 10,000-word service agreement for SBC Communications states:

This policy does not prohibit multiple DSL users from connecting to the Internet over the same DSL network connection using customer premise equipment such as a router or home networking equipment . . . The Service is provided for your use only (unless otherwise specifically stated) and you agree not to reproduce, duplicate, copy, sell, transfer, resell or exploit for any commercial purposes your membership in the Service, any portion of the Service, use of the Service, or access to the Service.[21]

SBC sells users WAPS as a standard part of their service contract yet continues to state to the media that it is illegal to share DSL lines. According to a March 2004 article in the *St. Louis Post Dispatch*, community wireless networks "could run afoul of mainstream providers of Internet access."[22] It is no surprise that this business practice causes confusion among end users—consumers are often required to sign a document stating that they are not allowed to share their line yet are provided by the same company with equipment whose only purpose is sharing. More importantly, if end users are paying only for the Internet *connection*, how is it the company's business what one does with this line? ISPs encourage business users to buy DSL or cable-modem connections and share them (at a café, bookstore, or fast-food restaurant, for example). In many ways, it is an open secret that once one buys an Internet connection, what you do with it is a private matter, yet few ISPs want users to know this.[23]

But the business model is changing. More and more service providers are moving away from the single-payer model (where each end user pays for Internet connectivity) toward more dynamic models. One of the largest corporations breaking this mold is Wayport. According to the wireless-industry analyst Glenn Fleishman,

Wayport was founded to put Ethernet into hotel rooms, and still derives most of its revenue from that business. But it's changing. With 12,000 McDonald's under contract to get WiFi service, thousands of UPS Store locations that they'll operate for SBC as a managed services provider, and a network of hotels and airports that will top 1,000 this year, Wayport is the last brand standing. Wayport has raised as much as $100 million in funding across its five-plus years in business.[24]

"Hotspots," or areas where one can connect to the Internet with off-the-shelf wireless hardware, are the mainstay of Wayport's business. In a May 2004 press release, Wayport announced a "significant change in how hotspot builders charge hotspot resellers and aggregators." "WiFi World [is] their name for a pricing model for partnering with retail chain stores and reselling access to aggregators and others for a fixed monthly fee per location instead of a per-connection rate. Resellers choose their own pricing for subscribers and do not share that revenue with Wayport."[25] Thus, major corporations have realized the logic of shared connectivity wireless networks. But what might an even better model look like? What would happen if communities owned their network infrastructure, in essence doing away with the middleman and passing the subsequent cost-savings on to residents? If the technology already exists to do this, what groups are actually implementing these networks?

The Alternative: The Community Wireless Network

"It is highly probable that many of the greatest inventions and improvements of the future will come from amateurs who, by experimenting, chance upon undreamed of things."[26] An alternative to profit-driven corporate models exists that is cheaper, is more reliable and flexible, and offers end users access to more bandwidth, services, and applications. This alternative is building Community Wireless Networks. Community Wireless Networks (CWNs) allow for open, freely accessible, nonproprietary systems to be built utilizing the buying power and economies of scale within neighborhoods, towns, and cities. CWNs are a way for residents to build resources into their communities, save money, and free themselves from the worst excesses of profit-driven business models. CWNs allow participants to buy bandwidth in bulk and share it among a community, create opportunities for building community Web resources (for example, streaming media servers, e-mail accounts, Web-hosting), help bridge the digital divide by eliminating one facet of the problem (namely end users having to pay directly for Internet access), and even help bridge the divide between Internet "resource-rich" and "resource-poor" areas by providing low-cost alternatives to wired communications infrastructures.

One internationally renowned not-for-profit group that has been exceptionally successful in these goals is the Champaign-Urbana Community Wireless Network (CUWiN). Since its founding in 2000, CUWiN has grown from a small group of local volunteers to scores of active participants, with a global following. The organization is composed of a coalition of researchers, programmers, entrepreneurs, and community activists who have built several next-generation communications networks that allow people to share bandwidth, publish media, and disseminate information by creating mesh, ad-hoc wireless networks throughout a geographical area using off-the-shelf wireless hardware. These systems form communications networks "on the fly"—creating a mesh of connectivity, much like a net or spider web, where multiple pathways exist for data to move between any two points. These networks can adapt to changing environments, routing data through different channels as network conditions change. CUWiN utilizes open-source software and open-architecture hardware, providing a nonproprietary system that anyone can utilize. CUWiN's network infrastructure allows anyone within range of the network to get on-line without paying monthly fees.

CUWiN's four-part mission is to: (1) provide wireless Internet connectivity to Network users; (2) develop software and hardware for use by other wireless projects throughout the United States and abroad; (3) disseminate software and hardware specs to nonprofit and community organizations; and (4) build and support sustainable not-for-profit community networks throughout the world. Tying in with its roots in the global-justice movement, the Champaign-Urbana Community Wireless Network is a program of the Urbana-Champaign Independent Media Center, supporting itself through donations from participants, supporters, foundational grants, and in-kind donations from institutions.

Software already developed by the CUWiN team has been integrated into the NetBSD operating system and CUWiN programmers have created multiple open-source drivers for wireless cards. Additional CWN uses have been downloading the CUWiN software to locations locally, across the country, and around the globe. Finally, the hardware developed by CUWiN is being utilized by multiple wireless projects worldwide. Since its inception, CUWiN has grown to become one of the leading sources for information, software, and hardware for building CWNs, as the coalition oversees the wireless domain and project of SourceForge.net at http://wireless.sourceforge.net (SourceForge is the world's largest open-source software development website).

Wireless Internet Options and Technologies[27]

The section that follows is an overview of different Community Wireless Networking options, with brief descriptions of the pros and cons of each choice. The intent is to provide a visual framework for comparing different types of infrastructure, from the wired networks built in previous eras up through the prototypes of "next-generation" wireless systems. Unlike the old wired systems, Community Wireless Networks require very little in the way of infrastructure. They do not require digging up streets to lay cables; they do not require investment in large towers or expensive broadcasting equipment; they do not even require the purchase of commercial software, since there are many open-source alternatives available. Of all the wireless options, a dynamic mesh using open source and open standards offers greatest adaptability, highest capacity, lowest cost, and greatest community benefits. Of course, this is not the system that commercial providers will choose, since it is not the best option for profit-making. But it is a system that local communities across America could build on their own and operate with limited resources and enormous social benefit.

FIGURE 1
Wired Infrastructure

Wired technologies have dominated the communications landscape since the age of the telegraph. In wired networks, cables strung along telephone poles or buried underground deliver services through physical connections to individual buildings. These wired networks are very costly and require enormous amounts of labor to deploy and maintain. Although antiquated, wired technologies are deeply entrenched in current communications systems and continue to be both expensive and disruptive to build.

FIGURE 2
Wireless Infrastructure

Because of the huge savings on infrastructure, industry, and research, leaders expect wireless technologies to rapidly replace wired systems. As documented in this chapter, major initiatives are already being undertaken to implement this transformation. "The strengths of a WLAN [Wireless Local Area Network] solution are ease of installation and wide-spread, low-cost technology."[28] For one-tenth to one-one hundredth the cost of tearing up roads or setting up towers, rooftop antennas with "smart radio" technology can be easily installed to deliver services using the airwaves. As more users come online and the wireless cloud spreads over an entire community, the network becomes cheaper and more robust. This is exactly the opposite of wired networks, which experience increased costs with each additional user.

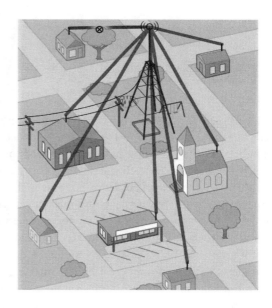

FIGURE 3
Hub-and-Spoke
Wireless Infrastructure

One of the earliest designs for wireless networks was the so-called "hub-and-spoke." Like the spokes on a bicycle wheel, these wireless systems connect users with line-of-sight antennas to a centrally located broadcast tower. Clients who cannot see the hub from their building (usually because line-of-site is blocked by trees or other buildings) cannot join the network. These networks are resource-intensive; they require a tower, specialized broadcasting equipment, and constant maintenance of the hub—an extremely vulnerable, single point of failure. Yet these relatively expensive and inefficient systems are the norm for wireless communications today. Following from the cell-phone model, WiMax system infrastructures will follow this model of connectivity, where the extra costs, downtimes, and "dead zones" are borne by end users.

FIGURE 4
Mesh Wireless
Infrastructure

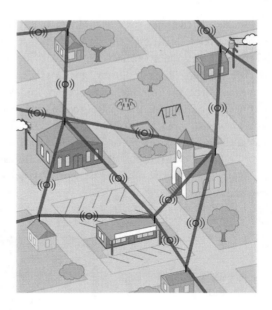

Mesh wireless systems offering multiple points of connection to the network can be built without a central tower. They connect to the larger Internet, not with a single tower, but with multiple points of wired connection at various points in the mesh. This arrangement dramatically reduces vulnerability to network failures. Within a mesh network, users can bypass such obstacles as hills, buildings, and trees by using different signal paths, in essence, routing *around* obstacles to reach all areas in a community. Mesh networks are easily expandable at very low cost. Mesh networks are often built with shorter distances between nodes (as compared with antiquated hub-and-spoke systems), a design by which each antenna can broadcast at lower power, creating less interference and allowing more users to communicate simultaneously. Mesh systems lower congestion, increase coverage, and are substantially less expensive to deploy and maintain than other wireless communications systems.

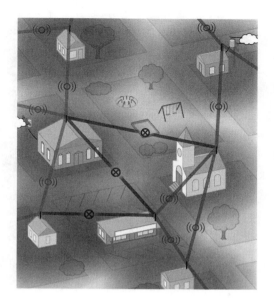

FIGURE 5
Proprietary Mesh Wireless
Infrastructure

Proprietary or "closed" networks do not communicate with each other. It would be as if two phone companies in the same community disallowed connection calls to their competitor's users. Even in a mesh system, these networks create unconnected wireless islands within a single neighborhood. Further, customers are often forced to overpay for incompatible equipment made by only one manufacturer. Companies purposefully attempt to "lock" consumers into a single system, following a Windows-esque business model of market domination, rather than an open system of interconnectivity and resource-sharing. Because the software provided by proprietary network developers is closed, innovation and collaboration among entrepreneurs and programmers is stifled. Proprietary networks overlook the public good that would come from providing compatible systems, often forcing companies to compete for market domination within a geographical area instead of collaborating to provide ubiquitous interconnectivity. Finally, closed software prevents expert programmers from adding innovations, fixing flaws, or closing security holes—leading to second-rate, often substandard software being released to the public.

FIGURE 6
Nonproprietary Mesh
Wireless Infrastructure

The success of the Internet itself demonstrates how open standards and open sourcing provide a foundation for building new wealth, a platform for innovation, and a basis for low-cost computing solutions. Early Internet developers utilized open-source software and open-standards—a fact that most proprietary wireless companies downplay or ignore outright. Had the Internet followed a proprietary development, the entire global communications system would have turned out much differently, costing end users much more. Open standards lead to interoperability of products, a necessity for efficient use of the public airwaves, resulting in lower costs for consumers. Current researchers have called for next generation networks to be open architecture,[29] and open-source code lends itself to innovation and development, a huge advantage for local developers with new ideas for community applications.

FIGURE 7
Static Nonproprietary
Mesh Wireless
Infrastructure

   Once cutting-edge technologies, static wireless networks are now seen as difficult to plan, build, manage, and expand. Developers must map out in advance the pathways that network signals will follow to ensure reliable service. This means that if an obstacle, like a growing tree or large truck, blocks a user's connection, or if new users wish to join the network, the network may need to be manually reconfigured to enable signals to reach them. Thus, it is a relatively inflexible system that is easily disrupted, resulting in an expensive, inefficient network with severe limitations on expansion.

FIGURE 8
Dynamic Nonproprietary
Mesh Wireless
Infrastructure

A dynamic wireless network constantly adapts its wireless links to cope with new conditions.[30] It automatically adjusts its pathways to integrate new homes and businesses, offering higher capacity to a wider coverage area. This system achieves the goal set by researchers of building a network that "offers the flexibility to reconfigure or add more nodes to the network without much planning effort and the cost of re-cabling, thereby making future upgrades inexpensive and easy."[31] This kind of network is strengthened as the subscriber base grows (a denser network of wireless nodes provides additional pathway options that can be utilized to provide connectivity). These networks can change routing patterns to bypass interference, blockage, or even network congestion. Dynamic networks achieve higher resilience and flexibility than comparatively rigid and fragile static networks.

Of the eight options discussed, dynamic, nonproprietary, mesh wireless networks offer individuals and communities the best alternative for sharing bandwidth or building a Community Wireless Network. However, WISPs (Wireless Internet Service Providers) are not building these types of systems because they are nonproprietary and thus allow users to choose their best option, creating true competition among service providers. The business model for almost all WISPs is to create network solutions that lock users into their service, making switching to other providers prohibitively expensive. Most wireless corporations are relying on marketing and barriers to entry as protection from lower-cost, more efficient, higher-quality competition. In this case, the best technology for the public good is not necessarily the best system for private profit.

The technologies involved may be fairly complex, but they are also highly intuitive and easily deployed; major telecommunications firms are counting on the general public to remain passive consumers of these technologies instead of seeking out and building viable, cheaper, locally owned alternatives. The challenge then is for an engaged public to build these cost-effective alternatives and become active agents in determining the future of the wireless telecommunications infrastructure.

Solutions and Conclusions

Any strong critique of existing structures should be accompanied with a vision for successful future systems. As this chapter has demonstrated, the future of wireless is an open question. However, there exist many opportunities for moving in the right direction that will help ensure that these infrastructures and technologies better serve the public good. Perhaps the most challenging first step is for more people to become smart consumers of wireless equipment and services. End users should search out independent and critical information on wireless equipment and services that allows consumers to easily compare the respective strengths and weaknesses of respective systems. Customers should demand that Internet Service Providers make this information available to users and independent consumers' groups.

Keep up with the wireless news: sites like http://www.wifinetnews.com, http://www.communitywifi.org, and http://www.muniwireless.com provide accessible information that is critical to understanding the complex wireless telecommunications world. Seek out services that allow sharing of connectivity and fight to remove existing gag rules that some ISPs place in their service contracts that prevent users from saving money. Dare to share your DSL or cable modem with your neighbor and community. Service providers want you to believe that sharing your network is a major security risk; but the fact is that wireless connectivity is no more of a security risk than the average cable modem connection. Major telecommunications companies' business models are based on making *everyone* pay (individually) for connectivity; they do not want users sharing their connections. While on a recent train ride from Vermont to Connecticut I found over fifty wireless access points along the railroad route—over 60 percent of these users shared their connectivity. Help to increase that percentage.

Second, remember that large business interests do not have a lock on the best technologies. In fact, many ISPs know far less about the technologies they are installing in their clients' homes than various improperly titled "amateur" WiFi enthusiasts and groups. A simple Google search for "Community Wireless Network" will pull up scores of websites that can provide invaluable knowledge and resources. Search out and actively support community wireless groups in your country, state, or community, these initiatives exist to benefit people, not profit margins.

Third, get involved in some way with wireless watchdog groups—CUWiN (http://www.cuwireless.net) is working hard to organize reforms of policies and regulations that restrict access to the public airwaves for community wireless groups.[32] Major telecommunications trade groups are actively working to influence national regulations.[33] Consumers should demand that public-service provisions be included in wireless networks; all wireless companies are using the public's airwaves and should provide ongoing compensation for that privilege. One constructive solution would be to require primary-frequency users to share their frequencies with nonprofit and individual users. In much the same way that an amplified lecturer can coexist with the whispers of audience members,[34] digital technologies have advanced allowing low-powered transmissions to coexist on the same frequency as primary transmissions. Corporations currently renting specific frequencies do not want this technology to be utilized because it allows additional access to this resource, thus undermining their ability to create artificial spectrum scarcity. A more innovative approach would be to make large sections of unlicensed bandwidth available only for nonprofit and individual use. Providing a swath of bandwidth that is reserved only for these uses will help prevent a "tragedy of the commons" by lessening the profit-driven exploitation of bandwidth from this spectrum.

A related and necessary development is for the FCC to create large swaths of additional unlicensed spectrum. It is abundantly clear that wireless communications will continue to grow in importance in our society; providing spectrum resources that meet the growing needs of our evolving telecommunications needs necessitates opening up far more unlicensed bandwidth than currently exists. Opening up more unlicensed spectrum will ease the congestion. The Federal Communications Commission (FCC) needs to proactively anticipate the future needs of consumers—waiting until the problem manifests itself is far too late. Because of the turnaround time on manufacturing and deploying new hardware, FCC staff should be asking what wireless network usage will look like in 10 to 15 years and making the bandwidth available today that will meet those needs. To ensure maximum access to unlicensed bandwidth and to prevent a few actors from unethically dominating this medium, it is important to place a low transmit power limit within unlicensed spectrum. In essence, the idea is that many broadcasters can transmit in the same space if none are exceptionally "loud."

Unlicensed spectrum is an extremely valuable resource. Historical precedence has demonstrated that without any checks and balances on industry excesses, this "commons" rapidly becomes assimilated into for-profit endeavors. Thus, reallocating existing industry spectrum for unlicensed spectrum use is an easy way to correct for past illegal business practices and abuses of this public good. Furthermore, creating ample unlicensed spectrum for educational and nonprofit use is an important strategy for supporting communications and information dissemination by community groups, governmental units, and civic and religious organizations. Much like public-access initiatives, this allocation supports many of the fundamental democratic processes of our society.

Current technologies allow manufacturers to produce software-controlled radios that can tune to uncongested bands automatically; however, this solution requires *continuous* unlicensed spectrum to be most effectively utilized. Equally, so-called smart antennas are under development that can help eliminate undirected transmissions.[35] Smart antennas can focus the radio transmission beam on-the-fly—allowing a single antenna to create focused beams to reach users, thus helping eliminate electromagnetic congestion. Power control already exists on several wireless microchips but is deactivated. Making this feature mandatory (and turned on by default) will ensure that individual transmitters "play well with others," "whispering" whenever possible, and only "yelling" when absolutely necessary (see below).

Setting a ceiling of 500 milliwatts prevents any one unlicensed spectrum user from "bullying" others from using the same band. Without this limit, a lowest common denominator of "might makes right" becomes normative, lessening access and preventing efficient use of this resource. Regulators should set a hard transmission power cap of 500 milliwatts within unlicensed spectrum. Congestion within existing unlicensed spectrum will increase; one "solution" that some shortsighted network deployers adapt is simply to broadcast at higher power levels. However, as anyone who has been in a large crowded room knows, inevitably this leads to everyone simply "speaking" louder, eventually resulting in more congestion, more interference, and less connectivity. Policymakers and regulators must anticipate this problem and proactively set transmit power limits to protect the public good. Furthermore, as users of this medium, it is in our own best interest to advocate for this change.

Regulators should build power control into existing wireless standards. Currently, almost all commercial radios transmit at the same power, regardless of the distance of the computer they are connecting with. When radios are close to the device they are connecting to, they should "whisper"—that is polite to other wireless users and will dramatically increase the number of users who can communicate at any one time within a set geographical area. A side effect of this simple change is that it will greatly improve security (since one would need to be much closer to the user to "listen in" on the user's communications). Variable power control (as this technology is called) already exists; why it has not been implemented by wireless card manufacturers is an open question.

Consumers must also be vigilant to see that unlicensed spectrum remains free from industry control or preferential treatment. Some business groups and trade organizations are already advocating that the first providers of wireless connectivity in a market receive privileged use of the spectrum. This idea is antithetical to the fundamental idea of unlicensed spectrum, but it has been gaining ground in some constituencies—especially by Wireless ISPs, who have built hub-and-spoke networks that cover long distances and are thus extremely vulnerable to minor electromagnetic interference. The problem is that many companies have a fairly limited understanding of the physics behind wireless technologies and the limitations of both their hardware and software; what worked in 2000 might not work within a congested wireless medium, might not scale well, or might not interoperate with new equipment or technologies. The problem is not with access to the medium, the problem is a bad business model that cannot compete with better practices.

Current usage of licensed frequencies is inefficient, given advances in wireless technology. Within any specific frequency, it is possible to have a primary user as well as one or more secondary (lower power) users, all without interfering with each other.[36] Existing frequencies can have a dominant carrier (such as a radio or TV station) and a low-power carrier (such as local access TV, low-power FM, or other licensed low-power usage) without interfering in any way with the dominant carrier. Utilizing existing spectrum more efficiently creates more openings for new broadcasters and uses without detrimentally impacting already available options.

The economies of scale that municipal wireless networks offer provide an opportunity to pass cost-savings to end users. Communities should work to set up locally owned wireless networks that utilize unlicensed spectrum and cutting-edge technologies to save local residents money. Since 2000, the growth of community-owned networks has been exponential as more and more neighborhoods have realized the benefits that these networks offer and are taking advantage of the opportunity to create local resources.

Familiarizing oneself with FCC rules and regulations is important for anyone interested in deploying CWNs. Timothy Pozar's "Regulations Affecting 802.11 Deployment"[37] is a brief, but in-depth resource for those seeking a straightforward overview of relatively recent FCC decisions, rules, and regulations. The rules and regulations that the FCC passes determine both existing options and the parameters for future wireless development. Given that communications technologies impact all of us, being knowledgeable about these laws is an important skill for any active citizen.

Finally, and perhaps most importantly, become an altruistic venture capitalist. Community wireless networks and those that are developing open-source alternatives to commercial products can make enormous strides with modest funding. Several nonprofit organizations already exist that are building these networks and developing next-generation wireless infrastructures. CWNs cost a fraction of many profit-driven counterparts; often all they need is a modicum of financial support to thrive. Supporting these institutions helps to build your community. Often local politicians need only a small push or a small-scale prototype to demonstrate the utility of these networks.

History provides numerous examples of the failings of unchecked, market-driven telecommunications network building. By becoming active agents in shaping the future of telecommunications, consumers can help ensure that history does not repeat itself. Most importantly, by arming ourselves with information about these new technologies and services, we can make wiser, more cost-effective choices from the options available. As the media reform movement continues to gather force, it is obvious that the wireless topography will grow in importance. This chapter provides only a first look at the issues facing society at the beginning of the twenty-first century and solutions that must be forthcoming. However, it is an important reference for expanding our understanding of what is possible with these new technologies, and arming oneself against the obfuscations and deceptions of some deceitful telecommunications companies.

Notes

1. See the *Business Week* special report on wireless: Heather Green, Roger O. Crockett, Steve Rosenbush, and Catherine Yang, "No Wires, No Rules New wireless technologies will soon reconfigure the Web using radio spectrum that doesn't cost a dime," April 28, 2004, available at: http://www.saschameinrath.com/sources/businessweek.html.
2. Ben Charny, "AT&T Wireless shareholders approve buyout," *CNET News.com*, May 19, 2004, http://zdnet.com.com/2100-1103-5216002.html.
3. Jon Van, "AT&T to Offer Wireless Services Using Sprint Network," May 19, 2004, *Chicago Tribune*, section 3(1).
4. Ibid.
5. Terence O'Hara, "Carlyle Group Embraces Telecom," June 22, 2004, *Washington Post*, p. E5.
6. Andrew Park and Steven Rosenbush, "Craig McCaw's Secret Plan: His Deals in Wireless Broadband Have the Telecom World Buzzing," May 24, 2004, http://www.businessweek.com/magazine/content/04_21/b3884110_mz063.htm.
7. Intel website available at: http://www.saschameinrath.com/sources/centrino.html.
8. From Atheros Communication's Whitepaper, "Centrino vs. Pentium M: The Battle for Wireless Notebooks," available at: http://www.saschameinrath.com/sources/CentrinovsPentium.pdf.
9. Karen Spring, "Face Off: US Next-Generation Wireless Services," March 7, 2003, available at: http://www.saschameinrath.com/sources/nextgenerationwireless.pdf.
10. Michele Zorzi, "Future Wireless Systems: Integrating Diverse Technologies into a Common Framework," *IEEE Wireless Communications*, (December 2003), p. 2.
11. See: http://www.wimaxforum.org.
12. See: http://www.wimaxforum.org/about/.
13. Ensemble Communications Incorporated and the Orthogonal Frequency Division Multiplexing Forum are officially cofounders of this industry group, but Nokia has maintained active control over the organization.
14. See the IEEE Whitepaper on 802.11b, "Part 11: Wireless LAN Medium Access Control (MAC) and Physical Layer (PHY) specifications: Higher-Speed Physical Layer Extension in the 2.4 GHz Band," September 16, 1999, available at: http://www.saschameinrath.com/sources/802.11bwhitepaper.pdf.
15. See Proxim's Whitepaper, "802.11a: A Very High-Speed, Highly Scalable Wireless LAN Standard," 2002, available at: http://www.saschameinrath.com/sources/80211awhitepaper.pdf, for a more in-depth discussion of 802.11a technology; See also Angela Doufexi, Simon Armour, Beng-Sin Lee, Andrew Nix and David Bull, "An evaluation of the performance of IEEE 802.11a and 802.11g wireless local area networks in a corporate office environment," *ICC 2003-IEEE International Conference on Communications*, 26, no. 1, (May 2003), pp. 1196–1200.
16. Spring (2003).
17. Michael Kanellos, "Korea's KT to Have Earth's largest Wi-Fi network," *CNET News.com*, May 20, 2004, http://zdnet.com.com/2100-1105-5217060.html.
18. From Synergy Research Group's Q1 2004 market share analysis, press release, "Enterprise WLAN Market Rebounds with Record Quarter," May 21, 2004, available at: http://webbolt.ecnext.com/coms2/description_29810_SRG210504_RCH.
19. See Green, Crockett, Rosenbush, and Yang (2004).
20. Spring (2003).
21. Archived online at: http://www.saschameinrath.com/sources/SBCagreement.html.

22. Jerri Stroud, "Linking Up a Town, *St. Louis Post-Dispatch*, March 24, 2004, available at: http://www.freepress.net/news/article.php?id=2906.

23. A notable exception to this business practice is Speakeasy, a Seattle-based Internet Service Provider that actively encourages end users to share their connections.

24. Glenn Fleishman, "Which Hotspot Networks Still Stand?" *Wifi Net News*, May 19, 2004, http://wifinetnews.com/archives/003355.html.

25. Glenn Fleishman, "Wayport's Wi-Fi World Switches from Per-Connection to Per-Venue Fees," *Wifi Net News*, May 24, 2004, http://wifinetnews.com/archives/003355.html.

26. A. Hyatt Verrill, *The Home Radio: How to Make and Use It* (New York, Harper & Brothers, 1922), p. iii.

27. This section was created with the help of the CUWiN development team (Bryan Cribbs, Zachary Miller, Victor Pickard, Ben Scott, David Young). Special thanks goes to graphic artist Darrin Drda who took our general ideas and turned them into these images. Full-color images and more information on Community Wireless Networks is archived online at: http://freepress.net/wifi/.

28. Zorzi, 2.

29. See Kyung-Hyu Lee, Kyu-Ok Lee, Kwon-Chul Park, Jong-Ok Lee, and Yoon-Hak Bang, "Architecture To be Deployed on Strategies of Next-Generation Networks," Paper presented at the 2003 IEEE International Conference on Communications, Conference Proceedings, pp. 819–822.

30. See Lakshminarayanan Subramanian and Randy H. Katz, "An Architecture for Building Self-Configuring Systems," August 2000, First Annual Workshop on Mobile and Ad Hoc Networking and Computing, Conference Proceedings, pp. 63–73. Benny Bing, Chris Heegard, and Bob Heile, "Wireless LANs," IEEE *Wireless Communications*, (December 2002), p. 6.

31. CUWiN recently filed comments to the FCC regarding "Establishment of an Interference Temperance Metric to Quantify and Manage Interference and to Expand Available Unlicensed Operation in Certain Fixed, Mobile and Satellite Frequency Bands" in response to Docket No. 03–237 and is hosting a National Conference on Community Wireless Networking in August 2004 to build a coalition of CWNs to further work towards policy and regulatory reform.

33. PowerPoint presentation "Adopted by Wireless Communications Association Board of Directors," 2002, archived online at: http://www.saschameinrath.com/sources/WirelessPRmission7-02.pdf.

34. See, for example the New America Foundation's "Cartoon Guide to Federal Spectrum Policy," April 10, 2004, http://www.newamerica.net/index.cfm?pg=article&DocID=1555.

35. For example, Motia (http://www.motia.com/) "is a fabless semiconductor company focused on enabling smart antennas for wireless systems providers. The Company's standards-compliant adaptive beamforming technologies easily integrate into customers' wireless products to enhance overall functionality and performance."

36. See http://www.saschameinrath.com/sources/TemperatureInterferenceComments.rtf for an in-depth analysis of the feasibility of this technology.

37. Tim Pozar, "Regulation Affecting 802.11 Deployment," Bay Area Wireless Users Group, June 6, 2002, available at: http://www.saschameinrath.com/sources/Regulations_Affecting_802_11.pdf.

COPYRIGHT REFORM:
THE NEXT BATTLE FOR
THE MEDIA REFORM MOVEMENT

GIGI B. SOHN, PRESIDENT, PUBLIC KNOWLEDGE

When we think about the media reform movement, we often think about efforts to ensure that control of television, radio, cable, satellite and the Internet are not placed in too few hands. What we don't normally put in this category are efforts to bring balance back to copyright, trademark, and patent law.

It is critical to understand how integrally linked traditional notions of media reform are to the reform of intellectual property law, particularly copyright (and trademark) reform. In a nutshell, both are about control over what you see and hear and what you can do with what you see and hear. In traditional media ownership debates, we seek to limit "big media" control over particular distribution mechanisms (broadcast licenses, cable systems), because such controls limit the public's access to the diversity of information and ideas vital to a democratic society. In debates over the proper balance in intellectual-property law, we seek to limit big-media control over specific content and the technology for viewing, hearing, and transforming that content (such as televisions, radios, and computers) because such control again limits diversity of information and ideas by prohibiting individuals to comment upon, transform, or otherwise engage in expressive conduct concerning that content. By trying to limit the use of technology, these big-media companies wish to keep us passive "consumers" of information, as opposed to active creators.

Threats to the Historical and Constitutional Balance of Copyright Law

Copyright laws are grounded in Article I, Section 8 of the Constitution, which gives Congress the power "[t]o promote the progress of science and useful arts, by securing for limited times to authors and inventors the exclusive right to their respective writings and discoveries." This language makes clear both that the main purpose of copyright protection is to benefit the public ("to promote the progress of science and the useful arts") and that any such protection will be "for limited times."

With this language, the framers sought to strike a balance: by giving artists and innovators a time-limited monopoly over their works, they sought to encourage creation of new works, while at the same time ensuring the development of a robust public domain of information and ideas that could be shared and built upon by others to create new works.

For many years, this "cultural bargain" worked well, and its fruits are all around us. For example, most American music post-1950 has its roots in other forms of music, particularly the blues, and many of our plays, films, and books derive from earlier works. *West Side Story* is Shakespeare's *Romeo and Juliet* set in a different time and place. Such artists as Andy Warhol, Roy Lichtenstein, and Barbara Kruger have enriched our artistic heritage by using consumer products and cultural icons as the foundations of their work. And a large number of Disney movies borrow from the public domain (*Alice in Wonderland*, *Little Mermaid*, *The Hunchback of Notre Dame*, and so forth). To paraphrase Sir Isaac Newton, American culture has flourished because artists, scholars, and innovators have stood "on the shoulders of giants."

For the past decade, however, the cultural bargain of copyright has been under siege, thanks to a variety of political, technological, and marketplace initiatives that seek to make access to scientific and artistic works either impossible or prohibitively expensive. Because we are in the "information age," the market value of information and its consequent creative works has increased. This has resulted in a movement by the "copyright industries" (largely the major motion picture, major recording, and large book publishing industries) to keep it in private hands for as long as possible. Their strategy for doing so has been to strengthen copyright and trademark laws. The result has been to stifle creative expression, civic discourse, scientific inquiry, and free speech.

Big Media Strategies for Tipping the Balance

Over the past decade, the copyright industries have been very creative and unrelenting in their effort to gain control over content and technology. They have used multiple strategies in federal and state legislatures, regulatory agencies, the courts, international bodies, and the marketplace to accomplish their goals.

Longer and Stronger Copyrights

Despite the clear constitutional mandate that copyright protection be for "limited times," the copyright industries have tried their very best to ensure that copyright terms last almost in perpetuity, or as one big media lobbyist put it, "forever less one day."[1]

The first copyright law, passed in 1790, imposed a term of fourteen years plus another fourteen-year renewal. Terms increased slowly over the next hundred and fifty years, but in the past forty years, copyright terms have been extended eleven times. The two most recent term extensions were imposed by Congress in 1976 and then again in 1998. The Copyright Act of 1976 extended copyright terms from twenty-eight years plus another twenty-eight-year renewal to fifty years beyond the life of an author. In 1998, the Sonny Bono Copyright Term Extension Act extended terms to seventy years beyond the life of an author for individual copyright holders, and ninety-five years for corporate copyright holders. In February 2003, the Supreme Court rejected a constitutional challenge to the Sonny Bono Act in *Eldred* v. *Ashcroft*.[2] The case was brought by an Internet publisher and others who argued that extending copyright terms retroactively was both a violation of the Constitution's "limited times" provision and a restriction on the First Amendment's guarantee of free speech. The Court disagreed, ruling that, among other things, Congress has wide latitude to set copyright terms.

The other significant change in copyright law has been the elimination of such "formalities" as the requirement that copyrights be registered and renewed. Thus, the minute I write something down on a piece of paper, it is copyrighted, regardless of whether I register it with the Copyright Office (registration is a prerequisite to bringing a copyright infringement suit). As a result, it is often extremely difficult, if not impossible, for an artist, scholar or other potential user of a work to know whether that work is still under copyright or even who owns the copyright. And it is no excuse for a user of a work to say that attempts were made to find the copyright,because infringement is a "strict liability" violation, and the costs for such a violation can be expensive—up to $150,000 per instance. This provision has a colossal chilling effect on creative and scholarly activity.

But changes in the law are not the only way that copyrights have become stronger over the past decade. Perhaps the most significant dilution of the public's rights under copyright has been the shrinking scope of "fair use." Fair use is a judicially created (now enshrined in the Copyright Act) exception to the copyright monopoly, which permits an individual to use portions of copyrighted works for certain purposes (such as educational) without securing the copyright owner's permission. But the practice of the copyright industries is such that they require permission (and usually a large sum of money) for even the most incidental use of a copyrighted work. Even though use of a work might clearly be considered "fair use" by a judge, many scholars and artists will change their work rather than risk the threat of a lawsuit or a significant licensing fee.

A great example of the shrinking scope of fair use can be found in Professor Lawrence Lessig's book *Free Culture*. The example involves Jon Else, a documentary filmmaker who made a documentary about Wagner's Ring Cycle. The scene at issue involved stagehands at the San Francisco Opera who are playing checkers. In a corner of the room, the television program *The Simpsons* is playing. When the film was completed, Else sought to "clear the rights" to use the few seconds of *The Simpsons*. It not only took a good deal of effort to find the copyright holder, but when he did, Else was told that it would cost him $10,000 to include the clip. Rather than risk a lawsuit, Else edited *The Simpsons* out of that segment of the documentary, even though it set a particular mood for that scene.

Stronger Trademarks

In trademark law, the most significant change over the past decade has been the passage of the Federal Trademark Dilution Act of 1995. Normally, the standard for trademark infringement has been consumer confusion; for instance, I cannot open up a fast-food hamburger stand with golden arches and call it McSohn's or sell sneakers with a swoosh logo.

But the Dilution Act went beyond the consumer-confusion standard and made it a violation of trademark law to "dilute the value" of a trademark. This standard has been used to deter social commentary or criticism about a product. Perhaps the best-known example was the suit that Fox News Network brought against the comedian Al Franken and his publisher over Franken's book *Lies and the Lying Liars Who Tell Them: A Fair and Balanced Look at the Right*.[3] Fox claimed that the book title "diluted" its trademark in the phrase "fair and balanced." Franken won the case, but few have the kind of means that he and his publisher have to fight such a lawsuit.

Privatizing Facts

In 1991, the Supreme Court ruled that nonoriginal databases, such as the telephone book, were not eligible for copyright.[4] In response to this ruling, for the past decade, large database publishers have attempted to create new intellectual-property protection for nonoriginal databases and, more importantly, for the facts underlying those databases. Thus, if I wanted to write a history of the Civil War using an encyclopedia as a resource, I might, under such a proposal, be forced to pay the publisher of the encyclopedia a licensing fee, or I might even be prohibited from using the facts found in that encyclopedia. The most recent attempt to give databases and the facts underlying them protection failed in the 108th Congress,[5] but efforts are now being made to enshrine such protection in an international treaty (see discussion below).

Technological Locks and Laws that Enforce Them

While the speed, ubiquity, and relatively low cost of digital technologies present greater opportunities to make works more widely available, they also present greater opportunities for the copyright industries to limit access to, and use of, copyrighted works beyond what the law would allow. For example, copy protection mechanisms on certain CDs do not permit them to be played on computers. Similarly, some online music and film services limit one's ability to burn files onto CDs, DVDs, or hard drives, and others simply cause the file to "disappear" after a specified time period. Copyright law does not permit a copyright holder to tell you how many times you can listen to or read content, for what length of time, or on what machine. But "technolocks" (sometimes known as "Digital Rights Management" tools) permit those very limits.

As if the technological locks themselves were not enough, the Digital Millennium Copyright Act (DMCA), passed in 1998, ensures that these locks are backed with the force of law. Under the DMCA, it is unlawful to break or "circumvent" these locks, even if an individual's reason for doing so is otherwise lawful. Indeed, the first court case involving the DMCA concerned a Norwegian teenager, Jon Johansen, who bought a DVD that would not play on his Linux-operated computer. Johansen broke the technological lock on the DVD for the sole purpose of playing it on his computer. Regardless of the fact that Johansen did not engage in any infringing conduct, he was still considered a criminal under the DMCA.

In addition to prohibiting the actual breaking of technolocks, the DMCA also prohibits an individual from "manufactur[ing], import[ing], offer[ing] to the public, provid[ing] or otherwise traffic[king]" in any tool that would circumvent such locks. This broadly worded "antitrafficking" provision has been used to stifle speech on several occasions. The best known of these involved a Princeton computer science professor, Edward Felten, who was invited by the recording industry to try and break the industry's "Secure Digital Music Initiative" ("SDMI") copy-protection scheme. After several weeks of effort, Professor Felten, working with researchers from Rice University, was successful in cracking SDMI. But when Professor Felten sought to publish a paper giving the details of how they did so, the recording industry threatened a lawsuit under the antitrafficking provision of the DMCA.

Licenses that Seek to Replace Copyright Law with Contract Law

Another way that the copyright industries seek to protect their works is through the use of so-called end-user license agreements. These are the icons that you click on when trying to access software or other digital content (click-through licenses), or the terms you agree to when breaking the shrink-wrap on your newest piece of software (shrink-wrap licenses). Without any negotiation, you are asked to waive rights reserved to you under the Copyright Act (such as "fair use") and agree to a list of restrictions, some of which can include a limitation on criticizing the work without the licensee's permission.

In common law, one-sided contracts of this kind are called "contracts of adhesion." But in the digital era, these licenses are used to extend the rights of copyright holders beyond those which is permitted by law. Like technolocks, these licenses can and do limit modification, excerpting, portability, and repeated access to content. As such, they can chill creative and educational activity.

Limiting Access to Content Via "Authorized Devices"

A recent strategy of the copyright industries is to try and ensure that every technology that can receive and retransmit its content is "authorized" to do so either by the industries or by the government (strongly pressured by the same copyright industries, of course). The idea works like this: if a television, radio, computer, or other digital device is not preapproved to receive or record content, then the technology is either illegal or will be otherwise rendered incapable of doing so.

The so-called digital television broadcast flag, scheme, adopted in November 2003 by the FCC, is a manifestation of this strategy.[6] The flag is a series of bits embedded in a digital television signal that prohibits the copying of that signal on a device other than that approved by the FCC. Thus, if I have an unauthorized Digital Video Recorder (DVR) hooked up to my authorized digital television set, my DVR will not be able to make a perfectly legal personal copy of a "flagged" digital television program. The flag also prohibits excerpting of digital television programming and redistribution of some or all such programming over the Internet. Thus, if a congresswoman wants to send a digital clip of her performance on *Meet the Press* to staff in her district office, she cannot do so if the show's creator embeds a flag in the signal. There is no exception for news or public-affairs programming.[7]

Similarly, the motion picture industry engaged in a three-year battle in state legislatures to have laws enacted that make it illegal to use devices not expressly authorized by cable companies and Internet service providers. Eight states currently have such laws on the books. Thus, if you own a TiVo, but your cable company wants to sell you its proprietary Digital Video Recorder, it could prohibit you from using your TiVo under these laws.

Limiting Use of New Technologies Through Increased Enforcement, Elimination of Anonymity, and Expansion of Copyright Liability

The rapid growth of new peer-to-peer (P2P) technologies have struck fear in the hearts of the copyright industries, and much of their efforts in the copyright realm over the past several years has been directed toward making these technologies unattractive to use. P2P file-sharing software programs allow a group of computer users to share text, audio, and video files stored on each other's computers. While there are many legitimate business, educational, and recreational uses for P2P technology (indeed, it is the technology that underlies the entire Internet), it is perhaps best known as a mechanism by which people share copyrighted music and movies without permission from the copyright holder.

The copyright industries have tried a variety of ways to hobble the use and growth of P2P technologies:

- *Lawsuits.* Since 2003, the recording industry has brought thousands of lawsuits against people who make multiple music files available over commercial P2P networks. The motion picture industry started bringing suits against those who upload movies in late 2004.

- *Increased penalties.* Several bills introduced in the 108th Congress would render the passive "making available" of even one copyrighted work on a computer network punishable by up to five years in prison.

- *Restricting Anonymity.* Eliminating the anonymity of the Internet generally, and P2P networks specifically, is a core goal of the copyright industries. The recording industry lost the first stage in this battle when a Federal Court of Appeals ruled that it could not force Internet service providers to give the recording industry the names of alleged file sharers without first going to court and providing a judge with evidence of illegal activity. The recording industry is trying a variety of legislative and judicial methods to reverse this decision.

- *Notice and Consent Requirements.* Some of the same bills discussed above would also require that P2P software companies provide notice that their networks are used to trade in copyrighted and obscene materials and that such software could not be downloaded without the specific consent of the downloader (or, in the case of a minor, his parent).

- *Legalizing Invasive "Self-Help" Technologies.* The copyright industries currently use a variety of legitimate technological measures to try and discourage illegal file trading. For example, a person downloading a copyrighted music file without permission may receive one that has cracks and pops in it ("spoofing") or which directs her to a website where the music can be purchased legally ("redirection"). In the 107th Congress, Rep. Howard

Berman (D-CA) introduced a bill that would make legal the use of technologies that would send viruses into hard drives to prevent an individual from making copyrighted files available to others ("interdiction"). The legislation produced a firestorm of protest, and the bill died in subcommittee.

- *Expanding "Secondary" Copyright Liability.* In 1984, in the seminal *Sony Betamax* case, the Supreme Court ruled that technology manufacturers could not be held responsible for copyright infringement engaged in by those using their technologies if those technologies were capable of "substantial non-infringing uses." In the 108th Congress, the copyright industries attempted an end run around this important doctrine through legislation that would have held responsible anybody who "aids, abets, induces or procures" copyright infringement, regardless of whether the technology at issue is capable of substantial noninfringing uses. The effort to expand secondary copyright liability is sure to continue, either through the courts[8] or through legislative means.

A Few Words about International Copyright Law

A long, detailed description of international intellectual property law is beyond the scope of this chapter. It is important to understand, however, how United States intellectual-property law influences international intellectual-property law and vice versa.

International intellectual property law is made primarily through three mechanisms:

- International policymaking bodies, like the World Intellectual Property Organization (WIPO) and the World Trade Organization (WTO);
- Multilateral trade agreements, like the Free Trade Area of the Americas;
- Bilateral trade agreements between the United States and individual countries.

The goal of the large copyright industries in the international realm is to impose the strongest possible copyright regime on foreign countries. If United States law provides the strongest protection, then the industries' goal is to export our law overseas. However, if United States policymakers have resisted the copyright industries' efforts to impose even stronger copyright and trademark protection, the industries will seek to have those stronger laws adopted first overseas and then seek to have them *imported* into the United States. This is how both the Sonny Bono Copyright Term Extension Act and the DMCA became law in the United States—they were imported from international agreements.

Another important thing to know about international intellectual property lawmaking is how integrally it is related to trade policy. This is no accident—the pharmaceutical industry convinced the United States government to tie intellectual property protection to trade in the 1980s. As a result, many countries—and particularly developing countries—will accede to the United States government's intellectual-property demands because they are simply more concerned about agricultural and other issues normally associated with trade. As a result, developing countries end up spending vast resources that could be used for education, safety, or creating their own cultural products on protecting the intellectual property of large multinational corporations.

Now for the Good News

Most of this essay has been devoted to describing the bad news about copyright and trademark law here and overseas. But there is also good news: the increasing privatization of culture that used to be available for public use over the past decade has resulted in a serious backlash. The past several years have seen the birth and the growth of a number of new organizations and initiatives inside and outside of the legal/policy arena that are working to bring balance back to copyright and trademark law.

The Rise of Copyright Activism and the Public Debate

Just six or seven years ago, the large copyright industries could accomplish their policy goals in Congress and the courts virtually unnoticed and unimpeded. That is no longer the case. New policy advocacy organizations, such as Public Knowledge (www.publicknowledge.org), were specifically created to combat the copyright industries' march to strengthen copyright and trademark law further. Moreover, existing civil-liberties organizations like the Electronic Frontier Foundation (www.eff.org) and the American Civil Liberties Union (www.aclu.org) began to engage in these issues because of their effect on freedom of expression, and consumer groups like the Consumer Project on Technology (www.cptech.org) began to work on international issues. Additionally, battles over new state laws that limit access to certain technologies have led to the formation and growth of such state and local grassroots organizations as Electronic Frontiers Georgia, the Tennessee Digital Freedom Network, and EFF-Austin (Texas).

Equally as important has been the radicalization of certain industry segments that have chafed under the copyright industries' desire to control their products and services. Chief among these are the consumer electronics industry (which had its first battle with Hollywood over the VCR in the early 1980's) and telephone-company Internet service providers, such as Verizon.

This activism has brought debates over stronger copyright and trademark to the attention of the press and into the public eye. Rarely a week goes by without major press coverage of copyright-related issues. Where copyright issues were rarely discussed outside of a congressional office or corporate boardroom just three years ago, they are now part of a much larger and more visible public debate.

Legal Proposals to Rebalance Copyright

As a result of this new activism and the resulting visibility of copyright reform, several bills were introduced in the 108th Congress that would bring some balance back to copyright law, including, among other things:

- providing an exemption to the anticircumvention and antitrafficking sections of the DMCA for noninfringing activity (H.R. 107, the Digital Media Consumers Rights Act);

- requiring registration of a copyrighted work fifty years after publication, with renewal required every ten years thereafter (H.R. 2601, the Public Domain Enhancement Act); and

- ensuring that digital media are subject to the "first-sale doctrine," which allows the owner of a copyrighted work to dispose of that work as she sees fit (S. 1621, The Consumers, Schools and Libraries Digital Rights Management Act of 2003).

Although the mere introduction of a pro-user copyright bill might be seen by cynics as nothing of consequence, the power of the large copyright industries was such just three years ago that even that activity would have been unheard of. Indeed, with the increasing resources that are being brought to efforts to reform copyright, there is reason to believe that this momentum will continue, eventually leading to the passage of one or more pro-user bills.[9]

Marketplace Mechanisms

Equally, if not more important than the legal and policy activity to rebalance copyright, is the work being done *outside* the legal and policy realm. These initiatives seek to create a new, less restrictive copyright regime using new technologies and marketplace forces.

- ***Creative Commons Licenses.*** The Creative Commons (www.creativecommons.org), founded by a number of legal scholars, has developed a series of licenses that allow copyright holders to retain control over their works but still make them available under terms more favorable than copyright allows. The copyright holder can choose to make the work available under a single license or a combination of licenses. For example, a copyright holder can permit use of the work only if it is used for noncommercial purposes and if the work is attributed to him, but not for derivative works. Or he could make it available for derivative works but require that the derivative works be made available under the same terms as the original.

- *Open-Access Publishing.* Open-access publishing refers to the free availability of scientific and other research data and analysis over the Internet in a searchable, downloadable form. This movement stands in stark contrast to proprietary print journals, which do not compensate researchers for their work yet charge libraries extraordinarily high subscription fees for their volumes. The crisis in this area is such that many libraries have stopped subscribing to certain academic journals.

- *Free and Open-Source Software.* In contrast to proprietary software programs like Windows, free software/open-source programmers make available to anyone the source code underlying their software. Other programmers can modify the code in any way they see fit, but they must make that future code available on the same terms as the original. This model eliminates the restrictive licensing and copy-protection controls that are inherent in proprietary software.

How *You* Can Make a Difference

For the most part, the copyright reform movement has been very top-down, with professional policy advocates, legal professors, and lawyers engaging in most of the work. However, there is a great need, and a lot of opportunity, for grassroots participation. Here are several ways that you can participate in copyright reform:

- *Get involved.* Organizations like Public Knowledge and the Electronic Frontier Foundation have "action centers" that allow you to send letters, e-mails, and faxes and make telephone calls to policymakers and corporate executives at the click of a mouse. If you sign up to be on their mailing lists, they will send you "action alerts" that keep you apprised of particular opportunities to get involved. In addition, several states and cities have grassroots technology-policy organizations, like Electronic Frontiers Georgia, the Tennessee Digital Freedom Network, and EFF-Austin, and over a dozen colleges have started "Free Culture" chapters dedicated to promoting the free flow of knowledge. If one doesn't exist in your city, state, or college think about starting one! The national organizations would be happy to help you get started.

- *Express yourself in the marketplace.* The power of the purse is often understated in dictating corporate behavior. When people refused to buy software with restrictive copy protection in the 1970s, software companies relented and made their software more flexible. If a music CD or a DVD has restrictive copy protection, don't buy it!

- **Walk the Walk: Explore alternatives to the current copyright regime.** If you are an artist, author, or other producer of content, consider licensing your work under a Creative Commons license. If you are an academic or student, consider making your research available over the Internet for free in an open access journal. When possible and practical, use free software or open-source tools for web content, software applications, and even your computer's operating system!

Conclusion

If media-policy advocates are successful in containing—or even rolling back—media concentration, they will have won just one battle of a much larger war. The war is over how artists, scholars and citizens will be able to express themselves in the twenty-first century. Will we merely be passive consumers of whatever huge media conglomerates want to feed us, unable to make our own political and social commentary about that content or even to create something new and different? Will we be "couch potatoes" tethered to our one-way television sets and radios, or will we take advantage of the flexibility and end-to-end nature of computers and the Internet, which empower us to distribute information and ideas cheaply, quickly, and ubiquitously? Will big media dictate how we can use digital technology, or will we? These questions are likely to be answered over the next decade.

The next, and equally important, battle for media-reform advocates is copyright and trademark reform. Hundreds of thousands of ordinary citizens have made their voices heard and have made a tremendous difference in the debate over media ownership. Imagine what could be accomplished if that many, or more, people speak out in favor of bringing balance back to copyright law. I urge you to join this burgeoning movement.

Notes

1. 144 Cong. Rec. 9946, 9952 (October 7, 1998), statement of Mary Bono quoting Motion Picture Association of America President Jack Valenti.
2. 537 U.S. 186 (2003).
3. *Fox News Network* v. *Penguin Group*, (SDNY 2003).
4. *Feist Publications, Inc.* v. *Rural Telephone Service Co.*, 499 U.S. 340 (1991).
5. This marked the ninth time since 1991 that large database providers tried and failed to obtain legislation giving protection to nonoriginal databases.

6. Nine public interest and library organizations have challenged the FCC's decision in federal court, alleging that the agency does not have the power under the Communications Act to adopt the broadcast flag scheme. A decision is expected by summer 2005. See *American Library Association* v. FCC, No. 04-1037 (D.C. Cir.).

7. The FCC is also considering a recording industry-backed proposal to require a similar kind of "flag" copy protection scheme in new digital broadcast radio services. See Digital Audio Broadcasting Systems and Their Impact on the Terrestrial Radio Broadcast Service, FCC No. 04-99 (released April 20, 2004) at pp. 67–69.

8. Indeed, in 2005, the Supreme Court will decide the case of *MGM* v. *Grokster*, in which the copyright industries seek to hold the creators and distributors of P2P software responsible for copyright infringement engaged in by users of the software. This case will test the vitality of the Sony Betamax case in the digital age.

9. Further evidence of this momentum is demonstrated by the fact that in January 2005, the Copyright Office began a proceeding that seeks to resolve the problems artists and scholars face when trying to locate the owner of a copyrighted work. The Copyright Office was asked to examine the problem of these "orphan works" by the four most powerful members of Congress with jurisdiction over copyright matters. See http://www.copyright.gov/fedreg/2005/70fr3739.html.

10. These college groups take their name from the most recent book by Lawrence Lessig, mentioned above.

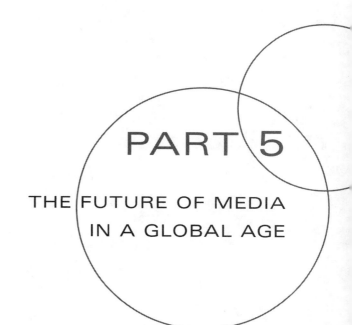

PART 5

THE FUTURE OF MEDIA IN A GLOBAL AGE

THE GLOBALIZATION OF MEDIA POLICY

Sasha Costanza-Chock

The broad public outcry in 2003–2004 against the Federal Communications Commission's attempt to allow even greater levels of media concentration ushered in an important wave of media-policy activism across the United States. The battle over consolidation and cross-ownership breathed new life into public-interest groups that have been pushing to democratize media policy for decades, galvanized organizations across the political spectrum, and generated new local and national media-policy advocacy organizations, networks, and coalitions. Parallel processes are unfolding at the international level, as media-policy activists from around the world organize around such global media-policy venues as the International Telecommunications Union (ITU), World Summit on the Information Society (WSIS), World Intellectual Property Organization (WIPO), United Nations Educational, Scientific, and Cultural Organization (UNESCO), Internet Corporation for Assigned Names and Numbers (ICANN), and the World Trade Organization (WTO). This chapter is intended to provide a basic synopsis of the issues, venues, and actors involved in global media policymaking. A brief introduction is followed by concise overviews of some of the key global media-policy venues, summaries of the powers they hold, and descriptions of recent efforts by activists to reform or replace them.

As media conglomerates expand their operations across borders, media policy is increasingly made outside of national regulatory agencies, in global venues that too often remain unscrutinized and poorly understood. Reform of global media policymaking will require the coordinated action of global networks of activists. It is imperative that United States media-policy activists, especially, begin to pay more attention to global media policy, since it is often the position of the United States government that prevails in global media-policy venues. Unfortunately, at present, most of the positions taken by the United States government in these venues represent the economic interests of the most powerfully entrenched United States communications conglomerates, rather than the best interests of people in the United States, let alone the best interests of the world's peoples in general. In fact, many of the positions taken by United States negotiators in global media-policy venues don't even represent the best technical solutions; instead, they support solutions favored by incumbents with the most money to hire lobbyists.

As global media-policy venues gain increased power, rules negotiated within them threaten to override national legislation, resulting in a process sometimes referred to as "harmonization." While this term may sound quite pleasant, in fact, harmonization is often accomplished by intense pressure from the most powerful players (particularly the United States), whose media and communications companies stand to benefit most from the revision of other countries' media, communications, and cultural policies. In practice, harmonization of media policy between poor countries and wealthy countries has often meant that the former rewrite their policies to give up public investment in noncommercial media, abandon local language requirements or support for local ownership, impose United States-style maximalist copyright law, drop subsidies for universal access to telecommunications, and even allow full privatization and takeover by the largest transnational media conglomerates. Who, for the most part, is writing these overarching global media policies? None other than the same big media firms that have been pushing in the United States to eliminate FCC ownership regulations.

Although the impact of corporate-controlled global media policy might be greatest in countries with weak domestic media, culture, and communications industries, it would be foolish to dismiss the potential domestic implications. As media multinationals gain greater and greater leverage over global media policy, the United States is not immune. Over the next decade, any domestic policy victories designed to move us toward a truly just, democratic media system with real diversity of content, local production, increased ownership of and employment at all levels within media firms by women and people of color, and a strong, noncommercial, public-interest media sector could be swept away if such victories are not paralleled by reform of the global media-policy venues that create and oversee international treaties, conventions, agreements, and standards. Big media lobbyists and lawyers will certainly be present to ensure that the interests of their clients are well represented. Who will be there to represent the rest of us?

Key Global Media Policy Venues

Crucial policies that affect the quality and nature of our media are made in a variety of global media-policy venues. The most important of these are the International Telecommunications Union (ITU), the World Summit on the Information Society (WSIS), the World Intellectual Property Organization (WIPO), the United Nations Educational, Scientific, and Cultural Organization (UNESCO), and the Internet Corporation for Assigned Names and Numbers (ICANN). Most powerful of all are the so-called free trade deals, where decisions that impact domestic media policy are made by ex-industry lawyers behind closed doors. The most well-known free trade institution is the World Trade Organization (wto); however, while in recent years, street resistance combined with increased solidarity among developing country delegates has created a crisis of legitimacy for the wto, the free trade agenda for the global media system is now being deployed more covertly through divide-and-conquer regional deals like the Free Trade Area of the Americas (ftaa), Central American Free Trade Agreement (cafta), and in a rash of bilateral, country-to-country Free Trade Agreements (ftas). For the most part, the United States media-policy agenda in all of these international venues is currently dictated by big media lobbyists.

Each of these venues has its own complicated history and relates in convoluted ways to all of the others. In-depth discussion of any of them is beyond the scope of this chapter; what follows is a brief overview of each, including a short description and a summary of recent demands by global media-policy activists. Hopefully, this will encourage activists in the United States to look beyond national borders in their thinking about how to create a better media system and a more just world.

The International Telecommunications Union (ITU)

Founded in 1865 as the International Telegraph Union, the itu was originally created as a way for European countries to develop consensus on technical standards for the telegraph—at the time, a key technology in empire building and colonial expansion. Later, the itu became the arena for negotiations over international technical standards for radio, followed by those for television, then for satellite communication and orbital allocation. In 1947, the itu became part of the United Nations. Currently, the organization is responsible for the coordination of international agreements on technical standards, the management of cross-border spectrum use, and the allocation of satellite orbits. The itu also runs programs that are intended to expand access to telecommunications in poor countries and maintains regularly updated country-by-country data on access, for example, the number of phone lines, television sets, and computers per capita, or the percentage of the population that uses the Internet. The itu is also the host organization for the World Summit on the Information Society (wsis, see below). itu headquarters are located in Geneva, Switzerland.

Historically, decisions made by the itu have been dominated by the interests of the most powerful countries and telecom companies. As a body made up of national delegates from member states, until decolonization, decisions were made for most of the world by the European colonial powers. While national delegates to the itu in general have always pushed for standards and agreements that would favor their own domestic communications firms, in recent decades the ITU has become increasingly open to direct participation by lobbyists from the private sector. This has taken place at the same time as a general shift in the telecommunications paradigm away from a system of dominant public or private national providers (one or a few in each country) to an ever smaller number of multinational telecom firms that dominate across borders. In the rush to privatization and liberalization that began in the Reagan-Thatcher years and continues today, public-interest and universal-service obligations have been largely trampled or, in many cases, eliminated entirely. Over the last decade, countries that have continued to support national providers or subsidize strong universal-access policies have faced increasing pressure from the ITU to adopt "best practices" of privatization and liberalization.[1] By the late 1990s, more than seventy countries had committed their telecommunications sectors to the WTO's General Agreement on Trade in Services (GATS), and the "voluntary" ITU recommendations were echoed by the new trade mechanism and backed by the threat of trade sanctions.[2]

At the same time, activists in recent years have increased pressure on the ITU to become more democratic, open, transparent, and accountable. Some specific demands have included: increased civil society participation, including a membership category for NGOs with rights equal to those of private sector members; sliding scale membership fees; scholarships to enable greater participation by NGOs from the global South; increased transparency in ITU decision-making, including at least observer rights for civil-society representatives during all meetings and online publication of all meeting notes; the inclusion of social-justice indicators in all data gathered by the ITU (for example, "phone access" cannot be measured simply by phones per capita but must include data on access stratified by income, gender, ethnicity or caste, age, physical disability, geographic location, and the like); and the creation of a global network of civil-society satellites, to be used for noncommercial, nonmilitary purposes, with permanent funding generated by charging private corporations fees for use of the scarce geosynchronous orbital space.

Activists' pressure for reform has yielded some success, albeit incremental. Beginning in 1996, a coalition of NGOs called the Platform for Cooperation on Communication and Democratization initiated a series of meetings with high-level ITU officials, submitted recommendations for ITU reforms to the United Nations' Secretary General, and by 1998 succeeded in pressuring the ITU to create a Focus Group on relations between the ITU and NGOs. Also in 1998, after years of pressure from many groups (spearheaded by the Association for Progressive Communications), the ITU finally formed a Focus Group on Gender Issues.[3] However, the opening of dialog, while a positive step, has not yet resulted in serious reforms. Technically, the ITU allows NGOs to register as "associates" in ITU-Development activities; for the most part, though, civil society input remains marginalized, and the costs of participation are prohibitive to all but the largest, best-funded international NGOs.

The World Summit on the Information Society (WSIS)

The WSIS, a United Nations process that will continue through the end of 2005, is intended to be a global gathering along the lines of previous UN Summits (for example, on the environment or on racism), where governments, the private sector, and civil society come together to discuss solutions to the so-called digital divide. I say so-called because the divide in question is not limited to the realm of the digital; now, in the most prosperous era of human history, there exists wealth inequality so great that the majority of the world's population has no access to a telephone, let alone a computer and high-bandwidth Internet connection. However, in December 2003, 10,000 delegates from around the world met in Geneva to discuss the "digital divide" and the future of the Information Society and to engage in heated debate on a range of issues, from community media to online privacy, from Free/Libre Open Source Software to information warfare, from the danger of allowing Internet governance to remain in the hands of a United States-based corporation (the Internet Corporation for Assigned Names and Numbers, discussed below) to the need for a Digital Solidarity Fund to support Internet rollout in poor countries. With only a few exceptions, media-policy activists from the United States were notably absent from the WSIS process.[4]

United States media-policy activists' scarce presence at WSIS might be explained by a general belief that the Summit would be more of a talk shop than a policy-making body. Indeed, the official WSIS Declaration and Plan of Action turned out, for the most part, to consist of lowest-common-denominator documents that reflected disagreement between the most economically and politically powerful countries over such important questions as universal access, copyright and patent law (Free/Libre Open Source Software was especially contentious), financial support for Internet infrastructure in the developing world, "information security," and Internet governance. However, while the "hard" policy outcomes of the first phase of WSIS appear to be limited, the Summit remains important in several respects. For one, it is a forum for the generation and exchange of ideas and positions between policymakers that will later be written into law. In addition, the summit provides a focal point for the growth of a global network of media-policy activists, who must learn how to take collective action in the face of globalized media policymaking. As an example, arguably the most compelling document to emerge from WSIS was the Civil Society Declaration, created through a two-year consensus process involving dozens of national and international Non-Governmental Organizations (NGOs) involved in media, information, and communication. Titled "Shaping Information Societies for Human Needs," the Civil Society Declaration did not focus on information and communication technologies (ICTs) as ends in themselves, but rather on the use of ICTs to advance human rights in every sphere from media democracy to health care.[5]

As the WSIS continues through its second phase, tensions are mounting over the high level of press censorship by the Tunisian government (host of the final Summit, scheduled for November 2005 in Tunis), the outcome of the Committee on Internet Governance (which some see as an attempt by the ITU to take regulatory authority over the Internet out of the hands of the United States-based ICANN), and the discussion of financing mechanisms for expanding Internet access in poor countries (with rich countries pushing for full privatization as the solution, against some poor countries seeking the creation of a major, UN-administered aid fund, and NGOs arguing for strong universal access commitments from states). The ability of media-policy activists to turn the vision elaborated in the Civil Society Declaration into strategy for organizing and winning victories in these and other WSIS debates remains to be seen.

Internet Corporation for Assigned Names and Numbers (ICANN)

ICANN is the organization responsible for coordinating the assignment of Internet domain names, IP address numbers, and protocol parameters and port numbers, as well as the root server system. In other words, ICANN regulates the domain-name system that sends users to the appropriate server when they type "www.indymedia. org" (or any website name) into their web browser. ICANN approves the creation of new top-level domains; for example, as of this writing, ICANN is considering whether to approve ten new top-level domains, including .mobi for websites designed for cell phone screens, .asia for sites relevant to the pan-Asian and Asia-Pacific region, and .xxx, for sexually explicit sites. The organization sets mandatory standards for Internet registrars (companies from which you can purchase a domain name). In addition, ICANN governs the way that disputes over domain names are resolved, through its Uniform Domain-Name Dispute Resolution Policy. Recently, ICANN adopted guidelines for a system of Internationalized Domain Names (IDN) that would allow registration of site names in all languages.

ICANN is formally a United States non-profit corporation, with a structure of Supporting Organizations and Advisory Committees meant to coordinate input from various constituencies. ICANN's byzantine decision-making structure is supposedly meant to provide input from governments, the scientific community, the corporate sector, and everyday Internet users. Over time, however, the board of ICANN has repeatedly voted to decrease the number of ICANN representatives from the nonprofit world and the general public, and the voice of the private sector has been strengthened. Meanwhile, the power and responsibilities of the organization have increased along with the worldwide expansion of the Internet.

ICANN is now coming under heavy fire from media-policy activists. Concerns include the well-documented bias of the current Uniform Domain-Name Dispute

Resolution Policy system toward wealthy corporations, which nearly always win domain-name disputes through the ICANN approved process;[6] the slide away from democratic decision-making as the number and power of the "at large" represen-tatives shrinks and the big media companies gain more clout; the organization's general lack of transparency and accountability; the problem that ICANN is a United States-based corporation but makes decisions that affect the Internet globally; and "mission creep," or the danger that, without a conscious decision by the people of the world, or even by their governments, ICANN will evolve, de facto, into the global regulatory authority for the Internet.

The creation of such a global regulatory body is an ongoing process being played out in several arenas, including ICANN, the ITU, and the WSIS. One outcome of the first phase of the WSIS was the creation of a UN Committee to, first, define "Internet governance," and then to make recommendations as to which organization should have these responsibilities—with the implication being that ICANN may in the coming years be replaced by some kind of UN body. That possibility might make Internet governance more formally accountable to a greater number of people, but, in turn, risks giving repressive governments more control over the Internet. Currently, media-policy activists are somewhat split between those who want to reform ICANN, those who advocate the creation of a new Internet governance organization, either within the UN system or independent of it, and those who favor decentralizing ICANN's authority as much as possible. Regardless, media-policy activists will have to organize to ensure that Internet governance, however it is defined and regardless of which venue(s) gain power, is held to high standards of democracy, accountability, and transparency.

World Intellectual Property Organization (WIPO)

WIPO is a UN organization whose mission is to "promote the protection of intellectual property throughout the world." It is responsible for the administra-tion of twenty-three international treaties on copyright, trademarks, patents, and other forms of so-called intellectual property rights. I say so-called because the term "*intellectual property*" obscures important differences between the various forms of legally enforced information monopolies. For example, copyright covers original artistic expressions of an idea, but not the idea itself, while a patent pro-vides the exclusive right to make, use, or sell an idea. In any case, WIPO monitors national and regional copyright and patent policies to ensure that they conform to international treaties, trains policymakers and regulators from the developing world and otherwise supports the adoption and strengthening of a United States-style maximalist copyright and patent regime across the world (I say *maximalist* because the United States positions on the length of copyright—life of the author plus fifty years, or in some cases nearly a hundred years—and the applicability of patents to "inventions" including genetic code and even living organisms, are extreme outliers in the range of existing national copyright and patent laws). WIPO also maintains a database of national copyright and patent policies. The organization counts 180 member nations and a staff of over 900, with an international headquarters in Geneva, Switzerland.

WIPO was created with the adoption of the WIPO Convention in 1967 but has roots going back to the first international intellectual-property treaty, the 1883 Paris Convention. By the 1980s, as the recently decolonized countries began asserting themselves within the UN system (including at WIPO), a private-sector alliance of pharmaceutical companies, the chemical industry, giant software firms, and the recording, broadcasting, and motion pictures industries developed and successfully implemented a plan to shift international copyright, trademark, and patent law away from WIPO and into what would become the WTO's Agreement on Trade-Related Aspects of Intellectual Property Rights (TRIPS).[7] Although TRIPS is a far more powerful mechanism because it carries the threat of trade sanctions for countries that fail to adopt United States-style copyright and patent law, WIPO remains important both because it cooperates extensively with TRIPS and in its own right as an institution devoted to promoting and enforcing an "intellectual property rights" regime that favors corporate interest over all other concerns. The governments of many poor countries, and many NGOs and activists, feel that the current WIPO model of "intellectual property" is contributing to the worldwide enclosure of the knowledge commons; in other words, the privatization of collectively produced information and knowledge that should belong to all of humanity. Indigenous movements and small farmers' associations have criticized WIPO's backing of the biotechnology industry in promoting the private ownership of genetic code, including plant, animal, and human genes; governments of southern countries, AIDS activists, and doctors' associations have attacked WIPO for supporting the pharmaceutical industry's attempts to prevent developing countries from producing cheap generic versions of desperately needed drugs to treat AIDS and other epidemic diseases; small software developers point out that WIPO seems to blindly support the spread of proprietary software, despite the advantages of Free/Libre Open Source Software (FLOSS). Some creative workers emphasize that the organization promotes a copyright system that gives long-term control of music and other audiovisual materials to big media conglomerates, undermines the rights of fair use, and limits the creative possibilities for artists, musicians, filmmakers, and everyday users.

Activists of all stripes can agree that WIPO reforms should include a fundamental reorientation of the organization to balance "intellectual property" protection with protection of the public domain, fair use, and the rights of creators and consumers over corporate owners, as well as increased transparency and civil society participation in decision-making. To that end, in 2004 a coalition of southern countries, led by Brazil and Argentina and supported by a large number of NGOs, introduced a proposal for a fundamental reform of WIPO toward a "development agenda." The proposed reforms would see the organization shift focus to promote the application of human knowledge toward achieving the UN Millennium Development Goals, rather than defend the profit margins of the media, software, biotech, and pharmaceutical industries. The period 2003–2004 may also have brought the first street protests targeting WIPO headquarters in Geneva. On June 7, 2003, three thousand people marched from the WTO to the International Organization of Migration to WIPO, to link the demand for freedom of information to the demand for freedom of movement. In December of 2003, during the WSIS summit, autonomous media activists and progressive NGOs stood together against the summit's formal endorsement of the existing copyright and patents regime. They projected the Negativland film *Gimme the Mermaid*, a satire of the copyright paradigm made from samples of Disney movies and phone conversations with greedy media company executives, while handing out Free Software CDs to international media, WIPO staff, and passersby.

Small advances have arguably been made in encouraging WIPO to seriously examine the benefits of alternative forms of "intellectual property" including copyleft, Creative Commons licenses, and Free/Libre Open Source Software. For example, in 2003, controversy swirled when the United States attempted to block WIPO from organizing a panel discussion on the possible economic benefits of open source software. However, these small openings by no means indicate that WIPO is an institution favorable to democratic media reform. In fact, one of the most serious global threats to media democracy in 2003–2004 was WIPO's proposed Treaty for the Protection of Broadcasting Organizations, which would give broadcasters—including cablecasters and webcasters—sweeping new rights to fixation, reproduction, and distribution of content, even when the content in question was previously in the public domain.[8] Public outcry organized by NGOs like the Consumer Project on Technology and IP Justice combined with Southern country delegates' resistance to giving even more restrictive powers to broadcasters has managed to slow the progress of this new treaty, but it remains on the agenda in 2005.

United Nations Educational, Scientific, and Cultural Organization (UNESCO)

UNESCO was created in 1945 to advance the goals of the Universal Declaration of Human Rights, and to support the advancement of economic, social, and cultural human rights across the globe. Its headquarters are in Geneva, with a worldwide system of National Commissions in 190 Member and Associate states. There are several ways that UNESCO affects media policy around the world.

UNESCO gathers country-by-country data on media policy and supports the development of comprehensive cultural, media, and communications policies in the developing world. The organization sponsors training programs designed to help poor countries create professional media organizations, build community technology centers, and adopt "best practice" media policies. In addition to the programs for which it is directly responsible, UNESCO serves as a forum in which international declarations, conventions, treaties, and other forms of international law that affect domestic media policies are proposed, debated, and approved or rejected.

Of all the global media-policy venues, UNESCO has historically been the one most aligned with media-policy activists' desire to see a truly free and diverse press dominated neither by the state nor by giant media conglomerates. In fact, UNESCO has a long and contentious history as a forum for worldwide debates concerning media policy and press freedom. In the late 1970s, UNESCO became a battleground for the newly decolonized countries, the Soviet bloc, and the United States, during what are now known as the New World Information and Communication Order (NWICO) debates. Concerned by the domination of global television, radio, and wire news services by the United States and Europe, developing countries demanded a restructuring of information flows that would reflect the reality of the majority of the world's population rather than the interests of the wealthy minority in the North. The United States, fearing the potential loss of control over information flows and a potential drop in income from media exports, denounced the demand for a NWICO as a communist plot to control media systems worldwide. In 1986, this battle culminated in the United States' withdrawal from UNESCO, followed shortly by the withdrawal of the United Kingdom and by a large reduction in UNESCO funding and power. The United States finally reentered UNESCO in 2003, on condition that a number of UNESCO staff considered "unfriendly" to United States interests be purged. This took place just at a time when, ironically, the debate over global information flows began brewing again in the form of a proposed treaty on Cultural Diversity (see the discussion of the Convention on Cultural Diversity, below). In 2005, media-policy activists need to demand transparency and participation in the newly reconstituted United States National Commission for UNESCO, which is supposed to be the interface between US civil society and UNESCO but was assembled in a bizarre back-room process involving the National Security Council.

World Trade Organization (WTO)

Of all the global media-policy institutions, the World Trade Organization (WTO) is the most powerful. The WTO is a trade agreement between 148 countries that is designed to eliminate government controls over imports and exports of goods and services and over foreign investment, to create pressure to liberalize and privatize state-owned enterprises and public services, and to enforce its rules by imposing multimillion-dollar trade sanctions on governments that fail to comply with commitments they have made. It was created in 1995 as the latest manifestation of a longer process of trade negotiations that began after World War II.

The primary mechanisms of the WTO are the General Agreement on Tariffs and Trade (GATT), which covers trade in goods, the General Agreement on Trade in Services (GATS), which sets out rules on trade in services—defined broadly to include everything from health care to telecommunications—and the Agreement on Trade-Related Aspects of Intellectual Property (TRIPS), which covers copyright, patents, and other forms of information monopoly. WTO rules are enforced through the binding Dispute Resolution process, which is a kind of court where countries bring complaints against each other for breaking WTO rules. The Trade Policy Review Mechanism is the process for ensuring that national policies comply with WTO terms.

The WTO has become a symbol of corporate globalization because of its closed-door decision-making, massive imbalance in influence between the developing countries and the countries of the north, and its attack on public services based on the professed blind faith, not espoused even by mainstream economists, that markets, left to themselves, will serve the needs of all. The United States government's position in the WTO, in particular, has been attacked as highly hypocritical, because of its own massive subsidies to companies in export-oriented sectors. The most attention has been given to United States government subsidies of agribusiness, which undermine whole economies and the livelihoods of millions of small farmers around the world. Less attention has been given to the gigantic subsidies handed out to media conglomerates, which trample on media democracy at home and abroad with equal zeal.

Activists from the global South have long fought against the WTO (and its precursors). However, the WTO first became a household word in the United States in 1999, when it was targeted by street protests during its ministerial meeting in Seattle. A broad coalition of organized labor, environmentalists, students, feminists, anarchists, and many others combined forces in the streets, while delegates from developing countries refused to bow to the demands of wealthy nations. The trade negotiations collapsed, the WTO's legitimacy was called into question, and the global justice movement was launched into the media spotlight, opening a broad debate in the United States' public consciousness on the benefits, costs, and injustices of corporate-led globalization.

Most media policies, including national or state support for public-interest media, local content requirements, national ownership requirements, and other public-interest policies and programs, are currently exempt from the WTO under what is known as the "cultural exception." Even with this exception, the WTO has ruled several times against national public-interest media policies, including local content requirements for Canadian magazines—and even against fair-use provisions in United States copyright law. Not satisfied, even while evidence of the WTO's ability to undermine the domestic public interest mounts, the office of the United States Trade Representative (USTR) is currently pressuring to eliminate the "cultural exception." If that happens, domestic public-interest media policy, in the United States and around the globe, could come under heavy fire behind the closed doors of the WTO Dispute Resolution process. Local content requirements, local ownership requirements, and public funding for nonprofit media could all be attacked. Governments could face multimillion or multibillion dollar trade sanctions for maintaining democratically created public-interest media and cultural policies. (For a more in-depth treatment of the impacts of the WTO on media democracy, see the chapter in this book by Lori Wallach and Chris Slevin).

In response, media activists around the world are stepping up the fight to keep media policy out of the WTO, out of related regional "free trade" deals like the Free Trade Area of the Americas (FTAA), the Central American Free Trade Agreement (CAFTA), and out of country-to-country bilateral Free Trade Agreements (FTAS). The next section of this chapter deals with the proposed convention on cultural diversity, an international treaty being developed in UNESCO that would allow each country to set its own cultural and media policy without fear of trade reprisals.

Convention on Cultural Diversity (CCD)

One of the most interesting recent developments in global media policy is the growing momentum toward the creation of a convention on cultural diversity (CCD), officially titled the Convention on the Protection and Promotion of the Diversity of Cultural Contents and Artistic Expressions. The CCD, promoted heavily by Canada and France and now backed by an increasing number of states, is meant to be a binding international legal instrument that would allow each country to exclude its cultural sector, including media, from forced liberalization or privatization under the WTO or other so-called free trade deals. The CCD has the potential to be a powerful buffer against the persistent attempts by the office of the United States Trade Representative (USTR) to fully incorporate what is termed "audiovisual services," or the production, reproduction, and distribution of television, film, radio, internet, or other sound or image content, into the mandate of the WTO.

The CCD has served as an organizing focus for a global advocacy network that includes cultural ministers from over eighty countries linked in the International Network on Cultural Policy, the NGO forum International Network for Cultural Diversity, the small and medium sized industry-led Coalitions for Cultural

Diversity, with chapters in a dozen countries and growing,[9] and the campaign for Communication Rights in the Information Society. These networks, and the CCD itself, claim to be acting to counter the reduction of culture to a commodity and the consolidation of media and cultural industries in the hands of a few, mostly United States-based, conglomerates. They have articulated language for an international treaty that would allow governments to decide to what degree they wish to insulate their cultural sectors from the market and safeguard cultural and media policy, including local-content quotas, public broadcasting systems, and limits on foreign ownership, from attack via the WTO free trade regime.[10] In October 2003, a proposal to draft the CCD was approved by the General Assembly of UNESCO, with a target date of 2005 for completion. The proposal passed with overwhelming support, despite the United States delegation's initial attempts to shut it down. During subsequent negotiations on the draft text of the Convention, the United States' delegation to UNESCO has fought against the vast majority of UNESCO member States and attempted to water down the CCD by subordinating it to the WTO. In addition, the United States delegation has supported troubling amendments that could convert the CCD into an instrument for strengthening the "intellectual property" regime and instituting new, unbalanced "antipiracy" measures.[11] The outcome of negotiations over the text of the Convention will remain up in the air at least until the fall of 2005. However, the very fact that the convention drafting process is under way may be encouraging some countries to keep their cultural sectors out of the WTO, as they wait to see what the outcome will be.

In discussing the debate over free trade versus media democracy, it is important to understand that the real aim of United States trade policy in the media, communications, and cultural sectors has never actually been to eliminate state intervention in the cultural industries or to allow the market to take its course. Even if we believed this were the aim, we would have to recognize that, as in other sectors (like agribusiness), the United States possesses a powerful cultural industry that it plans to continue to subsidize for export. Simultaneously, it will deploy the instruments of free trade to eliminate cultural/media subsidies by less powerful states, in order to force open smaller cultural markets to unimpeded penetration by its own services and products. Indeed, the USTR is so keen on liberalizing the cultural sector because, after the flight of manufacturing overseas, cultural goods and services now form one of the largest United States export sectors. At the same time, United States media conglomerates continue to receive massive state subsidies in the form of free access to public airwaves, tax breaks, and other legislative and regulatory gifts.[12] As in other sectors, neoliberal principles in the cultural sphere do not simply result in reduced government control. Rather, neoliberal tools are deployed selectively by the most powerful media conglomerates and their armies of lobbyists in order to most effectively expand markets by sweeping aside state protection of national cultural industries. This process is opposed both by powerful moneyed players, including national communication industries and lower-tier media firms, and by smaller cultural producers, cultural workers, and media-policy activists.

It is true that the convention on cultural diversity can be seen as, in large part, internecine warfare between different segments of big media: on the one side, the largest media behemoths based in the United States; on the other, second- or third-tier national cultural industries of the European Union, Japan, Brazil, Canada, and others. The defense of small cultural producers, cultural workers, community media, and horizontal, democratic communication is not the primary aim of the authors of the CCD. It is important for us to recognize that the motivation behind many countries' support for the CCD may not be to create the most diverse and locally controlled media, but rather to consolidate control of their national media. The role for progressive United States media activists will be to put pressure on the United States government (the United States National Commission for UNESCO, the US delegation to UNESCO, the USTR, the US Patent Office, and Congress) to support the convention on cultural diversity, exempt our own public-interest media policies from the WTO, ensure that the CCD respects the cultural commons and doesn't become a vehicle for unbalanced antipiracy legislation, and encourage activists in other countries to do the same.

Conclusion

United States media-policy activists have been behind the curve when it comes to engaging with the larger battle over the global media system. The past few years, especially, have seen a marked increase in the number of organizations and international networks that are mobilizing for reforms and constructing true alternatives. It would be impossible to do justice to any of these developments here. For example, the international campaign for Communication Rights in the Information Society (CRIS), a coalition of NGOs that have been active in community media, ICTs, and development for decades, played a key role in mobilizing progressive civil society participation in the WSIS (discussed at the beginning of this chapter). In recent months, the campaign has begun to shift part of its energies to the WTO and "free trade" deals, while developing a progressive position on the convention on cultural diversity. The World Social Forum, which has brought together literally hundreds of thousands of activists from around the globe, has begun to place more emphasis on the need for social movements to retake control of media and communications, including the organization of an Information and Communication World Forum within the 2005 meeting of the WSF.

Increasingly, then, the global justice movement is realizing that the commercialization and concentration of media is a key part of neoliberal globalization.

Each day, more people are taking action to oppose the policies that give global corporations control over our media, working to develop concrete alternatives, and helping to build a worldwide movement to wrest control over communications from corporations. The great majority of people in the United States, in this respect, share a common cause with people all over the world with regard to media, communication, and cultural policy; we all want our media to reflect true diversity, localism, and the public interest. Accordingly, United States media-policy activists are forging greater ties with worldwide networks that take the battle for media democracy to the global stage. This is crucial, because many of the worst policies being developed at the global level are driven by United States negotiators who serve their corporate masters. It falls to us—activists in the United States—to fight to take the United States position in global media-policy negotiations out of the hands of big media and place it under the control of the people. The next few years will be critical for the development of global communications policy. Either multinational media conglomerates will write global policy in their own interest, or people around the world will organize and take action to ensure that communications technologies and global media policies truly serve the needs of people over the profit margins of corporations.

Notes

1. Sean O' Siochru and Sasha Costanza-Chock, *Global Governance of Information and Communication Technologies: Implications for Transnational Civil Society Networking* (New York: Social Science Research Council Program on Information Technology and International Cooperation, 2004), http://www.ssrc.org/programs/itic/governance_report/index.page.
2. Internet Service Provider's Association, "South Africa's commitments under the WTO's Basic Telecommunications Agreement." http://www.ispa.org.za/downloads/GATS.doc (2001).
3. Sean O' Siochru, "Establishing Relations between the ITU and NGOs," http://www.comunica.org/itu_ngo/ (1999).
4. See, for example, Electronic Privacy Information Center, *The Public Voice WSIS Sourcebook: Perspectives on the World Summit on the Information Society* (Washington, D.C.: The Public Voice, 2004); CRIS USA, *WSIS Reportback: Organizing for Social Justice and Human Rights in Global Media and Communications Policy* (2004), http://hubproject.org/uploads/wsis-us-report.pdf.
5. WSIS Civil Society Plenary, *Shaping Information Societies for Human Needs: Civil Society Declaration to the World Summit on the Information Society*, Geneva, December 8, 2003, http://www.itu.int/wsis/docs/geneva/civil-society-declaration.pdf.
6. Michael Gurstein, "Fair.com? An Examination of the Allegations of Systemic Unfairness in the ICANN UDRP." Brooklyn Journal of International Law 27, 903-38 (2002).
7. The Corner House, "Who Owns the Knowledge Economy? Political Organizing Behind TRIPS" (2004), http://www.thecornerhouse.org.uk.
8. Consumer Project on Technology, "The proposed WIPO Treaty for the Protection of the Rights of Broadcasting, Cablecasting and Webcasting Organizations" (2004), http://www.cptech.org/ip/wipo/wipo-casting.html.

9. "Coalition Currents," CCD *Coalition Currents*, 1, no. 4 (November 2003).
10. Ivan Bernier, "Audiovisual Services Subsidies Within the Framework of the GATS: The Current Situation and the Impact of Negotiations" (Quebec: Ministère de la Culture et des Communications, 2002), http://www.mcc.gouv.qc.ca/international/diversite-culturelle/eng/pdf/update0308.pdf.
11. See http://www.mediatrademonitor.org for in-depth discussion of the negotiations.
12. Robert W. McChesney and Dan Schiller, "The Political Economy of International Communications: Foundations for the Emerging Global Debate over Media Ownership and Regulation" UNRISD Project on Information Technologies and Social Development, April 2002, http://tinyurl.com/ysrxj.

OUR MEDIA IS NOT FOR SALE

LORI WALLACH AND CHRIS SLEVIN

For nearly a year prior to the World Trade Organization's 1999 Ministerial summit in Seattle, then-Commerce Secretary William Daley made trips to various American cities, promoting "free trade" and the upcoming Seattle meeting as if it were the Super Bowl or the release of a new blockbuster movie. Daley's road show, "Trade Globally, Prosper Locally," featured government officials and corporate executives visiting factories and schools as well as editorial boards and local television studios. Daley was pegged by President Clinton as the point person to forge a "national consensus" on trade before the administration hosted the WTO summit, where the United States and Europe would push a major expansion of the WTO's jurisdiction and powers. Millions in taxpayer dollars were spent on the public-relations blitz as Daley donned work goggles, sat in tractors, and otherwise appeared in newspapers and on televisions news across the country.

The message, that free trade generally, and the WTO specifically, creates jobs, raises wages, promotes democracy, cleans up the environment, improves health, and much more, was amplified nationwide, despite its total disconnection from fact or reality. The WTO is not a "free trade" pact, but rather a managed trade pact; in the main it is not about trade, per se, but about limiting domestic food and product regulations, protecting intellectual property, and deregulating or privatizing services—including limiting cultural diversity and any other regulatory protections promoting more democratic media. The proposed WTO expansion Daley was flacking concerned all nontrade issues, such as granting foreign investors new rights, limiting local control over local government procurement decisions, and limiting health and safety inspections at the border. Meanwhile, the WTO's then five-year record had begun to prove the opposite of each of Daley's rosy claims.

At the same time, organizers of the international mobilization against the WTO, including Public Citizen, trailed Daley around the country, with shadow events in Chicago, Milwaukee, Providence, Racine, Wichita, and Cincinnati, among other places. With savvy and persistence, trade activists earned newspaper space and local TV news airtime. This coverage focused mainly on the stunts and rallies organized to protest Daley, but occasionally it included coverage of the many vital domestic and international issues of economic justice, environmental, health, and human-rights policies under attack by the WTO.

With few exceptions, the mainstream media treated the people who protested Daley almost like zoo animals in their reports, using such words as "alleged" and "suggested" when it came to our arguments, despite being supported by examples and textual analysis about the damage being caused by the corporate-driven globalization and trade agenda. It did not matter that already a string of WTO rulings and reams of government economic data substantiated our points: according to the media, Daley's malarkey was *fact* and what the protestors said was *theory*.

Underlying the tone of coverage of WTO critics was a presumption that either we were stupid and ill-informed or alternatively were protectionist, isolationist, anticapitalist, or some other audience-warning -*ist*. Missing from the coverage of Daley's tour was the fact that he was using taxpayer funds to shamelessly promote the narrow agenda of special interests that had bankrolled a Clinton campaign whose priorities regarding WTO and globalization were diametrically opposed to the vast majority of Americans.

This pattern has characterized the attitude of the major United States national and regional media since the early 1990s. Yet, domestically, an array of consumer, environmental, labor, family-farm, and other organizations, as well as scholars and policymakers began awakening to what really was going on with several new "trade" agreements that were being proposed. When these voices sought to expose the trade agenda as a Trojan horse carrying a broad array of nontrade, retrograde domestic policies that had previously been rejected when pushed in the relative sunshine of Congress and federal agencies, the major press either largely ignored them or in some instances launched attacks on the messengers.

As a result, the press in the United States totally buried one of the biggest stories of the 1990s—the stunningly audacious corporate power grab accomplished through "trade" agreements. It remains a largely ill-understood backdrop to a sizable portion of today's domestic and international economic and political news—from the jobless recovery, evisceration of the middle class, and startling increases in United States income inequality, to the radical deregulation of services that contributed to the Enron and WorldCom corporate crime waves, to record-low commodity prices fomenting unrest in countries around the world, to the new flood of uninspected imported food that will result in the United States' facing a new trade deficit in food.

In the early 1980s, the ideological and business interests behind the Thatcher and Reagan "revolutions" were stymied as their radical campaign to slash the role of government and to "free" markets and corporations to rule the world faced stiff opposition. Citizens' movements and parliamentarians around the world were passionately opposed to subjecting basic human rights and needs to the mercies of markets and corporations. In scores of nations, the most extreme elements of the "neoliberal" agenda were rejected by public opinion and democratically elected legislatures.

Yet while few were even aware of obscure global trade negotiations, the frustrated promoters of the neoliberal agenda had shifted their arena of operation. The plan was to transform the General Agreement on Tariffs and Trade (GATT), a narrowly cast twenty-page trade agreement signed in 1947, into a powerful new system of global governance. Trade negotiators from scores of countries—surrounded by "advisers" from the world's largest corporations and the think tanks they funded—toiled behind closed doors for a decade.

What emerged from the Uruguay Round in 1994 were the World Trade Organization and 900 pages of one-size-fits-all rules, setting policy on matters extending far beyond trade. WTO rules granted new powers and rights to corporations and restricted government action on local economic development, the environment, food safety, public health, economic justice, and even ways in which nations' tax dollars could be spent. If such an autocratic, antidemocratic governance system had been imposed by force over elected governments around the world, human rights monitors and United Nations inspectors would have been dispatched and the *New York Times* and *Washington Post* would have sounded the alarms in news coverage and editorials. CNN would have launched twenty-four hour continuous coverage. Instead, the United States media stood complicit in enthroning the WTO's legitimacy and aiding the threat to democratically accountable policymaking and just economic development worldwide.

In scores of developing countries, where people had already suffered under a decade of similar rules imposed as conditions for obtaining loans from the International Monetary Fund (IMF), massive street protests erupted as opposition to joining the new global body grew. These protests were covered broadly in the press of these nations—where WTO passage often involved epic political battles, extremely close votes, and in some cases, perverted democratic processes to obtain approval. But the United States press ignored the anti-WTO fervor in other nations almost entirely. When there was a story, it focused on which United States agribusiness multinational's office building had been attacked in India, but not that the incident occurred during a half-a-million-person anti-WTO march.

Instead, the American public and press were marinated in a public-relations campaign touting the WTO as just a bigger, better trade deal that would create more jobs and cheaper products for all. Meanwhile, media coverage of the concurrently raging debate about NAFTA was largely of the same ilk, although its tone was even more vicious in painting NAFTA opponents as retrograde idiots or perhaps anti-Mexican racists. The pro-NAFTA predictions and promises were touted as fact. At the time, it seemed that the media bias was rooted in elite group-think: so many reporters, editors, and producers had the same college indoctrination that "free trade" was good, whereas any criticism of anything called free trade was "protectionism," an evil that had caused the Great Depression and world wars.

Thomas Friedman, the *New York Times* columnist and cheerleader for corporate globalization, infamously attacked the skeptics in print and anecdotally espoused the virtues of "free trade." It was clear with which side of these inaccurate caricatures one would want to be associated, even if one wasn't a true believer in the "free trade" cult. Yet with the wisdom of hindsight and research, what later became apparent were the direct financial interests of the "free" media in promoting such programs. For instance, at the time of the NAFTA and WTO debates, NBC was owned by General Electric and CBS was owned by Westinghouse. Both Westinghouse and GE were both members of USA NAFTA, the corporate front group that coordinated the multi-million dollar pro-NAFTA lobby. And even for those outlets that were not part of major industrial conglomerates, with direct financial interests in passage of NAFTA and WTO, the agreements promised significant business opportunities. At issue were binding international rules that would provide major media corporations with market access into more sectors of other nations' economies, namely media and audiovisual services. Further, these corporations would receive new rights to overcome local cultural-diversity rules that might otherwise limit foreign media takeovers. Once in these markets, the large multinationals would be given new intellectual-property rights to protect imported "cultural products."

So, in 1994, the United States Congress voted to join the WTO—exposing decades of hard-won environmental, worker, and consumer protections to be taken over by a global-governance system hostile to these values. This odious attack was cleverly rolled through Congress under the appealing cover of "free trade." Thanks to the media's complicity, the WTO coup d'etat was a success.

Following the shameful coverage of the 1993 NAFTA and 1994 WTO debates, there were occasional solid stories, although few of them from first-tier newspapers and none from network television. Then, in the mid-to-late 1990s, occasional stories appeared about the Multilateral Agreement on Investment (MAI), a proposed foreign-investor protection treaty so extreme that it suffered the same fate as Dracula when dragged out into the sunshine of public scrutiny. The MAI, which was conceived by and negotiated through the Organisation for Economic Cooperation and Development (OECD), was to be implemented and enforced by the WTO. It would have imposed worldwide the controversial investment provisions seen only in NAFTA and its proposed extension throughout the Americas. Facing enormous grassroots pressure, in February 1998, the Canadian and French governments began to publicly distance themselves from the MAI as it was drafted at the time. They refused to announce, even in principle, that they would sign the agreement. France proposed a cultural carve-out that would keep MAI provisions from applying to print and broadcast media and cinema. Public backlash, which built substantial political pressure against the agreement, ultimately resulted in its failure. However, following its defeat by citizen activism, the European Union, Japan, and the United States have tried to revive elements of the MAI into new WTO negotiations.

The MAI received column miles of coverage in Europe and Canada, especially in the *Toronto Globe and Mail*. Yet it became number one in Project Censored's "Top 25 Censored Stories" of 1999, a list that noted that the *New York Times*, the *Washington Post*, and the *Los Angeles Times* never deigned to write about the MAI. Instead, only obscure letters to the editor or opinion pieces penned by informed and outraged citizens appeared. Ronald Forthofer, a retired professor, who wrote of the MAI on October 13, 1997, in the *Rocky Mountain News*, "This proposed constitution lacks input from the world's citizens." Similar letters by active citizens appeared in pages of the *St. Petersberg Times* and the *Newark Star-Ledger*.

Enterprising reporters, such as Jane Bussey of the *Miami Herald*, Robert Collier of the *San Francisco Chronicle*, R.C. Longworth of the *Chicago Tribune*, and Bill Atkinson of the *Baltimore Sun*, literally broke stories to their readership, in the business pages, about the growing resistance to corporate-driven globalization and the MAI. *BusinessWeek* was the lone national publication that covered the story. Yet for every well-reported piece on the proposed MAI, the *Financial Times* reinforced support for it by printing letters or op-eds with such titles as "Never Say MAI" or "Wishlist for Investors."

As NAFTA hit its five-year mark, there were more frequent well-reported print stories on its corporate investor protections, the environmental damage it caused in Mexico, and big-name high-profile United States factories, such as Zenith and Levi closing down to relocate south of the border. Yet in the late 1990s, while the economy was expanding, reporting on job losses to trade simply seemed impossible. The Daleys and Clintons asserted that trade created new jobs, while the executives in major newsrooms around the country largely bought the "Trade Globally, Prosper Locally" pitch. Criticizing the WTO or NAFTA was insane to them.

It required more than 50,000 anti-WTO protestors from across the United States and around the world taking to the streets of Seattle to break the major print and broadcast media marginalization of criticism of corporate-led globalization. On December 1, 1999, the A sections in newspapers across the country ran above-the-fold stories on the large-scale protests. What had been a long-growing struggle against corporate globalization and the WTO in the United States suddenly burst onto center stage. It took a relatively superficial fight on the streets of Seattle to lure the world's major media into paying attention to the WTO and the worldwide struggle being waged against it.

While much of the Seattle coverage focused on the protests themselves, the sheer volume of coverage—and the need to explain why so many people had taken time off to protest an organization considered obscure as a result of the lack of prior press coverage—meant that during the Seattle Ministerial and for a few weeks following, WTO criticisms started to be covered as broad-based and legitimate concerns. Seattle marked a turning point in terms of media visibility, if not in accuracy.

To the majority of Americans, the political movement against the WTO they saw on the evening news was an overnight sensation. The reporting of the eventual collapse of the Seattle ministerial conference, and its immediate aftermath, were at times accurate but more often overshadowed by the media's focus on peripheral protest scenes and the Seattle police department's violent response. Organizers of the mobilization were afforded a brief moment to convey to the world a complex system and the international coalition seeking to change it.

While the mainstream media focused their attention on the violence in the Seattle streets, the WTO staff and the handful of large countries used to dictating WTO terms were struggling to crush the opposition by blocs of developing countries to proposed new global rules over procurement, services, investment, and more. Media conglomerates, among other corporate interests, would have directly benefited from the proposed WTO expansion. In the heat of the Seattle protests, the media had an enormous opportunity to investigate a clash inside the Ministerial and to probe the charges protesters made about the WTO's impact on the developing world. Some reporters and editors made great strides in connecting the dots between the WTO's claims, the protesters' claims, and the real-life results. In response, WTO proponents and the corporate publicity machine quickly went on a counteroffensive to frame the Seattle meetings in a way that dismissed the protests and delegitimized their arguments.

Many news organizations adopted the message of this counteroffensive. NBC News's correspondent in Seattle concluded his report, "No matter what comes out of this four-day meeting—and a lot of analysts don't think it will be much—world trade has such momentum, almost nothing can get in its way." The *Associated Press* reported the protesters' "far-fetched" claims. ABC's Peter Jennings signed off when the Ministerial ended: "Thousands of demonstrators will go home, or onto some other venue where they'll try to generate attention for whatever cause that moves them." The Seattle police public-information office earned a raise after the *Los Angeles Times* ran a front-page story three days into the Ministerial with the subtitle, "Police Commended for Restraint." Thomas Friedman, boiling, wrote of the Seattle demonstrators: "A Noah's ark of flat-earth advocates, protectionist trade unions and yuppies looking for their 1960s fix."

The pattern of covering the story of protest against corporate globalization by trying to marginalize or dismiss the critics and the substantive critique persisted after Seattle. In the protests that followed in Prague, Quebec, Genoa, and other locations, the coverage focused on the most pierced, most tattooed, most-clichéd protesters and sensational insinuations of links to terrorism, threats of violence, and evidence of one protester's ignorance being generalized to all critics.

Perhaps the most ironic line of the public-relations spin, reported hook, line, and sinker by many major media outlets, was that protesters were all rich, spoiled white kids trying to keep the poor in developing countries poor. Friedman referred to them as having "open-toe sandals and closed minds." Of course, the truth is that the movement against corporate globalization is led from the global south and is much stronger in developing countries. Looking north from the south, Seattle was viewed as a Johnny-come-lately event, a sign that civil society in northern countries was finally getting with the political agenda of halting further corporate globalization and reversing its effects. This struggle had long been waged in the south.

The silence before Seattle and the largely off-base coverage of trade and globalization since should be understood in concert with the fact that major media conglomerates use the WTO as a vehicle to push for greater consolidation of their industry. Reporters' and producers' corporate bosses were not interested in covering the criticisms of globalization's mass commodification of life given that multinational media corporations themselves were a major culprit in the bad news. Who would cover the role of media corporations in commoditizing "culture" in order to produce and sell it? It is not likely to be an industry run on advertising revenues drawn from campaigns to achieve global brand recognition through cultural homogenization. (Polling of very poor communities in Africa and Latin America has shown that United States luxury goods are considered a gateway to happiness.) Reporters who cover the critique of corporate globalization court the ire of the front office or are simply shut down by editors. A media system featuring a broad range of independent, local voices would surely focus on the efforts of the WTO in permitting multinationals to cannibalize locally owned media outlets. Yet, concentration of media ownership—a trend facilitated by pacts such as NAFTA and WTO—means there is no such diversity of voices, and therefore there is little press coverage of the larger trends.

Media and Global Trade Agreements

What are the international trade rules from which global media conglomerates would benefit? One of the seventeen agreements enforced by the WTO is the General Agreement on Trade in Services (GATS), which sets global rules for the entities that can own services and the ways in which governments can regulate them. Services are anything that you cannot drop on your foot—insurance, banking, transportation, retail, education, and health care, as well as publishing, broadcasting, film, and other media. GATS rules, which apply to service sectors committed by WTO member countries, create a right for foreign companies to purchase, set up, or otherwise control local businesses, with strict limits on government regulation in these sectors. One intention of this agreement was concisely stated in an outbreak of unusual candor by the United States Chamber of Commerce in a letter to the Office of the United States Trade Representative in 1996, "No country can be allowed to resist American cultural imperialism."

Thus, if a country commits "broadcast services" to GATS market-access rules, countries are forbidden from limiting foreign ownership of television networks, allowing global giants to acquire domestic outlets and control their content. Because the issue of cultural diversity was so politically explosive, some countries refused to take commitments in this area. This issue almost crashed the entire WTO negotiations when the powerful Motion Picture Association of America insisted that France and other nations, which set limits on foreign media and film content, eliminate such policies as part of the talks. Nonetheless, many countries (including France) kept aspects of their media outside the coverage of the WTO rules, or so they thought.

The broad threat trade agreements have on a country's right to preserve cultural diversity was put on full display in a 1997 WTO ruling against Canadian regulations aimed at ensuring the survival of a domestic news-magazine sector. Since 1965, Canada had levied a tariff on split-run magazines—special editions that contain foreign editorial content but sell space to domestic advertisers or aim advertising at the domestic market. Canada enacted the tariff to protect smaller Canadian-owned publications from losing advertising revenue to larger magazines and thus being forced out of business by United States-based publishing conglomerates.

Time Warner began to beam *Sports Illustrated* into Canada via satellite to avoid the tariff charged on magazines that crossed the border. In 1995, Canada responded by amending the 1965 law to impose an 80 percent excise tax on split-run magazines—meaning that the charge would apply regardless of how the foreign content entered the country. In 1996, the United States launched a WTO challenge against the tax and the 1965 tariff on split-run magazines. For good measure, Canada's policy of subsidizing postal rates for domestic magazines was also taken before the WTO. Through a program called Canadian Heritage, the government provided a financial subsidy to Canada Post enabling it to provide a preferential postal rate for Canadian magazines shipped within the country, in recognition of the challenges of distributing to a population that is widely dispersed geographically.

The United States argued that measures to "ensure 'original content' in magazines sold in Canada . . . would be contrary to the object and purpose" of the WTO and that Canada had no right to protect its culture or heritage. The market should be the sole determinant. From the Canadian perspective, at issue was the disappearance of local culture in the national magazine market.

In March 1997, a WTO panel found the Canadian measures to be in violation of rules under the General Agreement on Tariffs and Trade (GATT) that forbid discrimination and import restrictions. It found that Canada's 80 percent excise tax on split-run magazines was a discriminatory imposition and judged the provision of lower postal rates to Canadian magazine an illegal subsidy.

Instead of allowing the unrestricted import of magazines with American content and Canadian ads, the Canadian government maneuvered around the WTO ruling by proposing new domestic legislation that focused on regulating sales of "advertising services" rather than regulating the magazines as "goods." This strategy was aimed at implementing its cultural goal through policies that would be covered by GATS (the WTO's services rules) as opposed to the GATT (the WTO's goods rules). Since Canada was one of the countries that had acted to protect its domestic culture by refusing to make certain GATS commitments—including covering "advertising services"—this course of action would comply with the 1997 WTO ruling based on GATT yet maintain the goal of protecting domestic culture.

The United States was infuriated by Canada's maneuver and threatened $4 billion in import sanctions before formally challenging Canada's new policy at the WTO. Observers predicted that Canada's refusal to take on GATS commitments would safeguard its cultural goal, yet, unbelievably, the WTO panel performed a legal limbo to conclude that advertising was both a "good" and a "service," and therefore Canada's absence of GATS advertising commitments was simply irrelevant. This kind of "pick and choose" classification was far removed from public participation and comment, since WTO tribunals are closed to the press and the public. Moreover, under WTO rules, its "judges" are trade specialists who have served at the GATT or WTO or represented their governments there. Together, these structural biases ensure a commodification "über alles" perspective. The implications of this ruling are chilling, especially in such a sector as media, where a film or book can be defined as a good, thus eviscerating whatever protections countries thought they had obtained for television or film production.

In 1999, Canada was finally pressured into abandoning the new legislation and cut a deal that allows United States publishers to sell 18 percent of their advertising space to Canadian clients if a "substantial" level of Canadian content is maintained in the publication. "Substantial," however, is not defined, a fact that Maude Barlow, chairwoman of the Council of Canadians, a national consumer group, described as a "sell-out" of the Canadian publishing industry.

Following Seattle, the WTO began new negotiations to actually expand the scope of the GATS. The negotiations, called GATS 2000, are part of the WTO's "built-in" agenda, meaning that, despite off-and-on-again logjams in other WTO talks (known as the Doha agenda), multilateral talks are now under way at the WTO's Geneva headquarters to place more services, including media, under the jurisdiction of GATS' rules, the requirements of which may be expanded during these talks. In 2003, WTO member countries completed a Request/Offer stage of GATS negotiations. Countries first extend requests of service sectors they want to access, and months later receive responses regarding sectors ultimately offered. The United States has been a leader in pressuring countries to make offers in "audiovisual services," including: "theatrical motion pictures" (film production, pre- and post-production services, film distribution and delivery services, and cinema operation), "television" (content production, distribution rights, selling advertisements, direct to home-service providers), "home video entertainment" (content production, film and tape duplication, leasing of home entertainment for such business customers as airlines and bus companies), "transmission services" (from producers to broadcast stations, satellite uplink, cable systems) and "recorded music" (representation and signing of artists, sound production, tape duplication, distribution rights to radio and TV, wholesale distribution, distribution and program packaging for businesses). Also on the agenda of these negotiations are rules to more tightly limit countries' ability to regulate foreign service providers. Assorted 2005 deadlines have been set to push forward the GATS-2000 talks to lock in more service sectors under WTO rules.

Not surprisingly, the same names and faces pushing the Federal Communications Commission to deregulate the media are members of the Bush administration's trade advisory committees. The Motion Picture Association of America (MPAA), for example, which sits on the Bush administration's trade advisory committee covering services, has largely dismissed other countries' efforts to protect cultural diversity. "In today's world, with multiplex cinemas and multi-channel television, the justification for local content quotas is much diminished," states the MPAA. "And in the e-commerce world, the scarcity problem has completely disappeared. There is room on the Internet for films and video from every country on the globe in every genre imaginable. There is no 'shelf-space' problem on the net."

Yet the right of social, religious, cultural, and indigenous groups to preserve their practices, beliefs, artifacts, and artistic expressions is crucial to maintaining diversity within and among nations of the world. The position argued by the International Forum on Globalization is that cultural diversity and integrity are fundamental rights (like water) that nations should retain the ability to protect.

Multimedia information technology firms that lobby governments to advance deregulation see their best chance for success through trade negotiations, be they multilateral at the WTO or bilaterally, one nation to another. The United States has driven the proposed Free Trade Area of the Americas (FTAA), a proposed expansion of NAFTA to thirty-one countries, which if approved would likely to extend the same policies that restrict media localism, diversity, and pluralism. The six-nation Central American Free Trade Agreement NAFTA expansion also includes these service-sector regulatory limits. As well, in the signed (but not approved) CAFTA and proposed FTAA are rules allowing multinational conglomerates to seek cash compensation—paid for by taxpayer dollars—if a nation takes steps to protect localism and diversity on its airways that affect a foreign investor's plans in another country. By late 2004, the FTAA was in a stalemate because of resistance to these rules by developing countries. In 2004, the Bush administration did not have the votes to pass CAFTA, but it will try to do so in 2005.

Bilateral deals are the means by which the United States corporate-driven trade agenda most easily obtains new rights, outside of the prying eyes of citizens and local governments. The proposed United States-Australia Free Trade Agreement, which was negotiated in 2003, signed by the Bush administration in 2004, and put into effect in January 2005, eliminates restrictions on the ability to invest or acquire overseas media and communication resources, including basic telecommunications, cable networks, news agencies, film production, video leasing and rentals, sound recording, and music publishing. The agreement eliminates media cross-ownership restrictions and caps the levels of local content on "free-to-air" television, paid television, and radio. This provision includes limiting media content for children, the arts, and educational purposes to a maximum of 10 percent. Mainstream dramatic series would be limited to 20 percent.

The agreement and its radical rules on media sparked protests in Australia. The 2003 Logie Awards, which celebrate Australian achievements in film and television, were overshadowed by attendees wearing green-and-gold ribbons in unified opposition to the United States-Australia Free Trade Agreement, while the executive director of the Australian Screen Directors Association pulled support from the deal.

Globalizing the Media Reform Movement

In the era of corporate globalization, the fight against media consolidation cannot be seen as just a domestic effort. The fight for media activists are on multiple fronts at home and internationally—multilaterally, regionally, and bilaterally—but are focused on United States officials setting United States positions taken to Geneva, where the WTO enforces rules over services. While, in the United.States, the FCC has endorsed greater media consolidation, the same push for deregulation is being negotiated globally in Geneva. The potential WTO rules are the ultimate safety net for media conglomerates facing fervent opposition from media activists in the United States. As the media reform movement gains momentum in the United States, conglomerates and their well-paid lobbyists are not just working in Washington, but in Geneva at the WTO, and at the office of the USTR, where numerous bilateral negotiations are in process.

For example, certain measures that media activists may take to defend localism, diversity, and pluralism could be classified as "barriers to trade," meaning that other WTO nations have the ability to use the same binding dispute mechanism of the WTO illustrated in the Canadian magazines case. Decisions on trade disputes made by the WTO are enforced; nations must comply with WTO rulings or face potential punitive sanctions reaching millions of dollars.

A variety of measures crucial to delivering high quality public-service broadcasting would violate GATS rules if a country commits certain cultural service sectors. Limits on ownership, specific restrictions on foreign media ownership, and rules regarding cross-ownership would all be subject to challenge under GATS. The 2003 battle to restore old regulations on ownership at the FCC could be rendered moot if the battle is not also won at the WTO and in other trade-agreement negotiations.

In addition, federal and state programs, grants and loans to fund media projects, subsidies, tax preferences, and other initiatives that encourage independent film, public broadcasting, art, and other cultural innovation within a given market could be challenged using GATS rules. These could be cited as violations of non-discrimination rules if the same resources were unavailable to other WTO member nations with interests in the same market. Advertising commitments could also prevent the United States from regulating promotions that target minors, such as current laws limiting advertising during children's programming and prohibiting cigarette ads on television.

Even if the United States government exempts its broadcast regulations and programs that support media and culture from the current round of negotiations, the goal of the GATS is "progressive liberalization." Thus, there will be strong pressure to discard such exemptions in future negotiations. Further, efforts to improve the regulatory structure would be impaired, since these legally binding trade obligations virtually assure the regulatory status quo. Attempts to substantially alter regulatory structures to transform a drastically homogenous media landscape would face unprecedented hurdles. Any adjustments to the regulatory structure that could be viewed as rolling back foreign corporations' potential opportunities under United States commitments under GATS would require preapproval and compensation to all of our trading partners, according to the GATS text.

About twenty nations have tabled GATS proposals on audiovisual. The United States is most aggressively pursuing the communications aspect, though the European Union and Canada have been hesitant. Citizens in many nations, including within the European Union, have so far been successful in pressuring their governments to make no agreements that could impact their nations' media and cultural services. The European Union has gone on record that it will not make any GATS commitments in culture and media.

Under the broad area of "communication services," the United States has included offers on information services, defined as the offering of the capability for generating, acquiring, storing, transforming, processing, retrieving, and making available information, which includes Internet, voicemail, online information, and electronic data exchange. It also includes communication services, such as cable, one-way satellite transmission, radio and television broadcasting. This proposal does not include exemptions for domestic media regulations protecting public service broadcasting, such as the 45 percent or 35 percent cap on size that was the subject of the FCC vote in 2003.

The United States position to expand the scope of the GATS over media and audiovisual services has been entirely formed by the same lobbyists and special interests pushing for deregulation at the FCC. As pressure increased on the domestic front and the FCC's deregulatory efforts were blocked, media industry lobbyists are likely to redouble efforts to open the WTO, a venue more protective of industry and impervious to the democratic process.

The effort to stop deregulation at a global level will not be easy. The Seattle WTO protest catalyzed world consciousness about globalization and its resistance, creating a model in which organized opposition can take place effectively. It triggered extreme reaction from its proponents, its flacks and hacks in the media machine. The extreme reaction to Seattle also created a military model, evident in November 2003, when the first major trade ministerial summit in the United States since Seattle occurred in Miami. Trade ministers of 34 nations in the proposed FTAA met to advance the proposed hemisphere-wide NAFTA expansion, but they adjourned after one day when serious concerns were raised by Brazil.

Considering the heightened profile trade had taken in the United States by 2003—from media focus on the off-shoring of high-tech service sector jobs through the escalating trade deficit and creeping decline of the dollar to widespread opposition to the WTO abroad—Miami presented an opportunity for major mainstream media to take a step back and rethink previous notions of sweeping trade deals like the FTAA. All national newspapers have at least one trade and globalization reporter who was present in Miami.

Yet the major broadcast media nearly blacked out Miami, most running no more than short spots on the Ministerial's first (and only) full day, after a massive police mobilization shocked and intimidated a collection of demonstrators that included retired seamstresses, steel workers, and teachers. The *Miami Herald* (and *Nueva Herald*, its Spanish-language counterpart) gave the FTAA host committee $62,500 in cash, as well as thousands more in services, glowing pro-FTAA editorials and free advertising, earning itself a "Diamond" sponsorship. Organizers of the Ministerial estimated the cost of the event at $3.6 million.

This sum did not include the federal assistance the City of Miami won from the Bush administration to fund more than 3,000 police in armored riot gear and providing helicopters and weapons for forty agencies on hand to greet demonstrators. Taking a cue from the Pentagon, Miami-Dade police, led by a police chief who called demonstrators punks and knuckleheads, embedded dozens of reporters within their ranks. Independent video caught one such embedded reporter wearing a helmet and vest; after being crowded by protesters, he began to beat a demonstrator with a piece of equipment. A reporter for the Workers Independent News Service was shot with a pepper-spray bullet. Another reporter, for Pacifica's *Democracy Now!*, was caught in a mass arrest. As reported by a colleague, she wore her press credentials in plain sight and asserted to police that she was a journalist. To that she heard one of the officers say, "She's not with us, she's not with us," meaning that she was not embedded with the police, and she was duly arrested. A reporter for the *Miami New Times*, the city's independent weekly, was interviewing demonstrators when Miami police ordered her and the protesters to lie on the ground at gunpoint before herding them into police vans. Of over 238 arrests from two days in Miami, there has not been one conviction. In June 2004, an independent panel formed by Miami-Dade County found that police and law enforcement officials used "deplorable, unrestrained and disproportionate use of force," stating that "civil rights were trampled and socio-political values . . . were undermined."

The panel also faulted the *Miami Herald* and the local media for fueling an anticipation of violent protests. Yet despite the fiery condemnation from the panel, it does not have subpoena power or any real authority over the city or the police. The *Herald* responded with a short article on June 3, 2004 about the panel's damning report but has reported little more.

During the Miami Ministerial, the Independent Media Center taught the local and visiting mainstream media lessons in savvy and professionalism. Writers, producers, and camera operators of the IMC in Miami worked around the clock, exposing unprovoked police aggression, but also feeding camera footage of police provocateurs and their unprovoked violence to local Miami television, as well as to such national outlets as PBS. Its footage has also been used by the ACLU and by lawyers filing suits against the City of Miami for protesters who were injured by police violence.

But Independent Media coverage will not be sufficient to educate the public or to build the power to fight against corporate globalization and media consolidation. To effect change, broad-scale reform is needed to change the policies promoting media consolidation. The tools of communication needed in these fights are currently monopolized by major broadcast networks and newspaper conglomerates.

Media conglomerates and other promoters of further consolidation and homogenization of media through the WTO, FTAA and bilateral trade agreements point to a changing landscape, fueled by technological innovation and consumer choice, as justification for eliminating public oversight in the domestic realm and fostering further global consolidation of media via trade agreements. They face resistance, but not yet enough either from the media reform activists or global justice activists..

While citizens have proven their effectiveness in generating a fury of public opposition to extreme FCC deregulation proposals, media-reform activists must reconcile the fact that the corporate promoters of media consolidation will keep looking for alternate venues to enact legislation they find beneficial. And while citizens have proven their effectiveness in bringing down the MAI and stalling FTAA and WTO expansion, global-justice activists must also reconcile the fact that without more diverse, independent mass media, it will be difficult to build the power to change the rules of the global economy.

Free, diverse, local, and independent media are recognized as a fundamental requirement for a functioning democracy. There is no way to ensure this outcome without winning the globalization fight, and there is no way to win the globalization fight without a free and diverse press. These struggles must be waged together as oppositional forces organized around common principles of social justice. Success against the corporate powers stalking democracy in both of these forums can and must occur again.

INDEX

Page numbers referencing an illustration are set in italic.

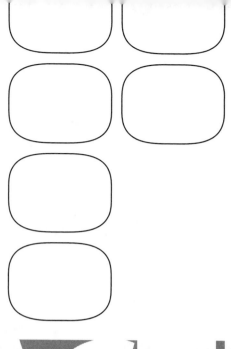

media
reform

ACTION GUIDE

Tired of a media system that puts

profits in front of the public interest?

This Action Guide contains

step-by-step instructions for media

reform strategies that get results!

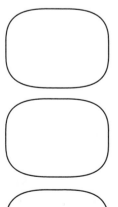

www.freepress.net

CONTENTS

◎ **Easy Targets.** These actions are great ways for someone new to media reform to get involved and make a difference.

INTRODUCTION

For far too long, our media has been shaped by policies made behind our backs and without our interests in mind. Information about our media system isn't in the press, and policymakers make crucial decisions about media behind closed doors.

This media system provides extraordinary profits and power to huge media corporations—and lets them shirk their responsibility to provide us with the quality journalism, diverse viewpoints, educational programs and public forums that democracy requires. They'd like to keep it that way.

But Americans increasingly understand how corrupt our media system is, and together we are starting to change it. Concerned people around the country are building an extraordinary movement to speak out and stand up for media reform.

This Action Guide was created to support the efforts of media reformers like you. Every action in this guide will help get your voice heard by the people who make the rules. And each action you take connects you to a growing rank of people who have the clout to transform the current media landscape.

There is much great work being done on many fronts—but still so much more to do. Armed with the will to speak up, we *can* build a better media system.

RAISE AWARENESS

Because we cannot rely on the media to educate us about their own failings—much less correct them—this task falls upon us, the citizenry, using every available channel of communication. One of the most important things you can do is to share your awareness of media reform with others.

Send a Letter to the Editor

Letters to the Editor are among the most widely read sections of the paper; in fact, many members of Congress scan these letters to gauge their constituents' interests and opinions.

Here's how you can increase the likelihood that your letter will be printed:

Check the specifications. Length and format requirements vary from paper to paper. Specifications are often printed on the editorial page, or you can call the paper to ask. Read the letters to the editor that get published in your paper to get ideas on successful style, format, etc.

Make it timely. For example, refer to a recent story where media ignored or mishandled a critical issue, or to a timely media policy issue. You could also respond directly to a story recently printed in the paper to which you're writing.

Make it local. Whatever you're writing about, relate it to local issues and illustrate how it will affect your community. For instance, you could refer to your local legislator's position on an issue or refer to a local media outlet.

Know your subject. Reference facts—don't make false or misleading statements.

Keep the tone reasonable. Use humor, irony, or even a hint of anger, but don't be nasty or offensive.

Keep it brief. Try to make just one point in your letter, and state the point clearly in your topic paragraph, followed by one or two paragraphs and then a conclusion. 200 words is a typical limit. Letters that are too long will either be edited down or not printed at all.

Make it easy for the paper. Include your full name, address, and daytime phone number. Without this info, your letter may not be printed. Find out how to send your letter—mail, fax, or e-mail.

See page 358 for a sample letter to the editor you can tailor and submit to your local paper.

Publish an Op-Ed, Guest Column, or Newsletter Article

Seek out venues to publish an opinion or commentary article that advocates for media reform. Many mainstream newspapers publish submitted articles in a "guest column" or accept op-ed submissions. (An op-ed is a brief essay that expresses a personal viewpoint, usually located on the page *op*posite the *edi*torial page). Alternative newspapers, magazines, and news web sites often accept and publish submissions as well. Or submit to an organization's newsletter: they might welcome an article that makes the connection between their primary issue and media reform.

Some tips on writing and publishing an op-ed:

Advocate. An op-ed is an opportunity to strongly state your position on an issue; do so emphatically but thoughtfully. Be timely and controversial, but not outrageous. You are trying to convince a middle-of-the-road audience to adopt your position.

Inform. Base your arguments on factual or first-hand information. Provide insight and understanding without preaching.

Write with verve. Use humor or emotion where appropriate. Employ an engaging anecdote or personal account. Choose clear, direct, powerful language. An engaging and well-written op-ed is much more likely to be published than a dry critique.

Use your professional affiliation or other title that suggests authority or shows your stake in the issue. If you work for an organization, get permission to sign your op-ed as a representative of that organization.

CATCHY TAGLINES

"Media IS the issue"

"It's the media, stupid"

"Media reform: democracy demands it"

"Don't trust the corporate media"

"Rich media, poor democracy"

"Commercial media is toxic to your health"

"Our democracy, our airwaves"

"What the FCC is going on?"

Write your own punchy title. Otherwise the editor may choose one that may not accurately sum up your argument.

Submit it after contacting the paper about their specifications. Length requirements are usually around 600–800 words. You can submit an op-ed to several different newspapers—even large national papers—but not to papers in the same market (for instance, submit it to either the *Boston Globe* or *Boston Herald*, but not both). Include a brief cover letter to the editor outlining your piece. Include your contact information and a brief bio.

For a guest column, article, or newsletter commentary, you can use the same general writing tips above, but check the other pieces in that publication to get a sense of the typical style, tone, length, and format of pieces they publish. Contact the publication's staff for information about how to submit a piece of writing.

See page 359 for a sample op-ed you can tailor and submit to your local paper or page 361 for a sample organizational newsletter article.

RESOURCE

- To find contact information for newspapers and other media, use the online database at www.congress.org/congressorg/dbq/media. Simply type in a zip code to get information for media outlets in a particular area.

Sticker the Message Around Town

Free Press' static-cling Warning Stickers (see below) are a great way to take media reform to the street (or the mall, or the airport . . .). They're thought-provoking, attention-grabbing, and totally legal—they don't use glue or adhesives so they won't destroy property.

Places to sticker:

BE BOLD!

A media reformer stickering TV's at a Best Buy store was caught in the act by a clerk—but when she explained the need for media reform to the worker, he allowed the stickers to stay!

- Newspaper boxes
- TV's at your local "big box" store (Best Buy, Circuit City, Wal-Mart, etc.)
- Outdoor advertisements for media (at bus stops, on subways & buses, etc.)
- TV's in public areas such as bus stations, laundromats, or doctors' offices

To order stickers, see www.freepress.net/tools or call us at 866-666-1533.

WARNING

This device may dispense corporate media that lacks the diversity, skepticism and alternative points of view required by democracy.

www.freepress.net

Host a Media Reform House Party

House parties are a great way to bring up media reform with your friends, neighbors, co-workers, and other community members. Use a video or speaker presentation as the main activity of your party. Free Press' DVD, *Mobilizing Media Reform*, is a 14 minute video created for just this purpose. (Order a copy at www.freepress.net/tools or by calling 866-666-1533).

Invite people. Either invite just people you know or open the event to the public. If it's an open event, publicize it in your local paper, post fliers around town, and/or advertise the event with local organizations. Include a phone number for questions. Request an RSVP if space is a concern.

Provide informational handouts. Download Free Press resources at www.freepress. net/tools or order by calling 1-866-666-1533. News articles are also useful.

Provide snacks or ask guests to bring some.

Play host. Once most people have arrived, ask everybody to introduce themselves to the group. Pass around a sign-up sheet to collect contact info.

House parties don't have to take place at your house—you can organize a presentation at a library, coffee house, community center, or local church.

Get people talking. After the video or presentation, facilitate a discussion about the issues addressed. The *Mobilizing Media Reform* DVD insert provides suggested questions for discussion.

Identify next steps. Encourage participants to visit the Free Press website (www.freepress.net) and sign up to receive our e-activist alerts via email. Better yet, collect email addresses and ZIP codes from participants and sign them up yourself. Identify a follow up "action" you'd be willing to organize, like a letter writing campaign (see page 322) or assembling a group to meet with your Representative in Congress (see page 324).

Most importantly, have fun! People should come away feeling energized, with the knowledge that they *can* change the media!

Give a Presentation about Media Reform

Whether it's a church group or a PTA, many groups—particularly those in which you already participate—might be interested in learning about media reform.

Contact the group's leadership to see if they'd allow you to give a brief presentation about media reform during an upcoming meeting.

State the connection between the group's main focus and media reform. Our failing media system impacts nearly every issue.

Set a date and publicize the presentation to group members through an email, announcement at a meeting, or newsletter blurb.

Prepare your presentation. Use the prepared speech or talking points provided on pages 363-67 of this guide. (Feel free to change the words so that you're comfortable speaking them.) Practice delivering your talk out loud before you give it. Also remember to bring some informational handouts for your audience. Free Press has resources you can download at www.freepress.net/tools.

NOT A SPEAKER?

If you don't feel confident giving a presentation yourself, there are probably some people in your community who might be able and willing to speak to your group:

- Professors from a nearby university's Communications, Journalism or Political Science department
- Representatives of local independent media (community radio stations, indymedia centers, independent newspapers, etc.)
- Local politicians who have been outspoken on issues of media reform
- Representatives of local media reform groups

Always have a "take-away" action that the group can do. Suggest that participants write letters to their members of Congress or another action that will seed their interest and motivate further involvement. This will provide you with a reason to follow up with them and a way to maintain a relationship. You can also encourage participants to sign up to be e-activists through Free Press' web site.

Some examples of groups to reach out to:

- Religious groups
- PTA groups
- Local political parties/organizations
- Book clubs

- Student groups
- Labor unions
- Neighborhood associations
- Senior citizen groups

See page 363 for a prepared speech or page 366 for sample talking points to guide your presentation.

Other Easy Ways to Raise Awareness

- E-mail articles, web site links, and e-petitions about media issues to your friends.
- Suggest that your book club read a book on media reform, such as Robert McChesney's *The Problem of the Media*.
- Post fliers and brochures around town.
- Give books, magazine subscriptions, and videos about media reform as gifts.
- Call in to radio talk shows and discuss media issues.

ADVOCATE FOR POLICY CHANGE

Media corporations spend billions on lawyers, lobbyists, and campaign contributions—all in the name of pressuring Congress, the courts, and the Federal Communications Commission (FCC) to craft policies that benefit their bottom line. We need to fight back by pressuring policymakers to make rules that support the public interest, not the bank accounts of Big Media moguls. Our pressure works. In 2003, Congress voted four times to roll back the FCC rules that let Big Media get bigger—because millions of Americans spoke up.

WHO'S IN CHARGE

	CONGRESS	FCC
Content on radio and TV	Can pass laws requiring broadcasters to air certain kinds of public interest programming, such as educational programs or election coverage.	Can fine TV and radio stations or revoke licenses if they don't follow Congress' rules—e.g. if they air obscene content or too little public interest programming.
Content in newspapers, movies, books, etc.	Minimal authority to regulate due to First Amendment protections.	No authority—FCC only governs broadcast media and telecommunications.
Ownership of media	Can overrule the FCC and make laws limiting consolidation of media ownership.	Can make or change rules that govern how much of the broadcast media a single company can own.
Public broadcasting	Can increase or decrease funding for public broadcasting. Can enact laws changing the way public broadcasting operates.	Can grant, renew, or revoke public radio and TV stations' licenses. Can fine noncommercial stations for violating rules about advertising and content.
Independent media	Can pass laws that allow more independent radio and TV stations to get on the air. Can allocate funds to subsidize independent media.	Can issue recommendations to allow increased use of the public airwaves for noncommercial use.
Advertising	Can pass laws limiting advertising on TV and radio. Can pass laws relating to political campaign ads.	Can punish stations if they air too many ads during childrens' pro-gramming or fail to offer political candidates "equal opportunities" to air ads.
Internet access	Can pass laws that foster improvements in Internet providers' service to communities or laws that require internet providers to let users visit any site they want to.	Recommends rules for regulating Internet provider systems (e.g., DSL, dial-up, cable modem). Can pass regulations that allow space on the airwaves for new technologies to provide affordable internet access.

A few examples of media policy jurisdiction

STATE/LOCAL	OTHER
Local cable authorities can negotiate to get public access channels that will let community members put their own programs on cable TV.	Media outlets themselves decide what specific content to broadcast.
No authority.	Media outlets themselves decide what specific content to publish.
Local authorities can decide which companies will be allowed to provide cable and telecom services to the community.	The Federal Trade Commission and the Justice Department can stop a merger from taking place.
States can allocate funding for public broadcasting.	The President appoints board members for the Corporation for Public Broadcasting (CPB). CPB allocates Congressional funds to public radio and TV stations and programming.
States can allocate funding to subsidize independent media.	IRS can grant tax-exempt, nonprofit status to independent media organizations.
Local authorities can limit billboards or advertising in schools.	Federal Trade Commission regulates the truthfulness of advertising. Federal Election Commission regulates political advertising.
Local authorities can require cable companies to provide free Internet access to schools and libraries. State and community governments can also create and sell their own Internet services to their communities instead of going through a commercial provider.	Citizen groups can take their own initiative and provide 'wireless' Internet access to communities via 'community wireless network' setups.

How Media Policy is Made

Media policy can be pretty complicated. In order to know where to put pressure, it's important for activists to know how lawmakers address these issues and who's in charge. A few key points on U.S. media policy:

Role of the First Amendment

The First Amendment protects free speech and freedom of the press. Hence, media outlets have the freedom to choose whatever kind of "content" (programs, music, articles, topics addressed, people in the programs, etc.) they want to express, with some exceptions. Congress can make laws to cover all sectors of the media system, but the First Amendment often prohibits government from regulating content.

Public Property and Public Responsibility

Some types of media are subject to stronger regulation than others because they use public property to distribute their messages. For instance, TV and radio use public airwaves to broadcast. Because they are the trustees of a public resource, they have a legal obligation to serve the public and Congress can dictate how they do so.

Different Medium, Different Rules

Different types of media (e.g., newspapers, TV, movies, Internet) are each regulated differently. The more dependent a media sector is on public property, the more power Congress has to enact public interest provisions. So, Congress has virtually no power to regulate newspapers (because newspaper publishers can do whatever they want with the paper and ink they buy). Broadcast television and radio are the most rigorously regulated because they get to use public airwaves for free. The FCC was set up to regulate broadcast media, but there is no parallel agency to regulate certain other types of media.

RESOURCE

- For more info on the FCC, check out the Media Activists' Guide to the Federal Communications Commission, prepared by the Prometheus Radio Project: www.prometheusradio.org/media_activists_guide.shtml.

How to Affect Federal Media Policy

Federal policies have the power to transform our nation's media system. Congress and the Federal Communications Commission (FCC) are the federal governing bodies with the greatest jurisdiction over media issues.

Call Your Members of Congress

If you've never contacted an elected official, you'll be surprised at how empowering it can feel—and it does make a difference. When a legislator receives numerous calls and/or letters on a certain issue, it does influence his/her vote.

Relax. Feeling nervous is normal. If it helps, write down what you want to say before you make the call, then simply read it to the Congressional staffer you'll speak with.

Identify yourself. Give your name and what city or town you live in, and say you are a constituent of the legislator you're calling.

Be brief and polite. State the media issue you're calling about and summarize your position clearly. Limit your call to one issue. Be direct but not argumentative.

Be specific. If you are calling about a specific piece of legislation, identify the name and number of the bill. For a comprehensive list of media-related legislation, go to www.freepress.net/washington. It's also OK to call without specific legislation in mind—instead you could ask about your officials' position on a particular issue.

Ask for an action. You may want to first ask if the legislator has a stated position on the issue. Then ask for a specific action on the part of your elected official: to vote for or against a particular bill, co-sponsor a bill, hold a hearing on an issue, or state a position on an issue. Mention that how they vote on media issues is a deciding factor in how you cast your vote.

GET THE SKINNY ON YOUR ELECTED OFFICIALS

You can get the name and phone numbers of your members of Congress by calling the Capitol Switchboard in Washington: 1-800-839-5276.

You can also get information on the Free Press Web site at www.freepress.net/washington which includes:

- The names of the Senators and Representative in your district
- Their contact information
- Which committees they serve on
- Links to their official web site, further biographical info, and fundraising info
- Whether they have co-sponsored media-related bills
- How they have voted on media-related bills
- Detailed info about specific media-related bills

Don't get discouraged. If you get a busy signal or can't get through, don't give up. Also, note that you will not be speaking directly to the legislator him/herself, but to his or her staffer who will relay the message.

Share feedback. If you learn anything about your Congressperson's positions, or have info to share about successful tactics, send us an email at action@freepress.net.

Send Letters to Your Members of Congress

A letter to your elected representatives in Washington is a tried-and-true way to work for change.

Use your own stationery. Don't use your company's letterhead unless the letter represents your company's formal position.

Address elected officials with their official titles. For Senators and Representatives, address the letter to "The Honorable [*full name*]." The greeting of your letter should be "Dear Senator [*last name*]" for a Senator and Dear Mr./Ms. [*last name*] for a Representative.

Be brief. A concise, one-page letter is more likely to be read. Don't ramble.

LETTERS ARE BETTER

Postal mail letters to your members of Congress are generally the most effective communication method because they're more likely to be read—and your letter will often receive a written response. This is not necessarily true for e-mail, faxes or phone calls.

Note: Postal mail gets caught up in security screening at federal buildings for weeks before it reaches its destination, so it's not the best choice if you're writing about a bill that's going to be voted on soon.

By writing a letter about local radio, cable rates, media diversity, or hyper-commercialism (just to name a few), you may start a process that compels your elected official to become aware of citizen concerns, get educated about the issues, and articulate a position about where they stand. If you're satisfied with their position, you can hold them accountable the next time they vote on the issue. If you're unsatisfied, you can write them again and ask them to reconsider. This is democratic dialogue, and it is essential that we engage in it as often as possible.

Use your own thoughts and stories. Although you can certainly use a form letter, it's better if you insert some of your own thoughts and words in the letter or write one from scratch. Reference a personal experience or talk about how the issue affects you or your community.

Be clear on your position. Write about only one issue. If you're writing regarding a specific bill, mention its number and name and the list of principal sponsors.

Request a specific action. Depending on the situation, ask your legislator to vote for/against a particular bill or amendment or to co-sponsor a bill. You can, however, ask him/her to simply state a position on an issue.

Include a return address. Be sure to include a complete return address in your letter so that your legislator can send you a response.

Mail the letter. On the Free Press Web site (www.freepress.net/washington) you can find addresses for both the Washington, DC, offices and primary home offices of your legislators. Send your letter to their Washington office, unless Congress is not in session—in that case, send it to their district office. Note that faxes tend to be ignored.

Let us know what you hear! If you receive a response, please share it with us via email at action@freepress.net. Also send us a copy if you've written a letter you'd like to share with other activists to use as a template.

See page 368 for a sample letter to your member of Congress that you can tailor and send.

Meet with Your Members of Congress

Most legislators are lobbied heavily by the media industry, so it's important that they hear the other side of the story. A face-to-face meeting with a group of constituents lets them know that voters care about the issue, and that if they want your vote, their stance on media issues is important.

Plan carefully. Assemble a small group of fellow constituents to organize the meeting with you, and agree on one particular issue to address, such as media ownership regulation, low-power FM radio, or public broadcasting.

> **TIP**
>
> The Committees that have power over media-related business in the Senate and House of Representatives are the Senate Commerce Committee and the House Energy and Commerce Committee. If your Senator or Representative serves on one of these committees, this makes them even more powerful when it comes to crafting media-related legislation.

Make an appointment. Call the legislator's home district office (not the DC office) and ask for the name of the scheduler. Fax a written request for a meeting to the scheduler's attention. In your fax, be sure to include your name and contact information, state that you are a constituent, note the issue you'd like to discuss during the meeting, and suggest a range of times that you can meet. Follow up with a call to the scheduler within a few hours of sending the fax.

Prepare. Agree upon a few key talking points and write them down. Find out how your legislator has voted in the past on the issue you will be addressing, and plan to note this during the meeting. Also prepare and make copies of fact sheets that you will bring with you to the meeting.

Expect a brief meeting. Plan to have each participant in your group briefly make one important and unique point during the meeting. Leave time for the legislator or staffer to ask questions and respond to your request for action. Note that meetings with a legislator can be as short as 10 to 15 minutes, though meetings with legislative staff may be longer.

Be pleasant, clear, and concise. Tell the legislator how the issue affects you personally, and provide facts and examples to support your argument. Don't be argumentative; keep the tone positive.

Ask for a specific action. For example, "Will you co-sponsor Senate bill *S 1046, the Preservation of Localism, Program Diversity, and Competition in Television Broadcast Service Act of 2004?*" Check www.freepress.net/washington for current information on pending legislation or see *10 Questions to Ask Candidates and Elected Officials* (on page 369) for a general guide. It's OK if the legislator or staffer wants to get back to you later with an answer, but be sure to follow up.

Leave written information. Leave fact sheets and other materials that provide accurate, concise information supporting your argument.

Follow up. Send a thank you note, and watch for your legislator's action on the issue. If they have made a commitment to you, make note of whether they follow through.

Let us know how it went. We'd love to hear about your meeting and help share your success stories or tactics with others. Send us a quick report at action@freepress.net.

> # TIP
>
> Try to set up a meeting in your legislator's district office (rather than DC office) around holidays or during August. This is when legislators tend to be home in their districts, and their staff may have less pressing schedules. They'll be more likely to give you the time you deserve.

Sign or Start Petitions

Legislators need your vote to stay in office—petitions are a way to show that many votes are at stake and that an issue has widespread support.

- The success of petitions hinges on *muscle* and *messenger*—the number of people signing, and the credibility of the group collecting signatures.
- Petitions are most effective when a group gathers the signatures and then delivers them in person as part of a visit to members of Congress. During the lobbying visit, the group presenting the petition will argue their position on the issue.
- Petitions are less effective when they are simply e-mailed or faxed en masse to a Congressional office.
- Petitions should include printed names, full mailing addressess (not P.O. Boxes), and signatures or the names may not be counted.

Ask Candidates About Media Policy

Asking candidates for elected office about their positions on media policy brings these issues onto the political agenda. It's important to let candidates know that we vote based on their positions on media issues.

- Pick one of the *10 Questions to Ask Candidates and Elected Officials* (see page 369) to ask during the Q&A portion of a campaign event. Or take the opportunity to ask these questions through meetings with elected officials and their staff, or through a phone call or letter to the candidate.
- If you'd like to ask a question during the Q&A portion of a campaign event, get in line for the microphone early—even before the Q&A segment of the program begins.

File Comments on FCC Rule Changes

Like other federal agencies, the FCC can't adopt new regulations without first notifying and seeking comment from the public. Unfortunately, the way the FCC solicits public comments can be confusing and often deters public participation. But that makes it all the more important that we file our comments. Often the FCC claims that they made industry-friendly rules because industry lobbyists were the only ones who offered opinions. By filing a simple comment in important proceedings, we effectively break this cycle of insider policymaking. It is a critical task.

Anyone can file and it requires no professional expertise. Comments from citizens describing their concerns, their experiences, and their desires for a better media system are both welcomed and highly important.

To find a list of FCC rulemakings open for comment, see the FCC's Electronic Comment Filing System page online at http://gullfoss2.fcc.gov/ecfs/Upload/. This provides a list of some of the more consumer-oriented rulemakings, with short descriptions of each.

> **TIP**
>
> When the FCC wants to gather information and comment on a broad subject, they issue a Notice of Inquiry (NOI). If they want to change a rule, they release a document called a Notice of Proposed Rulemaking (NPRM). These notices assign a docket number to the proposed rulemaking, explain what regulations are proposed, and set a deadline for public comment. The FCC accepts public comments by mail, e-mail, online, and through public hearings.
>
> For a fact sheet on the FCC's decision making process, see http://ftp.fcc.gov/cgb/dro/knownoi.html.

To learn more about a specific rulemaking, use the docket number to do a search on the FCC's web site for related information. You can also call the FCC at 1-888-CALL-FCC or e-mail them at fccinfo@fcc.gov with questions.

You can view comments submitted by others on the FCC's web site at this address: http://gullfoss2.fcc.gov/prod/ecfs/comsrch_v2.cgi. Looking at other comments will help you understand the arguments being put forth by the media industry as well as public interest groups and citizens.

EXAMPLES OF CITIZEN COMMENTS
FILED WITH THE FCC

Comments to the FCC can range from a short sentence stating your opinion to an entire legal or technical briefing. Here are just a few examples of brief comments filed on various issues by regular citizens across the country.

In FCC docket # 02-277 (Media Ownership Rules)

"The FCC was created to protect the public's interest for the public's airwaves. The original rules that limited media ownership were promulgated to insure diversity of opinion. Allowing the public airwaves to be consolidated under a few large corporate umbrellas will inevitably consolidate opinion & points of view.

I do NOT and never will believe that fewer points of view will be good for a free press or a free people. I believe that by succumbing to the blandishments of large media corporations to change the rules of ownership, the FCC would be not only violating its charter to protect the public's interest but will also harm the public good."

—Andrea P., Rapid City, SD

In FCC docket #04-261 (Violent Television):

"The level of violence continues to increase with no level of common sense to stop at. Since the industry doesn't control itself the government must step in with fines or loss of broadcast rights. The time of day doesn't mean a thing since children can stay up to watch at anytime, day or night."

—John S., Cedar Rapids, IA

In FCC docket # 03-202 (Rural Wireless):

"Use of available spectrum in rural areas is a great idea! Care should be taken to ensure that the 'new' spectrum does not simply end up under control of huge companies (wireless, broadcasters, telephone companies) who will use it simply to prevent the public from having an 'alternative'. Licenses should be given to true local entities.... I think that you'll see a lot of inventive uses and true public benefit if these ideas are followed. I have great hope for this initiative!"

—Joe T., San Diego, CA

In FCC docket # 02-153 (Spectrum):

"The FCC is supposed to regulate the spectrum as a public trust and in the public interest. We no longer have much educational programming and we certainly do not have diversity of opinion and music due in large part to the re-regulation of the Reagan Era, the Communications Act of 1996, and ongoing efforts by the current administrators of the FCC to remove further regulations to favor corporate interests over independent and non-commercial stations.

I would like to have additional support for creating and fostering community and LPFM stations. Non-commercial broadcasting should be subsidized with commercial licensing fees rather than, for example, giving away the digital television spectrum to the same corporations who have largely failed to offer programming that is educational, that provides information that aids in enriching and uplifting our communities, our families and our rapidly deteriorating democracy...."

—Frederic N., Syracuse, NY

File a comment online at http://gullfoss2.fcc.gov/ecfs/Upload/, via email at fccinfo@fcc.gov, or via fax at 1-866-418-0232. Comments sent via postal mail should be addressed to the FCC bureau that is handling the rulemaking docket and sent to that bureau's attention at 445 12th St., SW; Washington, DC 20554. Remember to include the docket number and your contact information with any comment.

THE EASY WAY TO FILE

The Free Press web site has an easy-to-use submission form designed to help people submit comments on certain important FCC proceedings. Check it out at www.freepress.net/action/fcc_comment.php.

Attend a Public Hearing

Though rare, the FCC occasionally holds public hearings to gather public input on a proposed rulemaking. In 2003 and 2004, the FCC held several hearings around the country on "localism" in broadcasting, soliciting testimony from the public about how well local TV and radio serve their communities' needs. Public comments at these hearings are generally entered into the public record and considered as the FCC reviews its rules. If an FCC hearing comes to your area, be sure to attend and deliver your own brief comments.

You can also invite FCC Commissioners or staff to come to your community for a hearing or conference you arrange. Email the FCC at fccinfo@fcc.gov, call 1-888-CALL-FCC, or contact Commissioners' offices directly (their information can be found at www.fcc.gov).

COMPLAINING ABOUT YOUR LOCAL MEDIA

Complaints you have about the programming on your local stations should be registered with the station itself and may also be sent to the FCC in a process different from filing comments on rule changes. For more info, see page 340 in this guide.

RESOLUTION OF THE CITY OF PHILADELPHIA

Activists succeeded in getting the following resolution passed by the City of Philadelphia in March 2003. Similar resolutions were passed in several other cities as well.

RESOLUTION

Supporting diversity in media ownership by urging the Federal Communications Commission to protect and preserve its ban on cross-ownership of print and electronic media, and by urging the Congress to exercise its oversight in the area of federal communications policy by holding public hearings on media ownership issues, and by enacting legislation to prohibit further media consolidation.

Whereas, freedom of the press and public access to diverse media are prerequisites for a functioning democracy; and

Whereas, the broadcast airwaves are owned commonly by the public, and should be managed to serve the public interest; and

Whereas, the public interest is best served by the availability of a broadly diverse range of viewpoints; and

Whereas, media diversity is seriously threatened by further consolidation of media ownership in an already highly concentrated market; and

Whereas, deregulation of radio ownership rules under the Telecommunications Act caused unprecedented consolidation, dramatically decreasing competition; and

Whereas, the Federal Communications Commission is currently considering an unprecedented rollback of media ownership regulations, including but not limited to rules which forbid companies from owning newspapers and TV stations—or TV and radio stations—in the same media market, and rules barring firms from owning TV stations that reach more than 35 percent of the nation; and

Whereas, the elimination or weakening of these regulations would further reduce competition, local accountability, diversity of content and voices, and the amount and quality of news coverage in broadcast and print media across the country, while providing windfall profits for a small handful of corporate media owners; therefore,

Resolved by the Council of the City of Philadelphia, that it urges the Federal Communications Commission to protect and preserve its rules banning cross-ownership of electronic and print media, and regulations that limit the number of stations one owner may hold; Resolved further, that the Council urges the Congress to exercise its oversight powers relating to federal communications policy through public hearings on media ownership issues, and to enact legislation prohibiting further media consolidation; and,

Resolved further, that a true and correct copy of this resolution be presented to all members of Philadelphia's congressional delegation as the true and sincere sentiments of this legislative body.

How to Affect Media Policy on the State and Local Level

Although decisions on media policy are made primarily at the national level, state and local authorities wield considerable power over policy on certain issues. This is particularly true as cable becomes the dominant provider of television and broadband Internet access, because cable is regulated at the local level.

ISSUES AT THE STATE LEVEL INCLUDE:

- Providing funding to public broadcasting stations.

- Earmarking funds for independent media, minority-owned media, educational opportunities for media literacy, etc.

- Building state broadband networks to provide Internet and other media access to underserved communities in rural areas or low-income areas.

- Guaranteeing the right of municipalities to offer broadband services.

- Some states handle cable TV franchise negotiations at the state level through Public Utility Commissions, while other states do this at the local level. (More info in the section "Pressure Local Governments for Better Cable" on page 333).

Contact State Legislators

The same techniques that are useful in pressuring Congress can also be applied to pressuring state legislators. See the information in the *Federal Media Policy* section of this guide for tips on calling, writing, and visiting legislators.

In working with state government, it's helpful to find out which committee in your state's legislature deals with media issues. Find out if your state Rep. and/or Senator serve on this committee. Even if they don't, you can still pressure your representatives to make decisions on media issues that benefit your community.

Work with City Councils & Local Regulatory Boards

Your town, county, or city council and local regulatory boards are good places to address concerns about the media in your community. Some ideas:

Go to city or town council/county board meetings. Become a regular participant in your local government to find out what media-related issues the council (or county board) is dealing with, or to propose that the council pass ordinances on issues important to you.

Join a local regulatory board. Local regulatory boards have the power to pass regulations that can have a real impact on local media policies. For instance, you could join your local cable board to help fight for a better deal with your com-

ISSUES ADDRESSED LOCALLY INCLUDE:

- Banning or reducing billboards and outdoor advertising within a community.
- Promoting city-wide Wi-Fi initiatives for Internet access.
- Negotiating cable franchise agreements (including cable rates, public access channels, production facilities for public access, etc.).
- Limiting advertising and commercialism in schools (including Channel One and agreements with vendors who want to advertise in schools).
- Bringing media literacy curricula into schools.

munity's cable company. Or you could join your local school board to push for media literacy curricula in schools or work to ban advertising and commercialism from schools.

Get your town, city or county to pass a resolution for media reform. Via resolutions, local governments can register disapproval of federal regulations and laws. Such resolutions against the FCC's loosening of media ownership rules in June 2003 were successfully passed in several communities (see page 330 for an example). Resolutions can also indicate the town/city/county's support for an ideal like diverse media or for a particular policy.

You can also pass a resolution for media reform in your union or in other organizations you're already active in.

Pressure Local Government for Better Cable

The cable TV service in your community is regulated by a city or county agency (often called a "local franchising authority" or LFA) that negotiates a contract with the cable company. The LFA allows the cable company to use public land and utility poles to lay their cable lines, and the cable company pays "franchise fees" and provides other services to the city in return.

During the contract negotiations between the LFA and the cable company (called "cable franchise renewal" negotiations), it's possible for your LFA to negotiate for various provisions in the contract such as providing channels that regular citizens can use to air their own programs (community access channels), providing funds for studios, staff, and equipment to help citizens make their own media, and offering technology access to schools, libraries, and local agencies.

However, many local franchising authorities fail to get good provisions for community media in the contract, missing an important opportunity for better media in their communities. You can help change that by pressuring your local government to approve better contracts during cable franchise renewals.

Find out who is in charge of regulating cable in your community. This information may be printed on your cable bill. You can also call your mayor or city councilors.

Get a copy of the current cable franchise agreement. This may be available from the cable board, Town Hall, or the county board. Look through the agreement to see what kind of provisions your city receives from the cable company.

WHAT YOU CAN GET FROM YOUR LOCAL CABLE FRANCHISE

- The cable company can be required to set aside a percentage of its channel capacity for community use. This channel capacity can be used to provide TV channels for public, educational, and government (PEG) programming and can also provide cable bandwidth for community agencies to send and receive data.

- If the cable company also offers Internet service, it can be required to provide free or reduced-price Internet service to public schools, libraries, computer centers, and other public facilities.

- The cable company can be required to pay 5 percent of its revenue to the local government for 'franchise fees.'

- Franchise fees can provide funding for a community TV studio that the public can use to produce their own TV programs, plus video and technical equipment and staff to run the studio and teach community members to make their programs.

- Franchise fees can fund programs that provide public access to computers and the Internet and offer technology skills training for low-income communities.

Find out when the current franchise agreement expires. This should be noted on your copy of the franchise agreement. Negotiations around the renewal of the cable franchise agreement can take anywhere from one to three years, so if the current agreement is set to expire within that time frame, you should plan to get engaged.

Find out who else in your community is advocating for improved public interest provisions. If there is a community access TV channel or government channel in your town, speak to their staff as they will most likely be involved. Other groups might include libraries, schools, community technology centers, and media activist groups.

If no one in your community is working on cable issues, think about sparking interest and *building a campaign yourself.* This might include:

- Building a coalition of organizations and interested community members to pressure local authorities to negotiate a better cable agreement.
- Researching the process of cable franchise renewal and the particular situation in your city.
- Determining your community's "wish list"—what provisions you and your neighbors want your city to get from the cable company during franchise negotiations.
- Trying to get yourself appointed to the board or commission that governs cable issues.
- Pressuring the mayor, city council members, and local cable authorities to negotiate for the provisions your community wants.

Let us know what you're up to. If you have information that might be useful to others waging battles in their communities, please share it in an email to action@freepress.net.

RESOURCES

A few good sources for information and support around cable franchise renewal are the Alliance for Community Media (www.alliancecm.org, 202-393-2650), the Young Americans and the Digital Future Campaign (www.techpolicybank. org, 202-429-0033), Reclaim the Media (www.reclaimthemedia.org/comcast, 206-709-0558) and the Our Cable website (www.ourcable.org).

CHALLENGE YOUR LOCAL MEDIA

If your media aren't living up to their duties, there are ways you can challenge them directly. Directly confronting your local media outlets can result in tangible changes in what you see or hear in your community's media.

Tell Media Outlets When You Don't Like What You're Getting

If you don't like what you're seeing on TV, hearing on the radio, or reading in your newspaper, make sure your media outlets hear about it! Free speech rights give media outlets authority to choose whatever kind of content they want, but that doesn't mean you can't object. Don't be shy about looking up a newspaper or station's address or phone number in the phone book and giving them some feedback.

Launch a Targeted Campaign Against a Media Outlet

More effective than a single complaint, a coordinated campaign may succeed in pressuring media outlets to alter their news coverage, air a popular program, or make other changes. If you and others in your community share the same complaint about your media, join forces and ramp up the pressure.

Determine the goal you're working toward and which media outlet to target. You'll be more effective if you start with a precise goal (e.g., bringing back a radio call-in show at a particular station or increasing coverage of local elections on Channel 5 news) than if you aim for broad changes in the media landscape.

Gather support from friends, colleagues, and allies in your community who share your concern. Build a coalition of citizens, activists, and representatives of organizations who are interested in the issue. Convene an initial meeting to discuss the issue and plan your actions.

Do some research to support your campaign. Your research might involve doing community surveys or interviews, starting a project to monitor your local media for their coverage of certain issues, researching the corporations who own your local media, or inspecting a broadcast station's public files. See the "Research" section in this guide for more information (p. 343).

Determine what actions will be most effective in reaching your goal. Start with tactics that engage the media outlet in a dialogue, but plan to turn up the heat if you don't get a response. Some tactics to consider might include:

- Coordinate a letter writing campaign.

- Invite the media outlet's management to meet with your group to discuss your concerns. Present your case and get agreement on ways the station or paper will work to solve the problem.

- Compile a report outlining your concern with data to support it. Send copies of the report to the media, policymakers, and other people who hold authority in your community.

- Get media coverage of your campaign. Work with members of your group to write letters to the editor of local papers, get op-eds placed, call in to talk radio shows, etc. (See the section on "Raising Awareness" in this guide for more information, or check out great resources from the SPIN Project: www.spinproject.org.)

- Raise public awareness by distributing fliers through the mail, e-mail, or by handing out leaflets in places where people gather.

- Conduct a boycott against companies who advertise on the media program or outlet you are targeting.

- If all other methods fail, think about holding a demonstration in front of the media organization's headquarters. Publicize your demonstration well to get good turnout. Use posters, signs, and slogans to get your message accross to people who see the demonstration and media who cover it.

Share information and success stories. Drop us an email at action@freepress.net if you have a story you think might be useful for other activists around the country.

RESOURCES

Fairness and Accuracy In Reporting (FAIR) has a Media Activist Kit that provides information on detecting bias in the media and organizing campaigns for change. Check it out at www.fair.org/activism/activismkit.html.

The Youth Media Council conducted a successful youth-led campaign to hold a San Francisco radio station accountable to local youth organizers. Read a report of their campaign at www.youthmediacouncil.org/publications.html.

Report Violations of FCC Rules

Not many FCC regulations are specific enough to be enforced, but there are a few with which radio and TV stations must comply. If you know that a local station is violating the following rules, you can report them to the FCC. The FCC will investigate, and if the station is found to be in violation, they may be fined or have their license revoked.

WHAT'S "OBSCENE"?

Congress has set out the following guidelines for the FCC to use in determining whether to punish a broadcast TV or radio station for obscene content:

- •"An average person, applying contemporary community standards, must find that the material, as a whole, appeals to the prurient interest;"

- •"The material must depict or describe, in a patently offensive way, sexual conduct specifically defined by applicable law;" and

- •"The material, taken as a whole, must lack serious literary, artistic, political, or scientific value."

Obscene content can't be aired at any time on broadcast TV and radio. There are separate guidelines for indecent or profane material. For more information, see the FCC fact sheet on obscenity, indecency, and profanity at: www.fcc.gov/cgb/consumerfacts/obscene.html

Some violations of FCC rules

Stations can't broadcast **obscene material** at any time of day, or indecent or profane content during certain times of the day (generally when children are likely to be watching).

Stations can't accept **payment in exchange** for airing a particular program or record unless they explicitly tell listeners/viewers who paid for the program to be aired.

Broadcasters must **keep a "public file"** at the station containing documents that describe the station's service to the community. They must also allow members of the public to inspect the public files at any time during normal business hours. (See the "Research" section of this action guide for more information on the public file).

TV stations (not radio) must air at least three hours per week of regularly scheduled **children's educational programming** between 7 AM and 10 PM.

TV stations (not radio) can't air more than 12 minutes per hour of **commercials during children's programs** on a weekday or 10.5 minutes on a weekend.

How to report

- To report violations of FCC rules, submit a complaint in writing to the FCC.

- Complaints should include the call letters and location of the station, a specific statement of the problem, and the name of anyone contacted at the station.

- If your complaint is about access to the public file (see below), also include the date, time, and address where you attempted to inspect the file, and the specific documents you were unable to view or obtain.

- If your complaint is about obscene programming, include a tape or transcript of the incident (or a very precise description). ·

- Mail your letter to:
  FCC—Enforcement Bureau
  Investigations & Hearings Division
  445 12th Street, SW
  Washington, DC 20554

- You can also email it to: complaints-enf@fcc.gov.

CHILDREN'S EDUCATIONAL PROGRAMMING

In exchange for their free use of the public airwaves, broadcast TV stations (but not cable networks) must air at least 3 hours per week of "Core Educational Programming" for children.

But because the TV stations themselves are allowed to define what is educational, stations often claim that shallow programs like "NFL Under the Helmet" and "Saved by the Bell" fulfill these requirements—squandering TV's capacity to serve as an educational tool for kids.

The requirements for "Core ed" programs include:

- The program must have education "as a significant purpose."
- The program must be aired between the hours of 7:00 AM and 10:00 PM.
- Advertising during the program must be limited to 10.5 minutes per hour on weekends and 12 minutes per hour on weekdays.
- The educational objective of the program and the target child audience must be specified in writing in the children's programming report ("FCC 398 report").

You can find out what your stations are showing to satisfy "core ed" requirements by looking at your local stations' "FCC 398" reports on the web. Simply go to http://gullfoss2.fcc.gov/prod/kidvid/prod/query1.htm and enter the 4-letter call sign for your TV station (e.g. 'WUSA' or 'KPIX').

File Objections When TV and Radio Licenses Are Up for Renewal

TV and radio stations get broadcast licenses for free—on the condition that they serve "the public interest." Every eight years, broadcasters have to submit a renewal, during which time citizens can object by filing comments with the FCC. If you're not happy with a local station's public service, you have one chance every eight years to challenge their license.

Unfortunately, policy changes pushed for by broadcast industry lawyers and lobbyists have made it almost impossible to successfully challenge a station's license, and stations now get their licenses renewed with very little scrutiny from the FCC.

WHY BOTHER?

While it's unlikely that a station's license would get taken away, it's still important to file comments so there is a record of public dissatisfaction with a station that is performing poorly. The more citizens participate in the license renewal process, the more likely it is that changes to the system will be implemented.

License renewals can also provide a good organizing opportunity for media activists. You can use the license renewal as a chance to analyze your broadcasters' service and educate your community about broadcasters' public interest duties.

- Find out when your TV and radio stations' licenses are up for renewal. License renewal dates are the same for all stations in a particular state. See the chart on page 342 to find out when radio and TV station licenses expire in your state.

- Choose either a formal "petition to deny" a license application, or an informal objection. Formal petitions to deny carry certain legal requirements and are best undertaken with the assistance of a lawyer. An informal objection is a better choice for most people.

- Plan to submit your comments two to four months before the license expires. Officially, you can file informal objections anytime after the station submits its renewal application and before the FCC grants the renewal. You can find out about the status of your station's application through the FCC's Consolidated Database System (CDBS), available at: http://gullfoss2. fcc.gov/prod/cdbs/pubacc/prod/cdbs_pa.htm.

- State your objection in a letter to the FCC. On the first page of the letter, include the station's call sign, city, and state, the station's facility number, and the station's license renewal application file number. You can find this info in the FCC's Consolidated Database System, mentioned above.

- In the body of your letter, provide specific information about the station's performance and why it should have its license revoked. Point out specific issues of community concern that were not covered, other inadequacies in the station's programming, or any actions by the station that are not in the best interests of your community. Remember that the FCC doesn't monitor stations' programming, so any specifics you can provide will be useful. Some research into your station's "public file" (see page 345) is highly recommended to help uncover specific information to support your objection. Also note the violations of FCC rules on page 338.

For radio stations, address your letter to:
Audio Division, License Renewal Processing Team
Mailstop 1800B
FCC, Office of the Secretary
445 12th St. sw
Washington, DC 20554

For TV stations, address your letter to:
Video Division, License Renewal Processing Team
Room 2-A665
FCC, Office of the Secretary
445 12th St. sw
Washington, DC 20554

- Send a copy of your comments to the station's managing director to let them know you're watching. Also send a copy to us at action@freepress.net, and share any information that might be useful for other activists challenging licenses around the country.

RESOURCES

Grand Rapids Institute for Information Democracy created a guidebook for residents of Grand Rapids, MI who will be challenging licenses in that community. Their resource has information useful for other communities as well: http://www.griid.org/pdfs/License_Renewal_Guide_Rev_2.pdf.

Media activist group Rocky Mountain Media Watch filed objections to the license renewals of four stations in Denver, CO. Read an example of their objections at: www.bigmedia.org/texts2.html.

The FCC has its own info sheet on participating in the license renewal process, available at: www.fcc.gov/localism/renew_process_handout.doc.

BROADCAST LICENSE EXPIRATION DEADLINES

Shown below are radio & TV license expiration dates. All deadlines occur on the first of the month. Plan to file informal comments 2 to 4 months before TV or radio stations' licenses expire in your state.

STATE	RADIO	TV	STATE	RADIO	TV
Alabama	Apr 2004	Apr 2005	Montana	Apr 2005	Apr 2006
Alaska	Feb 2006	Feb 2007	Nebraska	Jun 2005	Jun 2006
Arizona	Oct 2005	Oct 2006	New Hampshire	Apr 2006	Apr 2007
Arkansas	Jun 2004	Jun 2005	Nevada	Oct 2005	Oct 2006
California	Dec 2005	Dec 2006	New Jersey	Jun 2006	Jun 2007
Colorado	Apr 2005	Apr 2006	New Mexico	Oct 2005	Oct 2006
Connecticut	Apr 2006	Apr 2007	New York	Jun 2006	Jun 2007
Delaware	Aug 2006	Aug 2007	North Carolina	Dec 2003	Dec 2004
D. Columbia	Apr 2006	Apr 2007	North Dakota	Apr 2005	Apr 2006
Florida	Feb 2004	Feb 2005	Ohio	Oct 2004	Oct 2005
Georgia	Apr 2004	Apr 2005	Oklahoma	Jun 2005	Jun 2006
Hawaii	Feb 2006	Feb 2007	Oregon	Feb 2006	Feb 2007
Idaho	Oct 2005	Oct 2006	Pennsylvania	Aug 2006	Aug 2007
Illinois	Dec 2004	Dec 2005	Puerto Rico	Feb 2004	Feb 2005
Indiana	Aug 2004	Aug 2005	Rhode Island	Apr 2006	Apr 2007
Iowa	Feb 2005	Feb 2006	South Carolina	Dec 2003	Dec 2004
Kansas	Jun 2005	Jun 2006	South Dakota	Apr 2005	Apr 2006
Kentucky	Aug 2004	Aug 2005	Tennessee	Aug 2004	Aug 2005
Louisiana	Jun 2004	Jun 2005	Texas	Aug 2005	Aug 2006
Maine	Apr 2006	Apr 2007	Utah	Oct 2005	Oct 2006
Maryland	Oct 2003	Oct 2004	Vermont	Apr 2006	Apr 2007
Massachusetts	Apr 2006	Apr 2007	Virginia	Oct 2003	Oct 2004
Michigan	Oct 2004	Oct 2005	Washington	Feb 2006	Feb 2007
Minnesota	Apr 2005	Apr 2006	Wisconsin	Dec 2004	Dec 2005
Mississippi	Jun 2004	Jun 2005	West Virginia	Oct 2003	Oct 2004
Missouri	Feb 2005	Feb 2006	Wyoming	Oct 2005	Oct 2006

RESEARCH AND WATCHDOG

If you feel that your local media aren't doing an adequate job of serving the public interest, the results of a research or monitoring project can help back up your claims with evidence. This is a good start to any campaign to pressure your local media.

Investigate Ownership

Media ownership is becoming increasingly consolidated, with major conglomerates buying up more and more media outlets around the country. For many of your projects, it will be important to learn about the companies who control your media.

RESOURCES

- The Center for Public Integrity has a database called MediaTracker that will display information on who owns the TV, radio, cable, and print media in your community—simply by typing in your zip code. Check it out at: www.openairwaves.org.

- Free Press has an interactive chart at www.freepress.net/ownership outlining the media holdings of a handful of the biggest media conglomerates.

Monitor Media Content

You may want to launch a project to monitor your media for data on representation of diverse communities, coverage of important public affairs, corporate bias, or other concerns you have. There may be a research organization or professor in your community who could help develop a monitoring project. Two resources for monitoring projects are below.

RESOURCES

- Grade the News has developed a scorecard that can be used to grade local newscasts and analyze the results. Check it out online at: www.stanford.edu/group/gradethenews/feat/scoring.htm.

- FAIR provides useful tips on detecting bias in the news media at: www.fair.org/activism/detect.html.

Inspect TV and Radio Stations' Public Files

Local commercial stations make lots of money using our public airwaves to broadcast. The question is: Do they do enough for the community in return?

One way to find out is by investigating their "public file." There are certain FCC rules about what kinds of information must be in the file, including info about station ownership, community issues programming, educational programming, and public complaints.

Stations are required to show the public files to any citizen who shows up at the station and asks to see them—but since most citizens aren't aware of their rights, stations almost never receive such requests. This is a great way to find out about your local media and to monitor whether they're serving the public interest as required by the FCC. It's also a good first step in pressuring them for change.

Steps for inspecting a public file:

- Find out where your local stations are located through the Internet or the yellow pages.

- You may want to review (or bring a copy of) the FCC's "The Public and Broadcasting" guide, which discusses your rights to see the file, and the obligations of the station. The guide is available at www.fcc.gov/mb/audio/decdoc/public_and_broadcasting.html.

- You can show up at a station any time during regular business hours and simply ask to see the public file—they are required by the FCC to show it to you. However, it's a good idea to make an appointment in advance. When you call for an appointment, ask for the station's Public Affairs director. You don't have to explain why you want to see the files or mention your affiliation.

- Station staff will most likely be courteous and helpful. But if they're rude, unhelpful, or unwilling to show you the file, take note of this. Also take note if the public file is incomplete. Either of these is a violation of FCC rules.

- Station staff (usually the Public Affairs director) will either take you directly to the files, or they may ask you which files you're looking for, and bring those files to you. For this reason, it's important to know what you're looking for ahead of time (see "What to Look for in the Public File" on pages 348–49). They may leave you alone with the files, or they may stay with you as you inspect the files.

- The public file will most likely be in hard copy: papers in file folders. If parts of the public file are on a computer database, the station must provide you a computer terminal to look at them.

- You can either take detailed notes or request photocopies of all documents you're interested in. The station is required to make any photocopies that you request. They may make copies for free or may charge you a "fair price" (usually 10 or 25 cents per page). If you're asking for several copies, they may want to mail them to you later. The station must pay postage to send the photocopies, and must send them within seven days.

IT'S THE SYSTEM, STUPID!

After inspecting your local stations' public files, you may find that stations are making a lot of money off your airwaves and giving back little in return for this right to broadcast. This is largely due to lax policies that fail to hold stations accountable.

Tell your members of Congress and the FCC if you think there should be stronger public interest accountability rules.

• Should TV and radio licenses be reviewed more seriously before they are renewed every 8 years? Should there be more explicit rules about "public interest programming" and "treatment of community issues"?

• Should stations be required to air a certain amount of local issues programming or more educational children's programming?

• Should they be required to air some shows that are produced by community members?

• Should citizen surveys be required to determine what issues get covered?

• Should there be stricter rules about who can own media in your community?

Congress can develop policies that make better, more accountable media a reality in our communities—but they must hear it from you, because they certainly won't hear it from broadcast industry lobbyists.

What to Do With the Information You Find

If you found information in the public file that was interesting or surprising, share it with community groups, leaders, station owners, and even the press to start a dialogue with your community about media's obligation to the public.

You could prepare a report with some of the information you found, such as: Which company owns your station (and what else they control); what kind of programs and information the station thinks are most important to your community; how responsive the station has been to community concerns; what programs the station thinks fills its educational programming requirement for children, etc. Use it to:

- Bring community awareness and/or press attention to broadcasters' public interest obligations.

- Start a dialogue with your station about how they can better serve your community. Think about developing a "citizens' agreement" with your broadcasters if there is not already one in place.

- Provide data and examples to FCC and/or Congress that will encourage them to strengthen laws and rules that hold media accountable.

- Encourage the FCC not to renew a station's broadcast license.

WHAT TO LOOK FOR IN THE PUBLIC FILE

Citizen Agreements
Stations must keep a copy of any written agreements they make with local viewers or listeners. These "citizen agreements" deal with programming, employment, or other issues of community concern.

• Does the station have any citizen agreements? Is it adhering to these agreements?

Letters and E-Mail from the Public
Commercial stations must keep written comments and suggestions received from the public for at least 3 years.

• Is the station keeping all letters and e-mail from the public, or just the positive ones? (If you know of a prior negative comment that was sent, you might check to see if it's in the file).

• If there is consistent criticism from the public on a certain issue, did the station respond to these criticisms, or ignore them?

Material Relating to an FCC Investigation or Complaint
If the FCC is investigating a station or somebody has filed a complaint that the station has violated the Communications Act or FCC rules, the stations must keep related materials.

• Is the station being investigated for violating FCC rules?

Time Brokerage Agreements
A "time brokerage agreement" (also known as a Local Marketing Agreement or LMA) is a type of contract in which a station sells blocks of airtime to another company. The other company then provides the programming to fill that time block and sells the ads that run during the programming. (This is one of the deceptive ways that Big Media companies get around media ownership limits in local communities.) The station may also have this information in a "joint sales agreement."

• Who else is supplying programs on this station? Is another station providing the news for this station to cut costs? Does this reduce the number of different sources of information in your community?

Ownership Reports
The public file must contain a copy of the most recent, complete "ownership report" filed for the station.

• If the station is a subsidiary of another company, who is the ultimate owner?

• Is there a "Local Marketing Agreement" that allows another station to control some of this station's programming? (This information might be found in "time brokerage agreements").

• Does the file list any other interests of the owners that might conflict with the public interest requirements of broadcasting?

Issues/Programs Lists

Stations are required to keep a quarterly file of which local issues their programming covered and how those issues were covered specifically. This file will usually be separated by issue (for instance "public safety," "environment," etc.) with examples of when and how the issues were covered (usually as part of local news segments).

- What are the issues that are covered? Are they representative of the community and community concerns?

- Did some issues receive a great deal more coverage than others? What important issues are not being addressed?

- Are the issues that the station claims to be covering actually being covered adequately?

- Is important programming getting enough airtime? Is important programming on the air during prime times of day, or during times when nobody's listening or watching?

Political File

All candidates for public office must have equal access to broadcasting facilities. Also, stations must charge the lowest commercial rate available for political ads.

- Did the station provide more air time to one candidate than another? Did it provide free time to one candidate but not another?

- How much did the ads cost?

Employment Records

TV and radio stations must offer equal employment opportunity (EEO) and cannot discriminate on the basis of race, color, religion, national origin, or sex. Stations have to file reports saying how they comply with these policies.

- How is the station recruiting candidates for open positions? Are they taking steps to recruit a staff that represents the diversity of your community?

Children's TV Programming Reports

Commercial TV stations are required by the FCC to air a minimum of 3 hours per week (between 7 AM and 10 PM) of "core educational programming" specifically designed to educate and inform children and teens under 16. Stations must file "FCC 398" reports describing how their core educational programs have "education as a significant purpose." Note that the stations—not the FCC—decide what counts as educational programming.

- Does the station list at least 3 hours of educational programming for children, airing between 7 AM and 10 PM? Is it regularly scheduled for the same time every week?

- What kind of programs does the station air to fill its "core education" requirement? Are these programs legitimately educational, or are they fluff entertainment programs with some nominal information or morality component?

Records regarding advertising in children's programming.

There are limits on the amount and type of advertising in TV programs for children 12 and under. There cannot be more than 12 minutes of commercials per hour on weekdays and 10.5 minutes per hour on weekends during kids' programs.

- Did the station exceed ad time limits during children's programming?

PLUG IN

Our success in national and local battles will hinge on the strategic, coordinated actions of Americans working together. Plug in with established national organizations and local groups—or organize your own local group if there isn't one yet.

Join in National Advocacy Efforts

Free Press and other national advocacy groups monitor media policy and then organize large numbers of people to pressure Congress, the FCC, and others at crucial times in the policymaking cycle. Working with these organizations is a great way to ensure your voice will be heard.

- If you haven't already done so, join the Free Press e-activist network to be notified of important developments and opportunities for action. You can join by visiting freepress.net—the signup appears in the upper left on every page.
- Get your friends and neighbors to sign up, too!

RESOURCE

The Center for International Media Action (CIMA) created a directory of all the organizations that were involved in the 2003 fight against the FCC's attempt to allow more media ownership consolidation. You can download it at www.mediaactioncenter.org or call CIMA at (866) 470-2954 to order a copy.

Connect with Local Media Reform Groups

Coordinated, local grassroots activism is a driving force in all social change movements. Get involved!

- Check www.freepress.net/orgs for a directory of media reform groups, searchable by state.

- Hundreds of cities have action groups called "Fight Big Media MeetUps" that meet on the second Wednesday of each month. Go to www.fightbigmedia.meetup.com to link up with a group in your community or to find out how to start your own.

EXAMPLES OF LOCAL AND REGIONAL MEDIA ACTIVIST GROUPS

Chicago Media Action (www.chicagomediaaction.org, 1-866-260-7198) is an activist group dedicated to analyzing and broadening Chicago's mainstream media and to building that city's independent media.

Citizens for Media Literacy (www.main.nc.us/cml, 828-255-0182) is a North Carolina-based organization linking media literacy with the concepts and practices of citizenship.

Grand Rapids Institute for Information Democracy (www.griid.org, 616-459-4788), based in Michigan, does research on local media, provides media education workshops, trains community members in media relations and develops media strategy for local organizations.

Media Alliance (www.media-alliance.org, 415-546-6334) is a San Francisco-based media resource and advocacy center for media workers, non-profit organizations, and social justice activists.

Media Tank (www.mediatank.org, 215-563-1100), out of Philadelphia, promotes media literacy, policy education, and a vibrant local media culture through community workshops, lectures, screenings, forums, national organizing, speaking engagements, and resource materials.

Reclaim the Media (www.reclaimthemedia.org, 206-709-0558) is a coalition of independent journalists, media activists and community organizers in the Pacific Northwest, promoting press freedom and community media access as prerequisites for a functioning democracy.

Start an Action Group

If there isn't a local group working on media issues in your community, start your own! An awareness-raising event like those mentioned earlier in this guide could be a catalyst to launch your working group.

Lead the launch. Be the person who will organize people to come together for meetings and facilitate conversations about what the group will do. The success of your group will depend on others' involvement, but somebody has to get it all started.

Strengthen your organizing skills. Study up on some of the skills that will come in handy as you help launch your group, such as meeting facilitation, community organizing, and action planning. There are lots of great resources available on the web and in your local public library.

Use this action guide and the other resources referenced here to help plan your group's actions.

RESOURCE

The Media Empowerment Organizing Manual, produced by the Media Empowerment Project of the United Church of Christ, provides information on the basics of community organizing and resources for media activism. You can download it at www.ucc.org/ocinc/mep/orgman.htm or call the Media Empowerment Project at 800-778-9214 to order a copy.

Tap in Using Listservs, Blogs, and Online Forums

Blogs (online journals where people can post entries about their personal experiences and interests), listservs (automatic mailing lists which allow people sharing an interest to subscribe to a given discussion), and online forums (electronic bulletin boards) are all great ways to get a good sense of who's doing what and what the hot issues are.

- Media Tank runs a national listserv for media activists to discuss timely media issues. Sign up at www.mediatank.org.
- MediaChannel.org hosts Citizen Media Watch, a web forum for debating and discussing media issues. You can tap in at http://64.225.103.105/forum/.
- AlterNet has a MediaCulture discussion forum with several sub-topics. Check it out at http://forums.alternet.org.

Participate in Media Reform Events

Attending conferences, lectures, hearings, fundraisers, rallies, and other events about media reform is a great way to plug into the media reform movement. Visit www.freepress.net/action/calendar.php for a listing of events (and to contribute other events to the calendar as well). Independent media (including alternative newspapers, community radio stations, and public access TV channels) are also good places to check for information about local media-related events.

APPENDICES

Sample Letter to the Editor

Dear Editor,

Information is the lifeblood of democracy. We depend on our media to provide us with what we need to know, so that we can make informed decisions about the things that affect our lives.

Over the past several weeks, I've seen local TV, radio stations, and newspapers devote plenty of time to [insert a reference to a major "infotainment" story you've seen recently, such as celebrity gossip or sensationalistic court cases]. Coverage of these stories may be good for ratings or advertising dollars, but they have absolutely no impact on the lives of [insert city or region] residents, and they obscure the real issues that are crucial to our families and our communities. The media aren't telling us what's really going on in our statehouse, in Washington, and around the world!

I don't blame this problem on the reporters and editors, because I know journalists often get pressure from corporate headquarters to cover what's most profitable—instead of what's most important. The real blame goes to the policymakers in Washington who have let our media system become totally corrupted by profit motives of big media companies. We as citizens need to let our members of Congress—and the FCC—know that our media system is failing and they need to fix it. Media *is* the issue.

Sincerely,

[Your name]
[Your address]
[Your daytime phone number]

Sample Op-Ed / Commentary

Make the op-ed timely by leading it off with a paragraph that references a current issue related to media. For instance, you might mention a media policy bill being debated in Congress or an action being taken by the FCC, a recent report or event related to media, or any current discussion about a particular media phenomenon or the media's role in covering an issue or event. Make this first paragraph a punchy and compelling hook into the media issues discussed below.

Media is an important part of our lives. We read the paper to find out what's happening in our neighborhoods and in the world. We listen to the radio to hear music and find out about weather, traffic, and politics. We watch TV—on average, over 4 hours a day—to unwind, be entertained, and get the latest news.

Yet for all this media exposure, most of us are left in the dark when it comes to media policy.

For generations, the government policies that determine how we get our media, who owns it, and what they are able to do with it have been decided behind closed doors with virtually zero public participation. Why? These regulations are complicated, we're told. But there is no justification for excluding citizens from debates that affect what we hear, see, and read everyday.

The results of closed-door decision making have been disastrous. Without public involvement, policymakers have delivered control over the civic and political dialogue of our country (not to mention music, entertainment, and culture) to a handful of corporate conglomerates, while limiting our ability to develop viable alternative media systems.

In June of 2003, the Federal Communications Commission voted to gut media ownership limits. Had they been successful, almost all of the media outlets in a single community—the cable system, the newspaper, TV and radio stations, even the dominant Internet provider—could be owned by a single company. Realizing the impact of consolidating such complete power over information in a few hands, citizens across the country responded with outrage. Millions contacted their legislators to demand responsible public interest standards. Eventually the Courts reversed the FCC's decision, ordering the Commission to start over.

This uproar over media ownership alerted the public to a wide variety of media policy issues that not only affect us, but demand our involvement. When citizens are left out of the equation, we get policies that allow companies like Clear Channel to gobble up over 1200 radio stations, eliminating independent, local voices. We get cable rates rising five times faster than inflation with no local competition. We get politicians spending almost $1.5 billion on ads in the 2004 election cycle alone—because they're not afforded free airtime and their issues aren't covered adequately in the news. We get corporations sitting on copyrights for decades while art, culture, and innovation suffer. We get public broadcasting with a budget so small that it is forced to rely on corporate donations and advertising dollars to stay on the air.

As citizens committed to freedom and democracy, we need a media system that serves us better and provides us with a wider array of ideas and culture. Our democracy depends on it.

Sample Newsletter Article

I care about [*insert your priority issue or value here*]. I think it's imperative for our society to focus on these issues, discuss and debate them, and arrive at solutions to the problems. But it seems to me that more people on the street can carry a conversation about the latest Michael Jackson court case than [*reference issue*].

That's why I also care about the media—and media policy.

Today's media system is dominated by a small number of powerful corporations whose sole objective is making money, not providing citizens with the information we need to help guide our country. Journalism has been hijacked by celebrity gossip and sensationalism, and the range of political debate is shrinking. Without a media system that fosters democratic debate and dialogue on important issues from diverse perspectives, we'll never see the kind of public participation that it takes to bring about change in [*your issue*], or any other issue.

[*Optional: Insert a paragraph here detailing some facts, examples, or statistics that illustrate how your issue is poorly covered by the media. Note how this inadequate media coverage hinders success in achieving your goals or values.*]

The decline of our media system shouldn't just be blamed on journalists who fail to cover important stories, but on the root causes of media failure—the policies governing our media system which enable media corporations to evade their responsibilities.

For generations, Big Media corporations have successfully lobbied Congress and the FCC—behind closed doors—to make sure their profit motives are prioritized in government policies that determine how we get our media, who owns it and what they are able to broadcast. The results have been disastrous. Large media conglomerates have been granted enormous subsidies and free use of our public airwaves while public interest regulations are gutted and accountability measures relaxed.

As a result of corporate-driven media policy, we now get policies that allow companies like Clear Channel to gobble up over 1200 radio stations, eliminating independent, local voices. We get cable rates rising five times faster than inflation with no local competition. We get politicians spending almost $1.5 billion on ads in the 2004 election cycle alone—because they're not afforded decent airtime and their issues aren't covered adequately in the news. We get corporations sitting on copyrights for decades while art, culture, and innovation suffer. We get public broadcasting with a budget so small that it is forced to rely on corporate donations and advertising dollars to stay on the air.

In June of 2003, the Federal Communications Commission voted to gut media ownership limits. Had they been successful, one company could have owned almost all of the media outlets in a single community—the cable system, the newspaper, TV and radio stations, even the dominant Internet provider. Once people started hearing about the latest in disastrous media policy, they were outraged.

Over two million people spoke up to say they didn't want to let giant media conglomerates gain even more power. Groups from across the political spectrum— from the NRA to the National Organization for Women—spoke out too. Eventually the Courts reversed the FCC, ordering the Commission to start over. The politics of media ownership in 2003 have alerted the public that if more people are involved in the movement to change the media, the current system will fall apart like a house of cards. We must continue to stay engaged.

As citizens committed to freedom and democracy, we need a media system that serves us better, providing us with the information we need to play a role in government. Our [insert the value related to your issue here] and our democracy depend on it.

Prepared Media Reform Speech

I'm going to talk about an issue that affects your life as much as any other issue, but gets little attention: the media.

Television, radio, newspapers, books, movies and the internet are our windows to the world. They provide the information we use to form opinions and make crucial decisions about the issues we care about most—issues like health care, education, the economy.

But today's media system is dominated by a small number of powerful companies whose sole objective is making money, not serving the needs of a democratic society. Many people—myself included—are beginning to understand that the media system in our country is broken.

Journalism has become celebrity-obsessed fluff, and the range of political debate is shrinking. In fact, it's dreadful. The average adult knows more about the state of [*insert hot celebrity here*]'s love life than the state of the world.

Investigative journalism is declining, replaced by opinionated rants.

Entertainment has become overly violent and sensationalistic, or mindless cheap-to-produce drivel.

Commercialization of our culture is out of control, with over 30,000 advertisements bombarding the average American child each year. Our kids see ads in their schools, on their clothes, in the games they play, even on park benches.

The music we get to hear on the radio is no longer about how good a song is—but about who pays the most to have their client's song played 3 times in one hour. And forget about getting anything newsworthy from your radio. You could be driving through a toxic cloud of gas—and this did happen in North Dakota a few years ago—and no one would tell you about it on the radio because there's a good chance no one is at the radio station. These days radio giants like Clear Channel—with over 1200 radio stations across the country—slash costs by cutting staff and running their stations on pre-recorded autopilot.

I could go on and on about this sad state of affairs, but instead I'll sum it up like this: Unless we create a more diverse, independent, skeptical and competitive media system, all of the issues we care about most will not advance.

Most people think that, like death and taxes, you can't change the media—but we can. And it wasn't always like this.

When the postal service was first established, the nation's founders debated subsidizing the cost of mailing newspapers—which constituted 90 percent of the mail. The debate was not about how much to subsidize—but whether there should be any charge at all for sending newspapers through the mail. Because those who started our country knew that democracy would thrive only if ideas could thrive. And there was a fear that differing viewpoints would be silenced if you had to have money to distribute a newspaper.

What a difference a few centuries can make. Today, instead of subsidizing the media to create an even playing field, our government still subsidizes media, but in the form of giveaways to huge corporate media conglomerates. One example is that TV and radio stations are allowed to broadcast on the airwaves that legally belong to the public—free of charge. The airwaves belong to you and me—just like a national park is there for you and me—yet the media moguls are making billions of dollars off of them. Cable and satellite companies also get huge gifts of monopolies while they use our streets and public utilities to place their wires.

Our government gives media corporations free use of our airwaves and other public property under the condition that they use the media to serve the needs of their communities. But I know I'm not the only one who thinks the media aren't living up to their end of the bargain.

These giveaways are made behind closed doors in the most corrupt manner imaginable, and the worst part is that most of us don't even know it. The individuals who are responsible for this corrupt system want to make sure that people don't understand how the media cake is sliced—or even that there is a cake—because they know that once we know about this corruption, we won't stand for it.

In 2003, the FCC tried to quietly change the regulations to make it possible for one company to own virtually all the media outlets in one town—the cable system, the newspapers, TV and radio stations. And they inadvertently started a revolution. Once people started hearing about the proposal to allow consolidation of power over information in even fewer hands, people were outraged. Over two million Americans—from across the political spectrum—spoke up to say that they didn't want to let giant media conglomerates get even bigger.

The people won and these rule changes were stopped by the courts. Suddenly it became clear that the public could have a big impact. That if more people are involved in the movement to change the media, the current system will fall apart like a house of cards. But first we need to make more people aware that we do have the power to fight Big Media—because fighting big money takes big numbers.

What is necessary to win this fight is nothing new. Like other times of change in our nation's history, we need to educate, and activate. We must all understand how crucial media reform is to democracy. Americans like us must become actively involved, sending petitions, writing letters to the editor, meeting with our elected officials, calling Congress, hosting "house parties" to tell our friends, talking to local groups about media reform—just like I am now. It is about being actively involved in a democratic process that requires just that: active involvement.

Corporate control of the media is drowning out our democracy. . . . Join me. We can rescue our broken media system and the voices that deserve to be heard. To join this fight, please read the materials being handed out and then visit www.free-press.net to learn more about some simple steps you can take to make a difference. And it will make a difference. That's www.freepress.net or call 866-666-1533.

Thank you.

Talking Points for a Presentation on Media Reform

1. Television, radio, newspapers, books, movies and the internet are our windows to the world. They provide the information we use to form opinions and make crucial decisions about the issues we care about most—issues like health care, education, the economy.

By the age of 70, Americans will have spent 7 to 10 years of their lives watching TV. [1]

2. Today's media system is dominated by a small number of powerful companies whose sole objective is making money, not serving the needs of a democratic society.

Time Warner alone—in addition to its cable empire reaching 11 million subscribers—controls over 100 magazines, dozens of television networks and record companies, as well as major publishing, Internet, TV and movie production companies. [2]

3. The quality of our media is deteriorating. Journalism is celebrity-obsessed. Investigative reporting is declining. Cheap-to-produce, mindless "reality shows" are a fast growing genre.

Commercialization of our culture is out of control: Kids see ads in their schools, on their clothes, in the games they play, even on park benches.

The music we get to hear on the radio is determined by who pays the most to have their client's song played 3 times in one hour.

Local radio is being replaced with pre-taped programming to save money.

In 2002, a Minot, North Dakota train wreck resulted in a release of toxic gas. But the local radio station, owned by Clear Channel, was unable to issue any warnings because no one was at the station at the time. One person died. [3]

Clear Channel now owns 1200 radio stations—over 1 in 10 stations nationwide. [4]

The average person sees 400 to 600 ads per day, or 40 to 50 million by the time they are 60 years old. [5]

More than 1 out of 5 parents say that their kids began asking for brand name products by age 3. [6]

4. This decline is directly at odds to our nation's founding principle: that a healthy democracy depends on the free flow of a diversity of opinions and ideas.

When the postal service was first established, the nation's founders subsidized the cost of sending newspapers through the mail. There was a fear that if postage for news wasn't free, then differing viewpoints would be silenced.

5. Our government still subsidizes the media system—but in the form of unpublicized corporate giveaways and deregulations. The government gives a limited number of TV and radio broadcasters the right to use the airwaves free of charge, and allows cable and satellite monopolies to make extraordinary profits while using public streets and utilities to place their wires.

Between 1996 and 2000, the fifty largest media firms and the four media trade organizations spent $111 million on lobbying Congress. [7]

In the first five months of 2003, when the FCC was debating the media cross-ownership rules that were overturned in June of that year, the commercial TV and cable networks provided "virtually no coverage" of the issue, with the big networks typically airing nothing until a week before the FCC decision. [8]

6. Media reform is possible when the public becomes aware and involved in policy decisions. Last year the FCC tried to quietly change the regulations to make it possible for one company to own virtually all the media outlets in one town—the cable system, the newspapers, TV and radio stations. Over two million outraged citizens challenged this deregulation, which was ultimately stopped by the courts and Congress.

Prior to relaxing media ownership rules in 2003, FCC officials met behind closed doors 71 times with the nation's major broadcasters, but had only five such meetings with Consumers Union and the Media Access Project, the two major consumer groups working on the issue. The meetings were not recorded. [6]

7. Fighting Big Media—and Big Money—requires big numbers. In order to change the system, Americans must become actively involved—sending petitions, writing letters to the editor, meeting with your elected officials, calling Congress, hosting "houseparties," talking to local groups about media reform.

8. Join the fight to rescue our broken media system by learning more and taking action. Visit www.freepress.net to get educated and activated.

Notes

1. About-Face facts on the MEDIA.
2. *Columbia Journalism Review*, September 22, 2003.
3. *New York Times*, January 19, 2002
4. *Reuters*, July 22, 2004
5. About-Face facts on the MEDIA.
6. Center for a New American Dream Poll, July 1999.
7. The Center for Public Integrity, May 2003.
8. *American Journalism Review*, December/January 2004.

Sample Letter to Member of Congress

Dear Senator [*last name*] or Mr./Ms. [*last name*]:

I am writing as a constituent from [*your city and state*] to bring your attention to something which impacts every problem we face as a nation. I'm talking about the media—the venue of public debate and democratic deliberation. What we see, hear, and read has a profound effect on how we act as informed (or uninformed) citizens.

I have watched with great concern in recent years as the American media system has taken a turn for the worse. In a world of digital media with potentially millions of channels, our society seems to be even less well-informed, less conscious of diversity, and less attuned to local needs than ever before. In large part, these dire circumstances are the result of public policies. Despite the responsibility of the government to protect the democratic interests of the public in the structure of mass media markets, our public officials have failed miserably. They have bowed to the pressure of organized wealth and handed the keys to the kingdom to a handful of media conglomerates.

Certainly I support the First Amendment rights of all media producers. But I also insist on the First Amendment rights of all citizens—to speak for themselves and to hear the widest possible range of voices in the public media system. We have a Constitutional right to a media system that offers a diversity of voices over mainstream channels. We have a Constitutional right to open up the public airwaves to as many speakers as technology will permit, and a responsibility to ensure that our communications systems are open and accessible to all public speakers, great and small.

I ask you to consider these issues carefully. I ask you to respond to this letter with concrete ideas about how you intend to put media channels in the hands of local people. I ask for specific policy proposals which will promote diversity and competition. I ask for your ideas on how to promote open access, a broad non-profit and non-commercial media sector, and dedicated attention to the cultivation of independent voices.

I look forward to your response.

Sincerely,

[*Your name*]
[*Your address*]
[*Your city, state, zip*]

10 Questions to Ask Every Candidate and Elected Official

1) Media Ownership.
The United States has seen a massive wave of media consolidation over the past two decades. For example, Time Warner alone controls over 100 magazines, dozens of television networks and record companies, as well as major publishing, Internet, TV and movie production companies—in addition to its cable empire reaching 11 million subscribers.

Do you support setting limits on media consolidation—through antitrust law and ownership protections—to prevent large companies from having too much control over what Americans see, hear and read?

2) Public and noncommercial media.
Democratic discourse requires quality sources of information free from advertiser pressure. However, we provide less funding per capita for public broadcasting than most other industrialized countries—by a wide margin.

Do you support policies that would increase and preserve funding for public and noncommercial media, and eliminate commercial sponsorship of public radio and TV programs?

3) Marketing to kids.
Our children today are bombarded with advertising. Parents, teachers, and organizations dedicated to children's issues are growing increasingly concerned as evidence mounts connecting media exposure to a variety of health and behavior problems.

Do you support efforts to reduce commercialism and predatory marketing toward children, and to promote noncommercial educational TV programming for young children?

4) Cable rates.
Over the past 5 years, cable rates have risen over 40 percent nationwide. This is the direct result of government-granted monopolies and lack of competition. The government has stalled on setting reasonable cable ownership limits. Meanwhile, cable companies are increasing their profits as they eliminate communities' ability to negotiate public-interest-oriented cable agreements.

Will you promote consumer choice by setting limits on cable ownership and by supporting policies to encourage the development of competition in cable markets?

5) Internet freedom.

Big cable and telephone companies now want to restrict what users and providers can and cannot access on the Internet, all in the name of profit. The Internet exploded over the past decade in part because Internet Service Providers were required by law to allow access to all websites and users without discrimination.

Do you support open access rules that keep the Internet free and open, and that protect individual privacy from both government and corporations alike?

6) Campaign coverage.

The skyrocketing cost of buying ad time is a major reason candidates raise ever-higher sums of campaign money from wealthy special interests. This year, TV broadcasters—who are granted licenses to use publicly-owned airwaves, free of charge—will rake in a record $1.47 billion from political ads alone. At the same time, news coverage of campaigns, especially on radio and television, has plummeted.

Do you support requiring broadcasters to provide significant free airtime for candidates and public debates as a condition of receiving their government-granted licenses?

7) Community radio.

Many communities find themselves and their concerns misrepresented or ignored by major broadcasters. Citizens need to hear their own voices over their own airwaves, and the capability exists to fulfill this demand. Legislation can create thousands of new low-power FM radio licenses.

Do you support giving more communities the ability to broadcast their own locally-based programming through an expanded low-power radio and television service?

8) Minority ownership.

Minority ownership of media is at a 10-year low, down 14 percent since 1997. Today, only 4 percent of radio stations and 1.9 percent of television stations are owned by people of color. And studies show that the glass ceiling for women is firmly in place at communications companies.

Do you support providing incentives to increase diversity in media ownership and leadership?

9) Media workers.

Media consolidation pressures media workers to abandon their professional values in order to generate maximum short-term profits. Trade unions are especially important in media industries because they serve both to protect the rights of workers and to insulate the media's role in our democracy from economic pressure.

Do you support laws that make it easier for media workers to form trade unions and ensure they are paid for their overtime?

10) Copyright.

Existing copyright law serves the interests of large corporations to the detriment of public information, culture, and innovation. Legislation has kept the past 80 years' worth of copyrighted works and ideas out of the public domain, depriving new thinkers of the chance to build on old ideas. If copyright laws being considered today had been in effect a few generations ago, recording a show on your VCR or photocopying a news story may have been illegal.

Do you support policies that will shorten the terms of copyright and lend balance to the law by allowing fair use for nonprofit and noncommercial purposes?

become a
MEMBER

The Free Press Action Fund, the advocacy arm of Free Press, is a member-supported organization. By contributing, you will be directly supporting our efforts to promote public-interest media policy in Congress and at the FCC.

To join, visit www.freepress.net/support or complete and mail this form, along with a check payable to Free Press Action Fund, to:

Free Press Action Fund, 100 Main Street, P.O. Box 28, Northampton, MA 01061

Our Way of Saying "Thanks"

Regular membership includes a free copy of *The Problem of the Media*, written by Free Press co-founder Robert W. McChesney. Supporting members also receive McChesney's *Rich Media, Poor Democracy*. Contributing members receive those books plus Upton Sinclair's *The Brass Check*. All membership levels include advance notice of Free Press special events and conferences, as well as optional subscriptions to Free Press electronic mailing lists. *Please note gifts are subject to substitution based on availability.*

FREE PRESS ACTION FUND MEMBERSHIP FORM

Contribution Type:
- [ ] $20 Introductory
- [ ] $50 Regular
- [ ] $100 Supporting
- [ ] $200 Contributing
- [ ] Other: $_____

Membership fees are not tax-deductible as charitable contributions for federal income tax purposes.

_____
NAME

_____
ADDRESS

_____
CITY, STATE, ZIP

_____
EMAIL (*note, we do not share our email lists*)

Make checks payable to Free Press Action Fund. Mail to Free Press Action Fund, P.O. Box 28, Northampton, MA 01061.

ABOUT THE AUTHORS

MATT BARRANCA is an applied anthropologist and research director at Context-Based Research Group, an ethnographic consulting company in Baltimore, Maryland. Previously, he was a program associate at the New America Foundation, where he researched and wrote about the role of unlicensed spectrum in grassroots wireless networking.

MICHAEL CALABRESE is Vice President of the New America Foundation, a nonpartisan policy institute in Washington, D.C. As Director of the Spectrum Policy Program, Calabrese oversees New America's efforts to improve our nation's management of publicly-owned assets, particularly the radio frequency spectrum. He is the coauthor of three previous books on policy and politics and has published opinion articles in the nation's leading news outlets.

JEFF CHESTER is executive director of the Center for Digital Democracy, a nonprofit organization devoted to ensuring that the digital media serve the public interest. A former journalist and filmmaker, his work has appeared in many publications, on radio and on TV. He has played a leading role in debates about media policy in numerous forms for upward of two decades and was named by *Newsweek* one of the Internet's fifty most influential people.

DR. MARK COOPER is Director of Research at the Consumer Federation of America and a Fellow at the Stanford Law School Center for Internet and Society, the Columbia Institute on Tele-information, and the Donald McGannon Communications Research Center at Fordham University. He is the author of numerous articles on digital society and telecommunications issues and of five books, and has provided expert testimony in over 250 cases for public-interest clients in the United States and Canada on telecommunications and energy policy.

MICHAEL COPPS currently serves as a Democratic member of the Federal Communications Commission. He previously served as Assistant Secretary of Commerce for Trade Development at the U.S. Department of Commerce and prior to that as administrative assistant and chief of staff to Senator Fritz Hollings (D-SC). Before coming to Washington, Copps was a professor of United States History at Loyola University of the South. Copps received a B.A. from Wofford College and earned a Ph.D. from the University of North Carolina at Chapel Hill.

SASHA COSTANZA-CHOCK is the Global Communication Project coordinator for Free Press. He has worked for many years with youth-arts activists, social-justice organizations, and media-reform activists. He holds a BA from Harvard University and recently finished his MA in Communications at the Annenberg School at the University of Pennsylvania, where he studied the political economy of media with a focus on transnational social movements and new communications technologies. Currently, he sits on the international organizing committee of the campaign for Communication Rights in the Information Society.

MALKIA A. CYRIL is a twenty-nine-year-old African-American organizer and Brooklyn native. She is Executive Director of Youth Media Council (www.youthmediacouncil.org), where she works to build media capacity in the Bay Area's vibrant youth movement while holding local media outlets accountable for their participation in youth policy debates.

JOHN DUNBAR is director of the Center for Public Integrity's telecommunications project. He came to the Center in 1999 from the *Florida Times-Union* in Jacksonville, where he was chief investigative reporter. Since joining the Center, Dunbar has worked on the 50 States Project, the Center's Enron and Harken Oil investigations, and a report on the California energy crisis. A recipient of several awards for investigative reporting, Dunbar is a graduate of the University of South Florida in Tampa.

HAROLD FELD is the Senior Vice President of the Media Access Project. He joined in 1999, after practicing communications, Internet, and energy law at Covington & Burling. Mr. Feld served as cochair of the Federal Communications Bar Association's Online Committee, and has written numerous articles on Internet law and communications policy for trade publications and legal journals. Mr. Feld won the 2000 Burton Award for excellence in writing by a nonacademic. A *magna cum laude* of both Princeton University and Boston University Law School, Mr. Feld clerked for the Hon. John M. Ferren of the District of Columbia Court of Appeals.

LINDA FOLEY has been president of The Newspaper Guild-CWA since 1995. She is also a vice president of the Communications Workers of America, AFL-CIO and is the first woman to hold the Guild's top post. Foley also is vice president of the International Federation of Journalists, a global organization with affiliates in more than one-hundred countries. She is secretary-treasurer of the AFL-CIO's Department for Professional Employees. Foley currently serves as a member of the Board of Advisors to Northwestern's Medill School of Journalism, where she received her journalism degree in 1977.

PETER HART is the activism director at FAIR (Fairness & Accuracy In Reporting), the national media watchdog group based in New York City. He is also a cohost and producer of FAIR's syndicated radio show *CounterSpin*, and the author of *The Oh Really? Factor: Unspinning Fox News Channel's Bill O'Reilly* (Seven Stories Press, 2003).

VIDYA KRISHNAMURTHY has served as Legislative Coordinator for the media reform group Free Press and Communications Director for the campaign reform group Alliance for Better Campaigns. She holds a journalism degree from Northwestern University and a degree in public affairs from Princeton University.

GARY O. LARSON, an Oakland-based researcher-writer affiliated with the Center for Digital Democracy in Washington, D.C., has written extensively on the role that the nonprofit sector can play in the broadband revolution. He has taught graduate and undergraduate courses at the University of Minnesota, the University of Maryland, and American University and is the author of *The Reluctant Patron: The United States Government and the Arts, 1943–1965* (1983); *Lifelong Journey: An Education in the Arts* (1996); and *American Canvas* (1997).

CHERYL A. LEANZA serves as Principal Legislative Counsel for the National League of Cities. Ms. Leanza is a leader in public-interest advocacy, fighting for diversity in ownership, and other policies furthering First Amendment principles. She has taken leadership roles in the area of media ownership, low-power radio and cable Internet open access. She graduated *cum laude* from the University of Michigan Law School and simultaneously earned a Master of Public Policy degree from Michigan's Institute of Public Policy Studies. Ms. Leanza has been elected to serve on the Executive Committee of the Federal Communications Bar Association Foundation

MARK LLOYD is a Senior Fellow at the Center for American Progress focusing on communications policy. He is also an Adjunct Professor at the Georgetown University Public Policy Institute. Lloyd is a communications attorney with twenty years of experience as a broadcast journalist. He received his undergraduate degree from the University of Michigan and his law degree from Georgetown University.

ROBERT W. MCCHESNEY is Research Professor in the Institute of Communications Research at the University of Illinois at Urbana-Champaign. He is the Founder and President of Free Press, a nonprofit organization working to involve the public in media policymaking and to craft policies for a more democratic media system. He is the author of numerous books on media policy including the multiple award-winning *Rich Media, Poor Democracy* (1999), and most recently, *The Problem of the Media: U.S. Communication Politics in the Twenty-First Century* (2004).

SASCHA MEINRATH is a community organizer, media activist, and researcher. He is the treasurer for the Global Indymedia Network. He cofounded the Urbana-Champaign Independent Media Center Foundation and the Tactical Media Fund, an international nonprofit organization that is engaged in strategic funding, making disbursements to grassroots media producers in the Global South. He is the founder and coordinator of the Champaign-Urbana Community Wireless Network (CUWiN). He holds a master's degree in psychology and is currently completing a Ph.D. at the University of Illinois' Institute for Communications Research.

BILL MOYERS is one of Americans finest and most admired journalists. His work has won more than thirty Emmy awards, and he has been recognized by the National Endowment for the Humanities "for outstanding contributions to American cultural life." Before establishing Public Affairs Television in 1986, he served as executive editor of the *Bill Moyers' Journal* on public television, senior news analyst for the CBS Evening News, and chief correspondent for the acclaimed documentary series, CBS *Reports*. Before entering broadcasting, Moyers was Deputy Director of the Peace Corps in the Kennedy Administration and Special Assistant to President Lyndon B. Johnson from 1963 to 1967, including two years as White House press secretary. He left the White House in January 1967 to become publisher of *Newsday*, was for twelve years a trustee of the Rockefeller Foundation, and now serves as president of The Schumann Center for Media and Democracy.

RUSSELL NEWMAN serves as Campaign Director for Free Press. He oversees initiatives ranging from grassroots organization to new research projects, tracking current media issues and creating content for the Free Press website. He was a Waterston Scholar at Suffolk University's Sawyer School of Management with specializations in the political economy of mass communication, nonprofit management, and documentary production. Previous to joining Free Press, he was a professional multimedia designer. Russ also served as production designer on several independent films and was active in radio for nearly a decade. Russell holds a degree in Brain and Cognitive Science from MIT.

BARBARA RENAUD GONZÁLEZ is a writer and journalist living in San Antonio, Texas. She was the first—and only—Chicana to write a monthly column for the Opinion Section of a major newspaper before being censured by the *San Antonio Express-News*. She believes that she can change the world, and so can you.

REP. BERNIE SANDERS is an Independent Congressman from Vermont. He was elected to the House of Representatives in 1990. He sits on the House Committee on Government Reform and the Financial Services Committee, where he is the Ranking Minority Member of the Subcommittee on Financial Institutions and Consumer Credit. In the 104th Congress, he formed the Progressive Caucus, with fifty-eight members, calling for progressive tax reform, a single-payer health care system, a 50 percent cut in military spending over five years, and a national energy policy. He was the first member of Congress to hold town meetings on media issues, and he was the primary sponsor of legislation to overturn the FCC's media ownership rules.

BEN SCOTT is a Policy Director in the Washington office of Free Press. Previously, he served as a Legislative Fellow in the House of Representatives, handling telecommunications policy in the office of Congressman Bernie Sanders (I-VT). He is also currently completing his doctoral work at the Institute of Communications Research at the University of Illinois, Urbana-Champaign. He has written several articles on the history of American journalism and media policy making. Most recently, he is the editor, with Robert W. McChesney, of *Our Unfree Press: 100 Years of Radical Media Criticism* (2004).

ANDREW JAY SCHWARTZMAN is the President and CEO of the Media Access Project. From 1978 through 1996, he served as MAP's Executive Director, and is recognized as one of the nation's foremost authorities on telecommunications public policy. He is called upon often to be the public representative at congressional and FCC hearings on telecommunications issues. In 1993, Mr. Schwartzman received the Everett C. Parker Award for his career contributions to the public interest in communications. Most recently, he led the team of attorneys who scored a major victory for public interest limits on media ownership in *Prometheus Radio Project* v. FCC.

CHRIS SLEVIN is Deputy Director of Public Citizen's Global Trade Watch and has served as spokesman of Global Trade Watch since 2002, including at the 2003 Cancún WTO Ministerial and 2003 Miami FTAA Ministerial. He has studied at Villanova University and at University College, Dublin.

GIGI B. SOHN is the president and cofounder of Public Knowledge, a nonprofit organization that addresses the public's stake in the convergence of communications policy and intellectual-property law. Gigi previously served as a Project Specialist in the Ford Foundation's Media, Arts and Culture unit. Prior to joining the Ford Foundation, Gigi served as Executive Director of the Media Access Project (MAP), a Washington, D.C., based public-interest telecommunications law firm, and was appointed to serve as a member of Bill Clinton's Advisory Committee on the Public Interest Obligations of Digital Television Broadcasters (Gore Commission).

LORI WALLACH is Director of Public Citizen's Global Trade Watch, which for ten years has been a United States leader in promoting progressive trade policy and has worked with international partners in defeating the Multilateral Agreement on Investment (MAI), the proposed "Millennium Round" of World Trade Organization negotiations at the Seattle Ministerial in 1999, and the proposed WTO expansion defeated at the 2003 Cancún WTO Ministerial. Wallach is the author of *Whose Trade Organization? A Comprehensive Guide to the WTO* (The New Press, 2004).